The Book of Latin American Cooking

Elisabeth Lambert Ortiz was born in London but has lived and worked as a journalist all over the world, including England, the United States, Mexico, the Caribbean, the Far East (principally Bangkok), South and Central America and Australia. She is at present living in England with her husband, Cesar Ortiz-Tinoco, a Mexican journalist and a former high official of the United Nations.

Mrs Ortiz has written numerous cookery books, on the Caribbean (her book *Caribbean Cooking* is also published by Penguin), Mexico, Japan (with Mitsuko Endo), Latin America and France, on herbs and spices and on fibre. She has also translated, edited and prepared recipes for *Masterpieces of French Cuisine* and has contributed chapters to many cookbooks, including *Masterclass*. She was a principal consultant for the Time-Life Foods of the World series and a consultant for the Time-Life Good Cook series. Mrs Ortiz has been called a culinary anthropologist and a food historian because of her interest in the origins and history of food throughout the world but describes herself simply as a food writer. She writes regularly on food and travel for the American magazine *Gourmet* and is at present working on a book on British chefs.

The Book of
Latin American Cooking

ELISABETH LAMBERT ORTIZ

PENGUIN BOOKS

Penguin Books Ltd, Harmondsworth, Middlesex, England
Viking Penguin Inc., 40 West 23rd Street, New York 10010, U.S.A.
Penguin Books Australia Ltd, Ringwood, Victoria, Australia
Penguin Books Canada Ltd, 2801 John Street, Markham, Ontario, Canada L3R 1B4
Penguin Books (N.Z.) Ltd, 182–190 Wairau Road, Auckland 10, New Zealand

First published in Great Britain by Robert Hale 1984

Published in Penguin Books 1985

Made and printed in Great Britain by
Cox and Wyman Ltd, Reading

For my husband and colleague, César Ortiz-Tinoco, whose knowledge and enthusiasm were of inestimable help in writing this book, and for Jill Norman, valued friend and editor

Contents

Acknowledgements   9
Introduction   11
Ingredients   25

HORS D'OEUVRES AND APPETIZERS   39

Entremeses

SOUPS   68

Sopas

FISH AND SHELLFISH   92

Pescados y Mariscos

MEATS   113

Carnes

POULTRY   180

Aves

SUBSTANTIAL DISHES   213

Platillos Fuertes

VEGETABLES AND SALADS   249

Verduras y Ensaladas

BREADS AND DESSERTS   276

Panes y Postres

SAUCES   298

Salsas

DRINKS   314

Bebidas

Shopping Guide   322
Index   323

Acknowledgements

It is hard to know where to begin with thanks. Surely no one has had friends more generous with their time, their knowledge, and their kitchens than I have had. I would like to thank Mr. and Mrs. José Fernández de Córdoba, Mr. and Mrs. Belisario Fernández de Córdoba, Mr. and Mrs. Arturo Montesinos, Mr. and Mrs. Galo Plaza, Col. and Mrs. Edmundo García Vivanco, Mr. and Mrs. Vincente Umaña Méndez, Margarita Pacini, Cecilia Blanco de Mendoza, Mr. and Mrs. Guillermo Power, Jorge Manchego, Mr. and Mrs. Genaro Carnero Checa, Noreen Maxwell, Dr. and Mrs. Alberto Gormaz, Alejandro Flores Zorilla, Mr. and Mrs. Salvador Ferret, Dr. Raúl Nass, Mr. and Mrs. Carlos Augusto León, Simón Reyes Marcano, Raymond Joseph Fowkes, Lolita de Lleras Codazzi, Phyllis Bird, Emma Vásquez, Mirtha Stengel, Mr. and Mrs. Gilberto Rizzo, Mr. and Mrs. Raúl Trejos, María J. Troconis, Jeanne Lesem, José Wilson, Copeland Marks, Lua de Burt, Josefina Velilla de Aquino, María Teresa Casanueva, Mr. and Mrs. Abél Quezada, Mr. and Mrs. Humberto Ortiz Reyes, Humberto Ortiz Azoños, Mr. and Mrs. Héctor Fernández, Mr. and Mrs. Efraín Huerta, Dr. and Mrs. Antonio Delgado, Raquel Braune, Victor Simón Bovier, James A. Beard, Mr. and Mrs. Victorino A. Althaparro, Dr. Raúl Noriega, Dr. and Mrs. Andrés Iduarte, Elizabeth Borton de Treviño, Mr. and Mrs. Julio César Anzueto, Lucy de Arenales, Mr. and Mrs. Jason Vourvoulias, Mr. and Mrs. Mario Montero, Ruth Kariv, Mr. and Mrs. Antonio Carbajal, Mr. and Mrs. Eugenio Soler Alonso, Ambassador and Mrs. Mario Alvírez.

I am deeply indebted to Dr. David R. Harris of London University and Dr. Wolfgang Haberland of Munich for their scientific findings on the origins of agriculture in Latin America and for their advice and encouragement, and to Walter Sullivan, who first brought this new work to my attention. My thanks to my friend and colleague the late Dr. Alex D. Hawkes for helping me with botanical problems relating to tropical plants and herbs. I am immensely grateful to Alan Eaton Davidson CMG, that great authority on fish and shellfish and writer of cookbooks on the subject, and to Alwynne Wheeler of the British

Acknowledgements

Museum of Natural History, who both helped me on the identification of the Chilean fish *congrio*.

I also want to thank Dr. Charles B. Heiser, Jr., Distinguished Professor of Botany at Indiana University, Bloomington, Indiana, for telling me about new work that is being done in plant origins and for letting me know that it was the Mexican green tomato (*Physalis*) that is known from 700 A.D. since, archaeologically, the ordinary red tomato has not yet been found. I would have been lost without the work done by Dr. Jorge Hardoy, of Argentina, and Dr. Leopoldo Castedo, of Brazil, who make brilliantly clear the urban nature of the great civilizations of pre-Columbian Latin America. I owe them a great debt.

My thanks also to Felicia Pheasant for her help in editing the book and in finding sources for exotic ingredients.

London

ELISABETH LAMBERT ORTIZ

Introduction

I first became interested in Latin American food when I was at school for some time in Jamaica. It was the flavour of hot peppers that beguiled me, especially one that Jamaicans call a Scotch bonnet—small, lantern-shaped, fiery, and full of flavour. I also had Cuban and Brazilian friends who gave me a tantalizing glimpse into this enormous cuisine that stretches from the Rio Bravo (Rio Grande) to the Antarctic. It wasn't until shortly after I was married, twenty odd years ago, and my husband was transferred from headquarters in New York to another United Nations assignment in Mexico, that I was able to pursue my research into flavours I have never been able to forget. So it was chance that I started with Mexico, perhaps the most complex and unique cooking of the whole region. Even now, when I have travelled to all the world's continents, Mexican food is still the most exotic.

Mexican cooking still rests firmly on its Aztec, and to a lesser extent Mayan, origins, interwoven with the cooking of Spain. But Spain itself was for almost eight hundred years dominated by the Arab empire, so its food has a strong Middle Eastern influence. All through my investigation of Mexican cooking I kept stumbling into the Middle East. Later on I went to the Middle East, Spain, and Portugal to sort out the influences. So many strands are woven into this complicated tapestry that I still find it hard to unravel them completely.

But no matter the sources, the reward is in the eating. From the start I was enchanted by the dishes of the corn kitchen, the most purely Mexican aspect of the food. My palate was utterly bewitched by simple snacks like *quesadillas de flor de calabaza* where an unbaked tortilla is stuffed with a savoury mixture of cooked pumpkin flowers, folded over, and fried, or more rarely, baked. I had mouth-watering deep-green peppers stuffed with mashed beans, batter-coated, and fried; or even more exotic, stuffed with meat and masked with a fresh cheese and walnut sauce and garnished with pomegranate seeds. I had *huachinango a la Veracruzana*, beautiful red snapper with mildly hot *jalapeño* peppers in a tomato sauce very lightly perfumed with cloves and cinnamon. And *Mole Poblano de Guajolote*, that extraordi-

11

nary mixture of different types of dried peppers, nuts, herbs, spices, and a little bitter chocolate made into a sauce for turkey and originally a favourite dish at Montezuma's court. It was wholly unfamiliar, wholly delicious.

I found wonderful descriptions of the markets of pre-Conquest Mexico in the monumental work of a Spanish priest, Fray Bernardino de Sahagún, who was there before the Conquest was consolidated. A lively writer, he brought the markets to life, even describing how the local prostitutes lounged about, clicking their chewing gum. I hadn't realized that *chicle* (chewing gum) from the *zapote* tree was also a Mexican gift to the world, and that this same tree bears the pleasant *chico zapote* (sapodilla) fruit. Father Sahagún characterized and identified all the various kinds of tortillas on sale, and clearly he was not averse to sampling some of the cooked foods since he described a shrimp stew and other dishes with such relish one can almost taste them. I needed no more urging—I went off to the markets, realizing they were still the best places in which to learn.

Because peppers, along with corn and beans, play such a vital role in the Mexican cuisine, and because my palate was still haunted by the flavour of the hot Jamaican peppers of my school days, I began to research this fascinating fruit. Botanically it is *Capsicum annuum* or *Capsicum frutescens* of the *Solanaceae* family, to which potatoes, tomatoes, and aubergines also belong. There has never been an accurate count of peppers, which were first cultivated as far back as 7000 B.C. The reason is that they cross-fertilize easily, and since they have been doing this for thousands of years, there are now a great many different kinds. Some botanists put the number as low as sixty, while others can name over a hundred. Long before Columbus they had spread all over the Caribbean, as well as Central and South America. And since Columbus they have sprung up all over the world and have become so thoroughly naturalized that their national origin has been forgotten. They are sweet, pungent, or hot. They are first green, then change to yellow or red as they ripen — and some of them have all three colours in their cycle. They range from ¼ to 7 inches in length. They are used fresh or dried. Some are wrinkled; some are smooth; and quite apart from sweetness, pungency, or heat, they have flavour.

My first visit was to the large San Juan market. It was a blaze of colour. There were enormous piles of ripe crimson tomatoes; and heaps of yellow pumpkin flowers, soft green courgettes, ripe red peppers and pimientos, bright green peppers and darker green *poblanos;* stalls selling the dried, wrinkled red peppers—*ancho, mulato,* and *pasilla*—brick red *chipotle* and *morita,* smooth red *guajillos,* and the little peppers, *cascabel* and *pequin*. There were more kinds than I could possibly take in at a single visit.

The sellers were mostly women with their dark hair in plaits, dressed in full cotton skirts and snowy white blouses with the traditional *rebozo* (stole) around their shoulders. Some, sitting on the ground, had before them only tiny piles of herbs or spices, or a pyramid of purple-skinned avocados. Others, often with husbands and children, had proper stalls laden with oranges; grapefuit; the paddles of the *nopal* (prickly pear) cactus, *nopalitos;* or its fruit, *tuna*—globes of green or purplish red. They called to me as I passed: *"Qué va a llevar, marchanta?"* ("What are you going to buy, customer?") and when I explained that I wanted to learn about Mexican food, they were generous with their help. I found the pepper I had remembered from my school days. It came from Yucatán and was called, paradoxically, *habanero* (pepper from Havana), a migrant returned. Later I found it all over the Caribbean, the Bahia in Brazil, and in Guatemala where it is called *caballero*, gentleman pepper—one clearly to be reckoned with.

I bought peppers of all kinds, took them home, photographed them, learned their names, and cooked them. I have listed them in the ingredients section—not all, of course, only the ones I think it useful for the cook to know about.

That first day I asked one of the market women how to make *quesadillas de flor de calabaza* (pumpkin flower turnovers), and she was delighted. She shouted to a tortilla seller to come over, and gradually gathered all the ingredients needed, then showed me how to put them together, folding the pumpkin-flower mixture in a tortilla and then frying it. She was careful to explain that she was using an already baked tortilla for convenience. Whereupon she sent me off to a stall to buy a fresh lump of tortilla dough, which is made from the special cooked and ground corn that is sold dried as *masa harina* (literally "dough flour," in markets such as this one, it is already mixed with water). That was a lovely day and I became a regular visitor to markets whether in La Merced, San Juan, or Medellín in Mexico City; in Guadalajara, Querétaro, in Mérida, Yucatán; or in Cuernavaca. Wherever I went I found wonderfully knowledgeable teachers, good friends who introduced me with great generosity and enthusiasm to all manner of new foods.

Tortillas are an essential accompaniment to Mexican food. I learned easily to make them from packaged *masa harina,* using a tortilla press, which is a splendid colonial invention. Mexican cooks can pat a tortilla with their hands into a thin pancake, then slap it on to a *comal* (griddle)

13

to bake. But I found I could make only rather thick, clumsy ones this way, so I tried using a cast-iron tortilla press (the original presses were made of wood). It works very well and can be bought in this country. (See page 322.)

Beans are also an integral part of Mexican food, whether served in bowls as a separate course—not dry, rather soupy—or mashed and fried in lard to make *Frijoles Refritos*, a rich-tasting bean paste, used in all sorts of delectable ways.

A key ingredient is the tomato, and I can't imagine Mexican cooking without it, whether it is the familiar red or yellow tomato of everyday use, or the little Mexican green tomato *(Physalis ixocarpa)*—a small pale-green or yellow tomato covered with a papery husk, whose flavour develops only as it is cooked, and which is only available to us canned. Both types of tomato are used in cooked and fresh sauces, and in *Guacamole*, the avocado salad cum sauce that is another essential on the Mexican table.

Mexico, and indeed all of Latin America, adopted rice enthusiastically and it goes excellently with the *mollis* (Mexican stews) and most other dishes. Cooks all over the continent pride themselves on their rice. No matter what method they use to cook it, each grain is tender and separate.

During the years I lived in Mexico I travelled all over the country, from the northern cattle ranges where my husband's family comes from to Mayan Yucatán, from the Caribbean to the Pacific, in enthusiastic pursuit of recipies from family, friends, strangers, markets, and restaurants, captivated as I was by the exuberance of this wonderfully varied food. I worked happily in my kitchen to reproduce faithfully the dishes I found so seductive, and back in New York I put my discoveries into a cookbook. Then chance again, or should I say good fortune, took me to Central America, beginning with Guatemala—once the heart of the Mayan empire—and I realized there was a whole continent of intriguing new cookery, linked with Mexican food, still to discover.

My interest was stimulated by recent discoveries of food origins that showed that agriculture had been born simultaneously in the Middle East and in the Valley of Mexico about 7000 B.C. In the Middle East animals such as sheep, goats, pigs, and cattle were domesticated, and barley, wheat, peas, and lentils cultivated. Gradually this produce spread all over Europe and Asia. Rice was introduced from Asia about 3500 B.C. Peanuts, Guinea yams, and millet came from Africa some centuries later. At the same time in Mexico, that other cradle of agriculture, peppers, pumpkins, and avocados were the first cultivated food plants. A couple of thousand years later corn and the common bean followed, then lima beans, and later still, in 700 A.D., the green tomato. These foods gradually spread all over the Americas. Potatoes and sweet potatoes, cultivated in the Andean highlands by the predecessors of the Incas about 2500 B.C., spread through the continent, and so did manioc (cassava) and peanuts from Brazil. Peanuts, as a matter of fact, have a dual origin, as they were independently cultivated both in Brazil and West Africa by 1500 B.C., though of different genera, they behave the same in the cook pot. All this cultivation was, of course, a continuous process, with more and more fruits, vegetables, and crops being developed, so that by the time Columbus arrived, he found not only a whole new world, but a whole new world of food. These discoveries gave me an insight into the nature of the cuisine, for very soon after the Conquest there was a blending of cooking strains that evolved into the rich and varied cookery of Latin America today.

I knew it would take me a long time to travel the huge continent, to visit markets, to talk to cooks, to collect recipes, to learn about the food, and to cook it back home in my own kitchen. I also knew I would have a magnificent time doing so and I set off with enthusiasm, this book beginning to take tentative shape in my mind.

I found visiting the archaeological sites of the old Mayan empire a good way to trace the boundaries of the ancient cuisine. The Mayan empire began in Guatemala, spread to nearby Honduras, and into the states of Yucatán, Chiapas, and Campeche and the territory of Quintana Roo in Mexico. In this area today the cooking is Mayan, not Aztec Mexican. Since the civilization was already in decline at the time of the Conquest, not a great deal has survived. I wish more had, as it is subtle and delicate, except when it comes to fresh hot pepper sauce, which is really fiery. I love to cook with ground annatto seeds, which have a flowery fragrance when used whole, quite unlike the flavour of the coloured oil or lard made from just the reddish-orange pulp surrounding the seeds. The cooking of the rest of Central America—Belize, El Salvador, Nicaragua, Costa Rica, and Panama, which together with Guatemala and Honduras make a land bridge between North and South America—is a mixture of Mayan, Aztec Mexican, Colombian, and Spanish cuisines, with cosmopolitan influences from recent times. There is also a Caribbean influence, mostly from island people coming to work in the banana plantations.

The Caribbean seemed my next logical step, and I went off island-hopping and again found generous-hearted cooks who welcomed me with my notebook into their kitchens and shared their cooking secrets with me. Of that great arc of islands that stretches from Florida in the north to the coast of Venezuela in the south, and which Columbus discovered in 1492, only Cuba, the Dominican Republic, and Puerto Rico are part of Latin America. When Columbus arrived, first at Hispaniola (now the Dominican Republic and Haiti), the islands were inhabited by warlike Caribs and gentle Arawaks, both from South America. The Arawaks were good farmers and soon cultivated corn and peppers from Mexico, and sweet potatoes, yams, and manioc (cassava) which they must have brought with them. Their influence on the food of the islands persists in the wide use of root vegetables, hot peppers, allspice, and corn. African settlers brought okra and their own yams, but fundamentally the cooking of the Spanish-speaking islands is that of Spain—using a mixture of indigenous and introduced foods. It is a surprisingly rich and varied kitchen, particularly in the Dominican Republic where a *cocido* (stew) of chicken, beef, ham, and sausages, cooked with an assemblage of vegetables, is a veritable feast.

I could now see the pattern that the common heritage of Spain and Portugal and an early shared agriculture wove into the tapestry that makes Latin American food into a richly diverse unity. And so I set off on a series of journeys to South America, lucky to have friends all over the continent to help me. I began with the Andean countries—Venezuela, Colombia, Ecuador, Peru, Bolivia, and Chile—visiting them one by one.

The 4,000-mile mountain chain of the Andes, which runs along the Pacific coast of South America from Venezuela to the tip of Chile, dominates the continent. The foothills begin at the coast, which is lushly sub-tropical in the north and desert from Peru on south. The mountains rise range upon range interspersed with high plateaus and cut by wild mountain rivers, until they descend into the valley of the Amazon. It is awe-inspiring country, and travelling in it I felt as if I were in a sea of mountains. Before air travel became commonplace, journeys were difficult so that cuisines developed independently of each other. It was just as hard for people and goods to get from the coast to the highlands as from country to country, so there is a tropical and a temperate cuisine as well. Modern roads and transportation have changed this, blurring the distinctions.

Venezuela's cuisine is small, as there was no great indigenous Indian civilization. The country was discovered in 1498 by Columbus when he found the mouths of the Orinoco River. Spanish settlement began in 1520. The basis of the cookery is colonial more than anything else with borrowings and adaptations from other Latin American countries. Black beans are a great favourite and Venezuelans call their mashed black beans *caviar criollo*, native caviar, surely the ultimate culinary compliment. The national dish is as eclectic as the rest of the cooking. It is based on a sixteenth-century Spanish recipe, *Ropa Vieja* (Old Clothes), made from shredded flank steak in a rich tomato sauce—very good, despite its name—and is served with fried eggs, black beans, rice, and fried plantains. There is also a good avocado sauce, *Guasacaca*, derived from Mexico's *Guacamole*, and a fine fish dish, *Corbullón Mantuano* (Striped Bass in Sweet Pepper Sauce), that echoes Mexico's famous *Pescado a la Veracruzana* (Fish, Veracruz Style). The local corn bread is the *arepa*, made in a similar way to Mexico's tortillas but with a different type of corn. *Arepas* are much thicker, more like buns than pancakes, and the corn flavour is much less pronounced than in tortillas. German settlers of the last century are responsible for the very good cheeses of Venezuela and the excellent beer, for that matter. There is a delicious runny fresh cream cheese that turns an *arepa* into a feast when the corn bread is served hot, then pulled apart and stuffed with the cheese.

Colombia has a very grand geography with two seacoasts—one on the Pacific, one on the Caribbean—which gives the country a large choice of fish and shellfish. Three great mountain ranges, from six thousand to nineteen thousand feet, rise from the coast like the steps of a giant staircase, forming a series of plateaus at different heights so that the country has every type of climate and produces every kind of food. Wandering around the markets in the capital, Bogotá, I found piles of coconuts, bananas, plantains, pineapples, cherimoyas, papayas, sugarcane, avocados, guavas, and tropical root vegetables like yams, taros, sweet potatoes, cassava roots, and *arracacha* sharing space with peaches, pears, apricots, apples, grapes, and plums.

The conquering Spanish intermarried with the dominant Indians, the Chibchas, great gold workers who had a highly advanced civilization. The modern cuisine is very varied, sophisticated, and original. The coastal kitchen makes imaginative use of coconut milk—with rice, fish, meats, and poultry. I particularly like *Arroz con Coco y Pasas* (Rice with Coconut and Raisins) and its twin dish *Arroz con Coco Frito y Pasas* (Rice with Fried Coconut and Raisins): the rice is dry and quite firm, *bien graneado*, which is the equivalent of *al dente* in pasta. I also like the subtle flavour of *Sábalo Guisado con Coco* (Shad Fillets in Coconut Milk), which can be made either with shad or with another white-fleshed fish. The highlands produce wonderful stews, perhaps the most famous of which is *Ajiaco de Pollo Bogotano* (Bogotá Chicken Stew). There is the even grander *Sancocho Especial* (Special Boiled

Dinner) with a great selection of meats and vegetables, some from the tropics. It is a splendid dish for a family gathering or a party. As in all of Latin America, fresh coriander is used a great deal and there is always a fresh hot pepper sauce on the table to be taken at one's discretion.

My next trip was to Ecuador. The highland region was part of the Incan empire. The tropical lowlands were not conquered until the arrival of the Spanish. Quito, the capital, at nearly ten thousand feet lies within an extinct volcano, Pichincha, which rises to fifteen thousand feet. Eight volcanoes—among them the fabled Chimborazo, over twenty thousand feet, and Cotopaxi, over nineteen thousand feet—can be seen on clear days from Quito. The equator is only fifteen miles away, giving the highlands a gentle climate. There is a great contrast between tropical sea level cuisine and highland cookery, especially as one was Incan, the other not.

On the wall of the cathedral in the main plaza of Quito is a plaque that says that the glory of Ecuador is that it discovered the Amazon River down which Francisco de Orellana floated in a homemade boat, arriving at the source in 1541. I think it could also be claimed that the glory of the Ecuadorian kitchen is its *seviches* (fish "cooked" in lime or lemon juice). They are quite different from other countries' *seviches* mostly because of the use of Seville (bitter) orange juice in a sauce of onion, garlic, and oil. I tasted *seviches* made from bass, prawns lobster, and an interesting black conch. They are best accompanied by chilled beer. In Latin America there is never any problem finding beer of excellent quality with a nice bite to it, sharp on the tongue, refreshingly dry.

Potatoes play a large role in Ecuadorian highland cooking. A favourite dish is *Locro*, a thick potato and cheese soup that is sometimes served with avocado slices. I find it makes a splendid light lunch or supper if followed by a dessert or fruit. With Ecuadorian friends at midday dinner, still the main meal in most of Latin America, I had it as a course that followed a corn soufflé and preceded the meat. It was made with a little sweet paprika, but the coastal version uses annatto (achiote), which has a more pronounced flavour. Another good potato dish is *Llapingachos*, fried potato and cheese patties that are served with various accompaniments either as a first or as a main course according to what goes with them. They make an admirable addition to grilled meat, fish, or poultry. On the coast they are usually fried in annatto lard or oil. Coastal rice is also usually cooked with annatto, which turns it yellow.

Vegetables are highly esteemed in Ecuador and are served in that gentle climate at room temperature, several at a time. Since water at ten thousand feet boils at a much lower temperature than at sea level, vegetables are always crisply tender without the cook making a great effort. I think of this as a cuisine that builds bridges between the exotic and the known, using mustard in imaginative ways and contrasting texture and flavour. I was once served hot roast pork, cut into cubes and arranged in a circle on a serving dish, the centre filled with slightly chilled, chopped ripe tomatoes. Delicious. There is, as everywhere, a hot sauce, *Salsa de Aji*, to be taken or not as one pleases, this one made from fresh hot red or green peppers simply ground with salt and mixed with a little chopped onion.

Of all the Andean countries the cuisine of Peru is the most exciting, though in creating it the brilliant agriculturists of the region had a most formidable geography to contend with. The narrow coastal plain is desert except where rivers create a brief oasis. The mountains rise abruptly, completely barren, but they create fertile valleys with great rivers running through them, and wide plateaus with temperate farm- and pastureland, though already as high as eleven thousand feet. Higher still, at fourteen thousand feet, are only barren, windswept uplands.

It was in the temperate highlands, the steep mountainsides terraced to provide more land for crops, that the ancient people of the region developed the sweet potato and over a hundred varieties of the potato some time around 2500 B.C. They freeze-dried potatoes, using the cold of the Andean highlands to freeze the vegetables overnight, thawing them in the morning sun and squeezing out the moisture. The resulting rock-hard potatoes were called *chuño* and kept indefinitely. The only large domestic animals were the cameloids—the llama and the alpaca—used by the Incas for their wool, as pack animals, and for meat, and I believe they made a fresh cheese from their milk, though I can't prove it.

The Incan empire had an extensive highway system to which only the Roman is comparable, linking its more than thirty towns and cities. Farmers in this highly organized, highly urban society sent their produce to market in the town or city nearest them. A sophisticated cuisine developed with a characteristic use of hot peppers, *ají*. Peruvians like their food *picante* and are lavish in their use of peppers, of which they have a considerable variety, just about all of them hot. They are a wonderful sight in the markets, enormous piles of *rocotos* and *mirasols*, great heaps of sun yellow, flaming orange, or red as well as green peppers in various sizes, but it is the yellow ones that catch the eye. I like to speculate about the use of yellow in the food of countries that were sun worshippers before the Conquest brought Christianity. I don't think it can be an accident that Peru uses the *herb palillo*, ground to a sunshine-yellow powder, to colour and flavour food. And there are the yellow potatoes—true potatoes, not sweet potatoes—which have yellow flesh, as well as yellow sweet potatoes, and plantains, yellow when ripe. The yellows continue in the pumpkin family from the pale yellow of the huge *zapallo* to the deep yellow of other types, and in fresh corn. There are potato dishes that are a symphony of yellow and white, perhaps honouring the sun god and the moon goddess. In any case, they are lovely food in a cuisine full of marvellous dishes.

Little is known of the cooking of the Bolivian highlands, though this region was once the site of impressive civilizations. From the cook's point of view the altitude is rather daunting, for Bolivia tends to be high, higher, and highest. Lake Titicaca, which Bolivia shares with Peru, lies at 12,500 feet. Legend has it that an island in the lake is the legendary home of the Incas. Quite nearby are the ruins of Tiahuanaco, a pre-Incan city. After the Conquest Bolivia became part of Peru and was known as *El Alto Peru*, Upper Peru. With independence the name was changed to Bolivia to honour the liberator, Simón Bolívar. Like the Peruvians, the Bolivians like their food hot and are lavish in their use of hot peppers. Their most popular dishes are stews and hearty soups. However, my favourite is a very good chicken pie with a corn topping, *Pastel de Choclo con Relleno de Pollo*, which I recommend with enthusiasm.

The geography of Chile poses very different problems. The northern third of this stringbean of a country, twenty-six hundred miles long and sandwiched between the Pacific Ocean and the Andes, is unrelieved desert, the most total desert on earth. Flying over it, the shadows are so intensely dark they look like pools of water, a tantalizing illusion. It is strangely, movingly beautiful. The southern third is mountainous and storm-swept, with more rain than it needs, but the middle third is lovely, temperate, and fertile, with green valleys full of vineyards that produce very fine wines, splendid vegetables and fruits, among them notable strawberries. The southern part of this felicitous third is heavily forested with a series of lakes, a landscape of rare loveliness. And, of course, the snowcapped Andes make a permanently dramatic backdrop.

The cold Humboldt Current gives Chile the most unusual seafood in the world. I can only think of the giant sea urchins, *erizos*; giant abalone, *locos*, tender as chicken when properly beaten; of *picoroccos*, strange, beaked shellfish that taste like crabs; giant crabs; mussels;

clams; shrimp; *langostines*; oysters; and *congrio*, a splendid fish unique to these waters. Only in Chile can one enjoy these gifts of the cold current. All the same I found many interesting dishes that are not dependent on special ingredients—dishes like *Congrio en Fuente de Barro* (Fish with Tomatoes and Onions), *Pollo Escabechado* (Pickled Chicken), and *Porotos Granados* (Cranberry Beans with Corn and Pumpkin).

There was no great Indian civilization in what is now Argentina and Uruguay. Though they are today separate countries, before independence from Spain they were both part of the viceroyalty of the River Plate. Spanish cooking methods using indigenous and introduced ingredients produced the local cuisine, which has been somewhat modified by newer arrivals—Italian influence predominating. Like Chile, Argentina produces good wine, and its beef ranks with the best in the world. *Matambre*, which translates literally into kill hunger, and into kitchen parlance as stuffed rolled flank steak, is an example of what Argentine cooks can do with a comparatively humble cut of beef. And the *Empanadas*, the pastry turnovers, variously stuffed, are the best I've ever had. There are some unusual and good meat stews with fruits, such as *Carbonada Criolla* (Beef Stew, Argentine Style) with peaches and *Carbonada en Zapallo* (Veal Stew in Baked Pumpkin), which includes pears and peaches and finishes cooking in a large, hollowed-out pumpkin. It is a delicious combination.

Paraguay is a small landlocked country where Guaraní, the language of the Indians of the region, is co-equal with Spanish as an official language. The cooking is Spanish and Guaraní, with some international food, mostly French and Italian. My favourite Paraguayan dish is the magnificently named *So'O-Yosopy* (the last syllable is pronounced with an explosive PEH), that translates into Spanish as *sopa de carne* (beef soup). I know of nothing more restorative when one is worn-out. I'm almost as fond of *Sopa Paraguaya*, which is not a soup at all but a rich cheese and cornmeal bread that is traditionally served with steak; but as far as I am concerned, it is good by itself and goes with almost everything. Paraguay is also the home of *Mate* tea, a very ancient Indian drink that is pleasantly stimulating, since it has a good deal of caffeine.

Of all the cuisines in South America, the Brazilian is the most exuberant and varied. The country, taking up nearly half the continent of South America, is enormous, stretching from the tropics in the north to the temperate south, with great highlands and a long coastline. It bulges generously out into the South Atlantic toward Africa with which it is once believed to have been joined—perhaps accounting for the dual origin of the peanut. The ethnic mix is as varied as the climate, which ranges from torrid to temperate. There are the original Indians, the Portuguese, Africans, Italians, Germans, and so on. And there are all the foods of the world plus many cooking techniques, making a rich amalgam. The sheer size of the country has made for authentic regional cooking.

There was no great Indian civilization in Brazil. Today's cuisine has developed since the arrival of the Portuguese who in 1539 founded Salvador in the state of Bahia on the northeast coast, planted sugarcane, and brought in African slaves to work in the cane fields. From a combination of the foods and cooking methods of local Indians, Africans, and Portuguese, Brazil's most exciting cooking, the *cozinha baiana*, Bahian cookery, developed. The primary ingredients are *dendê* (palm) oil from Africa, which has a nutty flavour and colours food an attractive orangey-yellow, coconut, fresh coriander, fresh and dried shrimp, and nuts—almonds, cashews, peanuts—and of course, hot peppers. A hot sauce made with tiny *malaqueta* peppers steeped in *dendê* oil and *farofa* made from manioc (cassava) meal, often coloured yellow with *dendê* oil, is always on the table. Brazilians in all parts of the country sprinkle meat, poultry, and other dishes with *farofa*, as others might use grated Parmesan cheese.

The cooking of Rio de Janeiro which supplanted Salvador as the capital in 1763 seems almost subdued by comparison. It is closer to Portuguese, using local ingredients, except for *Feijoada Completa*, a regional recipe from Rio which is now recognized as the national dish. It is a very splendid, colourful meal of meats and black beans cooked together so that the many flavours are blended, and it is served, lavishly garnished, with sliced oranges, rice, cooked kale, *farofa*, and a hot pepper and lime juice sauce. I cannot think of a better dish for a party.

São Paulo and Minas Gerais to the south share a regional cuisine. It was the Paulistas who, in the seventeenth century, set out looking for gold and found it, together with diamonds and other mineral wealth in the mountainous country to the northeast. This is now the state of Minas Gerais, which means general mines, a succinct description of what the Paulistas found. It is hearty food, well suited to the cooler climate. One of its best dishes is *Cozido à Brasileira* (Stew, Brazilian Style), a splendidly robust pot-au-feu. The most famous dish is *Cuscuz Paulista*, an adaptation of the couscous that originated in Arabia and spread to North Africa. It is made with cornmeal (maize) instead of wheat, looks marvellously decorative, and is surprisingly easy to make.

Desserts all over Brazil are rich and very much in the Portuguese egg-yolk-and-sugar tradition with its strong Moorish overtones.

Throughout Latin America there are examples of the oldest form of cooking, the neolithic earth oven, now superseded for centuries by stoves of one kind or another from charcoal to electric or gas. It has persisted as holiday cooking. Country people in Mexico cook a whole lamb in an earth oven for a *barbacoa*, and less rural people have *barbacoa* parties on Sundays and holidays at special restaurants devoted to this form of cooking. In Yucatán the earth oven is called a *pib*; in the Andes it is called *pachamanca* from the Quechua words for earth and pot. In southern Chile they have a *curanto*, best described as a clambake like those in New England. It is often lavish and includes a suckling pig as well as Chile's magnificent shellfish.

Argentina, Uruguay, and Brazil all have barbecues. In Argentina there are splendid restaurants where meats are cooked on wall-size grills, and in Brazil there are *Churrascarias* where all manner of grilled meats are served. I think the best proof I ever had of the popularity of this form of cooking was on a main street in Montevideo, Uruguay, when I watched some road repairmen settle down to lunch. They made a fire, put a piece of wire netting on top of it, grilled a steak, opened a bottle of red wine, and with the addition of some good bread had an excellent meal.

Looking back to the day when I determined to collect Latin American recipes—true gems of cookery—into a book gives me a feeling of great pleasure. I have done what I so deeply wanted to do, to bring these delectable dishes within the reach of cooks everywhere, a practical aim since in our modern world many once exotic ingredients are now supermarket commonplaces. I have spent a long time on my research; I have made many exciting journeys and eaten a great deal of very good food. It has been infinitely worthwhile. I sought out the historical hows and whys of this intriguing cuisine and found academic answers which I recorded in my endless notebooks in a special kind of cook's shorthand. A fascinating analysis to be sure, of ancient peoples and cities, of the birth of agriculture, of the coming together, in the kitchen, of very different cultures. That was only part of what I sought. I found the rest quite simply in wonderful food, the focal point of family and social life. So the best part of my quest has been coming back to my own kitchen and bringing to life those scribbled words, turning them into dishes with the authentic taste of Latin American cooking.

It isn't food that is difficult to cook or bristles with complicated techniques. For the most part it is straightforward and easy, though there are some cooking methods that may seem odd at first, like frying a paste of peppers and other ingredients in lard or oil as a preliminary to making a Mexican *mole.* And I did have to learn about unfamiliar fruits and vegetables and seek them out in my own markets back home, where I found them without much trouble. I remembered flavours, and altered recipes until the taste was right, and had friends and family in to share splendid meals with me. It was a joyous experience and I have never been happier than when I received the accolade bestowed on good cooks in Latin America, *"tiene buena mano,"* "She has a good hand." It is my hope that readers will want to share my experience, and will cook, enjoy, and adopt these recipes as family favourites.

Ingredients

Most of the ingredients for Latin American cooking are the ordinary everyday ones available from our butchers and fishmongers, grocers and green grocers. But there are a few special ingredients for which it is worth searching. The supply position for exotic ingredients is changing so fast that last year's exotic is this year's commonplace. It is impossible to give very exact shopping instructions but, in general, markets in areas with a large immigrant population, such as Brixton or Shepherd's Bush in London, are splendid sources. Supermarkets can be surprisingly good hunting grounds and so can health food shops. Fortunately most of the hard-to-find ingredients are non-perishable and may be bought and stored for future use.

See page 000 for particularly useful sources of Latin American foods.

Aliño Criollo (Creole Style Seasoning Powder), a Venezuelan seasoning mixture made of herbs and spices, used with meat and poultry, in stews, and so on. Easy to make at home, see recipe, page 000.

Allspice or **pimiento** (*Pimenta officinalis*), the *pimiento de Jamaica* or *pimienta gorda* of the Spanish-speaking countries is the small, dark brown berry of an evergreen tree of the myrtle family found by the Spaniards growing wild in Jamaica. Most exports still come from the island. The dried berries, which closely resemble peppercorns, combine the flavour of cinnamon, nutmeg, and cloves. Available whole or ground.

Annatto is the English name given to the seeds of a small flowering tree of tropical America. Known as *achiote* in Spanish from the Nahuatl (Aztec) *achiotl*, the seeds are sometimes called *bija* or *bijol* in the Spanish-speaking islands of the Caribbean. The Caribs and Arawaks called the seeds *roucou*, a name by which they are still known in parts of the region. The hard orange-red pulp surrounding the seeds is used to make *Aceite o Manteca de Achiote* (Annatto Oil or Lard) and serves as a colouring and flavouring for meat, poultry, and fish dishes in the Caribbean, Colombia, Ecuador, and Venezuela. In Yucatán the whole seed is ground with various spices (such as cumin and oregano)

25

into a paste, giving a more pronounced flavour. The taste is hard to define, fragrant, light, and flowery.

Antojitos, literally little whims or fancies, the name given by the Spanish to the finger foods made with a base of tortillas that they found in Aztec Mexico. These foods fit perfectly into today's meal patterns as hors d'oeuvres or first courses. A large version, the *antojos*, whims or fancies, are ideal for light lunches or suppers.

Arepas, the corn bread of Venezuela, made from special flour of pre-cooked Venezuelan corn.

Arrowroot, the edible starchy powder made from the underground rhizomes of *Maranta arundinacea*, is a delicate thickening agent for soups, stews, and sauces.

Avocado (*Persea americana*), of the laurel family, was cultivated in Mexico as far back as 7000 B.C. and was known as *ahuacatl* in Nahuatl, the language of the ancient Mexicans. Today it is called *aguacate*. It spread to South America before Columbus arrived and was cultivated in the Inca empire, where it was called *palta*. Today it is known in Quechua by that name though in many parts of South America it keeps its Mexican name. In Brazil it is called *abacate*. The fruit may be rough or smooth-skinned, green or black. It is hard when unripe but ripens in a few days if put into a brown paper bag and left at room temperature. An avocado is ripe when it yields to a gentle pressure at the stem end. Once an avocado is cut, it discolours quickly. Sprinkling lime or lemon juice on it helps, and if you are going to try to keep an unused portion of an avocado, leave the skin on, let the stone rest in the cavity, rub the cut sides with lemon or lime, wrap tightly in plastic wrap, and refrigerate.

An easy way to mash avocados is to cut them in half, remove the stones, and mash them in their shells with a fork, holding the shell in the palm of the left hand. Scoop out the flesh with a spoon and mash any bits that may have escaped the fork. This method is much easier than having them slither round a bowl and gives a texture with character. Avocado leaves are sometimes used in Mexican cooking in the same way as bay leaves and there is also the charming bonus of being able to grow the seed into very beautiful house plants. To toast avocado leaves, place them on an ungreased *comal* (griddle) or a heavy iron skillet and cook on both sides over moderate heat for about 1 minute.

Bacalao, Spanish for dried salted codfish, called *bacalhau* in Brazil, is extremely popular in all of Latin America.

Bananas and banana leaves. Both green and ripe bananas are used in Latin American cooking, the green bananas as a vegetable. When a recipe called for plantains (page 15), bananas make a good substitute. Banana leaves are used as a wrapping in which to cook foods. Kitchen parchment or aluminum foil make good substitutes.

Beans, black (turtle), red kidney, pink, mottled pinto (light brown beans with pinkish markings sometimes sold as Crab Eye beans), haricot, or pea beans, all belong to the large grouping called *Phaseolus vulgaris* of the legume family, which originated in Mexico about 5000 B.C. They are an essential part of the Latin American kitchen and turn up in many guises. I usually follow the Mexican rules for cooking beans—namely, that they should not be soaked but should be put on to cook in cold water with their seasonings and that hot water is added as necessary during the cooking time. Salt should not be added until the beans are tender. It is impossible to give an exact time for cooking beans as it can vary from 1½ to 2½ hours according to the age of the beans. It is wise to buy beans from shops with a quick turnover, as stale beans may take a very long time to cook and even when cooked may have a dry texture. If there is reason to suspect that beans are stale, a desperate remedy may be in order. Soak them overnight in cold water with a little bicarbonate of soda (baking soda), ¼ teaspoon to 1 pound of beans, then rinse the beans very thoroughly before putting them on to cook in fresh water. It works wonders.

The Spanish and Portuguese brought chickpeas, sometimes called garbanzos or ceci (*Cicer arietinum*) also of the legume family, to the New World with them. These hard, round, yellow peas, native to the Middle East, do need soaking overnight in cold water before cooking. Another popular bean from the Middle East is the broad bean, also called fava or habas (*Vicia faba*). Other popular local beans are limas from Peru and cranberry or shell beans and, to a lesser extent, black-eyed peas, which originated in Africa. Whenever beans need soaking before cooking, instructions are given in individual recipes.

Calabaza, also called *ahuyama*, *zapallo*, *abóbora*, and, in English, pumpkin, is available from greengrocers and Caribbean shops.

Carne sêca is the sun-dried salt beef that is used in the Brazilian national dish *Feijoada Completa* (Black Beans with Mixed Meats). The salt beef used in *Sancocho Especial* (Special Boiled Dinner, see page 163) from Colombia could be used instead, or use ordinary salt beef.

Cassava (*Manihot utilissima*), also called manioc, mandioca, aipím, or yucca, is a handsome tropical plant whose tuberous roots, at least 2 inches in diameter and about 8 to 10 inches long, are best known as the commercial source of tapioca. Cassava originated in 1500 B.C. in Brazil and is widely used in the kitchens of Latin America. The

27

roots are covered with a brown, barklike, rather hairy skin. Cassava should be peeled under running water and immediately dropped into water, as its white flesh tends to discolour on contact with the air. It may be boiled and used as a potato substitute in stews, or to accompany meat and poultry dishes, or it may be fried and served like potato chips.

In Brazil manioc meal is used to make *farofa:* the meal is toasted and mixed with butter and other ingredients such as onion, eggs, or prunes and served with *Feijoada* or with poultry, steaks, or roasted meats. *Farofa,* which looks like coarsely grated Parmesan cheese, is as common on Brazilian tables as salt and pepper. Cassava meal is sold in West Indian shops as gari.

Chayote *(Sechium edule),* of the squash family, is also known as christophene, cho-cho, and chuchu. The vegetable originated in Mexico, and the name comes from the Mexican *chayotl.* It is now widely grown in semi-tropical regions throughout the world. About 6 to 8 inches long, and roughly pear-shaped, chayote is usually a light, pretty green (though there are white varieties), with a slightly prickly skin and a single edible seed. The texture is crisp with a delicate flavour a little like courgettes but more subtle. It is best when young and firm. Avoid soft or wrinkled ones. Available in West Indian shops and sometimes in supermarkets.

Chicha, a beerlike drink made from dried corn. Usually only slightly alcoholic. Popular throughout South America.

Chicharrones are fried pork rinds.

Coconuts and **coconut milk.** Choose coconuts that are full of liquid. Shake them to check. Nuts with little liquid are stale. Avoid those with mouldy or wet "eyes."

With an ice pick, screwdriver, or similar sharp implement, pierce two out of the three eyes of the nut using a hammer to bang it through if necessary. Drain out and reserve the liquid. Strain it before use as there may be bits of coconut fibre in it. A medium-sized coconut yields about ¼ pint liquid. Bake the coconut in a preheated hot oven for 15 minutes. Then put the coconut on a hard surface and hit it all over with a hammer. The hard shell will fall away. Lever out any bits that are left with a knife or screwdriver. If making coconut milk it is not necessary to peel off the brown inner skin, but if grated coconut is to be used in a recipe, peel this off with a small, sharp knife.

Chop the coconut pieces coarsely, then put into a blender or food processor fitted with a steel blade and grate as fine as possible. The grated coconut is now ready for use. If the coconut water is not to be used separately in a recipe, add it to the blender or food processor with the coconut pieces as this helps in the grating. This makes about 1½ pints per coconut.

To make thick (rich) coconut milk squeeze the grated coconut in a damp cloth, squeezing and twisting the cloth to remove as much liquid as possible. Set this aside. To make ordinary coconut milk put the squeezed-out coconut into a bowl and pour ½ pint boiling water over it. Let it stand 30 minutes. Squeeze out the liquid through a damp cloth and set aside. Repeat the entire process. Discard the coconut.

Unless a recipe calls for thick coconut milk to be used separately, mix the thick and ordinary coconut milk together and use. When thick coconut milk is left to stand, the cream rises to the top. This is delicious instead of cream with desserts. If the coconut water drained out of the nut at the beginning is not needed for any culinary purpose, it makes a wonderful mix with gin or vodka.

If coconuts are not available, desiccated coconut is an acceptable substitute for grated fresh coconut. Creamed coconut available from West Indian shops and delicatessens is a good substitute for coconut milk. Simply dilute to the desired consistency with warm water or milk.

Freshly grated coconut keeps well frozen.

Coriander *(Coriandrum sativum)*, of the carrot family, indigenous to the Mediterranean and the Caucasus, is a very old herb, mentioned in Sanskrit and ancient Egyptian writings. Its antiquity is proved by the fact that the Romans introduced it to Britain before the end of the first century A.D. It has spread throughout the world and is very important in Indian and Thai cooking, indeed in most of Asia including China.

It is often sold as Chinese parsley and though the leaves are a lighter green, it does resemble flat-leafed parsley, also the carrot family and a close relative.

Many Mexicans think of coriander as indigenous. Certainly it is hard to imagine the Mexican green tomato dishes or *Guacamole* (Avocado Sauce) without it. If there could be said to be a favourite herb in the Mexican kitchen it would be coriander, though oregano, cumin, and to a lesser extent the indigenous herb *epazote* are all popular.

I have never been able to find out when coriander first arrived in Mexico, but I think it was introduced after the Conquest and was adopted with enthusiasm. Certainly it is popular in all of Latin America. But there is a puzzle here. Coriander is not used in Spanish cooking today, although it is a favourite Middle Eastern herb and Spain was occupied for nearly eight centuries by the Arabs. In fact,

Columbus had discovered America before Spain had reconquered all its occupied provinces, so the Spanish of that time, eating Arab foods, may have brought coriander with them to the New World. Or it may have arrived via the Philippines, where it is popular; there was a great deal of trade between Mexico and the Philippines, then a Spanish possession, in early colonial times. Some kitchen mysteries may never be solved, though it is great fun trying. There is no mystery, however, about its arrival in Brazil, as it is a favourite Portuguese herb.

The fresh herb is increasingly available in greengroceries, Chinese and Cypriot shops. It is sold with its roots on and it does not keep well. The roots should not be removed for storage and the coriander should not be washed but simply wrapped in paper towels, roots and all, and stored in a plastic bag in the refrigerator. This is the simplest method and the one I use. Some recommend washing the coriander with its roots on, drying thoroughly, and refrigerating in a jar with just enough water to cover the roots. Others simply refrigerate roots and all in a glass jar with a screw top.

To have coriander available for flavouring soups and stews, I remove the roots, wash the coriander well, and purée it, including the stems, without the addition of any water in a food processor, then freeze the purée in an ice cube tray. When frozen, I store the cubes in a plastic bag. One cube is the equivalent of about 1 tablespoon of the freshly chopped leaves. This works well where flavour—not appearance—is what matters. Sometimes the coriander roots are quite sizeable. In Thailand, the country, incidentally, in which I became a coriander addict, they are scraped and used in curries. They add a very intense flavour. I always keep an eye out for these fat roots, a happy bonus.

The tiny brown seedlike fruits of coriander are also used in cooking, especially in curries, and to flavour gin. They are available in jars in the spice section of supermarkets and I have grown coriander from them.

Cornmeal, yellow maize flour, is sold in supermarkets and grocer's shops as cornmeal maize or coarse cornmeal maize. Italian shops sell it as polenta.

Crème fraîche. Venezuela has a lovely runny fresh cream cheese that is wonderful with hot *arepas* (corn bread). It is very like French *crème fraîche*. A good imitation of *crème fraîche* can be made by mixing 1 tablespoon of buttermilk with ½ pint double cream and heating the mixture to lukewarm in a small saucepan. Pour it into a jar and let it stand until it has thickened, about 8 hours in a warm room. It will then keep for several days refrigerated.

Dendê oil (palm oil), originally from Africa and very much used in Bahian cooking in Brazil. It is a deep, beautiful orange-gold and has a pleasant nutty flavour. Available in West Indian and African shops. It lends colour and some flavour to dishes but one can manage without it.

Epazote (*Chenopodium ambrosioides*), a herb used in Mexican cooking especially in black bean and tortilla dishes. The name comes from the Nahuatl *epazotl*. It is ubiquitous, growing wild all over the Americas and in many parts of Europe. It is easy to grow as a pot herb from seed and dries well. To dry it spread the leaves on paper towels and put into a dark, warm cupboard, or put on a tray in the oven with the pilot light on. Store in glass jars. There is no substitute but fortunately it is not vital to the success of the dishes. For supplier of seeds see page 322.

Flowers of the pumpkin family, those pretty golden yellow blooms of pumpkin, courgette or marrow plants, are much used in Latin American cooking. They are not the female blossoms, which would turn into little vegetables, but the male flowers, which if not gathered and cooked would die upon the vine. Female blossoms have recognizably pumpkin-like swellings behind them; male blossoms do not. The latter make a marvellous soup among other things.

Garlic. Peruvian garlic, purple-skinned, and Mexican garlic, sometimes purple-skinned, sometimes white, have quite enormous cloves, which comes in handy when one has to peel a number of them. The size of garlic cloves varies so widely, as does a taste for garlic, that I have adopted in most instances the system of simply giving the number of cloves needed so that those who are particularly fond of garlic may seek out the big ones with a clear conscience.

Guascas or **huascas** (*Galinsoga parviflora Lineo*) is a Colombian herb that grows in the Andes. It is sold in jars, dried and ground into a green powder, in Colombian food shops. Though it has no relationship whatsoever to Jerusalem artichokes, its smell is reminiscent of that vegetable. It adds a delicious flavour to soups and stews, particularly those made with chicken. Since delicatessens, health food shops and supermarkets constantly increase the range of their imports, I have included it here in case it should become available, but it is not essential to the success of any of the recipes in this book.

Hearts of palm, in Spanish and Portuguese *palmito*, are the tender heart buds of any one of several species of palm trees. Their delicate flavour is exquisite in salads and soups. Though they are eaten fresh in the countries of origin, they are always canned for export and are available in delicatessens.

Huacatay, a herb of the marigold family, is used in Peru in sauces and dishes such as *Picante de Yuca* (Cassava Root with Cheese Sauce). It is not available here and there is no substitute. The flavour is unusual and is certainly an acquired taste, rather rank at first try. I find I don't miss it.

Jerusalem artichokes, despite their name, are the edible tubers of a plant native to Canada and the northern United States. Their botanical name is *Helianthus tuberosus,* and they are a species of sunflower belonging to the daisy family. Jerusalem is apparently a corruption of *girasole,* the Italian word for sunflower. They are called *topinambur* in South America. They have a lovely crisp texture reminiscent of water chestnuts. They make a delightful soup, an excellent salad, and are a lovely change of pace from the more usual potatoes as a starchy root vegetable. They are a little tricky to peel since the small tubers are knobby in shape. I always pick out the largest and least knobby ones available, but I have also found recently that newer varieties are easier to peel. When I scrape them I'm not all that fussy about a bit of skin left on, as it is not at all unpleasant, and I just shave off the little knobs. It is very important not to overcook them since they lose their crisp texture and turn mushy.

Jícama, pronounced HEE-kama *(Exogonium bracteatum),* of the morning glory family, is a tuberous turnip-shaped root vegetable with a light brown skin, originally from Mexico, where it is usually eaten raw, sliced, with a little salt and a sprinkling of hot chili powder (cayenne), or in salads. It has crispy, juicy white flesh. Water chestnuts or tart green cooking apples are the best substitutes.

Malanga see **Taro**.

Mate, a tea made from the dried leaves of the South American evergreen *Ilex paraguayensis.* Especially popular in Paraguay, Uruguay, Argentina, and Brazil. Make according to package directions or see page 321.

Mole, pronounced MO-lay, from the Nahuatl (Mexican) word *molli,* meaning a sauce made from any of the peppers, sweet, pungent, or hot, usually a combination, together with other ingredients. The most famous of the *moles* is the *Mole Poblano de Guajalote,* the turkey dish from Puebla using bitter chocolate, but there are a host of others playing variations on a theme.

Nopal is the prickly pear cactus. The young paddles are used mainly in salads. Available tinned as *nopalitos.*

Oranges, bitter, sour, Seville, or Bigarade, to give this fruit all the names by which it is commonly known, are available in January and February. The large, rough-skinned, reddish-orange fruit has a delicate and quite distinctive flavour, but the pulp is too sour to be eaten raw. The juice, which is used a great deal in Latin American cooking, freezes successfully, and the peel need not be wasted but can be used to make marmalade. A mixture of one-third lime or lemon juice to two-thirds sweet orange juice can be used as a substitute.

Palillo is a Peruvian herb used dried and ground to give a yellow colour to food. Since so many Peruvian foods are yellow or white, I'm sure it is a reflection of pre-Conquest Inca sun (and moon) worship. *Palillo* is not available here but I have found that using half the amount of turmeric gives much the same result.

Pepitas, Mexican pumpkin seeds, available in supermarkets and health food stores.

PEPPERS

Peppers, sweet, pungent, and hot, all belong to the genus *Capsicum annuum* or *Capsicum frutescens* of the *Solanaceae* family, to which potato, tomato, and aubergine also belong. They were first cultivated in the Valley of Mexico about 9,000 years ago and their original name in Nahuatl was *chilli*. Varieties are legion and have not yet been fully classified botanically. They have spread all over the world and become naturalized so quickly that their national origin has been forgotten. Peppers are widely used in Latin American cooking, especially in Mexico and Peru. The number of varieties used is, fortunately, limited. They fall into two main categories, the dried and the fresh.

The Dried Peppers

Ancho. This is the most widely used of all the peppers in the Mexican kitchen. It is quite large, with a wrinkled skin, about 4 inches long by about 3 inches wide. It has a deep, lovely colour and a rich, full flavour. It is the base of many cooked sauces.

Mulato. Much the same size and shape as the *ancho* but darker in colour, closer to brown than red, and longer and more tapering. Its flavour is more pungent than the mild *ancho*. It is wrinkled.

Pasilla. This is a long, slender pepper, 6 to 7 inches in length and about an inch or so wide, and very much darker in colour than the *ancho*. Like ancho and mulato peppers, it is wrinkled and some varieties are so dark they are called *chile negro* (black peppers). It is very hot but at the same time richly flavoured. In Mexico these three peppers are often used in combination.

Chipotle and **morita.** These are dried wrinkled peppers, brick red in colour. Both are smaller than *ancho* peppers, with the *morita* smaller than the *chipotle*. Though they are available dried and sometimes ground, they are more usually canned. They have the most distinctive flavour of all the Mexican peppers and are very, very hot. If used sparingly, the exciting flavour comes through without excessive heat.

SMALL HOT DRIED PEPPERS

There are a number of small hot dried red peppers under various names, *cascabel*, *pequín*, *tepín*, which can be used interchangeably whenever dried hot red peppers are called for. One variety, a Japanese migrant, is called *hontaka* and should be treated with respect as it is very hot indeed. Hot paprika or cayenne pepper can be used instead: ⅛ teaspoon is about the equivalent of a whole *pequín*.

Mirasol. This is a medium-sized tapering, wrinkled, dried hot pepper from Peru, which may be either red or yellow. It is not available here, but dried hot red peppers are an excellent substitute. The larger ones like the Japanese *hontaka* are the most suitable.

How to Use Dried Red Peppers: The method used in Mexican cooking is the same for *ancho*, *pasilla*, *mulato*, *chipotle*, and *morita* chilies. Rinse in cold water, tear off the stem end, and shake out the seeds. Tear the chilies roughly into pieces and soak in warm water, about 6 to 1 cup, for half an hour. If they are very dry, soak them a little longer. Purée them with the water in which they have soaked in a blender or food processor fitted with a steel blade. The resulting almost paste-like purée is then ready to be cooked in hot lard or oil with the other ingredients specified in the recipe to make the sauce.

Canned *chipotle* and *morita* chilies are puréed right out of the can without soaking, or used as the recipe specifies. The small hot dried red chilies are usually just crumbled with the fingers.

Always wash the hands in warm soapy water after handling chilies. Hot chili accidentally rubbed in the eyes can be very painful.

Dried chilies are best stored in plastic bags in the refrigerator or other cool place. They dry out if exposed to the air.

The Fresh Peppers

HOT FRESH PEPPERS

A number of small and medium-sized hot green peppers are sold fresh in supermarkets and greengrocers all year round. They are not usually identified beyond being called hot peppers. In Mexico the most commonly used small fresh peppers are the *serrano*, about 1½ inches long, tapering, smooth-skinned, medium green, and the *ja-*

lapeño, which is slightly darker in colour and larger, about 2½ inches long. Both are quite hot. *Jalapeño* is sold interchangeably with *cuaresmeño*, a pepper so like it that some botanists classify them as the same. The shape is slightly different and I think the *cuaresmeño* is hotter. As most of the heat in these peppers is in the seeds and veins, remove them, unless fiery heat is wanted. These peppers are also sold canned and are very useful since they can be used when fresh peppers are not available.

There is a tiny hot pepper that in Brazil is called *malagueta*. It is fiery. A larger one, sometimes called cayenne chili, is widely available year round in greengrocers and can also be found in Chinese shops. These two are sometimes sold ripe, when they have turned red. They are then slightly less hot, and have a somewhat richer flavour.

In the West Indies there is a lantern-shaped pepper that the Jamaicans call Scotch Bonnet, usually quite small, about 1½ inches long, with a most exquisite flavour. It is the *habanero* of Yucatán and is also popular in tropical Brazil. This pepper is sold green, yellow, and red in its three stages of ripening. It is fiery hot but has a flavour that makes it worth seeking. I have found it fresh in West Indian shops and also bottled, usually imported from Trinidad. The bottled version keeps indefinitely in the refrigerator.

Any of these peppers can be used when fresh hot red or green peppers are called for.

Peppers vary a great deal in strength. There is only one way to find out how hot they are and that is by tasting. Nibble a tiny bit of hot pepper, and if it seems very fiery, use it sparingly. But tastes vary as much as peppers do, so the only true guide is to please yourself. As with dried peppers, always wash your hands in warm, soapy water after handling.

Visiting markets in Peru, I came upon great heaps of yellow peppers, *ají amarillo* (fresh hot yellow peppers), an astonishment to the eye. Surely nothing short of gold is as yellow as these peppers. Yellow peppers are not always available here. Fresh hot red or green peppers are just as good from the point of view of flavour.

SWEET FRESH PEPPERS

Perhaps the most widely used of all peppers is the green bell pepper, available year round everywhere. There is also a splendid Mexican pepper, the *poblano*, dark green and tapering and about the same size as the bell pepper, but it is not available here. It is used especially for stuffed peppers and the bell pepper makes a good substitute.

The green pepper turns red when ripe. A similar pepper, though a different variety, is the pimiento, tapering in shape. It is always sold canned or in jars, often labelled *pimientos morrones*. When red peppers are unavailable, use the canned pimientos. Already peeled and cooked, they can be used straight from the jar and make a very attractive garnish.

How to Peel Red or Green Peppers: Stick a cooking fork into the stem end of the peppers and toast them over a gas flame or electric burner, turning frequently, until the skin blisters and blackens. Wrap the peppers in a cloth wrung out in hot water and leave for 30 minutes. The burned part of the thin papery skin will rinse off easily under cold running water and most of the rest can be pulled away. If a few bits of skin remain, it does not matter. Toasting the peppers in this way also brings out their flavour.

Piloncillo, Mexican brown sugar packaged in pyramid-shaped pieces. Similar moulded brown sugar is called a variety of names. Use dark brown sugar instead.

Plantains, *plátanos* in Spanish, are members of the same family as bananas—bird-of-paradise *(Strelitzia)*. They are much larger and are not edible until cooked even when they are quite ripe and their skins are black. They are fried or boiled green, half-ripe, and ripe, and are usually served as a starchy vegetable to accompany meat, poultry, or fish. They also make a good cocktail nibble when green *(verde)*, thinly sliced, and deep fried.

How to Peel a Plantain or Green Banana: Neither plantains, except very ripe ones, nor green bananas peel readily by hand. The simplest method is to make shallow lengthwise cuts along the natural ridges of the fruit and pull the skin off in sections.

Potatoes. The people we call the Incas for convenience, though it was quite likely a much earlier civilization, now lost in time, first cultivated potatoes in the high Andes. They developed a bewildering variety, some of which survive today. Among the survivors are large, yellow-fleshed potatoes that look beautiful used in the Peruvian potato dishes. However, this is more a matter of aesthetics than flavour as any good-quality potato that takes to boiling can be used instead. Colombia has a small version of the Peruvian potato. They are also yellow-fleshed, are called *papas criollas*, and are the size of new potatoes. As they stay firm when cooked, Colombians use them in stews with other, softer potatoes, which disintegrate to thicken the gravy, leaving the *papas criollas* intact. Any good small new potato, especially a waxy one, does very well as a substitute.

Sausages. There are no problems in finding the right sausages for Latin American cooking. Chorizos, Spanish-style hot, spicy pork sausages, are available. Blood sausages are very little different from *morcilla*, and Polish *kielbasa*, boiling ring, available in supermarkets, is a splendid substitute for Spanish *longaniza* or Brazilian *linguiça*.

Shrimps (dried) are used a great deal in Bahian cooking in Brazil. They are tiny and are ground before being used in dishes like *vatapá*. A food processor fitted with a steel blade takes the hard work out of this chore. A blender can also be used. If the shrimp are very dry, a brief soaking in warm water helps. Available in Chinese stores.

Sierra (Spanish mackerel) is a large fish that can reach 10 to 15 pounds. It is very attractive, with yellow the predominating colour on its back scales instead of the steely blue of Atlantic mackerel. Found off Florida and the Gulf coast, it is a popular fish in South America and is used in *Sopa de Almejas* (Clam Soup) from Colombia. Use any firm fleshed non-oily white fish as a substitute, but not Atlantic mackerel, which is too strongly flavoured.

Smoked ham. When South American recipes call for smoked ham, the one most usually used is Spanish *jamón serrano*, which has been aged in spices. Italian prosciutto, German Westphalian, French and Belgian Ardennes, or Bayonne hams are perfect substitutes.

Sweet potato (*Ipomoea batatas*) is an edible tuber originally from tropical America, though its precise birthplace is not known. Only slightly sweet, it is in no way related to the potato family. The white sweet potato with dry white flesh and pink or white skin is known as *boniato* (pronounced bon-ee-AH-toe) and is the variety most popular in Latin America. It is widely available in tropical markets and increasingly in ordinary greengrocers. It makes a delicious substitute for potatoes.

Taro and **malanga** are tropical plants that bear edible tubers and are members of the very large *Arum* family. There are a great many of them and they have been cultivated for more than 2,000 years. I think of all the root vegetables they are, apart from potatoes, the most subtly flavoured, the most delicious. Taro can be found in West Indian shops and may be called *coco* or *eddo*. A closely related group, the malangas, which belong to the genus *Xanthosoma*, are known by a wide variety of names, malanga, tannia, dasheen and *yautía* being the ones most likely to be encountered here. The skins are usually brown, the flesh white to yellow, and they can be cooked like potatoes. When I first went looking for them in markets, I wrote down all the names and asked for them in a sort of litany. I found people very understanding and helpful, and they sorted things out for me in a charmingly good-humoured way.

Tomatoes, green or husk (*Physalis ixocarpa*), which have a loose, brown papery outer covering, should not be confused with ordinary green (unripe) tomatoes. Though members of the same family, they are a different species. The Aztecs called the fruit *miltomatl*, but today in Mexico it is usually called *tomatillo* (little tomato), as it is never very large, usually only about an inch across. It has other names, *tomate verde, tomatitto,* and *fresadilla.* In English it is sometimes called Spanish tomato. When the tomatoes, which cannot be skinned as nothing would be left of them, are marketed canned as peeled, it means that the papery brown husk has been removed. The green tomato is very important in Mexican, and to a lesser extent Guatemalan, cooking, giving a distinctive flavour to the "green" dishes and sauces. The flavour is delicate and slightly acid. It is not available fresh in this country. The tinned version needs no further cooking and is ready to use. The flesh is rather delicate and the can may be full of broken fruit. When this happens, use the liquid from the can in a sauce, reducing the amount of stock or other liquid, and save the whole fruit for sauces where no liquid is required. Green tomatoes are grown easily from seed. British seedsmen sometimes carry them. Also see availability list.

Tortillas and **arepas.** The tortilla of Mexico, and the *arepa* of Venezuela, and to a lesser extent Colombia, are unique in the world of bread since they are made from cooked flour. Dried corn kernels are boiled with lime (to loosen the skin), then the kernels are drained and ground, and, if not for immediate use, are dried and packaged as flour. Though the method of cooking the corn is the same for both tortillas and *arepas,* the end result is very different because of the difference in the type of corn used. The corn for *arepas* has very large kernels, giving a rather starchy flour. The packaged flours identify themselves very clearly as *masa harina* (literally dough flour) for tortillas, or flour for *arepas.* It is not possible to confuse them.

Yams are members of a vast assemblage of edible tubers of the Dioscorea family, which has about 250 different species, most of them originating in the tropical regions of the world. They can be as small as a new potato or weigh up to 100 pounds, though most of them weigh about a pound and are the size of a large potato. The skins are usually brown and may be rough, smooth, or hairy, and the shape is usually cylindrical. The flesh is white or yellow, the texture mealy, and the flavour pleasantly nut-like. They are available in West Indian and Indian shops and increasingly in supermarkets and greengrocers.

Hors d'Oeuvres and Appetizers

ENTREMESES

Hors d'oeuvres and appetizers in our modern sense were not a large part of the traditional cooking of Latin America. But there are innumerable small foods that were once used as accompaniments to main dishes or were served only to gentlemen in bars or eaten from stalls in the market, which have been adapted for comparatively new styles of eating: finger foods to go with drinks, or light first courses at lunch or dinner, often taking the place of soup.

From country to country they rejoice in a variety of names, which are as different and varied as the hors d'oeuvres themselves. They are known as *botanas*, meaning literally the stoppers on leather wine bottles; *bacaditos*, little mouthfuls; *antojitos*, little whims or fancies; *boquillas*, things to stop the mouth; *fritangas*, fried things and fritters; *tapados*, nibbles; *picadas*, things on a toothpick; *entremeses*, side dishes; *entradas*, dishes to be served at table; *salgadinhos frios*, small, cold, salty things; and *salgadinhos quentes*, small, hot, salty things.

These are the hors d'oeuvres I find exciting, not the almost universal modern canapes, which are mostly borrowed or adapted from our own cocktail foods and have become popular throughout Latin America in recent years as industrialization has changed social patterns from feudal to modern. One comes upon canapes of caviar, ham, shrimp, anchovies; even *crudités* turn up. There are clam or

39

onion-soup dips, cheese cubes alternating with pineapple on tooth-picks, tiny frankfurters, salmon caviar with sour cream, and grilled bacon-wrapped prunes. They appear in recipe books under the heading *Cocina Internacional*, International Cookery, and have a certain glamour in Latin America because they are foreign and unfamiliar, which is very understandable.

But fortunately they have not elbowed out the traditional appetizers with exciting flavours that are new to us. These traditional foods range from the simplest of nibbles—toasted corn, fried chickpeas, tiny fried potatoes, French fried plantain slices, yucca and banana chips—to the heartier *Empanadas* (Turnovers) and the *seviches* (fish cooked in lime or lemon juice), which make particularly splendid first courses for summer dining. And the *antojitos* (little whims or fancies) and *tacos, chalupas, sopes, quesadillas,* which all derive from some form of tortillas imaginatively stuffed and seasoned, can compose a whole cocktail buffet or informal luncheon.

All of these appetizers are easy to make and most of them are served at room temperature. They can be prepared ahead of time, and some, like the *empanadas,* can be made well in advance and frozen. They make ideal hors d'oeuvres for a cocktail party. I have enjoyed them in restaurants and in the homes of friends throughout Latin America. They fit perfectly into the pattern of today's living, where meals tend to have fewer courses and be less elaborate than in the past, and where the habit of having drinks before lunch or dinner is increasingly accepted.

It is surprising that the hors d'oeuvres of the region owe so little to their Spanish heritage. Though one might have expected the *tapas* of Spain to appear on New World tables changed, but recognizable, this has not happened. It always surprises me in the world of culinary borrowings, what gets taken, what gets left—and this is especially true of appetizers. After nearly eight centuries of Moorish domination, Spain gained its independence and united its provinces into a nation, turning its back at the same time on the *mezze,* the hors d'oeuvres of the Middle East, which are one of the most attractive features of the food of that region. Latin America, with a few exceptions such as *empanadas,* has behaved in much the same way, so that it is the ancient dishes of the pre-Columbian kitchens and the dishes of the creole cuisine that have been adapted as today's appetizers.

The old tradition of foods eaten in the market has survived in Latin America in a very charming way. Snack foods, cakes, and drinks of all kinds are served in *confeitarías* in Brazil, in *sandwicherías* in Uruguay, and *whiskerías* in Argentina, while each station on the subway in Buenos Aires has a stall selling coffee, a variety of drinks, and snack foods. In Chile *empanadas*, cakes, and snack foods of all kinds are sold in *salas de onces*. *Onces* (*once* is the number eleven), named for the English custom of having tea or coffee and biscuits at eleven in the morning, have become, by some extraordinary transmutation, afternoon tea, so that a *sala de onces* is a tea shop. Ecuador has restaurants devoted to its famous *seviches* while Mexico has its *taquerías*, with an astonishing variety of fillings for the simple *tortilla*.

Anticuchos

SKEWERED OX HEART   *Peru*

These are without doubt the most famous of all the Peruvian *entradas*, or appetizers—dishes traditionally served sometimes before, sometimes after the soup, but before the roast in the days when appetites were more robust than they are now. Many of the *entradas* make excellent lunches or suppers; some, like these spiced pieces of ox heart that are skewered and grilled, make a good first course but are also fine as a snack or an accompaniment to drinks. When served as lunch or supper they may be accompanied by corn on the cob, boiled sweet potatoes, and boiled yucca (cassava), bland foods that go very well with the spicy ox hearts. Peruvians like their *picante* foods to be really hot and *anticuchos* are no exception. The dried chili used is *mirasol*, not available here. I have found the Japanese *hontaka*, dried hot red chili peppers, to be an admirable substitute.

The amount of peppers given in the recipe, 1 ounce, will make a very fiery sauce just the way Peruvians like it but too hot for most of us. A good idea is to begin with 2 tablespoons peppers. If the sauce seems too bland, add more peppers. Peppers themselves vary a great deal in hotness, and I have found when dealing with them it is wise to experiment.

Anticuchos are a very old, pre-Columbian dish; I suspect they used to be made with llama hearts since there were no cattle until after the Conquest. The name translates from the Quechua into "a dish from the Andes cooked on sticks."

My favourite place to buy *anticuchos* is from stalls outside Lima's *plaza de toros*, built in 1768 and said to be the second oldest bullring in the world. Eaten right there, accompanied by beer and rounded out with a dessert of *picarones*, deep-fried sweet potato and pumpkin fritters, they make a wonderful impromptu meal.

[Serves 8 to 10 as an hors d'oeuvre, or 6 as a main course]

*1 ox heart, weighing about 4
    pounds*
*1 head garlic (about 16 cloves),
    peeled and crushed*
*1 tablespoon fresh hot red or green
    peppers, seeded, coarsely
    chopped, and puréed in a blender
    or food processor*

1 tablespoon ground cumin
Salt, freshly ground pepper
½ pint red wine vinegar

FOR THE SAUCE

1 ounce dried hot red peppers
*1 tablespoon ground annatto
    (achiote) seeds*

1 tablespoon vegetable oil
Salt

Remove the nerves and fat from the ox heart, and cut it into 1-inch cubes. Place in a large bowl. Combine the garlic, fresh hot peppers, cumin, salt, pepper, and vinegar, stir to mix, and pour over the heart, adding more vinegar, if necessary, to cover. Refrigerate, covered, for 24 hours. Remove the heart from the marinade and set them both aside.

Shake the seeds out of the dried peppers and soak in hot water to cover for 30 minutes. Drain the peppers and put them into a blender or food processor with the annatto, oil, and about ¼ pint of the reserved marinade. Season to taste with a little more salt if necessary and blend until smooth. The sauce should be quite thick. Thread the heart cubes on skewers. Brush them with the sauce, and grill, turning to cook all sides, either over charcoal or under a gas or electric grill, about 3 inches from the heat, for about 4 minutes. Serve with the remaining sauce on the side. Accompany with boiled corn, sweet potato, and yucca (cassava root).

Acarajé

BLACK-EYED PEA FRITTERS   *Brazil*

Black-eyed peas are originally African, brought to the New World by slaves. The fritters turn up all over the Caribbean as well as in South America. The most elegant version, *acarajé,* comes from Bahia in Brazil and makes an unusual cocktail nibble. I have occasionally come across packaged black-eyed pea flour, *harina para bollitos,* which I have found very good indeed and useful when one is in a hurry. It is worth looking out for. As the flour is a ready mix and needs only the addition of water, it saves one all the bother of soaking the peas, rubbing off the skins, and grinding them. To make the fritters from the pea flour, simply follow package instructions. The *dendê* (palm) oil, used a great deal in Bahian cooking, is also an African contribution. A rich reddish-orange in colour, it turns the fritters a beautiful deep gold. They have a crispy texture and a nutty flavour with an attractive hint of shrimp from the sauce.

[Makes 24]
1 pound black-eyed peas
2 ounces dried shrimp

1 medium onion, chopped
Salt
Dendê (palm) oil

Soak the black-eyed peas overnight in cold water to cover. Drain. Rub off and discard the skins. Soak the shrimp in cold water to cover for 30 minutes. Put the peas, shrimp, and onion through the fine blade of a food grinder, or purée them in a blender or food processor. Season to taste with salt if necessary. The shrimp may be quite salty. Pour enough *dendê* oil into a deep fryer or saucepan to fill it to a depth of 2 to 3 inches. When the oil is hot, fry the mixture by the tablespoon, turning the fritters once, until they are golden. Drain on paper towels and serve at room temperature with *Môlho de Acarajé*.

Môlho de Acarajé

BLACK-EYED PEA FRITTER SAUCE   *Brazil*

[Makes about ½ pint]
2 ounces dried shrimp
1 medium onion, chopped
1 tablespoon crushed dried hot red
   peppers

½ teaspoon chopped fresh ginger
   root
3 tablespoons dendê *(palm) oil*

Soak the shrimp in cold water to cover for 30 minutes. Drain the shrimp and pulverize them in a blender or food processor with the onion, peppers, and ginger root. Heat the oil in a frying pan and sauté the shrimp mixture for about 3 minutes. Transfer to a bowl and serve with the *acarajé*.

Variation: For *Abará* (Steamed Black-Eyed Peas), make 1 recipe *Acarajé* (Black-Eyed Pea Fritters), but do not fry them. Beat the mixture thoroughly until it is fluffy with 3 tablespoons *dendê* oil and fresh hot red peppers, seeded, coarsely chopped, and puréed in a blender or food processor, to taste. Place tablespoons of the mixture in the centre of

43

6-inch squares of kitchen parchment or aluminium foil, push a whole dried shrimp into the centre of the pea mixture, then fold up into a neat package. If using parchment, tie securely with kitchen string. Steam the packages for 1 hour and serve directly from the packages at room temperature. Traditionally, banana leaves are used for *Abará*. Makes about 24.

Variation: There is a simpler, but very attractive version, *Buñuelitos de Frijol* (Bean Fritters) from coastal Colombia. The black-eyed peas are soaked overnight in cold water and the skins rubbed off and discarded. The peas are ground fine and seasoned with salt, then beaten with a wooden spoon until they are light and fluffy. They are deep fried by the tablespoon in vegetable oil or lard until golden brown.

Garbanzos Compuestos

TOASTED CHICKPEAS   *Mexico*

Chickpeas were brought to the New World by the Spanish and even though the common bean (red kidney, etc.) was first cultivated in the Valley of Mexico as early as 5000 B.C. and had long spread to other parts of the continent by the time of the Conquest, chickpeas were given a warm welcome and have been widely used in the kitchen ever since. I think, however, that toasted chickpeas as a cocktail nibble are a piece of culinary borrowing from South America, where a special type of large-kernel white corn was developed by the Incas, presumably sometime after corn reached them from Mexico, its birthplace. Called *cancha* in Peru, the corn is soaked, fried in lard, seasoned with salt, and served alone, or with *seviche*, *anticuchos*, and so on. In Ecuador the same dish is called *Maíz Tostado* and is always served with the *seviches*.

Two 1-pound cans of chickpeas, or   ¼ pint olive oil
   1 pound dried chickpeas, soaked   1 clove garlic
   overnight   Ground hot red pepper
1 teaspoon salt

Drain the chickpeas, cover with fresh water, and simmer for 30 minutes. Add the salt and continue cooking until the chickpeas are tender. Drain and cool. Heat the olive oil in a pan and sauté the chickpeas with the garlic until they are golden brown. Drain on paper towels and sprinkle with the hot pepper.

    If using cooked carned chickpeas, rinse, drain, and then fry them.

Patacones

GREEN PLANTAIN CHIPS   *Colombia*

Fried plantain slices are popular in many parts of Latin America under different names and cooked by slightly different methods. Sprinkled lightly with salt, they are served with drinks, or as an accompaniment to meat, fish, or poultry. My favourite is this one from the northern coast of Colombia.

1 large green plantain, peeled and cut into 1½-inch slices	*Vegetable oil for deep frying* *Salt*

Pour enough oil into a deep fryer or saucepan to fill it to a depth of 2 to 3 inches. When it is moderately hot, drop in the plantain slices and fry until tender, about 5 minutes. Lift out and drain on paper towels. Cover with wax paper and press until each is about ¾ inch thick. I find a clenched fist does as well as anything. In fact in Costa Rica, where the usual name is *tostones*, they are sometimes called *plátanos a puñetazos*, "plantains hit with the fist."

Raise the temperature of the oil to hot, and fry the slices until they are brown and crispy on the outside, tender inside, a minute or two. Traditional cooks dip the slices in cold, salted water before this second frying to make them crustier. I don't find this extra fussiness makes much difference. Sprinkle lightly with salt before serving.

Variation: In Venezuela the chips are called *tostones de plátano*, and cut into 1-inch slices. Some cooks put them in overlapping pairs after the first frying and before flattening them. This gives a very thick, soft centre with crispy edges. In lieu of the clenched fist, the heel of the hand, or a rolling pin; I've seen cooks on this coast use large stones from the beach to do the flattening for them.

Variation: *Tostones* in Puerto Rico, cut diagonally into ½-inch slices, are soaked for 30 minutes in cold, salted water before they are either sautéed, or deep fried in oil or lard. They are dipped again in salted water before the second frying.

Variation: Also in Puerto Rico green plantains are very thinly sliced, soaked in ice water for 30 minutes, drained, patted dry, deep fried until crisp in hot oil or lard, and sprinkled with salt before serving. Called *platanutri*, they are *tostoncitos* in the Dominican Republic and *chicharitas de plátano verde* in Costa Rica. Green bananas are often used in the same way. They make a pleasant change from potato chips.

Yuca Frita

CASSAVA CHIPS   *Colombia*

In Colombia hors d'oeuvres are called *picadas* and any fried *picada* is called a *fritanga.* Cassava chips, deliciously light and crisp and no trouble at all to make, are among the *fritangas* I enjoy most. This root vegetable is such an astonishment. First cultivated in northern Brazil in 1500 B.C. it has now spread all over the world. I once saw it growing outside a country pub in Wiltshire, where its tall spike of white flowers towered flamboyantly over roses and wallflowers. Latin America uses it widely, added to stews, boiled and mashed. Its squeezed-out juice is the basis of *cassareep*, used in the Guyanese national meat and poultry stew. And of course there is always a bowl of *farofa* (cassava meal) on the table in Brazilian restaurants and homes (see page 28). I like cassava in all its forms whether it is called yucca, manioc, mandioca, aipím, cassava, or botanically, *Manihot utilissima.*

1 pound cassava (yucca) root, about	*Vegetable oil or lard*
Salt	

Peel the vegetable under cold running water as it discolours quickly. Cut into 1-inch slices and boil in salted water to cover until tender, about 30 minutes. The pieces often break up during cooking but this does not matter. Drain, pat dry with paper towels. In a pan heat about ½ inch oil or lard and fry the pieces until they are crisp and golden all over. Serve at room temperature with drinks. The chips are also a pleasant accompaniment to meats or poultry.

For crisper chips, freeze the boiled vegetable for an hour or so before frying it and fry it frozen. The chips can be deep fried if preferred.

Variation: In the Colombian highlands *Papas Criollas Fritas* (Fried Creole Potatoes) are a popular appetizer. These are small local potatoes with yellow flesh; the smallest bite-sized ones are chosen and deep fried, skin and all, sprinkled with salt and eaten while still hot as an accompaniment to drinks. Very small new potatoes can be used as a substitute.

Variation: Puerto Ricans use breadfruit to make *Hojuelas de Panapén* (Breadfruit Chips). Peel and core a breadfruit and quarter it. Cut it into thin crosswise slices and drop into boiling salted water. Boil for 2 to 3 minutes, drain, and pat dry. Fry in deep oil or lard until the chips are golden and crisp. Sprinkle with salt and serve at room temperature. Canned breadfruit can be used, in which case simply pat it dry, slice, and fry it.

SEVICHE

Seviche or *ceviche*—the spelling varies—is raw fish marinated in lime or lemon juice. The fish loses its translucent look as the juice "cooks" it and needs no further cooking. It doesn't taste raw. The idea almost certainly originated in Polynesia and like all migrant dishes has evolved in its new home; I have found versions of it all over Latin America. The best *seviches* in Mexico are from the state of Guerrero, especially from Acapulco on the Pacific coast. The fish principally used are sierra, or Spanish, mackerel, pompano, and porgy. I am always rather surprised at how well the mackerel *seviche* comes out, with the full-flavoured and oily fish tempered by the lime or lemon juice. *Seviche* in Peru, served with sweet potatoes, lettuce, ears of corn, and toasted corn *(cancha),* is almost a meal in itself. The most popular fish there is bass, which makes a very delicate *seviche,* though octopus, conch, and scallops are also used. I've enjoyed *seviche* in restaurants overlooking Acapulco Bay, with its indestructible charm, and at a beach club in the strangely beautiful desert landscape of the Peruvian coast, but I think the best *seviches* I've ever had were in Ecuador. They are quite different from the Mexican variety though not wholly unlike those from Peru since bitter (Seville) oranges are used in both countries. Made from prawns, lobster, bass, and an interesting local black conch, they have a reputation for being a splendid pick-me-up, and one is encouraged to try them at noon with a glass of cold beer. Marinated fish or shellfish should be eaten 5 to 6 hours after the marinating was begun.

Aguacate Relleno con Seviche de Camarones

AVOCADO STUFFED WITH MARINATED PRAWNS   *Mexico*

This unusual variation on the standard *seviche* is from Acapulco and makes a rather grand and rich beginning to a special lunch or dinner. It would make an admirable light lunch served with soup as a first course and a dessert to finish.

[Serves 2]
½ pound shelled prawns
¼ pint fresh lime or lemon juice
1 medium tomato, peeled and
  chopped
1 canned jalapeño chili, rinsed,
  seeded, and cut in strips
1 pimiento, chopped
1 tablespoon fresh coriander
  chopped, or use parsley

½ small white onion, finely
  chopped
6 small green olives, halved
4 tablespoons vegetable oil
Salt, freshly ground pepper
1 large avocado, halved and stoned
Lettuce leaves

Put the prawns into a bowl with enough lime or lemon juice to cover. Refrigerate for about 3 hours, or until the prawns are opaque. Add the tomato, chili, pimiento, coriander, onion, olives, oil, and salt and pepper to taste. Toss lightly to mix.

Spoon the mixture into the avocado halves and serve on plates garnished with lettuce leaves.

Seviche de Camarones

MARINATED PRAWNS   *Ecuador*

[Serves 6]
2 pounds prawns, shelled
Salt
¾ pint bitter (Seville) orange juice*
1 medium onion, finely chopped

1 fresh hot red or green pepper,
  seeded and finely chopped
1 large tomato, peeled, seeded, and
  chopped
Freshly ground pepper

Drop the prawns into a large saucepan of boiling salted water and boil for 2 or 3 minutes, or until they are cooked. Drain and mix with the orange juice, onion, hot pepper, tomato, and salt and pepper to taste. Let stand an hour before serving. Serve with *Maíz Tostada* (Toasted Corn) on the side.

Seviche de Corvina (1)

BASS MARINATED IN LIME JUICE   *Ecuador*

[Serves 6 to 8]
1½ pounds fillets of bass or similar
  white fish, cut into ½-inch pieces
½ pint lime or lemon juice
½ pint bitter (Seville) orange juice*

1 fresh hot red or green pepper,
  seeded and finely chopped
1 medium onion, thinly sliced
1 clove garlic, chopped
Salt, freshly ground pepper
½ pint vegetable oil

Put the fish into a large glass or china bowl and add the lime or lemon juice to cover, adding a little more if necessary. Refrigerate for about 3 hours, or until the fish is opaque, "cooked" by the lime or lemon juice. Drain. Transfer to a serving bowl and mix with the bitter orange juice, pepper, onion, garlic, salt and pepper to taste, and the oil. Serve with *Maíz Tostada* (Toasted Corn) on the side.

Seviche de Corvina (2)

BASS MARINATED IN LIME JUICE   *Peru*

[Serves 8]
1½ pounds fillets of bass or similar
  white fish, cut into 1-inch pieces
Salt, freshly ground pepper
2 fresh hot red peppers, seeded and
  thinly sliced
1 teaspoon paprika

1 large onion, thinly sliced
½ pint lemon or lime juice
½ pint bitter (Seville) orange juice*
1 pound sweet potato, preferably
  the white type
2 ears corn, each cut into 4 slices
Lettuce leaves

Put the fish into a large glass or china bowl and season to taste with salt and pepper. Add 1 of the peppers, the paprika, and the onion, reserving a few rings for the garnish. Add the lemon or lime and bitter orange juice, mix lightly, cover, and refrigerate for about 3 hours, or until the fish is opaque, "cooked" by the juices.

Peel the sweet potatoes, cut into 8 slices, drop into salted water, bring to a boil, and cook until tender, about 20 minutes. Drop the slices of corn into boiling salted water and boil for 5 minutes. Drain and reserve the vegetables.

Line a serving platter with lettuce leaves. Arrange the fish on the platter, garnish with the reserved onion rings and the hot pepper strips. Arrange the corn and sweet potato slices around the edge of the dish. Serve with *cancha* (toasted corn).

*If bitter (Seville) orange juice is not available, use half lime or lemon juice and half orange juice.

Seviche de Sierra

MACKEREL MARINATED IN LIME JUICE   *Mexico*

[Serves 6]
1 pound skinned fillets of mackerel,
  or use sea bream, cut into
  ½-inch squares

4 canned serrano chilies, rinsed
  and chopped
3 tablespoons vegetable oil
1 teaspoon oregano

¾ pint lime or lemon juice, about
2 medium tomatoes, peeled and
  chopped

Salt, freshly ground pepper
1 medium onion, finely sliced
1 large avocado, peeled, stoned, and
  sliced

Put the fish into a glass or china bowl and pour the lime or lemon juice over it. There should be enough to cover the fish. Add a little more, if necessary. Refrigerate the fish for 3 hours, turning it from time to time. Add the tomatoes, chilies, oil, oregano, and salt and pepper to taste. Toss lightly to mix and divide among 6 bowls. Garnish with the onion slices and the avocado.

Seviche de Ostras

OYSTERS MARINATED IN LIME JUICE   *Guatemala*

[Serves 8]
4 dozen oysters, shelled
½ pint lime or lemon juice
3 large tomatoes, peeled and
  chopped
1 large onion, finely chopped

1 fresh hot red pepper, seeded and
  chopped
2 tablespoons mint, chopped
Salt, freshly ground pepper
Lettuce leaves

Put the oysters into a large glass or china bowl with the lime or lemon juice, cover, and refrigerate overnight. Strain the oysters, reserving the juice. In the bowl combine the oysters with the tomatoes, onion, hot pepper, mint leaves, and 4 tablespoons of the reserved juice. Season to taste with salt and pepper. Line a serving bowl with lettuce leaves and pour in the oyster mixture.

Siri Recheado

STUFFED CRABS   *Brazil*

A similar dish, *crabes farcies*, is popular in the French Caribbean islands. I think it is very probable that the original inspiration came from West Africa. Whether in the West Indies or in Brazil, I have never had exactly the same version of stuffed crabs, which makes eating them a perpetual adventure.

If live crabs are not available, use ¾ pound fresh, frozen, or canned crab meat, picked over to remove any shell or cartilage, and stuff scallop shells.

[Serves 3 to 6]
6 small, live crabs
Olive oil
2 tablespoons lime or lemon juice
2 cloves garlic, crushed
Salt, freshly ground pepper
1 medium onion, grated
2 spring onions, chopped, using
  white and green parts
2 medium tomatoes, peeled, seeded,
  and chopped

2 tablespoons fresh coriander,
  chopped
1 or 2 fresh hot red peppers, seeded
  and chopped
2 ounces fresh breadcrumbs
1 egg, beaten
Fine bulgar wheat
Lettuce leaves
Small black and green olives

Plunge the crabs into boiling water and boil for 10 minutes. Lift out and cool. Carefully remove the meat from the shells and claws, and chop. Discard the spongy fibre. Scrub the empty shells, dry them, and brush the insides with a little olive oil. Season the crab meat with the lime or lemon juice, garlic, salt and pepper to taste, and set aside.

Heat 2 tablespoons olive oil and sauté the onion, spring onions, and tomatoes until the mixture is soft and well blended. Cool to room temperature and combine it with the crab mixture. Add the coriander leaves, the hot peppers, and the breadcrumbs, and mix well. Stuff the crab shells with the mixture, brush with beaten egg, and sprinkle with a little bulgar wheat. Bake in a preheated moderate (350° F., 180°C., gas 4) oven for 30 minutes, or until lightly browned. Garnish serving plates with the lettuce leaves and olives. Serve as a first course.

Variation: Parsley is sometimes used instead of coriander leaves and mandioca (cassava, or manioc, meal) is used instead of bulgar wheat. In Bahia *dendê* (palm) oil often replaces olive oil.

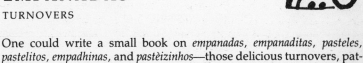

EMPANADAS
TURNOVERS

One could write a small book on *empanadas, empanaditas, pasteles, pastelitos, empadhinas,* and *pastèizinhos*—those delicious turnovers, patties, and pies, stuffed with meat, poultry, fish, shellfish, and other mixtures, and baked or fried, which are so popular throughout Latin

America. Each country has its own favourites and the *empanadas* of Argentina and Chile are as different as one turnover can be from another. They come in small sizes for cocktails, larger ones for first courses, snacks, light luncheons, or picnics. They are very versatile, and I often use a pastry from one country, a filling from another, according to my fancy. I am not attempting to give a representative selection of these delights, only those I have especially enjoyed making and eating.

I remember at Viña del Mar, on the Chilean coast, sitting on the terrace of a friend's house overlooking the sea in the cold winter sunshine and eating *empanadas de locos* bought from a small shop in nearby Quintero and washing them down with the local, very acceptable champagne. *Locos* are the enormous abalone of this coast, where the cold Humboldt Current makes for a fabulous harvest of fish and shellfish. There were also turnovers with other fillings, but it is the juicy onion-enriched abalone ones I remember best, and for which I have worked out an approximation. Use the recipe for the 6-inch Argentine *Empanadas* (Turnovers) pastry, page 57, with 2 tablespoons filling. Have ready equal amounts of coarsely chopped, canned abalone and finely chopped onion. Sauté the onion in *Color Chilena* (Paprika Oil), page 309. Add the abalone, salt, pepper, and a little chopped parsley. Place the filling across the centre of the pastry, top with 2 small black olives, stoned, and a slice of hardboiled egg.

As for the *empanadas* of Argentina, some of which I ate decorously in a *whiskería* (a felicitously evolved tea shop) in Buenos Aires, the crust was so light and flaky I felt the *empanada* might fly from the plate. The filling combined beef with pears and peaches—utterly delicious. I remember too taking some with me for an al fresco lunch on the banks of the River Plate, the Rio de la Plata, which looked like a vast sea of silver, not like a river at all. And on the other side of the river, later in Montevideo, in Uruguay, eating *empanadas* in a *sandwichería*, which again belied its name by selling all manner of marvellous small foods as well as drinks.

Empanadas of course have strong echoes of Spain, Portugal, and the Middle East. The *pasteles* of the Middle East, for example, are believed to have been taken to Turkey from Spain or Portugal by Sephardic Jews a long while ago. They are very like the *empadhinas* of Brazil, which are cousins of the *empanadas*. However, many of the turnovers incorporate foods of the New World—potatoes, tomatoes, peppers, even using corn for the pastry, thus linking them with the indigenous Indian kitchens.

EMPADHINAS and PASTÈIZINHOS
LITTLE PIES AND TURNOVERS

One of my pleasantest memories of Brazil is of eating *empadhinas* and *pastèizinhos*, little savoury pies and turnovers in a *confeitaria*, a pastry shop in downtown Rio which seemed to me to be full at all hours with people eating pies and cakes and drinking tiny cups of exquisitely strong coffee. The generic term for these pies and turnovers is *salgadinhos*, little salt things, and they form an enchanting part of the Brazilian cuisine, allowing the inventive cook endless freedom to experiment. If you make them in larger sizes, they are called *empadas* and *pastéis*, and they are fine for lunches.

Massa Para Empadhinas
PASTRY FOR LITTLE PIES   *Brazil*

[Makes about 30]
10 ounces plain flour
½ teaspoon salt
2 ounces lard

2 ounces butter
2 egg yolks
Water
1 egg

Sift the flour with the salt into a large bowl. Cut the lard and butter into little bits and rub into the flour with the fingertips to make a coarse meal. Make a well in the centre of the flour and stir in the egg yolks with enough cold water (4 to 5 tablespoons) to make a soft but not sticky dough or mix quickly in a food processor. Cover with wax paper and refrigerate for 1 hour. Roll out on a lightly floured surface to 1/16th-inch thickness and cut into circles 1½ inches larger than the circumference of the tart tin you are using. Cut an equal number of circles the same size as the tins. Press the larger circles into the tins. Add enough filling to come about three-quarters of the way up the tin, and if the recipe calls for it a small piece of sliced hardboiled egg and a slice of stoned olive. Moisten the edges of the pastry with a little egg beaten with ½ teaspoon water, cover with the smaller circle of pastry, and seal firmly with the fingers. Brush the tops with egg and bake in a preheated moderate (350°F., 180°C., gas 4) oven for 30 minutes or until golden brown.

The pastry may be used to make 1 large double-crust pie, in which case use a 9-inch pie tin and bake the pastry for about 10 minutes longer.

Picadinho de Carne

MEAT FILLING

Chopped beef fillings are popular all over Latin America. In this one the meat is steamed, making it moist and giving it a softer texture and more delicate flavour than its namesake, Mexican *picadillo*.

1 tablespoon olive oil
¾ pound lean minced beef
Salt, freshly ground pepper
2 cloves garlic, crushed
1 medium onion, grated

2 tomatoes, peeled and chopped
1 fresh hot red pepper, chopped
* (optional)*
2 hardboiled eggs, sliced
Sliced black or green olives

Heat the oil and add the beef, salt, pepper, and garlic, mixing well. Sauté for a minute or two, then add the onion, tomatoes, and the hot pepper, if liked. Stir to mix, cover, and cook over low heat until the meat is tender, about 20 minutes. Allow to cool. Then fill the pies three-quarters full and put a piece of sliced egg and a slice of olive on top of each before covering with the top crust.

Recheio de Sardinhas

SARDINE FILLING

1 tablespoon olive oil
1 medium onion, finely chopped
2 medium tomatoes, peeled, seeded,
* and chopped*
½ fresh hot red pepper, seeded and
* chopped*
Salt, freshly ground pepper

2 cans (4-ounce) sardines, drained
2 teaspoons lime or lemon juice
2 tablespoons chopped fresh green
* coriander*
2 hardboiled eggs, chopped
4 black or green olives, sliced

Heat the oil and sauté the onion until it is softened. Add the tomatoes and the pepper, season to taste with salt and pepper, and simmer, stirring from time to time, until the mixture is thick and well blended, about 10 minutes. Cool. Mash the sardines with the lime or lemon juice and coriander, and fold into the tomato mixture with the eggs and olives.

Recheio de Camarão Baiano

SHRIMP STUFFING, BAHIAN STYLE

4 tablespoons dendê *(palm) oil*
1 medium onion, finely chopped
1 medium sweet green pepper,
  seeded and chopped
1 fresh hot red or green pepper,
  seeded and chopped
1 pound fresh shrimps, peeled and
  chopped

Salt
Palm heart, chopped
2 egg yolks
¼ pint thick coconut milk (page 29)
1 tablespoon fresh green coriander,
  chopped

Heat the palm oil and sauté the onion and the peppers until they are softened. Add the shrimp, salt to taste, and palm heart, and cook for a minute or two. Beat the egg yolks with the coconut milk and stir into the shrimp mixture. Add the coriander and cook, stirring over low heat until the mixture has thickened. It should have the consistency of a medium white sauce. If necessary thicken with ½ teaspoon arrowroot or cornflour dissolved in 1 teaspoon water and cook for a minute or two longer. Cool.

Recheio de Galinha

CHICKEN FILLING

1 ounce butter
2 ounces mushrooms, finely
  chopped
4 spring onions, trimmed and
  chopped, using white and green
  parts

½ pound finely diced cooked
  chicken breast
½ pint thick béchamel sauce (page
  313)
1 tablespoon grated Parmesan
  cheese (optional)

Melt the butter and sauté the mushrooms over fairly brisk heat until they have given up all their liquid and are very lightly browned, about 4 minutes. Stir the mushrooms, spring onions, and chicken meat into the béchamel sauce, which should be highly seasoned. Add the grated cheese, if liked. Cool before using.

I sometimes like to follow the example of Brazilian cooks who vary the sauce by using equal amounts of chicken stock and milk, making the sauce lighter with a beautiful chickeny flavour.

Recheio de Queijo

CHEESE FILLING

¾ *pound ricotta*
Salt, freshly ground white pepper
½ *teaspoon sweet paprika*
4 *spring onions, trimmed and*
  chopped, using white and green
  parts

3 *egg yolks, lightly beaten*

Mix all the ingredients together. Chill slightly before using.

Massa Para Pastéis Fritos

PASTRY FOR FRIED TURNOVERS   *Brazil*

[Makes 50 to 60 turnovers]
½ *pound plain flour*
½ *teaspoon salt*

1 *ounce butter*
2 *eggs, lightly beaten*
Vegetable oil for deep frying

Sift the flour with the salt into a large bowl. Cut the butter into little bits and rub into the flour with the fingertips to make a coarse meal. Make a well in the centre of the flour and pour in the eggs. Stir with a fork to mix and add enough water (about 1 tablespoon) to make a soft but not sticky dough. Knead until the pastry is elastic. A food processor may be used to mix and knead the dough; spin until the dough forms a ball. Cover and allow to stand for 1 hour. Roll out on a floured surface to a thickness of 1/16 inch, cut into 3-inch rounds with a pastry cutter, or a glass, and stuff with 2 teaspoons of any of the fillings. Moisten the edges with water or milk, fold over, and press together. Seal with the tines of a fork.

To fry: Pour enough oil into a fryer or saucepan to reach a depth of 2 to 3 inches. Heat to moderate. An easy way to check the temperature is to stir the oil with wooden chopsticks, then wait to see if tiny bubbles form on the sticks. If they do, the temperature is right. Fry the turnovers, a few at a time, until golden brown, turning once, cooking a total of 4 to 5 minutes. Drain on paper towels and keep warm.

Empanadas

TURNOVERS   *Argentina*

[Makes 16 first-course or luncheon-size turnovers]

FOR THE PASTRY

1 pound plain flour
2 teaspoons baking powder
1 teaspoon salt

¾ pound lard, or half lard and half
  butter

Sift the flour, baking powder, and salt into a large bowl. Cut the fat into small pieces and rub into the flour with the fingertips to form a coarse meal. Mix to a fairly stiff dough with cold water, gather into a ball or mix in a food processor, and refrigerate, covered with wax paper, for 1 hour. Roll out on a floured surface to about ⅛ inch thick. Cut into 6-inch circles using a small plate or bowl as a guide.

FOR THE FILLING

2 medium onions, finely chopped
2 medium raw potatoes, finely
  diced
1 pound good quality lean mince
Salt, freshly ground black pepper

3 tablespoons beef stock
1 egg, beaten with ½ teaspoon
  water

Mix all the ingredients, except the egg, together. Spoon 2 tablespoons of the mixture across the centre of each circle of pastry, leaving ¼ inch at the edges. Moisten the edges of the pastry with the egg and fold the pastry over to make a turnover, pressing the edges firmly together. Curve the turnover slightly to form a crescent shape, then turn about ¼ inch of the pastry back over itself, pinching it between the thumb and forefinger to form a rope-like pattern round the edge. Prick the tops of the turnovers 2 or 3 times with the tines of a fork and brush with the egg mixture. The *empanadas* are now ready to bake and may be frozen until ready to use. Let them thaw for 3 hours at room temperature before cooking.

To bake: Bake the turnovers on an ungreased baking sheet for 10 minutes in a preheated hot (400° F., 200° C., gas 6) oven. Reduce the heat to 350° F., 180° C., gas 4 and bake for 30 minutes longer, or until golden brown.

ANOTHER FILLING

1 ounce butter
1 *medium onion, finely chopped*
1 *sweet green pepper, seeded and*
   chopped
1 *pound lean mince*
1 *large tomato, peeled and chopped*

1 *large pear, peeled, cored, and*
   chopped
2 *large peaches, peeled, stoned, and*
   chopped
Salt, freshly ground pepper
4 *tablespoons dry white wine*

Heat the butter and sauté the onion and pepper over moderate heat until softened. Add the meat, breaking it up with a fork, and sauté for a few minutes longer. Add all the remaining ingredients and cook for 5 minutes over low heat. Cool and stuff the turnovers with the mixture in the same way as for the other filling. If using both fillings, double the amount of pastry.

Variation: In Cuba a similar pastry is enlivened by the addition of ¼ pint dry sherry, 2 eggs and 2 egg yolks, and a tablespoon of sugar. The lard and butter are reduced to 1 ounce each. This is a very old recipe from colonial times and an attractive one. The fillings used are any cooked meat or poultry, chopped and mixed with chopped onion, sautéed in butter, peeled and chopped tomatoes, raisins, olives, capers, and chopped hardboiled eggs, combined and seasoned with salt and pepper. Wonderful for using leftovers.

Empanaditas

LITTLE TURNOVERS   *Venezuela*

[Makes 75 cocktail turnovers]

FOR THE PASTRY

¾ *pound plain flour*
½ *teaspoon salt*

6 *ounces butter*
1 *egg and 1 yolk, lightly beaten*

Sift the flour with the salt into a large bowl. Cut the butter into small pieces and rub into the flour with the fingertips to form a coarse meal. Or use a food processor. Make a well in the centre of the flour and add the egg and yolk, stir to mix, and add water, tablespoon by tablespoon, mixing with a fork, to make a soft but not sticky dough. Form the dough into a ball and refrigerate it, covered, for 1 hour. Roll out the dough on a floured surface to 1/16th inch thick and cut into 2½-inch squares. Put a teaspoon of filling into the centre of each square, fold over, and seal the edges. The turnovers may be frozen at this point until ready to use. Let them thaw for 3 hours at room temperature before cooking. If preferred, they may be completely cooked and simply reheated in the oven just before serving.

To fry: Fry as for the Brazilian fried turnovers, page 56.

FOR THE FILLING

1 pound lean pork, chopped
2 tablespoons vegetable oil
1 medium onion, finely chopped
1 sweet green pepper, seeded and finely chopped
2 medium tomatoes, peeled and chopped
1 tablespoon small pimiento-stuffed green olives, chopped

1 tablespoon capers, chopped
1 tablespoon seedless raisins
Salt, freshly ground pepper
Aliños criollos en polvo, to taste*
¼ pint dry sherry
1 hardboiled egg, chopped

Put the pork into a saucepan with water barely to cover and simmer, covered, until tender, about 30 minutes. Drain, reserving the pork stock. In a frying pan heat the oil and sauté the onion and pepper until they are softened. Add the pork and sauté for a minute or two longer. Add the tomatoes, olives, capers, raisins, salt, pepper, *aliño criollo* to taste, and the sherry. If the mixture seems a little dry, add some of the reserved pork stock. Simmer, uncovered, until the liquid has almost evaporated. Allow to cool. Add the egg, mixing well.

Variation: Chile has a turnover very similar to the Venezuelan one. It may be fried or baked. Make the pastry in the same way. Use chopped sirloin steak or topside instead of pork, omit the green pepper, the capers, and the *aliño*, and add 1 tablespoon sweet paprika, ½ tablespoon hot paprika, and ½ teaspoon ground cumin (or to taste). Cut the pastry into 5-inch rounds using a small bowl or plate as a guide, stuff with about 1½ tablespoons of the mixture, paint the edges with a little egg mixed with ½ teaspoon water, fold over, and seal firmly, pressing the edges with a fork. Cut 2 or 3 slits in the top, brush with the egg mixture. To bake, place the turnovers on an ungreased baking sheet in a preheated hot (400° F., 200° C., gas 6) oven for 10 minutes, then reduce the heat to 350° F., 180° C., gas 4

Aliños criollos en polvo is a Venezuelan seasoning sold ready made. It is a mixture of sweet paprika, cumin, black pepper, ground annatto, garlic powder, oregano, and salt. Add a little of all or any of the ingredients to the filling according to taste. It makes a characteristic and remarkably pleasant addition to soups, stews, etc., and also adds a little colour. It is easy to make at home (see page 310).

and cook for about 20 minutes longer, or until golden brown. The turnovers may be fried in the same way as the Venezuelan and Colombian ones.

A great many different fillings are used for turnovers in Chile; a piece of cheese, such as mild Cheddar, very thick béchamel sauce, highly flavoured and mixed with grated Parmesan cheese, or with chopped cooked green vegetables such as green beans, spinach, Swiss chard, or with shrimp, fish, or any of the marvellous shellfish that the coast of Chile is blessed with. The seafood is often mixed with a thick béchamel seasoned with tomato.

Some turnovers are even simpler. Just a little chopped onion, salt and pepper, the shellfish, and its natural juices, baked in a pastry shell. There is no end to the inventiveness of Chilean cooks when it comes to *empanadas*.

Pastelitos Rellenos de Cerdo

PORK-FILLED TURNOVERS   *Colombia*

[Makes about 100]

FOR THE PASTRY

½ pound plain flour
½ teaspoon salt
¼ pound butter

½ teaspoon lemon juice
¼ pint lukewarm water
Vegetable oil for deep frying

Sift the flour and salt into a large bowl. Cut the butter into small pieces and rub into the flour with the fingertips to form a coarse meal. Mix the lemon juice with the water. Using a fork, stir in the water quickly to make a soft dough. Gather into a ball and refrigerate, covered with wax paper, for 30 minutes. Roll out the pastry on a floured surface to a thickness of 1/16 inch and cut into 2½-inch circles with a pastry cutter or glass. Put ½ tablespoon of filling in the centre of each pastry circle, fold the pastry in half to make a turnover, and seal the edges by pressing with the tines of a fork. The turnovers may be frozen at this point until ready to use. Let them thaw for 3 hours at room temperature before cooking.

To fry: Follow the instructions for Brazilian fried turnovers, page 56.

If preferred the *pastelitos* may be baked. Brush with egg yolk beaten with a little water in a preheated hot (400° F., 200° C., gas 6) oven for 5 minutes. Reduce the heat to 350° F., 180° C., gas 4 and bake for 15 minutes longer, or until golden brown. Serve as an accompaniment to drinks.

They may also be cooked and later reheated in the oven just before serving. A food processor may be used to make the pastry.

FOR THE FILLING

½ pound minced pork
1 large onion, grated
4 tablespoons capers
1 hardboiled egg, finely chopped

¼ pound devilled ham or finely
 chopped boiled ham
Salt, freshly ground pepper to taste

Thoroughly mix all the ingredients together. Instead of pork, minced beef, chicken breast, or drained, canned tuna fish may be used. If using tuna, omit the ham and use 2 hardboiled eggs instead of 1.

ABOUT TORTILLAS

If one were to compile all the recipes that are in existence for tortilla-based appetizers, one would end up with an encyclopedia that would dizzy the reader. So I am giving here only my favourites, though I confess the choice has not been easy.

The Spaniards named them *antojitos*, little whims or fancies, and to me they are perhaps the most exciting aspect of pre-Columbian Mexican cooking. We have some very good descriptions of the markets of old Tenochtitlán, now modern Mexico City, before the Conquest was completed, when the city was virtually untouched by the invaders. In his *Historia General de la Cosas de Nueva España* Fray Bernardino de Sahagún, a Spanish priest, tells, among other things, of the types of tortilla on sale in the market; it is enough to make one's head spin—with envy. That marvellous early war correspondent, Bernal Díaz del Castillo, a captain who was with Cortés before and during the campaign, gives in his memoirs, *Historia de la Conquista de Nueva España*, a remarkable picture of dining in Mexico, so we do know that there was a great deal more, now alas lost, of this cuisine.

However, loss was soon balanced by gain, as post-Conquest Mexicans made good use of the foods the Spanish brought from Europe and Asia, and their *antojitos* were enhanced by beef, pork, chicken, olives, almonds, raisins, and so on.

With the exception of *arepas*, the corn bread of Venezuela, tortillas are unique among breads in being made from a cooked, not a raw, flour. Dried corn is boiled with lime until the skins are loosened and the cooked, skinned kernels are then dried and ground to make the *masa harina*, dough flour, that is used for tortillas. Happily for anyone wanting to make them, it is sold packaged by the Quaker Company. The flour is mixed with water to a fairly soft dough, pressed on a tortilla press or patted into a flat pancake by hand, and baked on a *comal*, an ungreased griddle, for a minute or so. It is not possible to speak of a raw tortilla, only of an unbaked one. Tortillas for those who don't want to make them are available frozen.

Arepas are also made from a cooked flour, and since it was in the Valley of Mexico in 5000 B.C. that corn was first cultivated, not arriving in South America until about 1500 B.C., it is a safe bet that the technique of cooking the corn before making it into flour was established in Mexico long before Venezuela invented *arepas*. In any event they are quite different.

Tortillas for *antojitos* are made in a variety of shapes and sizes and with a variety of fillings. Sternly traditional cooks parcel the fillings out among the shapes with some rigidity. However, when we make such things, we should have the freedom to follow our own whims and fancies.

A selection of *antojitos* makes a fine buffet lunch when accompanied by a dessert.

Tortillas
Mexico

Mexican cooks pat out tortillas by hand. They take a small ball of tortilla dough and with quick, deft movements pat the dough from one hand to the other, transforming it in no time at all into a thin pancake, which is then baked. I have managed to produce a recognizable tortilla by this method, though most of my hand-patted ones were a little on the thick side. I am pretty sure that if I had spent two or three years at it I could have mastered the art of making tortillas by hand! However, since colonial Spain had faced the problem and come up with the solution in the form of a tortilla press, I gave up trying and bought myself a press. The old colonial ones were made of wood. Mine is cast iron. It works extremely well and many Mexican cooks who can hand-pat a tortilla use it for convenience. I use a plastic liner on the press—a plastic bag cut in half is ideal. However, some people prefer to use greaseproof paper.

[Makes about eighteen 4-inch tortillas]
10 ounces masa harina   ½ pint lukewarm water

Put the *masa harina* into a bowl, pour in three-quarters of the water, and stir to mix to a soft dough. Add the remaining water if necessary, as it probably will be. It is impossible to be absolutely precise about the amount of water needed. If the *masa harina* is very fresh it will need less water, and I have even found that an extremely humid day has its effect. The corn flour picks up moisture from the air. The dough should be flexible and hold together nicely. If it is too wet, it will stick to the tortilla press, in which case simply scrape it off the plastic sheet or greaseproof paper, add to the dough with a little more flour. The dough is not hurt by being handled. If the dough is too dry, floury bits will show up on the cooked tortilla. Sprinkle the dough with a little more lukewarm water. Traditionally salt is not added to tortillas. However, a teaspoon of salt may be added to the flour by those who find the unsalted tortilla insipid.

Divide the dough into balls the size of small eggs and flatten on the tortilla press between 2 sheets of the plastic or paper to thin pancakes about 4 inches across. Peel off the top piece of plastic or paper. Put the tortilla, paper side up, in the palm of the left hand, peel off the paper, then flip the tortilla onto a moderately heated, ungreased *comal* or griddle. It's a knack, but very easily learned. Cook until the edges begin to curl, about 1 minute, then, using a spatula or the fingers, turn the tortilla over and cook for about a minute longer. It should be very lightly flecked with brown. The side that is cooked first is the top. Pressing the first side with a spatula while the second side is cooking will turn it into an *inflado*—meaning something swollen with air; it subsides on being taken off the *comal*—which is said to be good luck. It certainly makes the stuffing of *panuchos* easier.

As they are done, stack the tortillas in a cloth napkin. When a dozen are stacked up, wrap them, napkin and all, in foil and put them into a preheated barely warm (150° F., 70° C.) oven, where they will stay warm for hours. If you have a gas oven put it on the lowest Regulo setting, ¼. This is 240° F., higher than necessary, but no harm will be done. If it is necessary to reheat cold tortillas, dampen the hands and pat the tortillas between them. Place the tortillas over direct, fairly low heat, turning constantly for about 30 seconds.

For appetizers use a piece of dough about the size of a walnut and flatten it out to about 2 inches. Even smaller tortillas may be made if desired, using a piece of dough about the size of a large grape.

Variations

Tacos. Make 4-inch tortillas, stuff them with any filling, roll them into a cylinder, and eat by hand, or secure them with a toothpick and fry them in shallow oil or lard until crisp. Usually called soft and fried tacos.

Sopes. Pinch off a piece of tortilla dough about the size of a walnut, roughly 2 teaspoons, and pat or press it into a pancake about 2 inches in diameter. Bake it on an ungreased griddle, or *comal* until it is lightly flecked with brown on both sides, about 1 minute a side. Pinch up a ¼-inch border all around the *sope*, then fry in vegetable oil or lard on the flat side. Stuff with any filling, the most usual of which is *Frijoles Refritos* (Refried Beans), page 239, topped with a little grated cheese, a little chopped white onion, and a hot chili sauce with a radish slice for a garnish. The basic tortilla dough for *sopes* is often mixed with another ingredient. A few tablespoons of cottage cheese may be added to the dough, or 2 or 3 *ancho* chilies, soaked and ground, or 2 or 3 *serrano* chilies, seeded and ground in a blender or food processor.

Chalupas (little canoes). These are oval tortillas with a pinched-up rim. Pinch off a piece of tortilla dough, about 2 tablespoons, and roll it into a cylinder about 4 inches long. Flatten it into an oval on a tortilla press or pat it into shape by hand. Bake on a *comal* or griddle in the usual way, then pinch up a ¼-inch rim all the way round. Fry in vegetable oil or lard on the flat side. Some cooks spoon a little hot fat into the *chalupa* when frying it. Use any filling, but the most usual is shredded chicken or pork, crumbled or grated cheese, and a red or green chili sauce.

Totopos. Ordinary tortillas cut into 4 or 6 wedges, fried until crisp in lard or vegetable oil, and used for dips or with *Frijoles Refritos* (Refried Beans) are usually called *tostaditas*. However, in Mexico's Federal District they are often called *totopos*. This leads to some confusion as there is an entirely different *antojito* also called a *totopo*. To make *totopos* remove the seeds from 3 *ancho* or *pasilla* chilies, soak them in hot water, and purée them in a blender. Mix the chilies with the *masa harina* and 3 ounces cooked, mashed red kidney beans. Season with salt and make into rather thicker than usual tortillas using about 2 teaspoons of dough for each *totopo*. Fry the *totopos* in hot lard or vegetable oil on both sides. Drain on paper towels and spread with *guacamole* topped with grated Parmesan cheese, or use any topping.

Tostadas. These are 6- or 4-inch tortillas fried until crisp in hot lard or vegetable oil and topped with various combinations of poultry, meat, fish, or shellfish and various garnishes, lettuce, chili sauce, and so on. Use 2-inch tortillas for appetizers.

FILLINGS

The most popular fillings are shredded chicken, shredded pork, or *Picadillo* (Chopped Beef), combined with various sauces such as *Salsa Cruda* (Uncooked Tomato Sauce), *Salsa de Tomate Verde* (Green Tomato Sauce), and *Salsa de Jitomate* (Cooked Tomato Sauce); chilies such as *serrano* or *jalapeño*, available canned; shredded lettuce, cos or iceberg; grated cheese such as Parmesan or Cheddar; and *Frijoles Refritos* (Refried Beans). *Guacamole* can be added to almost any *antojito* to advantage. Radishes, sliced or cut into radish roses, and olives are a popular garnish.

Chorizo. Skin chorizos (hot Spanish sausage) and chop coarsely. Sauté in vegetable oil with a little chopped onion, and tomato if liked. Drain any excess fat. Mix with a little grated Parmesan or Pecorino cheese (in Mexico *queso de Chihuahua* or *queso añejo* would be used). If not using tomato, add a little tomato sauce, red or green. Garnish with shredded lettuce.

Sardine. Sauté a medium onion, chopped, in 1 tablespoon vegetable oil, add 2 medium tomatoes, peeled, seeded, and chopped, and chopped *serrano* or *jalapeño* chilies to taste. Cook until thick and well blended. Mash in ½ pound *Frijoles Refritos* (Refried Beans), page 239, mixing well. Fold in 1 can sardines packed in olive oil, drained, boned, and chopped. Sprinkle with Parmesan cheese.

Cream cheese. Mash 3 ounces cream cheese with 3 tablespoons double cream and combine with ½ pound chopped pork or chicken. Top with a tomato sauce or a bottled chili sauce and garnish with shredded lettuce.

Panuchos

FRIED STUFFED TORTILLAS   *Mexico*

Panuchos are one of the most popular appetizers in the Mayan cuisine of the Yucatán peninsula. The garnish may vary slightly, but black beans are always used. They make a fine snack or light meal, and I have found that if I make my tortillas a little thicker than usual, they are easier to stuff. Pressing down lightly on the tortilla with a wooden spoon, or a spatula, when it is baking makes it puff up and this puffed-up layer is easy to lift up to insert the stuffing.

[Serves 4 to 6]
6 ounces black beans
1 teaspoon epazote *(see page 31), if available*
Salt
1 medium onion, thinly sliced
¼ pint mild white vinegar

Twelve 4-inch tortillas
¼ *pound lard or* ¼ *pint vegetable oil*
Shredded lettuce, cos or iceberg
1 *whole cooked chicken breast, boned and shredded*
12 *slices tomato*

Wash the beans and pick them over. Put into a saucepan with cold water to cover by about ½ inch, add the *epazote*, crumbled, and simmer, covered, until tender, adding a little hot water from time to time if necessary. Add salt when the beans are tender and continue cooking, uncovered, until almost all the liquid has evaporated. Mash to a thick paste. Keep warm.

Chop the onion and soak it in salted water for 5 minutes. Drain. Transfer the onion to a small saucepan, pour in the vinegar, bring to the boil, remove from the heat and cool. Strain, discard the vinegar, and set the onion aside.

Using the point of a small sharp knife, lift up the top skin of the tortilla, leaving the skin still attached to the tortilla on one side. Carefully spread a layer of beans inside each little pocket. Replace the tortilla layer. Heat the lard or oil in a frying pan and fry the tortillas, bottom side down, until lightly browned. Drain on paper towels. Place a layer of lettuce, chicken, and onion on each tortilla, and top with a slice of tomato.

Variation: If liked, a slice of hardboiled egg may be put on top of the beans. Use 2 eggs for 12 tortillas. Cooked chopped pork may be used instead of chicken breast.

Sambutes

STUFFED MINIATURE TORTILLAS   *Mexico*

Sambutes, sometimes spelled *salbutos*, are another Yucatán speciality—they taste just as good no matter how they are spelled.

[Makes about 18]

FOR THE FILLING

2 tablespoons vegetable oil
½ pound lean minced pork
1 medium onion, chopped

2 medium tomatoes, peeled and
  chopped
Salt, freshly ground pepper

Heat the oil and sauté the pork until it is lightly browned. Purée the onion and tomatoes in a blender or food processor and add to the pork. Season to taste with salt and pepper and simmer, uncovered, until the mixture is thick and fairly dry. Set aside.

FOR THE TORTILLAS

10 ounces masa harina
1 teaspoon salt

4 tablespoons plain flour
Vegetable oil for deep frying

Mix the *masa harina*, salt, and flour together. Add enough water (about a teaspoon) to make a fairly stiff dough. Pinch off pieces of the dough about the size of walnuts and roll into balls. Flatten on the tortilla press into miniature tortillas not more than 2 inches across. Do not bake. Holding one tortilla in the palm of the hand, place a tablespoon of the filling on it. Cover with another tortilla and pinch the edges together. Continue until all the tortillas and the fillings are used up.

Into a fryer or saucepan pour enough oil to reach a depth of 2 to 3 inches. Heat the oil and fry the stuffed tortillas, a few at a time, turning once, until they are golden brown, about 3 minutes. Drain on paper towels and eat hot.

If liked, these can be made even smaller, an inch across, pinching off a piece of dough not much bigger than a good-sized grape. Fill with 1 teaspoon of the stuffing.

Sambutes are often served as an appetizer accompanied by the same pickled onion as in *Panuchos* (page 00) and with a tomato sauce made by peeling and chopping ½ pound tomatoes and reducing them to a purée in a blender or food processor with 1 fresh hot seeded pepper, or 1 canned *serrano* chili. The sauce is not cooked and is spooned on top of the stuffed tortilla, which is then topped with a little onion. They make a marvellous accompaniment to drinks.

Soups

SOPAS

Soup is extremely popular in Latin America, and most people there would regard a main meal without soup as a poor thing indeed. Soups were not part of the indigenous cooking but were introduced in the colonial period and range from the bowl of richly flavoured amber chicken consommé, so highly esteemed at the beginning of Sunday or holiday midday dinner in Mexico, to the hearty soup-stews, the pot-au-feu dishes that Colombia, particularly, excels in, and that are a meal in themselves.

From a very large array of soups, I have made a small selection of those I have particularly enjoyed. The varied soup repertoire evolved from local ingredients, chayote, courgettes, pumpkin flowers, sweet red peppers, corn, coconut, pumpkin, yams, yucca, hearts of palm, and from the fish and shellfish of the region's coasts. They are not run-of-the-mill soups, of which Latin America has its full share—the soups one could call universal—vegetable, onion, cream of tomato, celery, watercress, green pea. No matter how good these may be, their Latin American cousins have not changed enough from the versions with which we are all familiar to make it worthwhile including them. My choice has been soups that will introduce new combinations of flavours, refreshing to any palate that is pleased with change.

Latin American cooking methods have a pleasant bonus for the soup maker. Many dishes are cooked on top of the stove because, in the past, cooking was done mostly over charcoal, and ovens were not greatly used. As a result, when poaching a flank steak for a

Venezuelan *Pabellón Caraqueño*, or a chicken for a Mexican *mole*, I get stock as an extra. I seldom freeze it, just refrigerate it, though I make a point of boiling it up and simmering it for 3 or 4 minutes if it hasn't been used in 2 or 3 days, which doesn't happen often as one always seems to need stock in the kitchen. And a nice thing is that stock does not sneer at leftovers or bits of this and that but welcomes them. When I boil up a refrigerated stock, I take the opportunity of adding any extras I may have around. The good rich stock comes in very handy for soup making.

Sopa de Aguacate

AVOCADO SOUP   *Mexico*

Avocado soup is popular in Latin America from Mexico all the way south to Chile. I don't think I've ever had an avocado soup I didn't enjoy. The beautiful pale green colour and the buttery richness of the flavour are seductive, yet one of my favourite avocado soups is also one of the simplest. It comes from Mexico and is good hot, marvellous chilled. It is vitally important when making the soup not to let the avocado cook, as cooked avocados tend to develop a bitter taste. I like the soup garnished with chopped fresh coriander leaves.

[Serves 6]
2 large, ripe avocados
1¾ pints rich chicken stock
¼ pint double cream
Salt, freshly ground white pepper

1 tablespoon fresh green coriander, finely chopped (optional)
6 tortillas, quartered and fried crisp in lard or oil

Peel and mash the avocados and put them through a sieve. Place them in a heated soup tureen. Heat the chicken stock with the cream. Pour the stock into the avocados, stirring to mix, or beat lightly with a wire whisk. Season to taste with salt and pepper. Sprinkle with the coriander, if desired. Serve immediately with the crisp tortillas.

For summer dining the soup is splendid chilled. In which case do not heat the tureen and make sure that the chicken stock has been skimmed of all fat. Combine the avocados, stock, cream, salt, and pepper in a blender or food processor and blend until it is smooth. Chill quickly and serve as soon as possible, as the soup tends to darken on top if left for long. If it darkens, simply stir it before serving. The flavour is not affected and the small amount of darkening won't show. Keeping air from the soup helps to minimize darkening, so it is useful to cover it with plastic wrap while it is chilling.

Variation: This *Sopa de Paltas* (Avocado Soup) from Chile is an interesting example of a culinary combination from the opposite ends of the earth. The avocado and the béchamel go very well together, producing a soup that is subtly flavoured. In a fairly large saucepan heat 2 ounces of butter and sauté 1 medium onion, finely chopped, until it is soft. Add 4 tablespoons flour, and cook, stirring, for about 2 minutes over low heat without letting the flour take on any colour. Gradually add ¾ pint milk, stirring constantly until the mixture is smooth and thick. Stir in ¾ pint chicken stock and continue to cook over low heat, stirring from time to time, for about 5 minutes. Cut 2 large, ripe avocados in half and remove the pits. Mash them in their shells, turn them into a warmed soup tureen, season with a little lemon juice, and continue to mash until they are quite smooth. Pour the hot béchamel mixture over the avocados, stirring to mix, or beat with a wire whisk. Season to taste with salt and pepper. Serves 4 to 6.

Variation: For *Sopa de Aguacate y Papas* (Avocado Vichyssoise) from Colombia, peel and dice 1 pound potatoes and put into a large saucepan with the white part of 2 leeks, washed and sliced, and 1 medium onion, sliced. Pour in 1¾ pints chicken stock, cover, and simmer until tender. Put the vegetables and broth through a sieve, return the mixture to the saucepan, stir in ¼ pint of double cream, and heat just to the boil. Peel and mash 2 large avocados and put them into a heated soup tureen. Add the hot soup and stir to mix thoroughly. Season to taste with salt and white pepper. The soup is also very good served chilled. Serves 6.

Variation: For *Sopa de Aguacate* (Avocado Soup) from Venezuela, scoop out the flesh of 2 large avocados and put into a blender with ¾ pint fish stock, ¾ pint chicken stock, ¼ pint single cream, and salt and white pepper to taste. Blend until smooth, chill, and serve garnished with a little chopped parsley and a little sweet paprika. If preferred, omit the cream and use a little more chicken stock. Serves 6.

Sopa de Creme de Palmito

CREAMED HEARTS OF PALM SOUP   *Brazil*

Hearts of palm are a commonplace in Brazil, where their delicate flavour and texture is taken for granted. I will always think of them as a luxury, even though most delicatessens have them canned. I particularly like to serve this soup when I am having a beef dish as a main course and want something elegantly light in contrast to the robust flavour of the meat. The soup can be prepared ahead of time and finished at the last minute. It is simplicity itself.

[Serves 6]
2 tablespoons rice flour
½ pint milk
A 14-ounce can hearts of palm

2 pints chicken stock
Salt, white pepper
2 egg yolks

In a small bowl mix the rice flour with the milk. Drain and chop the hearts of palm and purée in a blender or food processor with ½ pint of the chicken stock. Pour the mixture into a saucepan and stir in the rice flour mixture and the rest of the chicken stock. Season to taste with salt and pepper and cook, stirring, over low heat until the soup is smooth and thickened slightly. In a bowl beat the egg yolks. Beat in a little of the hot soup, then pour the egg yolk mixture into the soup, and cook, stirring, for about 1 minute. Do not let the soup boil as it will curdle.

Antonia's Sopa de Chayote

CHAYOTE SOUP   *Mexico*

This soup from Cuernavaca in the state of Morelos has a lovely light texture and delicate flavour. The main ingredient, chayote, the pale green pear-shaped vegetable, is worth looking out for in West Indian shops.

[Serves 6]
2 large chayotes, peeled and sliced
Salt
1 medium onion, finely chopped
1 clove garlic, chopped

1 ounce butter
1 tablespoon flour
1½ pints chicken stock
White pepper

Put the chayotes in a saucepan with salted water to cover and simmer, covered, until they are tender, about 20 minutes. Transfer the chayotes to a blender or food processor with half the cooking liquid and blend until smooth. Discard any remaining cooking liquid.

In a saucepan sauté the onion and garlic in the butter until the onion is soft. Stir in the flour and cook, stirring, for a minute without letting it brown. Add the chicken stock and cook, stirring, until the mixture is smooth. Combine the stock with the chayote mixture, season to taste with salt and white pepper, and simmer, covered, for 5 minutes longer, stirring from time to time. If liked, the soup may be put through a sieve for a finer texture.

Variation: I found an interesting variation of this soup in Nicaragua. It is made in exactly the same way except that just before serving about ½ pound cooked, shredded chicken breast is added and heated through, and the soup when served is garnished with croutons.

Sopa de Jitomate

TOMATO SOUP   *Mexico*

This is a very fresh, simple tomato soup from Mexico, where the tomato originated and where it is sold large and ripe and sweet. I wait until the tomato season reaches its peak before cooking this, or better still until some home-grown tomatoes are ripe. I sometimes add a tablespoon of dry sherry to each serving, but mostly I prefer the unadorned flavour of tomato.

[Serves 6]
1 ounce butter or 2 tablespoons vegetable oil
1 large onion, finely chopped
1 clove garlic, chopped
6 large ripe tomatoes, peeled and coarsely chopped
1½ pints chicken or beef stock
Salt, freshly ground pepper
6 tablespoons dry sherry (optional)

Heat the butter in a fairly large saucepan and sauté the onion and garlic until the onion is soft. Add the tomatoes and cook, stirring, for 2 or 3 minutes. Pour in the stock and simmer the mixture for 10 minutes. Cool slightly and purée in two or three batches in a blender or food processor. Reheat, add salt and pepper to taste, and serve in bouillon cups with the sherry, if liked.

Sopa de Pimientos Morrones

SWEET RED PEPPER SOUP   *Mexico*

When I was first married and my husband was transferred to Mexico for some years, my mother-in-law found me a cook who had long associations with the family. Her name was Francisca and she was a Zapotecan Indian from Oaxaca, a tiny woman with a beautiful tranquil high-cheekboned face, framed by long plaits, quite gray. This soup was one she made for me. It is important that the peppers be smooth and shiny, as even slightly wrinkled peppers will have less flavour and the texture of the finished soup will not be so smooth. It is a beautiful soup to look at with its deep, rich colour. The addition of hot peppers to the pot is a matter of taste—I prefer it without.

[Serves 6]
2 tablespoons vegetable oil
1 medium onion, finely chopped
3 large ripe red peppers
1½ pints chicken or beef stock

½ pint tomato juice
1 fresh hot red or green pepper, whole and with stem left on (optional)
Salt, freshly ground pepper

Heat the oil in a small pan and sauté the onion until it is soft. Set aside. Peel the peppers according to the instructions on page 36. Seed and chop coarsely. Purée the peppers with the onion and a little stock in a blender or food processor. Transfer the purée to a saucepan, add the rest of the stock, the tomato juice, and if liked the hot pepper. Season to taste with salt and pepper. Simmer, covered, for 15 minutes. Remove and discard the pepper.

Sopa de Flor de Calabaza

PUMPKIN FLOWER SOUP *Mexico*

Pumpkins and marrows, among the oldest vegetables in the world, originated in Mexico. The flowers used in this recipe are usually from courgettes, although blossoms from any member of the family can be used. These are the male flowers, which produce no fruit. It is the female flower that gives us the vegetable, so one may eat the blossoms with a clear conscience. The male blossoms are attached to short, thin stems; the female flowers are attached to miniature vegetables. *Epazote*, which adds a slight but distinctive flavour to the soup, will not be available unless you grow your own (see page 31), but the soup is still very good without it.

[Serves 6]
1 pound blossoms
2 ounces butter
1 medium onion, finely chopped

2 pints chicken stock
Salt, freshly ground pepper
1 sprig epazote (optional)

Remove and discard the stems from the blossoms and chop the flowers coarsely. Heat the butter in a saucepan and sauté the onion until it is soft. Add the flowers and sauté for 3 or 4 minutes longer. Pour in the stock, season to taste with salt and pepper, cover, and simmer until the blossoms are tender, about 5 minutes. Purée in a blender or food processor, in more than one batch if necessary. Return to the saucepan and reheat with the sprig of *epazote* if it is available. Discard the *epazote* before serving.

Variation: For *Sopa de Flor de Calabaza con Crema* (Cream of Pumpkin Blossom Soup), a rather richer soup, whisk 2 egg yolks with ¼ pint of double cream, then whisk ½ pint of the hot soup into the egg mixture, beat this into the soup, and cook, without letting it boil, until the soup is lightly thickened. Mexican cooks always use only egg yolks. I find whole eggs do a much better job, and I use them even though this is a departure from tradition.

Variation: For *Sopa de Flor de Calabaza con Jitomate* (Pumpkin Blossom and Tomato Soup), add 2 medium tomatoes, peeled, seeded, and chopped, to the onion with the blossoms. This makes a very pleasantly different soup with an interesting blend of flavours.

Caldo de Zapallo Tierno

COURGETTE SOUP   *Paraguay*

This lovely simple recipe was given me by a friend, Josefina Velilla de Aquino, when I visited her in Asunción, Paraguay. She is a gifted cook and teacher of cooking, with a great feeling for traditional cuisine. Another version of it, from a family cook in Cuernavaca, is even more simple, and I often make that one when I am alone, or in a hurry, and the more elaborate one when I have guests. I often leave the rice out of the Paraguayan recipe for a more purely vegetable flavour.

[Serves 6]   1 pound courgettes, grated
2 tablespoons vegetable oil   Salt, freshly ground pepper
1 medium onion, finely chopped   1 egg
1 clove garlic, chopped   3 tablespoons freshly grated
2 pints chicken stock   Parmesan cheese
3 tablespoons raw rice   1 tablespoon finely chopped parsley

Heat the oil in a fairly large saucepan and sauté the onion and garlic until the onion is soft. Add the chicken stock and the rice and simmer, covered, for 10 minutes. Add the courgettes. Season to taste with salt

74

and pepper and simmer until the courgettes are very tender, about 15 minutes. In a soup tureen beat the egg with the cheese and parsley, then whisk in the soup, mixing well.

Variation: Antonia Delgado's *Sopa de Calabacita* (Courgette Soup) from Cuernavaca, Mexico. In a saucepan sauté 1 medium onion, finely chopped, and 1 large spring onion, using the white and green parts, coarsely chopped, in 1 ounce butter until the onion is soft. Add 1 pound courgettes, coarsely chopped, and stir for a minute. Pour in 2 pints chicken stock and simmer, covered, until the courgettes are tender, about 15 minutes. Purée in two or three batches in a blender or food processor. Pour the soup back into the saucepan, season to taste with salt and pepper, and reheat. Remove from the heat and stir in 4 tablespoons double cream. Serve immediately. Serves 6.

Sopa de Crema de Coco

CREAM OF COCONUT SOUP   *Colombia*

This is a subtle and unusual soup from Cartagena in coastal Colombia, where coconut plays a large role in the kitchen. I like it especially as the beginning to a summer lunch or dinner.

[Serves 6]
1 coconut
2 pints chicken stock
1 ounce butter

1 medium onion, grated
2 tablespoons flour
Salt, freshly ground white pepper

Follow the instructions for extracting the thick milk from a coconut (page 29), and set it aside. There will be ¼ to ½ pint. Heat about ½ pint of the chicken stock and pour it over the grated coconut, from which the thick milk has been squeezed, and let it stand about 30 minutes. Squeeze out the liquid through a double layer of dampened cheesecloth. Repeat the process two or three times to extract as much flavour from the coconut as possible. Set aside. Do not mix the two lots of milk. Discard the grated coconut.

Heat the butter in a saucepan and sauté the onion until it is very soft. Stir in the flour and cook, stirring, over low heat for 2 minutes. Gradually whisk in the thin coconut milk made with the stock, and the rest of the stock. Add a little more stock if there is only ¼ pint of the thick coconut milk, to make 2½ pints in all. Season to taste with salt and pepper, cover, and simmer for 15 minutes. Stir in the thick coconut milk and heat the soup through but do not let it boil. Serve in bouillon cups.

Sopa de Lima

LIME SOUP *Mexico*

This soup is one of Mexico's great regional dishes. It comes from Yucatán, where the Mayan kitchen predominates, and it owes its unique flavour to a local species of lime that is seldom available, even in Mexico, outside the Yucatán peninsula. I have sometimes found these limes in the great Mexico City markets, but even then not regularly or often. Fortunately I've found that the soup loses very little of its authentic—and marvellous—flavour when made with other limes. In Mérida, Yucatán's capital, I had an interesting and very pleasant variation of the soup. Instead of the chicken gizzards and livers, a whole chicken breast, boned, poached, and shredded, was added. The chicken breast was cut in half, then simmered very gently in the stock for 10 minutes, allowed to cool, then skinned, boned, and shredded with the fingers. It was added to the soup just long enough to heat through before serving.

[Serves 6]

Lard or vegetable oil
1 medium onion, finely chopped
1 medium tomato, peeled and chopped
½ sweet green pepper, seeded and chopped
2 or 3 canned serrano chilies, chopped

2½ pints chicken stock
Juice of ½ lime and the shell
3 chicken gizzards
6 raw chicken livers, chopped
Salt, freshly ground pepper
6 tortillas, cut into thin strips
1 lime, thinly sliced

Heat 2 tablespoons of lard or vegetable oil in a saucepan and sauté the onion until it is softened. Add the tomato and sweet pepper and sauté for 2 or 3 minutes longer. Add the chilies, the chicken stock, the lime juice, and lime shell. Simmer for 2 minutes. Remove and discard the lime shell.

Put the chicken gizzards into a small saucepan with water to cover. Bring to the boil, reduce the heat, cover, and simmer gently until the gizzards are tender, about 30 minutes. Drain, remove the gristle, chop, and set aside. Add the gizzards to the soup with the chicken livers. Simmer until the livers are done, about 5 minutes. Season to taste with salt and pepper. Have ready the tortillas, fried until crisp in lard or vegetable oil and drained on paper towels. Serve the soup garnished with the tortilla strips and thin slices of lime.

Quibebe

PUMPKIN SOUP *Brazil*

This is a Bahian speciality. The *calabaza* (West Indian pumpkin) available in West Indian markets is closest in flavour to the varieties used in Latin America, but any pumpkin will do.

[Serves 6]
2 ounces butter
1 medium onion, chopped
1 medium tomato, peeled, seeded, and chopped
1 clove garlic, minced
1 or 2 fresh hot red peppers, seeded and chopped

2 pounds pumpkin, peeled and cut into ½-inch cubes
1½ pints beef stock
Salt
¼ teaspoon sugar
Parmesan cheese (optional)

Melt the butter in a large saucepan; add the onion, tomato, garlic, and hot peppers; and cook until the onion is softened and the mixture thick and well blended. Add the pumpkin and the stock to the saucepan, season to taste with salt, stir in the sugar, and simmer, covered, for 20 minutes or until the pumpkin has disintegrated and thickened the soup, which should retain some texture and not be completely smooth. If liked, the soup may be sprinkled with 1 tablespoon Parmesan cheese for each serving.

Variation: In Chile the pumpkin is cooked in stock or water, mashed until smooth, and combined with a sautéed onion and an amount of milk equal to the stock, 1¼ pints of each to 1 pound of pumpkin. At the last minute a well-beaten egg is stirred into the soup.

Variation: In Colombia 2 pounds of pumpkin are cooked in beef stock until the pumpkin is tender. The soup, which should be thick, is put through a sieve or reduced to a purée in a blender or food processor. A little butter is added just before serving.

Variation: In Argentina, as in Chile, the soup is a thinner one, using 1½ pounds of pumpkin to 1¼ pints each beef stock and milk. At the last minute 2 egg yolks beaten with a tablespoon or so of Parmesan cheese are stirred into the soup. It is served with croutons.

Variation: In Paraguay 2 ounces raw rice is cooked with the pumpkin. At the last minute a whole egg is beaten with a tablespoon or so of grated Cheddar or Parmesan cheese together with a tablespoon of chopped parsley and stirred into the soup.

Variation: In Ecuador the pumpkin is put on to cook with 1 sliced onion, 1 medium sliced tomato, peeled, 1 clove garlic, chopped, and water barely to cover, about 1¼ pints. When the pumpkin is tender, purée it in a blender with all the liquid and return the soup to the saucepan. Add ¾ pint milk and season to taste with salt and pepper. Mix 1 ounce butter with 2 tablespoons flour, and add, bit by bit, to the soup. Simmer gently, stirring, over low heat until the soup is thickened. Serve with grated Cheddar cheese.

Locro

POTATO SOUP   *Ecuador*

This is a highlands dish. There is a coastal version in which 1 teaspoon ground annatto is used instead of the paprika.

[Serves 6 to 8]
2 ounces butter
1 teaspoon sweet paprika
1 medium onion, finely chopped
4 pounds potatoes, peeled and sliced

½ pint milk and ¼ pint single
  cream
½ pound Cheddar cheese, grated
Salt

In a large, heavy saucepan heat the butter and stir in the paprika. Add the onion and sauté over moderate heat until the onion is softened. Pour in 1½ pints water, bring to the boil, add the potatoes, and simmer over low heat, uncovered, stirring occasionally. When the potatoes are almost done, add the milk and cream and continue to cook, stirring from time to time, until the potatoes begin to disintegrate. Stir the cheese into the potatoes, season to taste with salt, and serve immediately. Avocado slices are sometimes served with the *Locro*, on separate plates but to be eaten at the same time.

Variation: In coastal Ecuador prawn fritters are sometimes added to the potato soup. Peel 2 dozen medium prawns and set them aside. In a frying pan heat ½ ounce butter and sauté the prawn shells until they turn pink. Put the shells into a small saucepan with ½ pint water, cover, and simmer for 5 minutes. Strain, discard the shells, and stir the stock into the *Locro*. Chop the prawns. Grate a medium ear of corn. In ½ ounce butter sauté 1 medium onion, very finely chopped, with 1 medium tomato, peeled, seeded, and chopped, until the onion is tender and the mixture very thick and well blended. Allow the mixture to cool. Season to taste with salt and pepper, add the prawns, the corn, and 1 egg, lightly beaten. Fry by the tablespoon in hot lard or vegetable oil until lightly browned on both sides. Add to the soup when serving.

Sopa de Elote

CORN SOUP   *Cuba*

[Serves 6]
*The kernels from 8 medium ears
    corn, preferably fresh; if frozen,
    thoroughly defrosted*
1 pint chicken stock

¼ pint single cream
Salt, freshly ground white pepper
2 eggs, lightly beaten
2 tablespoons chopped parsley

Put the corn into a blender or food processor with the chicken stock and blend to a purée. Do this in two batches. Pour the purée into a saucepan, stir in the cream, and simmer over very low heat, stirring from time to time, for 5 minutes. Work the purée through a sieve, return it to the saucepan, and season it to taste with salt and pepper. If it is very thick, thin it with a little more chicken stock, and bring to a simmer. Stir ¼ pint of the soup into the eggs, then stir the egg mixture into the soup and cook, stirring, for 1 or 2 minutes. Serve garnished with a little chopped parsley.

Sopa de Maní

PEANUT SOUP   *Ecuador*

Peanut soup turns up all over Latin America, each version a little different from the others, though not very much so. My favourite is this creamy, delicate soup from Ecuador.

[Serves 6]
1 ounce butter
1 medium onion, finely chopped
*4 ounces toasted peanuts, finely
    ground*
*1 pound fresh potatoes, cooked and
    chopped*

1¾ pints chicken or beef stock
¼ pint single cream
Salt, freshly ground pepper
2 tablespoons chopped chives

Heat the butter and sauté the onion until it is soft. In a blender or food processor combine the onion and its butter, the peanuts, potatoes, and a little of the stock. Blend to a smooth purée, pour into

79

a saucepan, stir in the rest of the stock, and simmer gently, covered, for 15 minutes. Stir in the cream, season to taste with salt and pepper, and simmer just long enough to heat through. Pour into soup bowls and garnish with the chopped chives.

Sopa de Topinambur

JERUSALEM ARTICHOKE SOUP   *Chile*

Chile was the only country in South America where I encountered this soup. Though differently made, it reminded me of my mother's artichoke soup. Autumn is the season for Jerusalem artichokes and I have found the soup comforting on a blustery evening, though it is richly delicate rather than hearty.

[Serves 4]
¾ pound Jerusalem artichokes
1 large onion, finely chopped
1½ pints chicken stock

Salt, freshly ground white pepper
¼ pint double cream
2 tablespoons fresh coriander or
*   parsley, chopped*

Wash and scrape the artichokes and slice thinly. Put into a saucepan with the onion and the chicken stock, bring to the boil and simmer, covered, until the artichokes are soft, about 20 minutes. Reduce to a purée in a blender or food processor and pour back into the saucepan. Season to taste with salt and pepper, stir in the cream, and heat through. Pour the soup into bowls and garnish with the chopped coriander or parsley.

Sopa de Plátano Verde

GREEN PLANTAIN SOUP

Traditionally the plantains for this soup, which I first had in Puerto Rico, are grated on a grater but I find a blender or food processor does the job admirably. Recipes vary from country to country though not in essentials.

[Serves 6]
1 green plantain (see page 36)
2½ pints chicken or beef stock

Salt, freshly ground pepper

Grate the plantain on the second finest side of a grater, or chop it and purée it in a blender or food processor with a little stock if necessary. Pour the cold stock into a saucepan, add the plantain, and cook over moderate heat, stirring with a wooden spoon, until the soup is thick. Season to taste with salt and pepper and simmer, covered, for 10 minutes.

Sopa de Batata Doce

SWEET POTATO SOUP   *Brazil*

This is one of the most delicious soups I have ever had, whether as *sopa de camote* in Spanish-speaking Latin America or as *sopa de batata doce* in Brazil. It is a beautiful golden-yellow colour with a lovely tart hint of tomato flavour balancing the slight sweetness of the potato. The type of sweet potato used is the *boniato,* which has a pink or brownish skin and white flesh and is available in Caribbean shops—it is well worth looking for.

[Serves 6]

1 *pound* boniatos *(white sweet potatoes)*
Salt
2 *ounces butter*
1 *medium onion, finely chopped*

4 *medium tomatoes, peeled and chopped*
1½ *pints beef stock*
Freshly ground pepper
2 *tablespoons chopped parsley or fresh coriander (optional)*

Peel the sweet potatoes, slice thickly, and put into a saucepan with cold salted water to cover. Bring to the boil, reduce the heat, and simmer, covered, until tender, about 20 minutes. Drain thoroughly and chop coarsely.

Heat the butter and sauté the onion until it is soft. Add the tomatoes and cook for about 5 minutes longer. Put the mixture into a blender or food processor with the sweet potatoes and ½ pint of the stock and reduce to a smooth purée. Pour into a saucepan with the rest of the stock. Season to taste with salt and pepper and reheat. I have sometimes had the soup garnished with chopped parsley or coriander, and though it looks pretty I feel this really adds very little to the incomparable flavour of the soup.

So'O-Yosopy

BEEF SOUP   *Paraguay*

This is a wonderfully comforting soup and needs little more than dessert to make a light supper. Its name in Guaraní, an official language in Paraguay, translates in Spanish into *sopa de carne*. It is easy to make if the simple rules are followed.

[Serves 6]

2 *pounds minced lean sirloin or topside*
2 *tablespoons vegetable oil*
2 *medium onions, finely chopped*
1 *sweet green pepper, seeded and finely chopped, or 1 or 2 fresh hot peppers, seeded and chopped*

4 *medium tomatoes, peeled and chopped*
¼ *pound rice or vermicelli*
Salt
Grated Parmesan cheese

Have the butcher mince the meat twice, then mash it in a mortar to make sure it is completely pulverized, or use a food processor. Set the meat aside together with any juices.

Heat the oil and sauté the onions and pepper until the onions are softened. Add the tomatoes and cook until the mixture is thick and well blended, about 5 minutes longer. Cool the mixture slightly. Put the beef and its juices into a saucepan. Stir in the sautéed onions, pepper, and tomatoes, known as the *sofrito*, and 3¼ pints cold water, mixing well. Bring to the boil over moderate heat, stirring with a wooden spoon. Add the rice or vermicelli and simmer, still stirring, until tender, about 15 minutes. At this point, season to taste with salt. If salt is added earlier, the meat and liquid, which should be completely blended, may separate. Some cooks believe that constant stirring is the most important step, others that the point at which the salt is added is the vital factor. Superstition has it that if anyone who does not enjoy cooking is present in the kitchen they may cause the *So'O-Yosopy* to separate and spoil the dish.

Serve with a baked sweet potato or a thick slice of boiled yucca (cassava), or both, and *Sopa Paraguaya*, Paraguayan Corn Bread despite its misleading name. Sprinkle, if liked, with grated cheese. Water biscuits may also be served with the soup.

Variation: Omit the rice or vermicelli and add 2 thinly sliced carrots to the onion and tomato mixture with a teaspoon of oregano and freshly ground pepper.

Variation: *Chupi* (Meat Soup) from Argentina is a very simple but traditional soup, easy to make and grand in winter weather. It is obviously related to Paraguay's exotically named *So'O-Yosopy*. Heat

4 tablespoons vegetable oil in a saucepan and sauté 1 large onion, finely chopped, and 1 sweet red pepper, seeded and chopped (or use 2 canned pimientos, chopped), until onion and pepper are both tender. Add 1 pound lean beef, topside or sirloin, coarsely chopped in a food processor, or by hand, and sauté, stirring to break up the beef for a few minutes. Add 3 medium potatoes, peeled and cubed, 1 tablespoon chopped parsley, ⅛ teaspoon of cayenne (optional), 2½ pints beef stock or water, and salt and pepper to taste. Bring to a simmer and cook, covered, for 30 minutes, stirring once or twice during the cooking time. Serves 6.

Sopa de Garbanzo

CHICKPEA SOUP   *Mexico*

Though this is a regional Mexican dish from Oaxaca, its overtones are very Middle Eastern with its union of chickpeas and mint. It is clearly an old colonial dish. The fried egg is an interesting addition.

[Serves 6]
4 tablespoons vegetable oil
1 medium onion, finely chopped
1 clove garlic, minced
1 tablespoon fresh mint leaves, chopped, or ½ tablespoon dried
1¼ pints beef or chicken stock

2 cups cooked chickpeas (20 ounce can), or ½ pound dried chickpeas, soaked overnight in cold water
Salt, freshly ground pepper
6 eggs

Heat 2 tablespoons of the oil and sauté the onion and garlic until the onion is soft. Transfer to a blender or food processor, add the mint leaves, and ¼ pint of the stock, and reduce the mixture to a purée. Pour the mixture into a medium-sized saucepan.

Put the cooked chickpeas in the blender or food processor with the liquid from the can. If using dried chickpeas, cook these in water to cover until tender, about 1 hour. Purée the chickpeas in a blender with ½ pint of the water in which they have cooked. Add the chickpea purée to the onion mixture and stir in the remaining stock. Season to taste with salt and pepper, bring to a simmer, and cook, stirring from time to time, until the flavours are blended, about 5 minutes.

Heat the remaining 2 tablespoons of oil and fry the eggs. Pour the soup into bowls. Slide a fried egg into each bowl.

FISH SOUPS

The fruits of the sea, with which Latin America is so lavishly endowed, are used in some very fine soups, robust enough to be the main course of lunch or dinner. They may be enriched with corn, tomatoes, sweet peppers, or beans, with root vegetables like yams, yucca (cassava) root, or potatoes, with okra, courgettes, or other green vegetables, with coconut milk as well as stock, sometimes enlivened with a touch of hot pepper, and always with well-orchestrated seasonings, a symphony of flavours.

Sopa de Almejas

CLAM SOUP   *Colombia*

This clam soup is a coastal favourite in Colombia, which is richly blessed in having both the Caribbean and the Pacific wash its shores. I had it with Colombian friends at a family gathering when there were twelve of us to lunch. The day was hot, the sun brilliant, and the soup hearty, but this did not stop even more substantial dishes following. At home I like it as a winter soup and make it the central dish of a family lunch or dinner, serving larger helpings; this recipe would serve 3 or 4 as a main dish, 6 as a soup.

In Colombia the large Spanish mackerel (see page 37) is used. The stronger flavoured Atlantic mackerel won't do for this dish, so substitute any firm-fleshed non-oily white fish.

[Serves 6]

4 tablespoons olive oil
1 medium onion, finely chopped
1 clove garlic, chopped
1 red and 1 green sweet pepper, or use 2 red or 2 green peppers, seeded and chopped
3 medium tomatoes, peeled, seeded, and chopped
1 pound (about 3 medium) potatoes, peeled and sliced
Salt, freshly ground pepper

1 bay leaf
Pinch ground cloves
⅛ teaspoon cumin
½ teaspoon sugar (optional)
3 dozen clams, well washed (if fresh clams are not available, use canned clams, or fresh mussels)
2 pounds fillets of white fish cut into 12 pieces
¾ pint fish stock
¾ pint water
2 tablespoons finely chopped parsley

Heat the oil in a fireproof casserole and sauté the onion, garlic, and peppers until the onion is soft. Add the tomatoes and sauté for a minute or two longer. Add the potatoes. Season to taste with salt and pepper. Add the bay leaf, cloves, cumin, and sugar (if desired). Cover and simmer until the potatoes are almost tender, about 15 minutes. Add the clams, pieces of fish, fish stock, and water. Cover and simmer for 5 minutes longer, or until the clams have opened and the fish has lost its translucent look. Sprinkle with parsley and serve in soup bowls.

Sopa de Candia con Mojarras

OKRA AND POMPANO SOUP   *Colombia*

The foods of the Andean countries, Venezuela, Colombia, Ecuador, and Peru, have more distinctive regional characteristics because the countries, until recently, were so cut off from one another. Though now with modern transportation they enjoy one another's foods, the old regional kitchens have, happily, retained their identity. This is a typical coastal dish from Cartagena, which has a very lively cuisine. I first enjoyed it high up in Bogotá. For pompano, substitute any firm-fleshed, non-oily fish.

[Serves 6]

3¼ pints fish stock
2 medium onions, finely chopped
2 cloves garlic, chopped
1 large tomato, peeled, seeded, and chopped
2 fresh hot peppers, seeded and chopped
¼ teaspoon each ground cumin and allspice
Salt

4 tablespoons lemon juice
½ pound small, fresh okra, quartered
1 pound small yams, peeled and cut into 1-inch pieces
2 ripe plantains, peeled and sliced
1 ounce butter
6 fillets fish
2 tablespoons tomato paste
1 tablespoon Worcestershire sauce
Salt, freshly ground pepper

In a large pan combine the fish stock, onions, garlic, tomato, hot peppers, and cumin and allspice. Bring the mixture to the boil and simmer it, covered, for 15 minutes over low heat. To a saucepan of boiling salted water add the lemon juice and okra. Bring back to the boil, remove from the heat, drain the okra, and rinse it in cold water. Add the okra to the pan with the yams and plantains and cook, covered, over very low heat for 1 hour.

In a frying pan heat the butter and sauté the fish until the fillets are golden. Cut the fish into 1-inch pieces and add to the soup with the tomato paste, Worcestershire sauce, and salt and pepper to taste. Simmer for 30 minutes longer.

Variation: Coconuts are used a great deal in coastal cooking. Instead of the fish stock, use 1¼ pints thin coconut milk (see page 29), increase the cumin to ½ teaspoon, and omit the allspice. Add 1 pound yucca (cassava) root, peeled and cut into 1-inch pieces, when adding the okra. Omit the tomato paste and Worcestershire sauce. When the soup is ready, pour in ½ pint thick coconut milk and simmer for a few minutes longer.

Chupe de Corvina y Camarones

STRIPED BASS AND SHRIMP STEW   *Ecuador*

This is Ecuador's version of the Peruvian *Chupe de Camarones* (Prawn Stew), but a distinctively different dish.

[Serves 6]

1½ pounds bass fillets, cut into
   1½-inch slices
Flour
Salt, freshly ground pepper
4 tablespoons vegetable oil
1 pound shrimps
2 ounces butter

1 teaspoon sweet paprika
1 large onion, finely chopped
2 pounds potatoes, peeled and sliced
¾ pint milk or ½ pint milk, ¼
   pint single cream
½ pound Cheddar cheese, grated
3 hardboiled eggs, sliced

Rinse the fish and pat dry with paper towels. Season the flour with salt and pepper. Dredge the fish in the flour. Heat the oil in a skillet and sauté the fish slices until lightly browned on both sides. Set aside.

Shell the shrimps, reserving the shells. Cut the shrimps into ½-inch pieces and set aside. Melt a tablespoon of the butter in a saucepan, add the shrimp shells, and cook, stirring, until the shells turn pink. Add 1¼ pints water, bring to the boil, cover, and simmer for 5 minutes. Strain, discard the shells, and measure the stock. Bring it up to 1¼ pints with a little water if necessary. Set the stock aside.

Heat the rest of the butter in a large saucepan. Add the paprika and the onion and sauté until the onion is softened. Add the potatoes and the shrimp stock, cover, and simmer until the potatoes are tender, about 20 minutes. Add the milk, or milk and cream, to the saucepan and continue to cook the potatoes, stirring from time to time, until they are partly disintegrated. Add the cheese and stir to mix thoroughly. Season to taste with salt and pepper, then fold in the fish and the shrimps. Cook over low heat for about 3 minutes, or until the shrimps are cooked. Serve in bowls topped with slices of hard-boiled egg. This should be thick, but still recognizable as a soup. Thin with a little milk if necessary.

Variation: This is also Ecuadorian, a simpler version, *Chupe do Corvina* (Striped Bass Stew). Heat 2 ounces butter in a large saucepan. Add 1 tablespoon sweet paprika; 1 large onion, finely chopped; 2 cloves garlic, chopped, and sauté until the onion is soft. Add 2 pounds potatoes, peeled and sliced, and 1¼ pints water. Cover and simmer until the potatoes disintegrate. Season to taste with salt and pepper, stir in ¼ pint single cream and ½ pound grated Cheddar cheese or, if available, Spanish *queso blanco*, crumbled. Cut 1 pound bass fillets into 1-inch slices. Dust with flour and fry in vegetable oil until golden brown on both sides. Drain and fold into the potato soup. Serve garnished with slices of hardboiled egg, using 2 eggs. Serves 4 to 6.

Caldillo de Congrio

FISH SOUP   *Chile*

Congrio is a magnificent firm-fleshed fish found in Chilean waters. I have found cod to be the most acceptable substitute.

[Serves 4]

2 pounds cod, cut into 4 steaks
Salt
4 tablespoons lemon juice
2 carrots, scraped and thinly sliced
2 pounds small potatoes, peeled and
    thinly sliced
2 medium onions, halved and
    thinly sliced

2 cloves garlic, chopped (optional)
Freshly ground pepper
½ teaspoon oregano
½ pint dry white wine
1½ pints fish stock
4 tablespoons olive oil

Put the fish steaks into a casserole, preferably earthenware, large enough to hold them in a single layer. Season with salt and the lemon juice. Cover with a layer of carrots, then a layer of half the potatoes, then the onions and garlic, and the rest of the potatoes. Season with salt, pepper, and oregano. Pour in the wine, fish stock, and olive oil. Bring to the boil, reduce the heat, and simmer until the potatoes and carrots are tender, about 30 minutes. Serve in soup bowls accompanied by crusty bread and butter. With the addition of dessert, or cheese, this makes a splendid lunch or dinner.

Chupe de Camarones

PRAWN STEW   *Peru*

More like a bouillabaisse, this soup is really a meal in itself. The word *"chupe"* actually means a savoury stew containing potatoes, cheese, eggs, etc. Peru, Ecuador, and Chile all have magnificent *chupes*.

[Serves 6]

4 tablespoons vegetable oil
2 medium onions, finely chopped
2 cloves garlic, chopped
2 medium tomatoes, peeled and chopped
1 or 2 fresh hot red or green peppers, seeded and chopped
½ teaspoon oregano
Salt, freshly ground pepper
5½ pints fish stock
2 medium potatoes, peeled and cut into 1-inch cubes

2 pounds large prawns
¼ pound rice
3 large potatoes, peeled and halved
1½ pounds peas, shelled, or use one (10-ounce) package frozen peas, thawed
2 ears corn, each cut into 3 slices
3 eggs
¼ pint single cream
2 tablespoons finely chopped fresh green coriander or use parsley, preferably flat

Heat the oil in a large saucepan and sauté the onions and garlic until the onions are softened. Add the tomatoes, hot peppers, oregano, salt and pepper to taste, and cook for a few minutes, stirring to mix well. Add the fish stock and the diced potatoes. Peel the prawns and add the shells to the saucepan. Set the prawns aside. Bring to the boil, reduce the heat, and simmer gently, covered, for about 30 minutes. Strain through a sieve, pressing down on the solids to extract all the juices. Rinse out the saucepan and return the broth to it.

Add the rice, halved potatoes, and peas, cover, and simmer until the potatoes are tender, about 20 minutes. Add the corn and the prawns and cook for 5 minutes longer. Break the eggs into the soup, one at a time, stirring, so that the eggs coagulate in strips. Pour in the cream and cook just long enough to heat through. Pour into a warmed soup tureen and sprinkle with the coriander or parsley. Ideally this is served in large, deep, old-fashioned rimmed soup plates. Serve in large bowls holding about ¾ pint.

Variation: Use only 1 pound of prawns. Add six 1-inch slices of fillet of bass, fried in oil at the last minute. Leave out the stirred-in eggs and top each soup plate with a poached egg and, if liked, a strip of lightly sautéed sweet red or green pepper. Serves 6.

Variation: In Chile, that paradise of fish and shellfish, there is a simple, very pleasant version of these hearty fish soup-stews, *Chupe de Pescado* (Fish Stew). It is light enough to serve as a soup, not as a meal in itself. Peel, quarter, and boil in salted water 6 fairly small potatoes. Set aside. In a saucepan sauté 2 finely chopped onions in 3 tablespoons vegetable oil and 1 tablespoon sweet paprika until the onions are soft. Add 4 ounces freshly made breadcrumbs, 1 finely grated carrot (optional), 1¼ pints milk, ¾ pint fish stock or water, salt and pepper to taste, ½ teaspoon oregano, and 1 pound mackerel fillets or hake or cod, cut into 1-inch pieces. Add the potatoes. Cover and simmer gently until the fish is done, about 5 to 8 minutes. The *chupe* should be about as thick as a medium béchamel sauce. If it seems too thick, add a little more milk. Serve sprinkled with finely chopped hardboiled egg, using 2. Serves 6.

Sopa de Frijol Negro con Camarones

BLACK BEAN SOUP WITH PRAWNS   *Mexico*

This is a recipe from Oaxaca, where avocado leaves are often used in cooking. Since I find it hard to prune my potted avocado trees, lost as I am in affectionate admiration for their beautiful glossy foliage, I am grateful to recipes like this, which urge me to pluck a couple of leaves. The flavour they add is less pronounced than bay leaf, which is also often used. The leaves may be toasted lightly before they are added to the pot. Some cooks insist this is a vital step, but from experience I do not think it matters a great deal, if at all. The soup is absolutely delicious with a most exciting flavour, the richness of the black beans contrasting unexpectedly with the fresh flavour of the prawns.

[Serves 4]

5 ounces black beans, washed and picked over
⅛ teaspoon ground cumin
¼ teaspoon oregano
1 bay leaf, or 2 avocado leaves
2 tablespoons olive oil
1 medium onion, finely chopped

1 clove garlic, chopped
1 medium tomato, peeled and chopped
Salt, freshly ground pepper
¾ pint chicken stock
½ pound peeled raw prawns, cut into ½-inch pieces
4 tablespoons dry sherry

In a medium saucepan combine the beans, cumin, oregano, bay leaf or avocado leaves, with 1¼ pints water. Bring to the boil over moderate heat, reduce the heat to low, cover, and simmer until the beans

89

are very tender, about 2½ hours. Cool a little, remove, discard the bay leaf or avocado leaves, and pour the beans and liquid into a blender or food processor.

Heat the oil and sauté the onion and garlic until the onion is soft. Add the tomato and simmer until the mixture is well blended, 2 or 3 minutes. Season to taste with salt and pepper and add to the blender or food processor. If necessary do this in two batches. Reduce the mixture to a smooth purée and pour it into the saucepan. Stir in the chicken stock and bring to a simmer over moderate heat. Add the prawns and cook for 2 minutes longer. Serve immediately, as overcooking toughens prawns. Stir 1 tablespoon of sherry into each serving.

Fanesca

SPRING SOUP   *Ecuador*

A traditional dish for Lent, when spring vegetables—peas, green beans, and so on—are first available, this soup is a meal in itself.

[Serves 8 to 10]
1 *pound salt cod*
2 *ounces butter*
2 *medium onions, finely chopped*
1 *clove garlic, minced*
¼ *teaspoon oregano*
¼ *teaspoon ground cumin*
1 *bay leaf*
Freshly ground pepper
6 *ounces long-grain rice cooked in*
    ¾ *pint milk and water mixed*
Kernels from 2 medium ears corn
    (about 6 ounces), cooked
1 *pound cooked shredded cabbage*
½ *pound pumpkin, cooked, mashed*
¾ *pound cooked, chopped*
    courgettes

6 *ounces cooked broad beans or baby*
    lima beans, or use 10-ounce tin,
    drained
6 *ounces cooked green peas*
4 *ounces cooked green beans, cut*
    into ½-inch pieces
2 *ounces peanuts, ground*
1½ *pints milk*
¼ *pint single cream*
¼ *pound Spanish fresh cheese or*
    Caerphilly, white Cheshire or
    mild Cheddar, crumbled
Salt
3 *hardboiled eggs, sliced*
Grated Parmesan cheese

Soak the cod in cold water to cover for 12 hours or more, changing the water frequently. Drain the fish and put it into a saucepan with fresh water to çover. Bring to the boil, lower the heat, and simmer until the fish is tender, about 15 minutes. Drain, and reserve the fish stock. Remove any skin and bones from the fish and cut it into ½-inch pieces. Set aside.

Heat the butter in a large saucepan and sauté the onions and garlic until the onions are soft. Add the oregano, cumin, bay leaf, and several grinds of black pepper and sauté for a minute or two longer. Add ½ pint water, bring to the boil, and add the cooked rice, corn, cabbage, pumpkin, courgettes, broad or lima beans, peas, green beans, ground peanuts, the fish and fish stock, the milk, and the cream. Stir to mix and simmer very gently for about 5 minutes to blend the flavours. Add the crumbled cheese and salt to taste. The soup should be about as thick as a minestrone. If it seems too thick, thin it with a little more milk and simmer for a few minutes longer.

Pour the soup into a tureen and serve in soup plates. Garnish the servings with sliced hardboiled egg. Have the grated Parmesan cheese in a bowl on the table to be used as liked.

Fish and Shellfish

PESCADOS Y MARISCOS

As I have noted, fish and shellfish in Latin America are superb, with the cold Humboldt Current that runs up the coasts of Chile and Peru being responsible for some of the most magnificent seafood in the world. *Erizos*, the sea urchins of Chile, which often measure as much as 4 and 5 inches across, provide an unrivalled gastronomic experience. I remember having *erizos al matico*, raw sea urchins served with a sauce of chopped onion, parsley, oil, and lemon juice, a soup spoon, and a pile of thin, hot buttered toast, at the Hotel Crillon's dining room in Santiago, and marvelling not only at their exquisite flavour but at their astonishing size.*

It is the same with *locos* (abalone), which also reaches wildly generous proportions yet loses nothing in delicacy and flavour. At a beach club near Lima, Peru, I had huge scallops with their coral served on the half shell and accompanied only by the small tropical lemon-lime that I am sure is indigenous to tropical America, its flavour more lemon than lime, but muted, delicate. Shrimp, crabs, oysters, lobsters, clams, and scallops are found in abundance, and there are also strange shellfish like the *picoroccos*, beaked creatures that live in colonies of rocklike tubes and taste like crabs when cooked. Among the fish, *congrio* with its large head and tapering body is unique, and *corvina*, sea bass, is very fine. Mexico's waters produce excellent

Erizos (sea urchins) are sometimes available canned from delicatessens. Serve them with *Salsa de Perejil* (Parsley Sauce *page 307*).

shrimp, conch, red snapper, and other fish and shellfish, and the same is true of the waters off Ecuador, Colombia, Argentina, and Brazil.

Perhaps because of this abundance of good seafood, recipes are not as numerous, or as varied, as for meat and poultry dishes, since the best way to cook splendid fish and shellfish is often the simplest. But there are a number of very good, original recipes, especially those from Brazil, suitable for fish usually available in any fishmongers. And there are the *seviches*, fish and shellfish "cooked" in a marinade of lime or lemon juice, and the *escabeches*, lightly pickled fish.

Salt cod is as popular in South America as it is in Spain and Portugal, with cooks combining indigenous and introduced foods to create exciting new dishes. Mexico cooks salt cod with a sauce of the mild but richly flavoured *ancho* pepper and almonds. The north of Brazil marries coconut milk with tomatoes and sweet peppers for its salt cod Bahia style, in great contrast to the cod of Minas Gerais to the south, where tomatoes, sweet peppers, and cabbage are included.

Corvina a la Chorrillana

STRIPED BASS WITH VEGETABLES   *Peru*

This is bass in the style of Chorrillos, a resort 10 miles out of Lima. The annatto oil gives a distinctive flavour to this robust and satisfying dish. Chorrillos means literally "the little streams," which flow down from the Andes creating a green patch on this desert coast so that the town can exist—and hence the dish.

[Serves 6]

1 tablespoon annatto oil (see page 310)
2 large onions, finely sliced
2 cloves garlic, chopped
2 large tomatoes, peeled and sliced
2 large or 4 small fresh hot red or green peppers, seeded and sliced

½ teaspoon oregano
Salt, freshly ground pepper
3 pounds bass, or any firm-fleshed non-oily fish cut into 6 steaks
2 tablespoons peanut oil
Juice of 1 lemon

Pour the annatto oil into a heavy casserole so that it covers the bottom evenly. Make a layer of half the onions, garlic, tomatoes, and peppers. Sprinkle with half the oregano and season to taste with salt and pepper. Arrange the fish on top of the vegetables and cover with the remaining vegetables. Season with the rest of the oregano, salt and pepper, the peanut oil, and the lemon juice. Cover the casserole and cook over low heat for 20 to 30 minutes, or until the vegetables are tender. Serve with *Arroz Graneado* (Peruvian Style Rice) Page 244.

Variation: Omit the oregano and use 2 tablespoons finely chopped fresh green coriander instead.

Peixe em Môlho de Tangerina

FISH IN TANGERINE SAUCE   *Northern Brazil*

[Serves 4]

A 3-pound red snapper or bass, or
   any firm-fleshed, non-oily white
   fish, cleaned, with head and tail
   left on
2 tablespoons lemon juice
Salt, freshly ground pepper
Butter

1 tablespoon olive oil
½ ounce melted butter
¼ pound mushrooms, sliced
1 tablespoon chopped parsley
1 spring onion, chopped, using
   green and white parts
½ pint dry white wine
¼ pint tangerine juice

Season the fish with lemon juice, salt, and pepper. Put the fish in a buttered baking dish just large enough to hold it and pour over it the olive oil and melted butter. Sprinkle the fish with the mushrooms, parsley, and spring onion. Pour the wine and tangerine juice over it and bake in a preheated hot oven (400° F., 200° C., gas 6) for 25 to 30 minutes, or until it flakes easily when tested with a fork.

Pescado con Cilantro

FISH WITH CORIANDER   *Mexico*

Fresh coriander leaves give this dish a delectable flavour, especially for addicts of the herb, of which I am one. It is a colonial dish, and very easy to make, which is unusual as many of the older recipes are rather long-winded. Plain White Rice (*Arroz Blanco*), cooked in the Mexican style, is the perfect accompaniment (page 245).

[Serves 6]

3 pounds fillets of red snapper,
   striped bass, flounder, or any
   firm white-fleshed fish
Salt, freshly ground pepper
4 tablespoons lemon juice
5 tablespoons vegetable oil

1 medium onion, finely chopped
8 tablespoons chopped fresh
   coriander
3 canned jalapeño chilies, rinsed,
   seeded, and chopped, or 3 large
   fresh green chilies

Season the fish with salt and pepper and sprinkle with the lemon juice. Heat 4 tablespoons of the oil and sauté the onion until it is soft. Lightly film with oil the surface of a shallow ovenproof casserole large enough to hold the fish comfortably, in more than one layer if necessary. Arrange the fish fillets, with any liquid they may have yielded, in the casserole, cover with the onion and the oil, and sprinkle with the coriander and chilies. Drizzle with the remaining tablespoon of oil. Bake in a preheated moderate oven (350° F., 180° C., gas 4) for 20 minutes, or until the fish has lost its translucent look.

Pescado Frito con Salsa de Vino Tinto

FRIED FISH WITH RED WINE SAUCE   *Colombia*

The red wine and tomatoes combine here to make a full-flavoured sauce with the subtle hint of allspice that I find very attractive and out of the ordinary.

[Serves 4]

2 pounds fish steaks, cut into 4 pieces, using any firm-fleshed white fish
Salt, freshly ground pepper
Flour
4 tablespoons vegetable oil
2 medium onions, finely chopped

2 cloves garlic, minced
4 medium tomatoes, peeled and chopped
1 bay leaf
Pinch each cayenne pepper and ground allspice
½ pint dry red wine

Season the fish steaks with salt and pepper and coat lightly with flour, shaking to remove the excess. Heat the oil and sauté the fish until lightly browned on both sides. Transfer to a platter and keep warm. In the oil remaining in the pan (add a little more if necessary), sauté the onions and garlic until the onions are soft. Add the tomatoes, bay leaf, cayenne pepper and allspice, and salt and pepper to taste, and sauté, stirring from time to time, until the mixture is thick and well blended, about 5 minutes. Stir in the wine and bring to a simmer. Add the fish and simmer for 2 or 3 minutes. Transfer the fish to a warmed serving dish and pour the sauce over it. Serve with rice, potatoes, or any starchy accompaniment.

Pescado en Escabeche

FISH IN OIL AND VINEGAR SAUCE   *Peru*

Pescado en Escabeche is very popular throughout Latin America. The cooking technique is of Spanish origin, but cooks have changed re-

95

cipes adding an herb or vegetable, altering things a little, so that there is a whole group of New World *escabeche* dishes that make splendid appetizers or main courses.

[Serves 6]

3 pounds of any firm-fleshed white
    fish, cut into 6 fillets or 6 steaks
Salt, freshly ground pepper
Flour
1½ ounces butter or lard
½ pint olive oil or vegetable oil

3 medium onions, thickly sliced
1 or 2 fresh hot red or green
    peppers, seeded and cut into
    strips
¼ teaspoon oregano
4 tablespoons white vinegar

Season the fish with salt and pepper and dredge in flour, shaking to remove the excess. Heat the butter or lard and sauté the fish until lightly browned on both sides. Transfer the cooked fish to a shallow serving dish and keep warm. Heat the oil in a medium-sized saucepan, add the onions and pepper strips, and cook over low heat until the onions are soft and very lightly browned. Stir in the oregano and cook for a minute longer. Pour in the vinegar, stir, and pour over the fish. Serve immediately.

For a more robust dish, garnish with 3 ears of freshly cooked corn, each cut into 4 slices, 3 hardboiled eggs, halved, lettuce leaves, and olives.

Variation: This Argentine version, *Merluza a la Vinagreta* (Hake in Vinaigrette Sauce), is quite different from the Peruvian one. Wash and pat dry 3 pounds of hake or cod fillets, cut into 12 pieces. Sprinkle the fish with salt, preferably coarse salt, and let stand for 1 hour. Rinse and dry. Dredge in flour, shaking to remove the excess, and sauté in 3 tablespoons olive oil until the fish has lost its translucent look. A good rule is to measure the thickness of the fish and give it 10 minutes to the inch, 5 minutes on each side. Arrange the cooked fish in a shallow dish and pour on a sauce made by mixing 1 clove garlic, peeled and finely chopped, 4 cornichons, chopped, 2 hardboiled eggs, chopped, 2 tablespoons capers, 2 tablespoons finely chopped parsley, salt, freshly ground pepper, ½ pint wine vinegar, and ½ pint olive oil. Let the fish stand for at least an hour before serving. Serve, garnished with lettuce leaves, at room temperature. Serves 12 as a first course.

Variation: *Pescado en Escabeche* from Mexico can be made with mackerel, bream or similar fish. Cut 2 pounds of fish fillets into 8 pieces and sprinkle them with 3 tablespoons lemon juice. Let the fish stand for 15 minutes, turning the pieces once. Rinse gently in cold water and pat dry. Heat 4 tablespoons of olive oil and sauté the fish until it has lost its translucent look and is lightly browned on both sides. Lift the fish out and place in a dish.

In a saucepan combine 2 whole cloves, a 1-inch piece of stick cinnamon, 6 peppercorns, 2 cloves garlic, ⅛ teaspoon ground cumin, ¼ teaspoon thyme, ½ teaspoon oregano, 2 bay leaves, 2 whole fresh hot green peppers, preferably *serrano*, with stems left on, 6 sliced spring onions, using white and green parts, salt to taste, and ½ pint white vinegar. Bring to the boil, lower the heat, and simmer, uncovered, for 2 or 3 minutes, or until the spring onions are soft. Set aside. In another small saucepan heat ½ pint olive oil with 2 cloves garlic and fry the garlic over low heat until browned. Lift out and discard the garlic. Pour the oil into the saucepan with the vinegar mixture, heat to a simmer, and pour the mixture over the fish. Allow to cool, cover, and refrigerate for 24 hours. To serve, lift out the fish onto a shallow serving platter and sprinkle with a little oregano crumbled between the fingers, if liked. Garnish the platter with shredded lettuce tossed in vinaigrette sauce (page 314), 2 tablespoons capers, 2 canned *jalapeño* chilies, cut into strips, 1 bunch radishes, cut into flowers, and about 24 small pimiento-stuffed green olives. Serve with tortillas as an appetizer for 8. This makes a pleasant light lunch for 4.

Congrio en Fuente de Barro

FISH WITH TOMATOES AND ONIONS   *Chile*

Congrio, the very splendid large fish found in Chilean waters, is considered by Chileans to be the finest of all their food fishes. There are three kinds, *congrio colorado*, *congrio negro*, and *congrio dorado*, red, black, and gold fish. They made a fine sight when I saw them hanging up in a Santiago fish market, looking rather like eels with their big heads and tapering bodies—which explains their equivocal common name, for *congrio* is the Spanish word for eel. Eels these are not. They are *Genypterus chilensis*, living in the waters off Chile's long Pacific coast and existing as far north as Peruvian waters. Their only known relatives are a New Zealand fish known as ling, but not to be confused with the European ling to which it is not related.

The fish is firm-fleshed and when cooked breaks into large flakes. In my experience cod is the best substitute, though any firm-fleshed non-oily fish can be used successfully. The term *"fuente de barro"* simply means cooked in earthenware. Though any casserole may be used, the dish is better when cooked in earthenware.

[Serves 4]

2 pounds fillets of cod, cut into 4 pieces

Salt, freshly ground pepper

2 tablespoons lemon juice

1½ ounces butter

1 teaspoon sweet paprika

1 large onion, finely chopped

4 medium tomatoes, peeled and chopped

4 slices firm white bread, fried in butter, or 1 pound potatoes, boiled and sliced

2 hardboiled eggs, sliced

1 sweet red pepper, seeded and cut into strips

¼ pint milk (optional)

1 tablespoon chopped parsley

Season the fish with salt, pepper, and lemon juice, and set aside. Heat the butter, stir in the paprika, add the onion, and sauté over moderate heat until it is soft. Add the tomatoes and sauté for a few minutes longer. Butter an earthenware casserole and put a layer of the tomato mixture, then the fish, more tomato, the fried bread or potatoes, and more tomato. Repeat until all these ingredients are used up. Or you may have a casserole large enough to hold the fish in a single layer. Top with the sliced hardboiled eggs and pepper strips. Cover and bake in a preheated moderate oven (350° F., 180° C., gas 4) for 30 minutes. If the dish seems to be drying out during cooking, add up to ¼ pint milk. Sprinkle with parsley and serve.

Variation: I was quite astonished one day in Asunción, capital of land-locked Paraguay, to be given a dish remarkably like *Congrio en Fuente de Barro* from Chile, which is more seacoast than anything else and has a most remarkable harvest of fish and shellfish. The fish in this *Guiso de Dorado* was from the Paraguay River, a great, noble waterway. It seemed to me in flavour and texture very like the Spanish *dorado*, dolphin fish, and so it turned out to be, though not, of course, to be confused with the mammalian dolphin. *Dorado* is a famous fish of Paraguayan rivers and wholly delectable. Any firm-fleshed white fish would make a suitable substitute.

For *Guiso de Dorado* (Fish Stew), put 2 pounds fish, cut into 4 steaks, into a flat dish and season them with salt and pepper. Pour 4 tablespoons lemon juice over the steaks and let them stand 1 hour, turning once or twice. Lift out, pat dry with paper towels, and dust with flour. Heat ¼ pint olive or vegetable oil in a casserole and sauté the fish steaks until golden on both sides. Arrange half the fish steaks in the casserole. Have ready 2 medium onions, thinly sliced, 2 cloves garlic, minced, 2 tomatoes, peeled and sliced, 2 sweet red or green peppers, seeded and sliced, and 2 medium potatoes, peeled and thinly sliced. Arrange half of the onions, garlic, tomatoes, peppers, and potatoes over the fish. Top with a bay leaf, a sprig of thyme, and 2 or 3 sprigs of parsley. Season to taste with salt and pepper and top with the rest of the fish and the remaining vegetables. Season again with salt and pepper. Pour ¼ pint each dry white wine and fish stock, or water, over the fish, cover tightly, bring to a simmer, and cook for 20 to 30 minutes, or until the potatoes and fish are both tender. Check to see if the fish is drying out during the cooking time and add a little more stock or wine if necessary. Serves 4.

Corvina Rellena

STUFFED STRIPED BASS   *Argentina*

[Serves 4]

A 3- to 3½-pound striped bass, cleaned and boned, with head and tail left on, or use any firm-fleshed non-oily fish
Salt, freshly ground pepper
1 medium onion, finely chopped
2 cloves garlic, finely chopped or crushed

1 ounce (8 tablespoons) finely chopped parsley
2 ounces fresh breadcrumbs
Milk
½ ounce butter
1 tablespoon olive oil
½ pint dry white wine

Rinse the fish and pat dry with paper towels. Season the inside of the fish with salt and pepper. In a bowl combine the onion, garlic, parsley, breadcrumbs, and salt and pepper to taste. Moisten the mixture with a little milk and stuff the fish with the mixture. Fasten with toothpicks. Butter a shallow, heatproof casserole that will hold the fish comfortably, and arrange the fish in it. Dot the fish with the butter and pour the olive oil over it, then pour the white wine over it. Bake in a preheated hot oven (400° F., 200° C., gas 6) for 40 minutes, or until the fish feels firm when pressed with a finger. The wine will have reduced, combining with the butter and oil to form a sauce. Serve directly from the casserole. Accompany with rice or potatoes and a green vegetable or salad.

Mero en Mac-Cum

STRIPED BASS IN SAUCE   *Mexico*

This dish with achiote (annatto), cumin, and Seville orange juice is typical of the Mayan kitchen of Yucatán.

[Serves 4]
2 pounds striped bass, or any firm-
fleshed, non-oily white fish, cut
into 4 steaks
4 large cloves garlic, crushed
Black pepper
¼ teaspoon ground cumin
½ teaspoon oregano
1 teaspoon ground annatto
Salt
¼ pint Seville (bitter) orange juice,
about, or a mixture of two-thirds
orange juice to one-third lime
juice

1 fresh hot pepper, seeded and
chopped (optional)
¼ pint olive oil
1 large onion, thinly sliced
2 cloves garlic, minced
2 tomatoes, sliced
2 medium sweet red peppers, seeded
and sliced, or 2 canned
pimientos, cut into strips
2 tablespoons chopped parsley

Put the fish steaks on a platter in a single layer. Make a dressing of the garlic, 6 or more grinds black pepper, cumin, oregano, annatto, salt to taste, and enough orange juice to make a thin paste. Coat the steaks on both sides with the mixture and let stand for 30 minutes. Pour a little of the olive oil into a shallow baking dish large enough to hold the fish steaks. Use only enough oil to coat the bottom of the dish. Arrange the fish steaks, with any remaining marinade, in the dish. Top the steaks with the onion, minced garlic, tomatoes, and peppers. Pour the rest of the oil over the fish, cover, and cook over low heat until the fish loses its translucent look, about 15 minutes. Sprinkle with the parsley and serve with rice. Fresh hot tortillas may also be served.

Pescado a la Veracruzana

FISH, VERACRUZ STYLE *Mexico*

Pescado a la Veracruzana (Fish in the Style of Veracruz) is Mexico's best-known fish dish and rightly so for it is admirable. There are a great many versions of it, each one differing in minor details. This is the one I prefer and I never tire of it. When I first visited Venezuela, I realized I was meeting its culinary, and almost certainly younger, cousin, *Corbullón Mantuano*, made with striped bass, and in Buenos Aires the *Corvina a la Porteña*, also with bass, seemed to be the Argentine cousin. Subtle variations make all three worth trying; they come to table surprisingly different.

[Serves 4]
2 pounds red snapper fillets, or any
    firm-fleshed non-oily fish
Salt, freshly ground pepper
Juice of a small lemon or lime
6 tablespoons olive oil
2 medium onions, finely chopped
2 cloves garlic, chopped
6 medium tomatoes, peeled and
    chopped
3 tablespoons capers

20 small pimiento-stuffed green
    olives
2 or 3 canned jalapeño chilies, or
    fresh hot green chilies, seeded
    and cut into strips
12 small new potatoes, freshly
    cooked, or 6 medium potatoes,
    halved
3 slices firm white bread
Butter for frying

Season the fish with salt and pepper and the lemon or lime juice. Set aside. Heat the oil and sauté the onions and garlic until the onions are soft. Reduce the tomatoes to a purée in a blender or food processor and add to the pan with the capers, olives, *jalapeño* chilies, and the fish. Season with a little more salt and pepper and cook over very low heat until the fish is tender and the sauce slightly thickened, about 10 to 15 minutes. Transfer to a warmed platter and garnish with the potatoes. Cut the bread into 6 triangles, fry in butter until golden, and arrange as a border round the edge of the platter.

Variation: *Corbullón Mantuano* (Striped Bass in Sweet Pepper Sauce) from Venezuela. Remove the head and tail from a 2½-pound bass and cut it into 1½-inch slices. Season with salt and freshly ground pepper. Heat 4 tablespoons butter and 1 tablespoon olive oil in a large frying pan and sauté the fish until it is lightly browned on both sides. Transfer the fish to a platter and keep it warm. In the fat remaining in the pan sauté 2 medium onions, thinly sliced, and 1 green and 1 red sweet pepper, seeded and thinly sliced, until the onions are soft. Add 6 medium tomatoes, peeled and chopped, ½ small fresh hot red pepper, or ¼ teaspoon ground hot red pepper (cayenne), 2 tablespoons capers, and 20 small pimiento-stuffed green olives, and simmer for 2 or 3 minutes. Add ½ pint dry red wine and 4 tablespoons olive oil and simmer until the sauce is well blended, about 10 minutes. Add the fish and cook just long enough to heat it through. Arrange on a warmed platter. Peel and slice 1½ pounds potatoes and boil, covered, in salted water until tender, about 15 to 20 minutes. Drain and arrange around the edge of the platter with the fish. Serves 4.

Variation: *Corvina a la Porteña* (Striped Bass, Buenos Aires Style) is an Argentine cousin of both dishes. Cut a 2½- to 3-pound bass with head and tail removed into 1½-inch slices and dredge them in flour. Pour ¼ pint olive oil in a baking dish and arrange the fish slices in it. In a frying pan heat ½ pint of olive oil and sauté 2 medium onions, chopped, until softened. Add 2 tomatoes, peeled and chopped, 2 sliced sweet green peppers, a bay leaf, ½ teaspoon oregano, and salt and freshly ground pepper to taste. Simmer the mixture until it is thick and well blended. Pour the sauce over the fish and bake in a preheated moderate (350° F., 180° C., gas 4) oven for 20 minutes, or until the fish is done. Discard the bay leaf. Transfer to a warmed platter and sprinkle with a tablespoon of chopped parsley. Serves 4.

Pargo al Horno

BAKED RED SNAPPER   *Venezuela*

[Serves 4]
A 3- to 3½-pound red snapper,
  cleaned and boned, with head and
  tail left on, or sea or black bass
Salt, freshly ground pepper

2 ounces butter
4 tablespoons lime or lemon juice
½ pint fish stock
¼ pint double cream
1 teaspoon Worcestershire sauce

Rinse the fish and pat dry with paper towels. Season the fish inside and outside with salt and pepper. Using ½ ounce of the butter, grease a shallow, heatproof casserole that will hold the fish comfortably and arrange the fish in it. Combine the lime or lemon juice and fish stock and pour over the fish. Dot the fish with ½ ounce of the butter and bake in a preheated hot oven (400° F., 200° C., gas 6) for 30 minutes, or until the fish feels firm when pressed with a finger. Using 2 spatulas, lift the fish out onto a serving platter and keep warm. Pour the liquid from the casserole into a small saucepan. Stir in the cream and bring it to a simmer over moderate heat. Cut the remaining butter into small pieces and stir in. Taste for seasoning and add more salt and pepper if necessary. Spoon a little of the sauce over the fish and serve the rest separately in a sauceboat. Accompany with potatoes or rice and a green vegetable.

Sábalo Guisado con Coco

SHAD FILLETS IN COCONUT MILK   *Colombia*

Coconut milk is used a great deal in the cooking of coastal Colombia, giving dishes an interestingly different flavour, rich yet delicate.

[Serves 6]

3 pounds boned shad fillets, cut
  into 6 pieces
3 medium tomatoes, peeled, seeded,
  and chopped
1 medium onion, finely chopped
1 or 2 fresh hot red or green
  peppers, left whole with stem on

Salt, freshly ground pepper
1¾ pints thin coconut milk, about
  (see page 29)
½ pint thick coconut milk (see page
  29)

Arrange the fish fillets in a shallow flameproof casserole and cover with the tomatoes and onion. Lay the hot peppers on top. Season to taste with salt and pepper. Pour in the thin coconut milk, and simmer for about 10 minutes or until the fish is no longer translucent. A simple rule is to measure the thickness of the fish and cook it 10 minutes to the inch. Carefully lift out the fish onto a serving platter and keep warm. Discard the hot peppers. Reduce the liquid in the casserole to about ½ pint over brisk heat. Add the thick coconut milk and simmer just long enough to heat the sauce through. Strain the sauce but do not push the solids through the sieve. Pour the sauce over the fish. Serve with rice.

The fish may be cooked in a preheated moderate oven (350° F., 180° C., gas 4). In this case bring the liquid just to a simmer on top of the stove, transfer the casserole to the oven, and cook for 10 minutes to the inch, which will be about 10 minutes for fillets. Make the sauce in the same way. Any firm-fleshed white fish can be used for this dish when shad is not in season, making it *Pescado Guisado con Coco* (Fish Cooked in Coconut Milk).

If the peppers are very hot (nibble a tiny bit to check), the sauce may be too *picante* for some tastes. A simple solution is to take the peppers out of the sauce after 2 or 3 minutes instead of leaving them there for the full cooking time.

MOQUECAS

The mixture of indigenous Indian, African, and Portuguese cooking that makes up Bahian cuisine is particularly apparent in the *moquecas*, which I translate as stews for want of a better word. According to that great authority in the Bahian kitchen Darwin Brandão, *moquecas*

103

were originally Indian *pokekas*—dishes wrapped in banana leaves and cooked over charcoal. Africans brought over as slaves and working as cooks for the Portuguese in the great houses of the sugar plantations around Bahia modified the indigenous dishes, and today *moquecas*, whether of prawns, fish, crab, or whatever, are cooked in a saucepan on top of the stove. Coconut milk, *dendê* oil, and hot peppers are typical ingredients.

Moqueca de Camarão

BAHIAN PRAWN STEW   *Brazil*

[Serves 6]
4 tablespoons olive oil
1 large onion, finely chopped
2 small carrots, scraped and thinly
  sliced
1 sweet green pepper, seeded and
  chopped
1 sweet red pepper, seeded and
  chopped

4 medium tomatoes, peeled, seeded,
  and chopped
Salt, freshly ground pepper
2 pounds prawns, shelled and
  deveined
2 tablespoons dendê (palm) oil

Heat the olive oil in a large, heavy pan and sauté the onion, carrots, and green and red peppers until the onion is soft. Add the tomatoes and salt and pepper to taste, and cook for a few minutes longer over moderate heat. Stir in the prawns and the *dendê* oil and cook, turning the prawns once or twice, until the prawns are pink and have lost their translucent look, about 3 minutes. Serve on a warmed platter surrounded by white rice. Serve separately with *Môlho de Pimenta e Azeite de Dendê* (Hot Peppers in Palm Oil), page 302, or *Môlho de Pimenta e Limão* (Hot Pepper and Lime Sauce), page 302.

Moqueca de Peixe

FISH STEW   *Brazil*

[Serves 6]
3 pounds fillets of sole or any white
  fish
2 medium onions, chopped
1 or 2 fresh hot peppers, seeded and
  chopped
3 medium tomatoes, peeled and
  chopped

1 clove garlic, chopped
2 tablespoons fresh coriander
Salt
4 tablespoons lime or lemon juice
4 tablespoons dendê (palm) oil

Cut the fish into 2-inch pieces and place in a large bowl. In a blender or food processor combine the onions, hot peppers, tomatoes, garlic, coriander, salt to taste, and the lime or lemon juice, and reduce to a purée. Pour the purée over the fish, mixing lightly, and allow to stand for 1 hour. Transfer the fish and the marinade to a saucepan. Add ¼ pint cold water and 2 tablespoons of the *dendê* oil. Cover and simmer until the fish is done, about 8 minutes. Pour in the remaining *dendê* oil and cook just long enough to heat the oil through. Transfer the stew to a heated serving platter and surround with a border of plain white rice.

Variation: *Moqueca de Camarão* (Prawn Stew). This is a very interesting *moqueca*. Substitute 2 pounds raw prawns, shelled and deveined, for the fish. Shorten the cooking time to about 3 minutes, or just long enough for the prawns to turn pink and lose their translucent look. Stir in ½ pint thick coconut milk with the prawns. Omit the water. Serves 6.

PRAWN DISHES

Prawns in Latin America are magnificent in quality and abundant in quantity and in my experience almost always beautifully cooked, juicy, and well flavoured. It takes discipline in Bahia to eat anything *but* prawns, they are so delicious. Tomatoes and peppers, both sweet and hot, are used a great deal with prawns, but because each country uses different seasoning, or different ways of preparing them, the finished dishes are quite varied in flavour. Perhaps the most unusual is the *Vatapá de Camarão e Peixe* (Prawns and Fish in Coconut, Nut, and Shrimp Sauce), which illustrates the exuberance of this extraordinarily imaginative kitchen, where improbable combinations, such as dried shrimp and fresh prawns, almonds and cashew nuts, *dendê* oil and coconut milk, marry in an exciting way—a lovely dish for a party (and fortunately a food processor simplifies the work).

Vatapá de Camarão e Peixe

PRAWNS AND FISH IN COCONUT, NUT,   *Brazil*
AND SHRIMP SAUCE

[Serves 6 to 8]
¼ pound dried shrimp
4 tablespoons dendê *(palm) oil or*
olive oil
2 *medium onions, grated*
2 *cloves garlic, crushed*
¼ *pound cashew nuts, ground*
¼ *pound blanched almonds, ground*
2 *ounces fresh breadcrumbs*

1¾ *pints thin coconut milk (see*
page 29)
2 *or more tablespoons* dendê
(palm) oil
2 *tablespoons olive oil*
2 *pounds sea bass fillets, or other*
white fish
1 *pound prawns, shelled and*
deveined

Soak the dried shrimp in warm water to cover for 15 minutes. Drain the shrimp, then purée in a blender or food processor, or put through a food mill, using the fine blade. Set aside.

Heat 4 tablespoons *dendê* or olive oil in a heavy frying pan and sauté the onions, garlic, cashew nuts, almonds, and the puréed shrimp for 5 minutes. Stir in the breadcrumbs and the coconut milk, and simmer, stirring occasionally, until the mixture has the consistency of a thick béchamel sauce. Add more breadcrumbs if necessary. Remove from the heat and stir in 2 or more tablespoons of *dendê* oil to taste.

Heat 2 tablespoons olive oil in a frying pan and sauté the fish lightly. Add the prawns, and sauté for about 2 minutes, or until they turn pink. Fold the prawn and fish mixture into the coconut milk sauce. Serve with *Angú de Arroz* (Moulded Rice , page 247) and a hot pepper sauce (see pages 299–302), if liked.

Camarones Acapulqueños

SHRIMP, ACAPULCO STYLE   *Mexico*

[Serves 4]
1 *pound shrimp or prawns*
2 *ounces butter*
2 *cloves garlic, minced*
4 *tablespoons parsley, finely*
chopped

3 *medium tomatoes, peeled and*
chopped
3 *tablespoons tomato paste*
Salt, freshly ground pepper
5 *tablespoons brandy*

Peel and devein the shrimp or prawns and set aside. Put the shells into a small saucepan with ¾ pint water, bring to the boil, reduce the heat, and simmer, uncovered, for 20 minutes. Strain and discard the shells. Measure the liquid. There should be ½ pint. If necessary, reduce it over brisk heat or make up the quantity with water. Reserve.

Heat the butter in a casserole and add the garlic and parsley, and sauté for 2 minutes, taking care not to let the garlic burn. Add the tomatoes and simmer until the mixture is thick, about 10 minutes. Add the reserved shrimp stock and the tomato paste, stir to mix, season with salt and pepper, and add the brandy. Bring to a simmer, add the shrimp or prawns, cover, and cook for 2 to 3 minutes, according to the size of the shellfish until they are pink, taking care not to overcook. Serve on a bed of rice.

Camarão com Leite de Côco

PRAWNS IN COCONUT MILK   *Brazil*

A Bahamian dish that I find enticing.

[Serves 6]
1½ pounds prawns
3 cloves garlic, crushed
6 tablespoons lime or lemon juice
Salt, freshly ground pepper
4 tablespoons vegetable oil
1 large onion, grated

3 spring onions, chopped, using
   white and green parts
3 medium tomatoes, peeled, seeded,
   and chopped
½ pint plus 4 tablespoons thick
   coconut milk (see page 28)

Peel and devein the prawns, saving the shells. Put the prawns in a bowl with the garlic, lime or lemon juice, and salt and pepper to taste. Set aside.

Place the reserved shells in a saucepan with 1¼ pints water and simmer briskly, uncovered, for 30 minutes, or until the liquid is reduced to ¼ pint. Strain, discard the shells, and set the stock aside.

Heat the oil and sauté the onion and spring onion for 3 minutes, or until the onion is softened. Add the tomatoes and the prawn stock to the pan and simmer until the mixture is well blended and quite thick, about 5 minutes. Stir in the thick coconut milk and the prawns with their liquid, and cook, uncovered, until they are pink and have lost their translucent look, about 3 minutes. Turn the prawns over once or twice during the cooking. Be careful not to overcook them as they toughen very quickly. Taste for salt and pepper and add a little more if necessary. Serve on a bed of plain white rice.

Arroz con Mariscos

RICE WITH SHELLFISH   *Peru*

This is a really festive dish with its shrimp-flavoured rice and rich mixture of shellfish. The secret is in cooking the shellfish just until they are done and not a second longer as they toughen very quickly with overcooking.

[Serves 4 to 6]

4 tablespoons olive oil, about
1 large onion, finely chopped
2 cloves garlic, minced
2 fresh hot peppers,* preferably red, seeded and cut into strips
¾ pound long-grain rice
1¾ pints prawn stock

1 or 2 tablespoons fresh coriander, chopped
½ pound medium-sized prawns
½ pound scallops—if small, left whole; if large, halved
12 cherrystone or littleneck clams or mussels
12 oysters

Heat the oil and sauté the onion, garlic, and pepper strips until the onion is soft. Using a slotted spoon, transfer the onion mixture to a casserole. There should be about 2 tablespoons oil left in the pan. Add a little more if necessary. Add the rice and sauté until the rice has absorbed the oil, taking care not to let it brown. Transfer the rice to a casserole. Add the stock, bring to the boil over high heat, reduce the heat to low, and cook, covered, until the rice is tender and all the liquid absorbed, about 20 minutes. Add the coriander and the prawns, scallops, and clams or mussels folding them well into the rice. Cook, covered, over low heat for about 3 to 5 minutes, or until the prawns have turned pink and lost their translucent look. Add the oysters, folding them into the rice and cook just long enough to plump them, about 1 minute. Serve immediately.

To make prawn stock: In a small saucepan heat 1 tablespoon olive oil and toss the shells in this until they turn pink. Add 1 sprig parsley, 1 slice onion, or a sliced spring onion, using white and green parts, 1 sprig thyme or ⅛ teaspoon dried, 3 or 4 peppercorns, and 1¾ pints

---

*Peruvians for the most part like their food hot and are lavish in their use of *ajíes*, hot peppers, which in fact, lend flavour as well as heat. A wicked Peruvian friend of mine says that his compatriots like *picante* food as it gives them an excuse to quench the fire with *pisco* sours, a lovely local drink, or with anything else alcoholic. However, use just as much, or as little, of the hot pepper as suits your personal taste.

water. Bring to the boil, reduce the heat, and simmer, covered, for 30 minutes. Strain and measure. There should be about 1¼ pints. Measure the liquid from the oysters and clams or mussels. If there is more than ½ pint, reduce the prawn stock, uncovered, over brisk heat so that there will be 1¾ pints stock. Cool the stock and stir in the oyster and clam liquid. Season to taste with salt.

Cuajado de Camarones

SHRIMP AND POTATO OMELET   *Colombia*

Cuajado means a dish made in a frying pan with meat, fish, or fruit, and eggs to hold it together. "Omelet" seems the best word to describe it but the eggs do not play as large a role as they would in a French omelet, pushed off centre stage by the onions, tomatoes, potatoes, and shrimp. Though not a heavy dish, this is robust and satisfying and served with a green salad makes an excellent lunch or dinner.

[Serves 4]
1½ ounces butter
1 teaspoon sweet paprika
2 medium onions, finely chopped
3 large tomatoes, peeled, seeded, and chopped

Salt, freshly ground pepper
2 medium-sized new potatoes, cooked and cubed
4 large eggs, separated
1 pound raw shrimp or prawns, peeled and cut into ½-inch pieces

Heat the butter in a large (10-inch) frying pan, stir in the paprika and the onions and sauté over moderate heat until the onions are soft. Add the tomatoes and salt and pepper to taste and cook until the mixture is thick and well blended, about 5 minutes. Add the potatoes and cook for a few minutes longer. Beat the egg yolks until they are thick and lemony. In a separate bowl beat the egg whites until they stand in firm peaks. Fold the whites and yolks together with a spatula. Return the pan to the heat, fold the shrimp or prawns into the sauce, cook 2 minutes for small shrimp, 3 for prawns. Then fold in the eggs, mixing thoroughly. Cook until the eggs are lightly set.

SALT COD DISHES

Many fishmongers, some supermarkets, and most West Indian shops sell salt cod, so that it will be easy to duplicate these typical Latin American dishes. It is sold packaged by the pound, sometimes in a box, sometimes as a piece cut from a whole fish, often very large. There is no important difference between the two except that the packaged fish is usually boneless while pieces from the whole fish may be quite bony, involving a little extra work.

Bacalhau a Baíana

SALT COD, BAHIA STYLE *Brazil*

This Brazilian dish of salt cod cooked in a tomato mixture is the most original of these popular dishes, but other versions are good, too.

[Serves 4]
1 pound salt cod
3 tablespoons vegetable oil
1 medium onion, grated
1 clove garlic, crushed
2 sweet peppers, 1 red, 1 green, seeded and chopped
3 tomatoes, peeled and puréed

½ pint hot water
Salt, freshly ground pepper
1 tablespoon dendê (palm) oil
½ pint thick coconut milk (see page 29)
6 ounces spring onions, chopped, using white and green parts

Soak the cod in cold water to cover for 12 hours or more, changing the water frequently. Drain the fish and remove any skin and bones. Pat the fish dry with paper towels and cut it into 2-inch pieces. Heat the oil in a saucepan and sauté the onion, garlic, and peppers until the onion and peppers are soft, about 5 minutes. Add the tomatoes, fish, and hot water. Cover and simmer for 15 minutes, or until the fish flakes easily when tested with a fork. Season to taste with salt, if necessary, pepper, and *dendê* oil. Stir in the coconut milk and the spring onions and heat through without letting the mixture boil.

Variation: *Bacalao a la Criolla* (Salt Cod, Creole Style), from Venezuela. Prepare the cod as for *Bacalhau a Baíana*. Heat 4 tablespoons of olive or vegetable oil in a casserole and sauté 1 large onion, finely chopped, with 3 cloves garlic, minced, until the onion is tender. Add 3 large tomatoes, peeled and chopped, ½ teaspoon cumin, ½ teaspoon oregano, pepper to taste, and a bay leaf, and simmer for 5 minutes. Add the fish, ½ pint dry white wine, 2 tablespoons lemon juice, and salt if necessary. Simmer until the fish is tender, about 15 minutes. Accompany with rice. Serves 4.

Bacalao en Salsa de Chile Ancho y Almendra

SALT COD IN MILD RED CHILI AND ALMOND SAUCE   *Mexico*

[Serves 4 to 6]
2 pounds salt cod
1 medium onion, chopped
1 whole clove garlic

1 *recipe* Salsa de Chile Ancho y Almendra *(Mild Red Chili and Almond Sauce), page 300*
1 teaspoon red wine vinegar

Soak the cod in cold water to cover for 12 hours or more, changing the water 5 or 6 times. Drain the fish and put into a saucepan with the onion and garlic and cold water to cover. Bring to the boil, reduce the heat, and simmer, covered, for 15 minutes, or until the fish is tender. Drain the fish. Strain and reserve the stock. Remove any skin and bones from the fish and cut into 2- or 3-inch pieces.

Make the sauce and thin it with ¾ pint of the reserved fish stock, stir to mix, and simmer for a minute or two. Add the fish and the vinegar and simmer for 5 minutes. Serve with rice.

Bacalhau a Mineira

SALT COD AND CABBAGE, MINAS GERAIS STYLE   *Brazil*

[Serves 4]
1 pound salt cod
3 tablespoons olive oil
1 onion, finely chopped
1 clove garlic, crushed
1 sweet red or green pepper, seeded and chopped

3 medium tomatoes, peeled and chopped
4 tablespoons chopped parsley
¼ pint dry white wine
Freshly ground pepper
1 pound shredded cabbage
Salt

Soak the cod in cold water to cover for 12 hours or more, changing the water frequently. Drain the fish and remove any skin and bones.

111

Pat the fish dry with paper towels and cut it into 2-inch pieces. Heat the oil in a large frying pan and sauté the onion, garlic, pepper, tomatoes, and parsley for 5 minutes, stirring occasionally. Add the fish, wine, pepper to taste, and cabbage. Stir to mix and simmer, partially covered, until the cabbage is tender and the fish flakes easily when tested with a fork, about 15 minutes. Season with salt.

Pudim de Bacalhau com Ovos

SALT COD WITH EGGS   *Brazil*

This is an unusual and delicious first-course or breakfast dish. The salt cod in the tomato-flavoured white sauce makes a rich topping for the egg.

[Serves 6 as a first course, 3 as a breakfast]

½ pound salt cod fillets
2 tablespoons cornflour
¾ pint milk
2½ ounces butter
1 medium onion, grated
2 medium tomatoes, peeled, seeded, and chopped

2 tablespoons drained capers
Salt, freshly ground pepper
Butter for ramekins
6 eggs
3 tablespoons grated Parmesan cheese

Soak the cod in cold water to cover, changing the water several times, for 12 hours or more. Drain and rinse the fish. Put it into a saucepan with water to cover and poach it for 15 to 20 minutes, or until it flakes easily when tested with a fork. The water should just simmer. Drain and flake the fish and set it aside.

Mix the cornflour with a little of the milk, add the rest of the milk, and pour the mixture into a small saucepan. Add ½ ounce of butter and cook, stirring, over moderate heat until the mixture is smooth and lightly thickened. Set aside.

In another saucepan heat 2 ounces of butter, add the onion, and cook, stirring, for a few minutes. Add the tomatoes and cook until the mixture is thick and well blended. Stir in the béchamel sauce and the capers. Fold in the codfish and add a little salt if necessary. Season generously with pepper. Cool slightly.

Butter six 5-ounce ramekins and break an egg into each. Pour the codfish mixture over the eggs and sprinkle each ramekin with ½ tablespoon grated Parmesan cheese. This may also be cooked in a single shallow Pyrex dish. Bake in a preheated hot oven (400° F., 200° C., gas 6) for 8 minutes.

Meats

CARNES

Nowhere in Latin American cooking is there such a coming together of introduced and indigenous foods and cooking methods as in the meat and poultry dishes. All of South and Central America, as well as Mexico, was poorly supplied with animals for meat. There were no sheep, goats, or cattle, all of which had been domesticated thousands of years before in the Middle East, and no domestic pigs or chickens, which had been supplying meat for a long while in Asia.

But the Aztecs did cultivate turkeys, ducks, quails, and doves among other birds, and they hunted a type of wild boar. Yucatán was known as the land of *Faisán y Venado* (the curassow pheasant and deer). From Mexico on south there were many rabbitlike animals from the small *agouti* to the *ñeque* or *paca*, the *viscacha*, and the huge *capybara*, weighing up to 150 pounds; this may explain why modern Latin America has so many splendid rabbit recipes. The *cuy* (pronounced kwee), a type of guinea pig, is still popular in Peru and tastes like young rabbit. The Incas bred the llama, vicuna, and alpaca from *guanacos*, small camel-like animals that still roam wild in herds in the Andean highlands. They supplied milk, meat, and soft, fleecy wool, while the llama did extra duty carrying loads as well.

The Spanish introduced sheep, goats, cattle, pigs, and chickens quite soon after the Conquest, and these were welcomed with varying degrees of enthusiasm into the Aztec, Inca, and Chibcha kitchens, among others. Pork and chicken were the favourites, reflected in the cooking of today. The new meats were incorporated into existing local dishes and, as the colonial kitchens evolved, new dishes were created, some with echoes from Spain's own colonial past, when the country had been dominated for nearly eight centuries by the Arabs. The Middle Eastern influence can still be seen in meat dishes cooked with almonds, raisins, cinnamon, and cloves, or with fruits, either dried or fresh. In Brazilian meat dishes, once again you find the contributions of the rich Portuguese cuisine, the indigenous foods of Africa like yams, nuts, and palm oil, blending with the local produce of the Indians. Dried shrimp and nuts may be ground together and mixed with coconut milk and rice flour to form a sauce coloured gold with *dendê* oil—as luscious to the palate as to the eye.

The meeting of conqueror and conquered produced astoundingly rich and varied results, new food and old combined in a harmony of contrasting flavours, exuberant often, but never bland or dull. Chili peppers join chocolate to make an exotic sauce for Mexico's national dish, *Mole Poblano de Guajolote* (Turkey in Chili and Chocolate Sauce). Peppers and tomatoes used with nuts, and the herbs of both Old and New Worlds make aromatic sauces. In Peru, Brazil, and Ecuador shellfish, especially prawns, make fascinating combinations with both meats and poultry. Fruits, fresh as well as dried, enhance beef or veal stews in Argentina and may be cooked in a large, hollowed-out pumpkin, the vegetable itself becoming the cookpot. Tropical root vegetables, yams, taros, and sweet potatoes, transform everyday dishes into something unctuous, attractive, and different, and beans make all sorts of unusual combinations in dishes ranging from grand affairs like Brazil's *Feijoada Completa* (Black Beans with Mixed Meats) to simple ones like their *Tutú a Mineira* (Black Beans, Minas Gerais Style), where the vegetable dominates. Annatto and allspice, very much New World spices, enliven meat dishes.

Many traditional meat dishes in Latin America are types of stew, cooked on top of the stove, largely because reliable ovens are a comparatively new feature in kitchens where until recently tiled charcoal stoves were commonplace. Also much of the continent is mountainous and altitude is an important feature in cooking. It was discovered early that long, slow cooking gives very flavourful results, making meat tender and juicy. An advantage is that dishes can be prepared ahead of time and need little watching.

Argentina, which is famous for its beef, and Brazil, whose south is great cattle country, both have wonderful outdoor feasts, the *asado criollo* and the *churrasco*.

On this diverse continent there is a whole new world of flavours to be explored.

MEAT STEWS WITH VEGETABLES AND WITH FRUIT

There is a seemingly inexhaustible range of meat stews—made from beef, veal, pork, lamb, kid—with vegetables and with fruits in the Latin American kitchen. Taste, texture, and aroma are balanced in excitingly different combinations, gentle, pungent, fiery, earthy, or elegant. Unusual ingredients are put together in subtle partnerships to produce a wonderful array of dishes, splendid for everyday eating, grand for guests as all the work can be done ahead of time. And despite a rich complexity of ingredients, cooking is straightforward. Long, slow simmering makes even the cheaper cuts of meat juicy and tender. Orange juice, wine, or vinegar is used to tenderize, nuts to thicken the already richly flavoured cooking liquid, and fruits, fresh and dried, lend a hint of acid blended with sweetness to the robustness of meat.

Seco de Carne

BEEF STEW · *Peru*

This stew is very curiously named, since *seco* means dry. Once upon a time stews were very much more soupy than they are now and the *seco* here is simply to indicate that this is not a soupy stew like a pot-au-feu. The ingredients are not exotic but the taste of the finished stew is far from ordinary, as the garlic, hot pepper, fresh coriander, and lemon juice combine to give the sauce a fine flavour.

A similar stew made with kid, *Seco de Cabrito*, is a great favourite. Kid is more strongly flavoured than beef and Peruvian cooks take advantage of this, adding extra coriander and white wine or *chicha*, a sort of corn beer, as well as stock to the dish, with very savoury results. *Seco de Carnero* (Lamb Stew) and *Seco de Chancho* (Pork Stew) belong to the same family.

115

In Peru the potatoes used would be ones with yellow flesh, not to be confused with sweet potatoes. Though they are delicious as well as pretty, they taste the same as ordinary white potatoes.

[Serves 6]

2 ounces lard or 4 tablespoons
  vegetable oil
4 cloves garlic, finely chopped
1 medium onion, finely chopped
1 teaspoon ground hot pepper or
  cayenne
3 pounds beef chuck, cut into
  1-inch cubes

¾ pint beef stock
Salt, freshly ground pepper
2 tablespoons fresh coriander,
  chopped
Juice of 1 lemon
2 pounds potatoes, boiled and
  halved

Heat the lard or oil in a casserole and sauté the garlic, onion, hot pepper, and beef cubes until the beef is lightly browned. Add the beef stock, salt and pepper to taste, and the coriander. Cook, partially covered, over low heat until the beef is tender, 1½ to 2 hours. The liquid should be reduced so that the sauce is quite thick and not very abundant. Just before serving stir in the lemon juice and cook a minute or two longer. Heap the stew onto a warmed serving platter and surround with the freshly cooked, hot potato halves.

Variation: *Seco de Cabrito.* Make the stew as for the beef stew above, using 3 pounds kid cut into 1-inch pieces instead of the beef. Use 1 fresh hot red or green pepper, seeded and finely chopped, instead of cayenne pepper, and increase the amount of fresh coriander to 2 ounces. Use equal amounts of dry white wine and stock for the cooking liquid but use only enough barely to cover the meat. An authentic Peruvian touch would be to use *chicha* (corn beer) instead of wine. When the stew has been simmering, partially covered, for 2 hours, or when the kid is almost tender, add 6 medium-sized potatoes, peeled and halved, and cook for 20 minutes longer, or until both kid and potatoes are tender. Omit the lemon juice and add 6 ounces cooked green peas just before serving. The stew is cooked partially covered to reduce the liquid as the gravy should not be abundant. Serves 6.

Carne en Jocón

BEEF IN TOMATO AND PEPPER SAUCE   *Guatemala*

This is called *Carne en Adobo* in some parts of Guatemala.

[Serves 6]
4 tablespoons peanut oil
1 medium onion, finely chopped
2 cloves garlic, chopped
2 sweet red or green peppers,
  seeded and chopped
1 fresh hot red or green pepper,
  seeded and chopped
3 pounds lean, boneless beef chuck,
  cut into 1-inch cubes
A 10-ounce can Mexican green
  tomatoes and liquid from the can

4 medium tomatoes, peeled and
  coarsely chopped
1 bay leaf
2 cloves
½ teaspoon oregano
Salt, freshly ground pepper
¼ pint beef stock, more or less
2 stale tortillas, or 2 tablespoons
  masa harina or 2 tablespoons
  cornmeal

Heat the oil in a heavy saucepan or casserole and sauté the onion, garlic, and peppers until the onion is soft. Add the meat and all the other ingredients except the tortillas. The liquid should barely cover the meat. Add a little more stock, if necessary. Cover, and simmer gently until the beef is tender, about 2 hours. If using tortillas soak them in cold water, squeeze them out, and crumble like breadcrumbs. Add to the casserole and simmer, uncovered, until the sauce is thickened. If using *masa harina* or cornmeal, mix it with a little cold water and stir into the stew, cooking just until the sauce is thickened (cornmeal will take a few minutes longer to thicken). Serve the stew on a bed of *Arroz Guatemalteco* (Rice, Guatemalan Style), (page 247).

Tomaticán

BEEF AND TOMATO STEW   *Chile*

[Serves 4]
4 tablespoons paprika oil (Color
  Chilena), see page 309
1½ pounds lean, boneless beef, cut
  into 1½-inch cubes
1 tablespoon parsley, finely chopped
Salt, freshly ground pepper
8 medium tomatoes, peeled and
  chopped

1 large onion, chopped
1 clove garlic, chopped
½ teaspoon oregano
4 medium potatoes, peeled and
  quartered
6 ounces corn kernels

Heat the paprika oil in a heavy casserole and add the beef, onion, garlic, oregano, parsley, and salt and pepper to taste, and sauté, stirring frequently, for about 5 minutes. Add the tomatoes, cover, and cook over very low heat until the meat is almost tender, about

1½ hours. Add the potatoes and cook until both meat and potatoes are tender, about 30 minutes longer. Stir in the corn and cook for 5 minutes longer. If liked, the dish may be garnished with slices of hardboiled egg. Some cooks fry the potatoes in oil before adding to the casserole.

Ternera en Pipián Verde

VEAL IN PUMPKIN SEED SAUCE *Mexico*

Pipián is a stew of meat or poultry where the liquid is thickened with ground nuts or seeds—pumpkin, sesame, peanuts, almonds— whatever the cook chooses. It may be red or green according to the type of peppers and tomatoes used. This one has a delicious flavour and is a lovely colour. It looks truly elegant accompanied by rice, and green beans for their contrastingly darker green.

[Serves 6]

3 pounds lean boneless veal, cut into 2-inch pieces
¾ pint chicken or veal stock, about
5 ounces pepitas (pumpkin seeds)
1 medium onion, chopped
1 clove garlic, chopped
3 fresh hot green peppers, seeded and chopped (serrano or jalapeño peppers, if available)

8 tablespoons chopped fresh coriander leaves
A 10- or 12-ounce can of Mexican green tomatoes, drained
6 cos lettuce leaves, preferably the darker green outside leaves, chopped
2 tablespoons lard or vegetable oil
Salt, freshly ground pepper

Put the veal into a heavy casserole and pour in the stock, adding a little more if necessary barely to cover. Simmer over low heat, covered, until the meat is tender, about 1½ hours. In an ungreased frying pan toast the pumpkin seeds for a few minutes. Cool slightly and pulverize in a blender or food processor fitted with a steel blade. Add to the blender or food processor the onion, garlic, hot peppers, coriander, green tomatoes, and cos, and reduce to a pastelike purée. If necessary add a little of the stock.

Heat the lard or vegetable oil and cook the pumpkin seed mixture, stirring, for about 3 minutes. Thin the pumpkin seed mixture with about ¾ pint of the stock, or until it is the consistency of heavy cream. Season to taste with salt and pepper. Drain the veal and set the meat aside. Return the veal to the casserole, pour on the sauce, and cook just long enough to heat through.

Seco de Chancho

PORK STEW   *Ecuador*

[Serves 6 to 8]

2 tablespoons annatto oil or lard
  (see page 310)
3 pounds lean pork shoulder, cut
  into 2-inch cubes
1 large onion, finely chopped
2 large cloves garlic, minced
1 large tomato, peeled, seeded, and
  chopped
1 sweet red pepper, seeded and
  coarsely chopped, or 2 canned
  pimientos, chopped

1 fresh hot red or green pepper,
  seeded and finely chopped
1 tablespoon fresh coriander,
  chopped coarsely
½ teaspoon ground cumin
½ teaspoon oregano
Salt, freshly ground pepper
Pinch sugar (optional)
¾ pint beer

Heat the oil or lard in a heavy frying pan and lightly sauté the pork cubes. With a slotted spoon remove the pork pieces to a heavy flame-proof casserole. Remove all but 2 tablespoons of fat from the pan, add the onion and garlic, and sauté the mixture until the onion is soft. Add the tomato, the sweet and hot peppers, coriander, cumin, and oregano, and simmer until the mixture is well blended, about 10 minutes. Season to taste with salt and pepper and, if liked, the pinch of sugar. Pour over the pork, add the beer, cover, and cook over very low heat until the pork is tender, about 2 hours. The sauce should be quite thick. If it seems at all watery, partially uncover the casserole during the second hour of cooking. Serve with rice.

Chancho Adobado

SPICY PORK   *Peru*

[Serves 6]

1 whole head garlic
2 tablespoons ground annatto
2 teaspoons ground cumin
Salt, freshly ground pepper
½ pint white vinegar

3 pounds shoulder of pork, cut into
  2-inch cubes
2 tablespoons lard or vegetable oil
Juice of 1 Seville (bitter) orange, or
  4 tablespoons orange juice
1½ pounds sweet potatoes

Peel the garlic cloves and reduce them to a purée in an electric blender with the annatto, cumin, salt and pepper to taste, and vinegar. Put the pork pieces into a large bowl and pour the garlic marinade over them, mixing well. Marinate overnight in the refrigerator, covered.

119

Strain, reserving the marinade. Pat the pork cubes dry with paper towels. Heat the lard or oil in a large frying pan and sauté the pork pieces until golden brown all over, transferring them to a casserole as they are done. Pour the reserved marinade over the pork, add the orange juice, cover, and cook over very low heat until the meat is tender, 1½ to 2 hours. If the meat seems to be drying out, add a little water; 3 or 4 tablespoons will probably be enough. There should be very little gravy when the dish is finished.

Peel the sweet potatoes and cut them into slices about ¾ inch thick. Cook in boiling salted water until tender, 15 to 20 minutes. Drain.

To serve, heap the pork in the centre of a large warmed platter and surround with the sweet potato slices moistened with a little of the meat gravy. White rice is another traditional accompaniment to this dish.

Jamón del País

PERUVIAN FRESH HAM *Peru*

Though this is called ham *(jamón)*, it is really fresh pork spiced and cooked in a most unusual way—marinated, simmered until tender, then browned in hot fat. Very different and marvellous for a buffet either hot or transformed when cold into a delicious dividend, *Butifarras,* special Peruvian sandwich rolls. It can be made with a boned leg of pork but I find the shoulder a more manageable size. Incidentally, though the meat is stewed, the finished dish is more like a baked meat.

Peruvian and Mexican garlic have quite enormous cloves, which comes in handy when one has to peel a number of them. I have specified large cloves of garlic but if these are not available, a whole head of garlic should be used. It will not overpower the other flavours.

[Serves 12 or more]

12 *large cloves garlic, peeled, or 1 whole head*
2 *tablespoons annatto seeds, ground*
1 *teaspoon cumin, ground*

Salt, freshly ground pepper
About 6 pounds pork shoulder, or leg, boned and rolled
2 *ounces lard*

Crush the garlic cloves and mix to a paste with the annatto, cumin, and salt and pepper to taste. Spread this on the pork, put the pork into a baking dish, cover loosely with foil, and refrigerate overnight. Put the pork, and any liquid in the pan, into a very large saucepan and pour in enough water to cover it. Cover, bring to the boil, reduce the heat to low, and simmer gently until the meat is tender, 2½ to 3 hours. When it is cool enough to handle, remove it from the cooking liquid and pat it dry with paper towels. Heat the lard in a very large pan and sauté the pork until it is browned all over. Transfer the pork to a serving platter and serve hot, sliced with rice or potatoes, a green vegetable or a salad, or allow to cool and use to make *Butifarras* (Peruvian Ham Sandwiches).

Variation: For *Butifarras*, put thinly sliced onions into a bowl with an equal amount of thinly sliced radishes; fresh hot peppers, seeded and sliced; and salt and pepper to taste. Pour in enough white vinegar to cover the vegetables and let them stand at room temperature for 2 hours before using. The amount of hot peppers will depend on taste. Strain and discard the vinegar. Have ready crusty rolls, cut three-quarters of the way through. Butter the rolls if desired and place a lettuce leaf, a slice of ham, and a layer of the pickled vegetables in each roll. Serve as a snack.

Cordero Criollo

LAMB, CREOLE STYLE *Peru*

Lamb and kid are used interchangeably in Latin America, though kid requires a little longer cooking time. There are not a great many recipes calling for these meats, but the few that exist are very good indeed. Annatto lends fragrance to this Peruvian roast leg of lamb. The herbs and spices in the dressing are the same as those in *aliño criollo* (Venezuelan creole style seasoning powder), and I find the prepared version exactly right for this dish, though I add a large clove of crushed garlic to the mixture.

[Serves 6]
A 4-pound leg or shoulder of lamb or kid
2 tablespoons aliño criollo (see page 310)
4 tablespoons red wine vinegar

1 large clove garlic, crushed
¼ pint olive oil
3 large potatoes, peeled and halved lengthwise
Lettuce leaves, preferably cos
1 canned pimiento, cut into strips

Trim the lamb of all but a thin layer of fat. Mix the seasoning powder with the vinegar, add the garlic, then beat in the oil with a fork. Rub this marinade into the lamb and let it stand for at least 2 hours, turning the meat from time to time and spooning the marinade over it. When ready to cook scrape off and reserve the marinade. Put the lamb into a baking tin brushed over with oil and surround with the potatoes. Bake in a preheated moderate oven (325° F., 170° C., gas 3) for 1 hour (15 minutes to the pound), for rare lamb, 130° to 135° F. (54° to 57° C.) on a meat thermometer. Cook for 15 minutes longer if medium rare lamb is preferred. Baste every 20 minutes with the reserved marinade and any pan juices. Turn the potatoes halfway through the cooking time.

Remove the lamb to a carving board and let it stand 15 minutes before carving. Arrange the potatoes round the edge of a serving platter and keep warm in the turned-off oven. Slice the lamb and arrange it on the platter. Garnish the edge of the dish with lettuce leaves and strips of pimiento. Spoon the fat off the pan juices and put into a gravy boat with the juices from the meat as it is carved. Either spoon over the meat or serve as gravy. There will not be a greal deal.

Variation: A most delicious variation, which has overtones of the Middle East in its use of mint, is *Carnero o Cabrito al Horno* (Roast Lamb or Kid). Make a dressing of 3 tablespoons butter creamed with 8 large cloves crushed garlic, salt, freshly ground pepper, and 4 tablespoons finely chopped fresh mint. Spread over the lamb or kid and roast as above. Baste with ½ pint dry white wine instead of the marinade.

Cazuela de Cordero

LAMB CASSEROLE   *Chile*

This lamb stew is a Chilean standby, a family favourite, both rich and simple at the same time. The pumpkin slightly thickens the sauce, and the final whisking in of beaten eggs finishes it.

[Serves 6]

2 pounds boneless lamb for stew, cut into 2-inch pieces
1 onion, coarsely chopped
1 leek, sliced
1 carrot, scraped and sliced
Small stalk of celery with leaves
½ teaspoon oregano
Pinch of ground cumin
1 sprig parsley
1 bay leaf

6 small potatoes, peeled, or 3 large potatoes, peeled and halved
½ pound pumpkin, peeled and cut into 1-inch cubes
Salt, freshly ground pepper
3 small courgettes, cut into 1-inch slices
½ pound green beans, cut into 1-inch pieces
¾ pound fresh corn kernels
2 eggs, lightly beaten

Put the lamb, onion, leek, carrot, celery, oregano, cumin, parsley, and bay leaf into a large saucepan or casserole. Pour in enough water to cover, about 2½ pints, bring to the boil, skim off any froth that rises to the surface, lower the heat, cover, and simmer until the meat is almost tender, about 1½ hours. Lift out the pieces of lamb onto a plate and set aside. Strain the stock, pressing down to extract all the juices. Discard the solids. Rinse out and dry the casserole.

Return the lamb pieces to the casserole and add the potatoes and pumpkin. Pour in the strained stock, adding a little water if necessary to cover the lamb and vegetables. Season to taste with salt and pepper and simmer 15 minutes. Add the courgettes, beans, and corn, and simmer until the beans are tender, about 10 minutes.

Whisk a cup of the hot stock gradually into the eggs, then pour the mixture into the saucepan, stirring to mix. Do not let the liquid boil, as the eggs will curdle. Cook over very low heat until the eggs have thickened the sauce. The pumpkin will have disintegrated, also thickening the sauce slightly. Serve in soup plates, making sure that each serving has a little of everything.

Arvejado de Cordero

LAMB STEW WITH GREEN PEAS *Chile*

This Chilean lamb stew is characterized by the interesting use of paprika oil *(Color Chilena)*.

[Serves 6]

3 *tablespoons paprika oil* (Color Chilena), *see page 309*
2 *pounds boneless lamb for stew, cut into 1-inch pieces*
1 *large onion, finely chopped*

1 *tablespoon flour*
Salt, freshly ground pepper
¾ *pound fresh green peas*
2 *eggs, lightly beaten*
2 *tablespoons chopped parsley*

Heat the paprika oil in a casserole or large saucepan. Add the lamb pieces and the onion, and sauté until the onion is soft. Add the flour and cook for a minute or two longer, stirring with a wooden spoon to mix thoroughly. Add ¾ pint water, season to taste with salt and pepper, cover, and simmer until the lamb is almost done, about 1½ hours. Add the peas, bring back to a simmer, and cook for 15 minutes longer, or until the peas are tender. Transfer the meat and peas to a serving dish and keep warm. Stir the eggs and parsley into the liquid in the casserole and cook over very low heat, stirring constantly with a wooden spoon, until the sauce has thickened lightly. Do not let it boil, as it will curdle. Pour the sauce over the lamb and serve with boiled potatoes or any puréed root vegetable or plain rice.

Carnero en Adobo

LAMB IN CHILI AND VINEGAR SAUCE   *Mexico*

Lamb and kid are very popular in the north of Mexico, much of it mountain country well suited to these animals. Julia, the cook of my husband's uncle, General Procopio Ortiz Reyes, who lives in Torreón, Coahuila, cooked this for me and gave me her recipe. It is easy yet exotic. *Ancho* chili is mild and full flavoured, *mulato* chili a little *picante*. Using both gives a sauce full of character.

[Serves 6]
3 pounds boneless lamb (shoulder
    or leg), cut into 1½-inch pieces
Salt
3 ancho *and* 3 mulato *chilies*
⅛ teaspoon ground cumin

½ teaspoon oregano
2 medium onions, chopped
2 cloves garlic, chopped
3 or 4 sprigs fresh coriander
2 tablespoons red wine vinegar
3 tablespoons lard or vegetable oil

Put the lamb into a heavy saucepan or casserole with 1 onion, 1 clove garlic, the coriander sprigs, salt, and water barely to cover. Bring to the boil, lower the heat, and simmer, covered, over moderate heat until the meat is tender, about 1½ hours. Drain the lamb, strain the stock, and set aside. Rinse out and dry the casserole and return the lamb to it.

Prepare the chilies (page 34) and put them with the soaking water into a blender or food processor fitted with a steel blade. Add the remaining onion and garlic, the cumin, oregano, vinegar, and salt, and blend until fairly smooth. The mixture should be more of a paste than a purée. Heat the lard or oil in a frying pan and cook the mixture, stirring constantly with a wooden spoon, for about 5 minutes, over moderate heat. Thin with about ½ pint of the reserved lamb stock. The mixture should be the consistency of a medium white sauce. Add more stock if necessary. Pour the sauce over the lamb and simmer over very low heat for 20 minutes. Serve with rice, beans, and a green vegetable. Tortillas are good with this.

Variation: Mexican friends who like their food hot and very highly flavoured suggest adding a canned *chipotle* or *morita* chili to the blender when making the sauce. It makes a delicious change.

Variation: For *Carnero en Salsa de Chile Ancho* (Lamb in Mild Red Chili

Sauce) from Mexico, sauté the lamb in 2 tablespoons olive oil in a frying pan and transfer to a casserole. Prepare 6 *ancho* chilies (page 34) and put them with the soaking water into a blender or food processor fitted with a steel blade. Add 1 chopped onion, 1 clove garlic, and 4 medium tomatoes, peeled and chopped, and reduce to a purée. If necessary, add enough oil to the pan to make the quantity of fat up to 2 tablespoons. Add the chili mixture and cook, stirring constantly, for about 5 minutes over moderate heat. It has a tendency to splutter. Pour over the lamb, season to taste with salt and freshly ground pepper, a pinch of cinnamon, and ⅛ teaspoon of cloves. Cover and simmer over low heat until the lamb is tender, about 1½ hours. Soak a dozen small, pimiento-stuffed olives in cold water for 15 minutes to get rid of the brine, drain and halve them. Put the lamb in a serving dish and garnish with the olives and ½ ounce slivered, toasted almonds. Serve with rice and a green vegetable. Depending on the juiciness of the tomatoes, it may be necessary to add a little more liquid to the lamb, though the sauce should not be abundant. Add tomato juice, stock, or water. Serves 6.

Seco de Carnero

LAMB STEW   *Peru*

Don't be afraid of the amount of garlic used here. The flavour will not be at all aggressive, indeed it will be quite gentle as the pungent oils cook out. The coriander, garlic, fruit juices, and hot peppers combine into a most delicious sauce.

[Serves 6 to 8]
2 ounces fresh coriander, chopped
2 or 3 fresh hot red or green
   peppers, seeded and chopped
1 whole head garlic, peeled and
   chopped
¼ pint olive oil
2 medium onions, finely chopped
4 pounds lean, boneless lamb

(shoulder or leg), cut into 1-inch
   cubes
Salt, freshly ground pepper
¼ pint Seville orange juice, or use
   two-thirds fresh orange juice and
   one-third lime or lemon juice
2 pounds potatoes, peeled and sliced
1 pound green peas, or 2 packages
   frozen peas

In a blender or food processor combine the coriander leaves, hot peppers, and garlic, and reduce to a purée. Set aside. Heat the oil in a casserole and sauté the onions until they are soft. Stir in the coriander mixture and cook for a minute or two longer. Add the lamb pieces and cook for about 5 minutes, turning the pieces to coat them with the sauce. Season to taste with salt and a generous amount of pepper. Add the orange juice and enough water to cover, about ½ pint. Cover and simmer until the lamb is tender, about 1½ hours. The stew may be cooked to this point a day ahead and refrigerated so that any fat may be removed. Let the casserole stand until it reaches room temperature before reheating.

Boil the potatoes in salted water until they are tender. Drain and add to the casserole. Boil the peas in salted water until they are tender, drain, and add to the casserole. Bring the casserole to a simmer and cook just long enough to heat it through.

Posta en Frutas Secas

BEEF AND DRIED FRUIT STEW   *Colombia*

This is one of the Latin American meat and fruit stews that have links, via Spain when it was a Moorish colony, to ancient Persia, where these delectable dishes were first concocted. Interestingly there are also links with the cooking of present-day Morocco, where dishes very similar to those of ancient Persia survive. Most Colombians take advantage of modern marketing and use a package of dried mixed fruit, but you can make the mixture yourself.

[Serves 6]

An 11-ounce package mixed dried fruit (prunes, dried apricots, peaches, and pears)
3 tablespoons olive or vegetable oil
3 pounds lean beef, preferably topside, cut into 1-inch cubes
1 medium onion, finely chopped

1 clove garlic, minced
1 medium carrot, scraped and chopped
Salt, freshly ground pepper
½ pint dry red wine
½ ounce soft butter (optional)
1 tablespoon flour (optional)

Put the mixed dried fruit into a bowl with about ½ pint warm water and leave to soak for 1 hour, turning the fruit from time to time. Drain, reserve the soaking water, and set the fruit aside.

Heat the oil in a heavy casserole and sauté the beef, onion, garlic, and carrot for about 5 minutes. Season with salt and pepper. Pour in the wine and the reserved soaking water from the fruit. Bring to the boil, reduce the heat to low, and simmer, covered, for 2 hours, or until the beef is almost tender. Add the fruit. The prunes and apricots should be left whole, the pears and peaches halved or quartered. Cover and simmer 30 minutes longer. If the sauce is too thick, add a little more wine. If you want a slightly thicker sauce, mix the butter and flour together and drop a few smooth pieces into the casserole, blending well. Serve with rice.

Carne con Salsa de Frutas

BEEF IN FRUIT SAUCE   *Ecuador*

A particularly delicious beef stew, with the flavours of the fruits and the tomatoes subtly blended and enriched by the cream, though still nicely tart.

[Serves 6]

6 tablespoons vegetable oil
1 large onion, finely chopped
3 pounds beef chuck, cut into
    1-inch cubes
½ pint dry white wine
½ pint beef stock
Salt, freshly ground pepper
2 quinces, peeled, cored, and

chopped, or 2 peaches, peeled,
    stoned, and chopped
2 apples, peeled, cored, and chopped
2 pears, peeled, cored, and chopped
2 large tomatoes, peeled and
    chopped
Sugar to taste
¼ pint double cream

Heat 4 tablespoons of the oil in a frying pan and sauté the onion until it is soft. Using a slotted spoon transfer the onion to a casserole. In the oil remaining in the pan sauté the beef until it is browned on all sides. Add it to the casserole with the wine, stock, and salt and pepper to taste. Cover and simmer until the meat is tender, about 2 hours. Arrange the meat on a serving platter and keep warm. Reserve the stock.

Heat the remaining 2 tablespoons of oil in a saucepan and add the fruit, including the tomatoes. Cook for a few minutes, stirring. Add a little sugar, if liked. The sauce should be quite tart. Add enough of the reserved stock barely to cover, and simmer, stirring from time to time, until the mixture is thick and well blended. In the old days cooks had to work the mixture through a sieve, a tedious procedure; today a blender or food processor does the job. Return the purée to the saucepan and taste for seasoning, adding a little salt if necessary. Stir in the cream and cook just long enough to heat through. Pour the sauce over the meat. Serve with rice.

Variation: Guavas or nectarines may be used instead of quinces or peaches; pork loin instead of beef. The sauce is also pleasant served with grilled lamb chops. If preferred, serve with *Llapingachos* (Potato Cakes, page 265) instead of rice.

127

Ternera en Salsa de Ciruelas Pasas

VEAL IN PRUNE SAUCE   *Mexico*

This is an old colonial dish that I particularly like to serve when friends are coming to dinner. The prunes give the dark sauce a rich, subtle flavour.

[Serves 6]

¾ pound large, stoned prunes,
  chopped
½ pint dry red wine
4 tablespoons lard or vegetable oil
2½ to 3½ pounds boneless veal
  roast, preferably leg

2 medium onions, finely chopped
2 cloves garlic, chopped
3 medium tomatoes, peeled, seeded,
  and chopped
¾ pint beef or veal stock, about
Salt, freshly ground pepper

Put the prunes to soak in the wine for at least 2 hours.

Heat the lard or oil in a heavy casserole and sauté the veal until it is golden brown all over. Lift out of the casserole and set aside. In the oil remaining in the casserole sauté the onions and garlic until the onions are soft. Add the tomatoes and cook until the mixture is well blended. Add the prunes and wine. Add the veal and pour in just enough stock to cover. Simmer, covered, over low heat until the veal is tender, about 2 hours. Lift out the veal to a serving platter, slice, and keep warm. Season the sauce to taste with salt and pepper. During cooking the prunes should have disintegrated, thickening the sauce. If necessary, cook the sauce over fairly brisk heat, stirring, for a few minutes to amalgamate the solids and reduce the sauce a little. It should be thick but not completely smooth. Spoon a little sauce over the veal slices and serve the rest in a sauceboat. Serve with rice or any starchy root vegetable.

Ternera con Aceitunas

VEAL WITH OLIVES   *Mexico*

The stuffed green olives add a distinctive flavour to this dish.

[Serves 4 to 6]

4 tablespoons olive or vegetable oil
2 pounds shoulder of veal, cut into
  1-inch cubes
2 ounces boiled ham, coarsely
  chopped

1 medium onion, finely chopped
1 clove garlic, chopped
8 tablespoons chopped parsley
36 small pimiento-stuffed green
  olives

½ *pint dry white wine*   *Salt, freshly ground pepper*
½ *pint beef stock*   *2 eggs*

Heat the oil in a frying pan and sauté the veal with the ham. Lift out
into a casserole. In the oil remaining in the pan sauté the onion and
garlic until the onion is soft. Add to the casserole with the parsley.
Soak the olives in cold water for 10 minutes, drain, and add to the
casserole. Pour in the wine and stock, season to taste with salt and
pepper, cover, and simmer until the veal is tender, about 1½ hours.
Lightly beat the eggs, then whisk ¼ pint of the hot liquid into them.
Pour the mixture back into the casserole and cook, stirring, until the
sauce is lightly thickened. Do not let the sauce boil, as it will curdle.
Serve with rice or a starchy root vegetable and a green vegetable or
salad.

Chuletas de Cerdo con Frutas

PORK CHOPS WITH DRIED FRUIT   *Dominican Republic*

The use of dried fruits, especially apricots, in meat dishes is very
much a Middle Eastern thing. In Iran lamb and dried apricots are
used together in a most delectable dish. A lot of old dishes have
survived in the Dominican Republic and this one was obviously
brought over by the Spanish, using pork instead of lamb. It works
beautifully.

[Serves 4]   *Salt, freshly ground pepper*
¼ *pound stoned prunes*   *2 tablespoons vegetable oil*
¼ *pound dried apricots*   *1 medium onion, finely chopped*
¼ *pound dried pears*   *1 clove garlic, chopped*
4 pork loin chops, weighing 2   ½ *pint chicken stock*
   pounds   ½ *pint dry white wine*

Put the prunes in a bowl with the apricots, halved, and the pears,
quartered. Pour in enough cold water barely to cover and let soak for
30 minutes.

   Season the chops with salt and pepper. Heat the oil in a pan and
sauté the chops until golden on both sides. Transfer the chops to a
casserole. In the fat remaining in the pan sauté the onion and garlic
until the onion is softened. Add to the casserole. Arrange the fruit
over and around the pork chops. Pour in the chicken stock and wine,
adding a little more of each if necessary to cover. Cover the casserole
with aluminum foil, then the lid, and bake in a preheated moderate

oven (350° F., 180° C., gas 4) for about 1½ hours or until the pork is tender.

Chirmole de Puerco

PORK STEW WITH PEPPERS AND GREENGAGE PLUMS   *Mexico*

[Serves 6]

3 pounds lean pork, cut into 2-inch cubes
6 ancho *chilies*
3 fresh or canned hot green serrano *peppers, seeded*
2 cloves garlic, chopped
1 large onion, chopped
¼ teaspoon ground cinnamon
Salt, freshly ground pepper

1 pound greengage plums
4 medium tomatoes, sliced
½ teaspoon crumbled, dried epazote (optional)
4 tablespoons masa harina
4 tablespoons Seville orange juice, or use two-thirds orange juice and one-third lime juice
2 tablespoons lard or vegetable oil (optional)

Put the pork into a large, heavy saucepan or casserole, add water barely to cover, and simmer, covered, until almost tender, about 1½ hours.

Pull off the stems and shake out the seeds from the peppers and tear them into pieces. Rinse and put into a bowl with ¼ pint hot water. Let the peppers soak for 1 hour, turning them frequently. Combine the *ancho* chilies, the water in which they were soaked, the *serrano* peppers, garlic, onion, and cinnamon in an electric blender or food processor and reduce to a coarse purée. Drain the pork, reserving the stock, and return the meat to the saucepan. Add enough of the stock to the purée to make a thin sauce. Season to taste with salt and pepper and pour over the pork, mixing well. Stone the greengages and cut each plum into 4 pieces. Add them to the pork. Add the tomato slices, and if it is available the *epazote*. Simmer, covered, until the pork is tender. Mix a little of the remaining stock with the *masa harina*. Stir the orange juice into this mixture and add to the pork stew. The lard or vegetable oil may be added at this time, if liked. Simmer, stirring gently, for a minute or two longer.

SKIRT STEAK DISHES

South Americans hold goose skirt (flank) steak in high esteem for its fine flavour and adaptability. It may be braised, stewed, and grilled, stuffed, baked, or shredded. And it may be served hot or cold. It is used for the national dish of Venezuela with the traditional accompaniments of rice, black beans, and fried plantains. It is stuffed with spinach, or even more exotically with an omelette, asparagus tips, and strips of pimiento to make a party dish that is not only satisfyingly hearty but elegant in appearance. It has the added merit of being a lean and tender cut that is also economical.

Matambre

STUFFED ROLLED SKIRT STEAK   *Argentina*

This translates literally as "kill hunger" and it is indeed a very satisfying dish whether eaten hot as a main course, or cold with salads, ideal for a picnic. In more modest amounts, it makes an unusual first course.

[Serves 4]

1 teaspoon oregano
2 cloves crushed garlic
1½ pounds goose skirt (flank) steak
Salt, freshly ground pepper
¼ pound spinach leaves
1 small carrot, thinly sliced
1 hardboiled egg, thinly sliced
Cayenne pepper (optional)
3½ pints beef stock

Mix the oregano and garlic and spread over the steak. Season the steak with salt and pepper to taste, then cover with the spinach leaves, leaving about a ½-inch margin. Top the spinach with the carrot and egg and sprinkle with a little cayenne pepper, if liked. Roll up with the grain and tie with kitchen string at about 1-inch intervals. Place in a casserole into which it fits comfortably but quite snugly. Pour in the beef stock. There should be enough to cover the steak. Bring to the boil, skim off any froth that rises, reduce the heat, and simmer gently for 1½ to 2 hours, or until the beef is tender. Lift out, remove the strings, slice, and serve hot, moistening the steak with

131

a little of the stock. Serve with potatoes or rice. Or allow the steak to cool in the stock and serve cold, sliced, with salad. Reserve the leftover stock for another use. Serve with *Salsa Criolla* (Creole Sauce), page 309.

Variation: For *Matambre al Horno* (Baked Goose Skirt Steak), put the stuffed steak into the casserole with 1½ pints stock. Bring the stock to the boil on top of the stove, cover the casserole, and transfer to a preheated moderate oven for about 1 hour, or until the steak is done.

Variation: In Uruguay, where the dish is also popular, the steak is sometimes just seasoned and stuffed with spinach.

Variation: *Matambre a la Cacerola* (Casseroled Goose Skirt Steak). Heat 1 ounce butter in a pan, add 1 small onion, finely chopped, 1 stalk finely chopped celery, and 1 small carrot, scraped and finely chopped. Sauté until the onion is soft, about 5 minutes. Remove from the heat and stir in 2 tablespoons finely chopped parsley and 2 cups cubed bread. Season with salt and pepper. Stir in 2 tablespoons beef stock, mix well, and spread over the steak, leaving a ½-inch margin. Roll up with the grain and tie at 1-inch intervals with kitchen string. Heat 2 tablespoons vegetable oil in a casserole large enough to hold the steak, and brown the steak all over. Pour in enough stock, about 3½ pints, to cover, and simmer for 1½ to 2 hours. Or cook in a preheated moderate oven for 1 hour or so, in which case add only enough stock to come about one-third of the way up the steak, about 1½ pints. If liked, thicken about 2 cups of the stock with a beurre manié (see page 312). Serve with carrots and potatoes and a green vegetable.

Variation: *Malaya Arrollada* (Rolled Goose Skirt Steak) is a Chilean version of *Matambre,* and why this particular cut of steak is called a *malaya* in Chile is entirely beyond me. Admittedly, women in Malaya wear sarongs and sarongs are wrapped around ladies, while the *malaya* is wrapped around a filling, but this is surely stretching a linguistic point too far. Season the steak with salt, pepper, and 1 teaspoon oregano. Cover it with 1 onion, finely chopped, 1 stalk celery, finely chopped, 1 carrot, scraped and finely sliced, and 1 hardboiled egg, thinly sliced. Roll up with the grain, tie with string, and place in a flameproof casserole that holds it snugly. Pour in enough stock to cover and simmer until it is tender, 1½ to 2 hours. Let it cool in the stock. Lift out, remove the string and slice. Serve as a first course with any salad. Serves 8.

Pabellón Caraqueño

STEAK WITH RICE, BLACK BEANS,
AND PLANTAINS   *Venezuela*

This national dish of Venezuela is said to look like a flag (*pabellón*)
because of the different colours of meat, rice, beans, and plantains.
It is a robust and satisfying dish.

[Serves 6]

1½ pounds goose skirt (flank) steak
½ pint beef stock
1 medium onion, finely chopped
1 clove garlic, minced
2 medium tomatoes, peeled, seeded,
   and chopped
Salt
2 tablespoons olive oil

1 recipe Arroz Blanco (*White
   Rice*), page 244
6 eggs, fried in olive oil
1 recipe Caraotas Negras (*Black
   Beans*), page 239
1 ripe plantain, or 2 underripe
   bananas
2 tablespoons vegetable oil

Cut the steak into 2 or 3 pieces to fit conveniently into a saucepan,
and add the stock to cover. If necessary add a little more. Bring to
a simmer and cook, covered, over very low heat until the meat is
tender, 1½ to 2 hours. Allow to cool in the stock, drain, reserve the
stock for another use, and shred the meat with the fingers. Combine
the meat with the onion, garlic, and tomatoes. Season to taste with
salt. Heat the oil in a pan and sauté the meat mixture until the onion
is cooked and the mixture is quite dry. Put the rice in the centre of a
large, warmed platter and heap the meat on top of it. Arrange the fried
eggs on top of the meat. Surround the rice with the black beans and
decorate the edge of the platter with the fried plantains or bananas.

To fry the plantains or bananas: Peel the plantains and cut them
in half lengthwise, then crosswise into thirds. If using bananas, peel
and cut into thirds. Fry the plantains or bananas in the oil until golden
brown on both sides, about 2 or 3 minutes.

Sobrebarriga

SKIRT STEAK   *Colombia*

[Serves 4 to 6]

A 2-pound goose skirt (flank) steak,
   with layer of fat left on
1 medium onion, chopped
2 cloves garlic, chopped

2 medium tomatoes, chopped
1 carrot, scraped and chopped
1 bay leaf
2 or 3 sprigs parsley

½ *teaspoon thyme*   *Beef stock or water*
½ *teaspoon oregano*   *½-1 ounce butter, softened*
Salt, freshly ground pepper   *2 ounces fresh breadcrumbs*

Put the steak into a large saucepan with the onion, garlic, tomatoes, carrot, bay leaf, parsley sprigs, thyme, oregano, and salt and pepper to taste. Add enough stock or water to cover the meat and cook it, covered, over low heat for about 2 hours, or until it is tender. Remove the meat from the liquid, pat it dry with paper towels, and place it in a grill pan, fat side up. Spread the butter over the meat and cover with breadcrumbs. Grill until the crumbs are golden brown. Slice the steak and arrange it on a heated platter. Strain the hot seasoned liquid into a sauceboat. Serve with *Papas Chorreadas* (Potatoes with Cheese, Tomato, and Onion Sauce) and *Ensalada de Aguacate* (Avocado Salad).

Sobrebarriga Bogotana

SKIRT STEAK, BOGOTÁ STYLE   *Colombia*

[Serves 4 to 6]
1 *medium onion, finely chopped*   1 *teaspoon Worcestershire sauce*
2 *cloves garlic, chopped*   *Salt, freshly ground pepper*
2 *medium tomatoes, peeled and*   *A 2-pound goose skirt (flank) steak,*
  chopped   *trimmed of all fat*
1 *tablespoon parsley, chopped*   ¾ *pint beef stock or water*
½ *teaspoon thyme*   ¾ *pint dark beer*
1 *bay leaf, crumbled*   1 *ounce butter, softened*
1 *teaspoon prepared mustard*   2 *ounces fresh breadcrumbs*

Mix together the onion, garlic, tomatoes, parsley, thyme, bay leaf, mustard, Worcestershire sauce, and salt and pepper to taste. Spread the mixture on the steak. Roll the steak up with the grain and tie securely with string. Place in a flameproof casserole, cover, and refrigerate until the following day. Cover with equal quantities of beef stock or water, and dark beer. Bring to the boil, reduce the heat to a bare simmer, and cook, partially covered, until the steak is tender and the liquid reduced, about 2 hours. Remove the steak from the casserole, brush it with the butter, and roll it in the breadcrumbs. Arrange the steak in a baking tin and bake in a preheated hot oven (400° F., 200° C., gas 6) until the crumbs are lightly browned, about 15 minutes. Heat the sauce remaining in the casserole and serve in a sauceboat. Slice the steak and arrange on a warmed platter.

Roupa Velha

OLD CLOTHES   *Brazil*

This is the Brazilian version of the Spanish dish *Ropa Vieja* (Old Clothes). Ideally skirt steak is used since the cooked meat should be shredded, as old clothes can be said to shred into rags and tatters. The dish is infinitely more appetizing than its name, and occurs very widely in Spanish- and Portuguese-speaking countries, varying from place to place. The Brazilian version, though it is not as rich as, for example, the Cuban version, is very good. Traditionally leftover beef from a *cozido* (pot-au-feu), or similar dish, is used, and if you have some, by all means use it.

[Serves 4 to 6]

A 2-pound goose skirt (flank) steak, or 2 pounds cooked boiled beef	1 sprig parsley
	1 bay leaf
1 medium onion, stuck with a clove	1 clove garlic
1 carrot, scraped and halved	6 peppercorns
1 stalk celery	1 tablespoon salt

Put the steak into a flameproof casserole with the onion, carrot, celery, parsley, bay leaf, garlic, peppercorns, and salt and enough cold water to cover. Bring to the boil, simmer for 5 minutes, and skim the froth that rises to the surface. Cover, lower the heat, and simmer for 1½ hours, or until the steak is tender. Leave the steak in the stock until it is cool enough to handle. Lift it out of the stock onto a chopping board. Strain the stock into a jar and refrigerate for another use. Cut the steak in half crosswise, then shred it along the grain into strips. Set aside.

FOR THE SAUCE

4 tablespoons olive oil	8 tablespoons finely chopped parsley
2 medium onions, thinly sliced	Salt, freshly ground pepper
2 medium tomatoes, peeled and sliced	Pinch of sugar
	2 tablespoons vinegar
	Tabasco sauce (optional)

Heat the oil in a frying pan and sauté the onions until they are lightly browned. Add the tomatoes, parsley, salt and pepper to taste, and the sugar. Cook the mixture for 5 minutes longer, stirring occasionally. Add the steak, vinegar, and a little Tabasco sauce, if liked, and cook, stirring, until the steak is heated through. Transfer to the centre of a heated platter and surround it with plain white rice.

PORK LOIN DISHES

Pork is one of the best-liked meats in Latin America, and pork loin one of the favourite cuts. In my view pork shoulder is just as attractive and much more economical though it will need a little longer cooking time. Recipes are quite varied, ranging from an Ecuadorian dish where the meat is larded with raw shrimp and braised, reminding one of the flavours of Chinese food, to an Argentine dish where the meat is baked in milk and emerges deliciously tender with a creamy sauce, to pork simmered in orange juice, tender and delicate, to pork loin, Chilean style, served with a fiery pepper sauce to be taken with discretion.

Lomo con Camarones

PORK LOIN WITH SHRIMP   *Ecuador*

The combination of pork and shrimp braised in wine is unusual and exciting—the flavour exquisite. This is one of my party favourites.

[Serves 6]
A 3-pound boned loin of pork
½ pound raw shrimp, peeled and
  coarsely chopped
1 hardboiled egg, chopped
Salt, freshly ground pepper
2 cloves garlic, crushed
2 ounces butter
¾ pint dry white wine
1 tablespoon flour
White wine or chicken stock

With a steel, or with a sharp, narrow knife, make holes about the thickness of one's thumb all over the loin, almost to the centre of the meat. Season the shrimp and egg with salt and pepper. With your fingers, stuff half the holes with the shrimp, the other half with chopped egg, or mix the shrimp and egg together and use as a stuffing. Season the loin with salt, pepper, and the crushed garlic. Heat 1½ ounces of the butter in a flameproof casserole large enough to hold the loin comfortably (an oval casserole is best) and sauté the meat until it is golden all over. Pour in the wine and bring to a simmer. Remove from the heat. Cover with aluminum foil and the casserole lid and bake in a preheated moderate oven (325° F., 170° C., gas 3) for 2 hours, or until the pork is tender. Lift the pork onto a warmed serving platter and remove the string. Slice the pork and keep warm. Mix the flour with the remaining butter and stir it, over moderate heat, into the casserole, stirring until the sauce is lightly thickened. If the liquid has reduced a great deal during cooking and the sauce is too thick, add a little wine or chicken stock to thin it to medium consistency. Taste, and season with more salt and pepper, if necessary. Spoon a little of the sauce over the pork slices, and pour the rest into a sauceboat. Serve with shoestring potatoes, sliced tomatoes, and *Ensalada de Habas* (Fresh Broad Bean Salad) page 271.

Lomo en Jugo de Naranja

PORK LOIN IN ORANGE JUICE   *Ecuador*

[Serves 6]

1½ ounces butter
1 large onion, finely chopped
1 clove garlic, minced
A 3-pound loin of pork, boned
Salt, freshly ground pepper
1 tablespoon grated orange rind

1 fresh hot red or green pepper,
    seeded and ground, or 1 teaspoon
    hot pepper sauce such as Tabasco
¾ pint orange juice
Chicken stock
2 teaspoons cornflour

Heat the butter in a frying pan and sauté the onion and garlic until the onion is soft. With a slotted spoon transfer the onion and garlic to a flameproof casserole large enough to hold the pork loin. Season the pork with salt and pepper and brown all over in the fat remaining in the pan. Add the pork to the casserole with the grated orange rind, the hot pepper or hot pepper sauce, orange juice, and enough stock barely to cover. Bring to a bare simmer and cook, covered, over very low heat for about 2 hours, or until the meat is tender. Put the meat on a serving platter, slice it, and keep it warm. Measure the liquid in the casserole and reduce it over brisk heat to ¾ pint. Mix the cornflour with a little water and stir it into the sauce. Cook, stirring, over moderate heat until the sauce is lightly thickened. Spoon a little of the sauce over the pork and serve the rest separately in a sauceboat. Accompany the pork with a salad made of cooked sliced beetroot, carrots, and potatoes in a vinaigrette sauce made with a teaspoon of Dijon mustard. If liked, toss the vegetables separately in the vinaigrette sauce and arrange them in heaps on a bed of lettuce leaves on a platter. Or serve with plain rice and a green vegetable.

Chancho a la Chilena

PORK LOIN, CHILEAN STYLE *Chile*

[Serves 6 to 8]

4 tablespoons vegetable oil	*1 bay leaf*
4 pounds boneless pork loin	*½ teaspoon oregano*
2 medium onions, sliced	*½ teaspoon thyme*
2 cloves garlic, chopped	*¼ teaspoon ground cumin*
1 carrot, scraped and sliced	*Salt, freshly ground pepper*
1 stalk celery, cut into 1-inch pieces	*¼ pint red wine vinegar*

Heat the oil in a large flameproof casserole and brown the meat lightly all over. Add all the other ingredients to the casserole with enough water to cover. Bring to the boil, cover, reduce the heat, and simmer gently until the meat is tender, about 3 hours. Allow the meat to cool completely in the stock, then remove to a serving platter. Reserve the stock for another use.

Serve the pork sliced with *Salsa de Ají Colorado* (Red Pepper Sauce), page 299, separately. In Chile the pork slices would be covered with the sauce. But since it can be quite incendiary if the peppers used are very hot, it is wiser to test one's palate with a little at a time.

Lomo de Cerdo a la Caucana

PORK LOIN BAKED IN MILK *Argentina*

This is an unusual version of a meat cooked in milk. The lemon juice curdles the milk slightly and also tenderizes the pork. At the end of the cooking time there are about 1¼ pints of slightly thickened milk in the baking dish. This makes a very light and attractive sauce when reduced. Boned shoulder of pork, a more economical cut, can be used, in which case increase the cooking time by half an hour.

[Serves 6]

2 pounds boned pork loin or shoulder	*4 tablespoons lemon juice*
1¾ pints milk	*Salt, freshly ground pepper*
	1 ounce butter

Put the pork into an oblong Pyrex or other flameproof baking dish that will just hold it comfortably. Mix the milk with the lemon juice and pour it over the pork. Cover the dish lightly and leave overnight in a cool place. When ready to cook, lift the pork out of the milk mixture and pat it dry. Season with salt and pepper. Heat the butter and brown the pork lightly all over. Put the pork back into the dish with the milk together with the pan drippings, and bake it, uncovered, in a preheated moderate oven (350° F., 180° C., gas 4) for 1½ to 2 hours, or until the pork is tender. Lift the pork out onto a warmed serving platter and remove the string tying it up. Skim the fat from the sauce and pour the sauce into a saucepan. Reduce it over brisk heat to ½ pint. Pour it into a sauceboat and serve separately. Slice the meat and serve hot with rice or potatoes and a green vegetable.

This is also good served cold with *Guasacaca* (Avocado Sauce) from Venezuela (page 304) or *Guacamole* (Avocado Sauce) from Mexico (page 303 and salad.

MINCED MEAT DISHES

Picadillo
SEASONED CHOPPED BEEF   *Mexico*

Picadillo is a great favourite throughout Latin America and every country has its own version. In Mexico it is much appreciated as a filling for tacos, *empanadas*, tamales, and green peppers. In the north of the country it is popular on its own and is eaten as a main dish, accompanied by rice, beans, *guacamole*, and tortillas.

[Serves 6]
3 tablespoons olive or vegetable oil
2 pounds lean minced beef
1 large onion, finely chopped
1 clove garlic, finely chopped
3 medium tomatoes, peeled and chopped
1 or more fresh hot green peppers, seeded and chopped, or 2 or 3 canned jalapeño chilies, seeded and chopped

2 tart cooking apples, peeled, cored, and chopped
3 ounces raisins, soaked 10 minutes in warm water
3 ounces pimiento-stuffed olives, halved crosswise
½ teaspoon oregano
½ teaspoon thyme
Salt, freshly ground pepper
½ ounce butter
2 ounces slivered almonds

Heat the oil in a large, heavy frying pan. Add the beef and sauté until it is lightly browned, stirring to break up any lumps. Add the onion and garlic and sauté for 5 minutes longer. Add all the remaining ingredients except the butter and the almonds. Mix well and simmer, uncovered, over moderate heat, stirring from time to time, for 20 minutes. In a small pan heat the butter and sauté the almonds until they are golden brown. Mound the beef onto a serving platter and sprinkle with the almonds. Surround it with a border of *Arroz Blanco* (White Rice) page 244.

Variation: Instead of oregano and thyme, use a pinch or two of cinnamon and ⅛ teaspoon ground cloves. This makes an interesting difference in flavour, giving the dish an almost Middle Eastern taste.

Variation: In Chihuahua, the apple is left out and 4 medium potatoes, cooked and cubed, and ¾ pound cooked green peas are added to the beef at the end of the cooking time for just long enough to heat them through. This makes a nice one-dish meal.

Variation: *Picadillo de la Costa* from the state of Guerrero, best known for the beach resort of Acapulco, uses the tropical fruits in which the region abounds, and instead of beef uses an equal mixture of minced pork and veal. The method is the same but the meats, with the onion, garlic, tomatoes, hot peppers, salt, and pepper, are cooked, uncovered, for 15 minutes. Then ½ pound pineapple chunks, 2 pears, peeled, cored, and cut in chunks, and 2 bananas, peeled and sliced, are added and the mixture simmered for 15 minutes longer over low heat. Sprinkle with almonds just before serving. This is a delicious summer dish, good with plain rice.

Albóndigas

MEATBALLS   *Uruguay*

Albóndigas enjoy great popularity in Latin America and are obviously inspired by the Middle East, where the range of variety of delicious meatballs seem inexhaustible. The countries of Latin America, adding their own very special touches, make their meatballs with beef, veal, or pork or a combination. They are usually lightly sautéed first, then cooked in a broth or sauce, seasoned quite differently from the meatballs themselves, thus creating a counterpoint of flavours that is very intriguing. Often there is the added richness that wine gives to the sauce. In Mexico the full-flavoured yet mild *ancho* chili or the peppery, exotic *chipotle* adds unusual flavour to the sauces. With such variety in seasonings it would be hard to tire of them.

[Makes about 18 meatballs, serves 4 to 6]

5 tablespoons vegetable oil	2 ounces fresh breadcrumbs
1 medium onion, finely chopped	4 tablespoons grated Parmesan cheese
1 medium tomato, peeled and chopped	2 ounces seedless raisins
1 fresh hot red pepper, seeded and chopped	¼ teaspoon grated nutmeg
1 teaspoon sugar	2 eggs
Salt, freshly ground pepper	Milk, if necessary
1 pound veal, finely minced	Flour

FOR THE BROTH

1 tablespoon vegetable oil	¼ teaspoon oregano
1 medium onion, finely chopped	1 bay leaf
½ pint beef stock	Salt, freshly ground pepper
½ pint dry red wine	Additional stock and wine, if necessary
¼ teaspoon thyme	

In a frying pan heat 2 tablespoons of the oil and sauté the onion until it is soft. Add the tomato, hot pepper, sugar, and salt and pepper to taste. Cook, stirring from time to time, until the mixture is thick and quite dry. Let the mixture cool. In a bowl mix together the veal, breadcrumbs, Parmesan cheese, raisins, nutmeg, and the tomato mixture. Add the eggs, mixing thoroughly. If the mixture is too dry to hold together, add a very little milk. Form into balls, about 2 inches in diameter, and flour them lightly. Heat the remaining oil in the frying pan and sauté the meatballs until lightly browned. As they are done, lift them out and set aside.

To make the broth: Heat the tablespoon of oil in a saucepan and sauté the onion until it is very soft. Add the stock, wine, thyme, oregano, and bay leaf, and simmer for a few minutes to blend the flavours. Season to taste with salt and pepper. Add the meatballs, cover, and cook over low heat until they are done, about 30 minutes. If necessary to cover the meatballs, add more stock and wine in equal amounts.

Serve the meatballs with rice or any starchy vegetable, using the broth as gravy. The broth may be a little thin, or too abundant, in which case lift out the meatballs to a serving dish and keep them warm. Reduce the broth over brisk heat until it is slightly thickened. If any is left over, I find it comes in handy for use in other sauces. *Ensalada de Habas* (Fresh Broad Bean Salad) from Ecuador makes a very pleasant accompaniment (page 271).

Variation: For *Albóndigas* from Chile, use minced beef instead of veal and mix the beef with 1 finely chopped onion, 2 ounces fresh breadcrumbs, salt, pepper, and 2 eggs, adding a little milk if the mixture is too dry. Form into balls, and poach in beef stock until tender, about 30 minutes. While the meatballs are poaching, make a sauce: In a saucepan heat 1 ounce butter and sauté 1 onion, finely chopped, until it is soft. Add ¾ pint beef stock and ½ pint dry red wine, 1 very finely grated carrot, ¼ teaspoon ground cumin, 1 bay leaf, and salt and pepper to taste. Bring to the boil and simmer, covered, for 30 minutes, then strain. Return the sauce to the pan and thicken with a beurre manié. Mix 2 teaspoons flour with 2 teaspoons butter and stir it into the hot sauce bit by bit. Reserving the poaching stock for another use, remove the meatballs to a serving dish and pour the sauce over them. Serve with rice. Serves 4 to 6.

Variation: For *Albóndigas en Caldo* (Meatballs in Stock) from Paraguay, thoroughly mix together 1 pound minced beef, 4 ounces cornmeal or 2 ounces fresh breadcrumbs, 1 onion, finely chopped, 1 clove garlic, minced, 2 tablespoons finely chopped parsley, 1 fresh hot red pepper, minced, ¼ teaspoon oregano, salt and pepper to taste, and 2 eggs. Add a little stock if the mixture seems too dry. Form into balls, about 2 inches in diameter, putting a piece of hardboiled egg in the centre of each ball. Set aside. Heat 1 tablespoon vegetable oil in a saucepan and sauté 1 onion, finely chopped, 2 medium tomatoes, peeled and chopped, 1 fresh hot red pepper, seeded and chopped, and salt and pepper, until the onion is soft. Add 1¼ pints beef stock and bring to the boil. Add the meatballs and simmer until they are done, about 30 minutes. Serve with rice. Serves 4 to 6.

If liked the meatballs may be made small, 1 inch in diameter, and the amount of stock increased to 3½ pints. Cook the meatballs with 3 tablespoons well-washed rice for 20 minutes and serve in soup plates, with the stock as a soup. The cornmeal will give this version a slightly drier texture, the breadcrumbs a very soft one. Both are good. Serves 4 to 6.

Variation: For *Albóndigas Picantes* (Peppery Meatballs) from Paraguay, put 1½ pounds lean beef, minced twice, in a bowl with 2 cloves garlic, minced, 2 ounces fresh breadcrumbs, ½ teaspoon each ground oregano and cumin, salt and pepper to taste, and a beaten egg. Mix very thoroughly, adding a little milk or stock if the meat mixture seems too dry. Make into balls 1½ inches in diameter and roll lightly in flour. Sauté the balls in vegetable oil until lightly browned all over and set aside.

Next make a sauce: Heat 3 tablespoons vegetable oil in a saucepan and sauté 2 medium onions, finely chopped, 1 sweet pepper, seeded and chopped, preferably red (if red peppers are not available, use 2 canned pimientos, chopped). Add 2 fresh hot red or green peppers, seeded and chopped, or use 1 teaspoon cayenne or 1 teaspoon hot pepper sauce such as Tabasco. (If using cayenne or Tabasco, add these later with the tomato purée.) When the onion is soft, add 1 bay leaf, 1 teaspoon sugar, and salt and pepper to taste. Stir in ¾ pint beef stock and 3½ pints thin tomato purée or tomato juice and simmer, covered, for 15 minutes. Remove and discard the bay leaf and purée the liquid in a blender or food processor. Return to the saucepan and bring to a simmer, add the meatballs and simmer, uncovered, for 15 minutes longer, or until the meatballs are done. Serve with white rice. There should be a generous amount of sauce to go over the rice. It may be reduced over brisk heat or thickened with a little flour if it is too abundant. Serves 4 to 6.

Variation: Perhaps of all the meatballs in Latin America, the Mexican ones are the most exotic. There is one version with a choice of sauces—either a gentle *ancho* chili sauce or a hot *chipotle* or *morita* chili sauce, so that all tastes are accommodated happily.

For *Albóndigas Mexicanas*, in a bowl thoroughly mix together ½ pound each twice-minced beef, pork, and veal. Add 1 ounce fresh breadcrumbs, 1 medium onion, finely chopped, ½ teaspoon oregano or ground cumin, according to preference, salt, freshly ground pepper, and 1 egg, lightly beaten. Mix thoroughly, adding a little milk if necessary. Form into 1½-inch balls, roll lightly in flour, and set aside. If liked, a little cooked rice, a little hardboiled egg, or a slice of green olive, or a combination of all three, may be put in the centre of each meatball. Makes 24 meatballs.

For the Ancho Chili Sauce: Pull the stems off 3 dried *ancho* chilies, shake out the seeds, and tear the peppers into pieces. Rinse and put to soak in a bowl with ¼ pint warm water. Leave to soak for about 1 hour, turning from time to time. Put into a blender or food processor with the liquid and reduce to a purée. Set aside. Heat 3 tablespoons vegetable oil and sauté 1 medium onion, finely chopped, with 1 clove garlic, minced, until the onion is soft. Add the puréed *ancho* chili and

1¼ pounds peeled, seeded, and finely chopped tomato, and sauté, stirring frequently, for 5 minutes over moderate heat. Pour the mixture into a fairly large saucepan, add ½ pint or more of beef stock to thin the mixture to a souplike consistency. Season to taste with salt, pepper, and ¼ teaspoon sugar. Bring to a simmer, add the meatballs, and simmer, uncovered, until the meatballs are tender, about 20 minutes. Serve with rice. Serves 4 to 6.

For the Chipotle or Morita Chili Sauce: Follow the instructions for the preceding sauce, but omit the *ancho* chili. Put the 1¼ pounds peeled, seeded, and chopped tomato in a blender or food processor with 1 *chipotle* or 2 *morita* chilies, coarsely chopped, and blend to a purée. Sauté with the onion and thin with the beef stock, adding more stock if necessary. The sauce will be quite hot, and very much thinner than the mild but full-flavoured *ancho* sauce.

Variation: For *Albóndigas* from Venezuela, in a bowl combine 1 pound finely minced lean beef, ¼ pound boiled ham, minced, 1 finely chopped onion, 1 ounce fresh breadcrumbs, 2 lightly beaten eggs, and salt and freshly ground pepper to taste. Mix thoroughly and form into balls about 1 inch in diameter. Heat 4 tablespoons vegetable oil and sauté the meatballs, in batches, until they are browned all over. Transfer to a flameproof casserole or saucepan. In a blender or food processor combine 1 onion, chopped, 1 tablespoon chopped parsley, 4 medium tomatoes, peeled and chopped, salt and freshly ground pepper to taste, and ½ pint dry white wine. Blend until the mixture is smooth. Pour over the meatballs, adding a little beef stock if necessary to barely cover. Simmer, covered, over low heat until the meatballs are cooked, about 20 minutes. Serve with rice or potatoes, and a green vegetable or salad as a main course. Serves 6.

The meatballs may be made half size, speared with toothpicks and served as an accompaniment to drinks. Drain them thoroughly and reserve the sauce for another use.

Picadinho de Porco

PORK HASH *Brazil*

[Serves 6]

½ ounce butter
1 medium onion, grated
2 large tomatoes, peeled, seeded, and chopped
2 pounds minced pork

½ pound chorizo or other spiced, smoked pork sausage, skinned and chopped
4 tablespoons lemon juice
Salt, freshly ground pepper

4 *tablespoons chopped parsley*	3 *large bananas, peeled*
2 *hardboiled eggs*	*Butter*

Heat the butter and sauté the onion for 2 minutes. Add the tomatoes and cook, stirring occasionally, until the mixture is thick and well blended. Add the pork and the sausage and continue cooking for 20 minutes until the pork is cooked through, breaking up the meat with a fork. Add the lemon juice and salt and pepper to taste and cook for a few minutes longer. Transfer the hash to a warmed serving dish and sprinkle with the parsley, the egg whites, finely chopped, and the egg yolks, sieved. Keep warm.

Halve the bananas crosswise, then lengthwise, and sauté in butter until lightly browned. Surround the hash with the bananas.

If preferred, omit the bananas and serve with *Angú de Farinha de Milho* (Moulded Cornmeal) page 243, or include both.

RABBIT DISHES

Rabbit, with its lean, flavourful meat, is very adaptable, taking happily to a wide variety of seasonings. In Latin America, where it is a favourite, having superseded its indigenous relatives like the *agouti* or *paca* in modern markets, it may be cooked with white wine in the simplest of ways, or exotically with sweet peppers and thick coconut milk, with annatto, with orange juice, or even more exotically with ground peanuts. A friend of mine uses peanut butter, but I prefer the texture of the sauce when homeground nuts are used. Excellent quality frozen rabbit cut up in ready-to-cook pieces is available in supermarkets. However, a whole rabbit is very easy to cut up.

Usually the head has already been removed. If not, cut it off using a sharp, heavy knife. Split it in two and use it to enrich the dish. There is a small amount of meat on it and the brains can be eaten separately. Cut off the forelegs—easy, as they are not jointed. Cut across the rabbit just under the rib cage, then cut the rib cage in half. Cut across the section with the hind legs, then split it in two, separating the legs. Cut the part remaining, the saddle, into two pieces crosswise. One piece will contain the kidneys. There will be eight pieces in all but the two rib pieces have very little meat.

Guiso de Conejo

RABBIT STEW   *Peru*

[Serves 4]
6 cloves garlic
1 teaspoon each cumin, oregano,
  and rosemary
Salt, freshly ground pepper
¼ pint vegetable oil

4 tablespoons white wine vinegar
A 2½-pound rabbit, cut into
  serving pieces
3 rashers bacon, chopped
¾ pint dry white wine
12 small white onions, peeled

Grind the garlic, cumin, oregano, and rosemary together with a mortar and pestle or in a small blender jar. Add salt to taste and a generous amount of pepper. Mix with 4 tablespoons of the oil and all the vinegar. Put the rabbit pieces in a bowl and pour the mixture over them. Cover with plastic wrap and marinate overnight in the refrigerator, turning once or twice. Lift out the rabbit pieces, pat dry. Reserve the marinade.

In a frying pan heat the remaining 4 tablespoons of oil and sauté the bacon until it is crisp. Push it to one side and sauté the rabbit pieces in the fat until they are golden. Transfer the rabbit and the contents of the pan to a flameproof casserole or heavy saucepan. Add the marinade, the wine, and the onions. Cover and simmer until the rabbit is tender, about 1½ hours. Arrange the rabbit and the onions in a serving dish and keep warm. Reduce the sauce over brisk heat until it is slightly thickened. Pour over the rabbit. Garnish if liked with black olives and parsley sprigs and serve with boiled potatoes.

Conejo Guisado con Coco

RABBIT STEW WITH COCONUT MILK   *Colombia*

In Colombia this is made with *ñeque* or *paca*, an animal like a hare, but rabbits are enough like hares for the substitution to succeed.

[Serves 4]
1½ ounces butter
A 2½-pound rabbit, cut into 8
  serving pieces
1 large onion, finely chopped
2 cloves garlic, chopped
1 sweet green pepper, seeded and
  chopped

1 fresh hot red or green pepper,
  seeded and chopped
1 large tomato, peeled and chopped
1 pimiento, chopped
Salt, freshly ground pepper
¾ pint beef or chicken stock
¼ pint thick coconut milk (see page
  29)

Heat the butter in a frying pan and sauté the rabbit pieces until they are lightly browned. Transfer the rabbit to a flameproof casserole. In the fat remaining in the pan sauté the onion, garlic, and the sweet and hot peppers. Add to the casserole with the tomato, pimiento, salt and pepper to taste, and the stock. Bring to the boil, cover, and cook over very low heat until the rabbit is tender, about 1½ hours. Remove the rabbit pieces to a serving dish and keep warm. Over brisk heat reduce the liquid in the casserole to about half. Lower the heat and stir in the coconut milk. Cook, stirring, for a few minutes, then pour the sauce over the rabbit. The sauce should be quite thick. Serve with rice.

Variation: Omit the coconut milk, and reduce the amount of stock to ½ pint and add ½ pint red wine instead. Reduce the liquid in the casserole in the same way, as the sauce should not be abundant.

Conejo con Maní

RABBIT IN PEANUT SAUCE   *Chile*

[Serves 4]
4 tablespoons vegetable oil
1 tablespoon sweet paprika
A 2½-pound rabbit, cut into
   serving pieces
2 large onions, finely chopped
1 clove garlic

¼ *pound roasted peanuts, finely*
   ground
Salt, freshly ground pepper to taste
½ *teaspoon ground cumin*
1 *tablespoon white wine vinegar*
¾ *pint chicken stock*
½ *pint dry white wine*

Heat the oil in a heavy casserole and stir in the paprika, taking care not to let it burn. Add the rabbit pieces and sauté lightly. Lift out and set aside. Add the onions and garlic to the casserole and sauté until the onions are softened. Return the rabbit pieces to the casserole. Add all the other ingredients, mix well, cover, and simmer until the rabbit is tender, about 1½ hours. Serve with rice and a salad.

Variation: Peru has a *Conejo con Maní* using the very hot yellow peppers that are a feature of this kitchen. It can however be made with fresh hot red or green peppers instead. Sauté the rabbit pieces in a mixture of 2 tablespoons vegetable oil and 1 ounce butter. Transfer the rabbit to a casserole. In the fat remaining in the pan sauté 3 medium onions, cut into thick slices, and add to the casserole with 1 or 2 hot peppers ground in a blender with 2 cloves garlic and 1 teaspoon salt. Cover with chicken stock or water, ¾ to 1¼ pints, and simmer for 1 hour. Add 4 ounces roasted ground peanuts and simmer until the rabbit is tender, about 30 minutes longer. Just before serving, add 8 small whole cooked potatoes. The peanuts will thicken as well as flavour the stew.

Conejo en Salsa de Naranja

RABBIT IN ORANGE SAUCE   *Chile*

[Serves 4]
2 tablespoons vegetable oil
A 2½-pound rabbit, cut into
    serving pieces
2 medium onions, finely chopped
1 clove garlic, chopped
¾ pint dry white wine

½ pint orange juice
Salt, freshly ground pepper
1 tablespoon flour
½ ounce butter
2 eggs, lightly beaten
1 hardboiled egg, finely chopped
1 tablespoon chopped parsley

Heat the oil in a frying pan and sauté the rabbit pieces until they are lightly browned. Transfer to a flameproof casserole. In the oil remaining in the pan, adding a little more if necessary, sauté the onions and garlic until the onions are softened. Add to the casserole. Pour the wine into the pan and scrape up all the brown bits. Pour into the casserole. Add the orange juice to the casserole and season to taste with salt and pepper. Cover and simmer until the rabbit is tender, about 1½ hours. Transfer the rabbit pieces to a serving dish and keep them warm.

Work the flour and butter into a paste. Add it to the liquid in the casserole and cook over low heat, stirring, until it is lightly thickened. Beat ¼ pint of the sauce into the eggs, then pour the eggs into the casserole, stirring constantly. Do not let the sauce come to the boil, as it will curdle. Pour the sauce over the rabbit and sprinkle with the egg and parsley. Serve with rice, potatoes or noodles, and a green vegetable.

INNARDS, OR OFFAL
Tripe Dishes

Of all the *interiores* (innards) none is so popular in Latin America as tripe, understandably so since few dishes are as appetizing when well prepared from an imaginative recipe. Tripe, which generally means the first and second stomach of the cow, comes to the market from the packing house, ready prepared and partially cooked. The best kind is honeycomb, but plain tripe is also good. Pig and sheep tripe are also sometimes sold. Tripe is quite tough and needs to be simmered 2 or more hours to tenderize it unless it is bought pre-cooked. Nibble a bit and if it is fully cooked and watery cook in the sauce with little or no added liquid. If precooking it, test from time to time so as not to overcook it. It should be tender but with a good, firm texture, a nice bitey resistance. Overcooked tripe has no character.

I have chosen a group of recipes that come from Mexico and all over South America—all deliciously appetizing, easy to cook, earthy dishes to be enjoyed at any time of the year. They need little in the way of accompaniment, potatoes if they are not already included in the recipe, or perhaps rice, a green vegetable, or a salad. And your excellent dish of tripe has the added merit of being inexpensive.

Tripa de Vaca a Brasileira

TRIPE WITH VEGETABLES, BRAZILIAN STYLE   *Brazil*

This is another rather fancy dish made special by the fresh coriander and the dry Madeira.

[Serves 6]

3 pounds honeycomb tripe
4 tablespoons lime or lemon juice
1¼ pints beef broth
3 tablespoons olive oil
1 large onion, finely chopped
1 large clove garlic, chopped
1 sweet red pepper, seeded and
   chopped

3 medium tomatoes, peeled and
   chopped
1 bay leaf
3 tablespoons fresh coriander,
   chopped
4 tablespoons dry Madeira
18 small stoned black olives
2 ounces grated Parmesan cheese

Wash the tripe in cold running water and cut it into strips about ¾ inch by 2 inches. Put the tripe into a flameproof casserole and add the lime or lemon juice, stir to mix, and leave for 5 minutes. Add the beef broth to the casserole. Simmer the tripe in the broth over a low heat until it is tender. Drain the tripe and set it aside. Reserve the broth. Rinse out and dry the casserole. Heat the oil in the casserole and sauté the onion, garlic, and sweet pepper until the onion is soft. Add to the casserole the tomatoes, bay leaf, fresh coriander, Madeira,

149

tripe, and ¾ pint of the reserved stock. Simmer, partially covered, until the tripe is tender and the sauce slightly thickened, about 1 hour. Stir from time to time with a wooden spoon to prevent the tripe from sticking. Add the olives and cook for a minute or two longer. Stir in the cheese. Serve with *Angú de Farinha de Milho* (Moulded Cornmeal) page 243.

Mondongo Serrano

TRIPE, MOUNTAIN STYLE   *Mexico*

This is quite a fancy dish from northern Mexico, with a wonderful blending of flavours and a fine aroma.

[Serves 6 to 8]

3 pounds honeycomb tripe, cut into 1-inch squares
4 tablespoons lemon juice
1¼ pints beef stock
¼ pint vegetable oil
1 large onion, finely chopped
4 chorizos (hot Spanish sausages), coarsely chopped
A ½-pound piece boiled ham, cut into ½-inch dice
A 1-pound can cooked chickpeas, or ½ pound dry chickpeas, soaked overnight and boiled until tender (about 2 hours)

2 ounces seedless raisins
1½ ounces ground almonds
¼ pint orange juice
2 fresh hot green peppers, seeded and chopped, or canned Mexican serrano or jalapeño chillies
3 ounces small pitted green olives, halved
Pinch each ground cloves and cinnamon
¼ teaspoon thyme
¼ teaspoon oregano
1 bay leaf
Salt, freshly ground pepper
Freshly grated Parmesan cheese

Wash the tripe in water mixed with the lemon juice, rinse, and put into a heavy saucepan or casserole with the beef stock, adding a little more if necessary to cover. Cover and simmer over low heat until the tripe is barely tender, about 1 to 2 hours. Test often for doneness, as the cooking time for tripe varies greatly. Lift the tripe out of the stock with a slotted spoon and pat dry with paper towels. Reserve the stock.

Heat the oil in a frying pan and sauté the onion and chorizos until the onion is soft. Lift out with a slotted spoon and put into the casserole. In the fat remaining in the pan sauté the tripe and add to the casserole with all the remaining ingredients except the cheese. Pour in the reserved stock, cover, and simmer over very low heat for 30 minutes, or until the tripe is tender. Add a little more stock if necessary as the sauce should be quite abundant. Serve in rimmed soup plates with the cheese served separately. Accompany with crusty bread and a green salad.

Chupe de Guatitas

TRIPE STEW   *Chile*

A stew with a modestly fiery accent from the hot pepper combined with the richly subtle flavour of sweet red peppers. Chileans often use breadcrumbs, as is done here, to thicken sauces.

[Serves 4 to 6]
2 *pounds honeycomb tripe*
¼ *pint paprika oil* (Color Chilena), *page 309, made with olive or vegetable oil*
1 *medium onion, finely chopped*
1 *sweet red pepper, seeded and chopped, or 2 canned pimientos, chopped*

4 *tablespoons parsley, chopped*
½ *teaspoon oregano*
1 *fresh hot red pepper, seeded and chopped, or* ½ *teaspoon cayenne*
Salt, *freshly ground pepper*
2 *ounces fresh breadcrumbs*
½ *pint milk*
2 *ounces grated Parmesan cheese*
1 *hardboiled egg, sliced*

Put the tripe into a large saucepan or flameproof casserole with cold, unsalted water to cover, bring to the boil, lower the heat, and simmer, covered, until the tripe is barely tender, about 1 to 2 hours. Test during the cooking period as tripe varies greatly. Drain, cut the tripe into strips about ½ inch by 2 inches, and set aside. Reserve the stock.

Heat the paprika oil in the saucepan and add the onion and sweet pepper. If using pimientos, add later with the parsley. Sauté until the onion and pepper are soft. Add the parsley, oregano, hot pepper or cayenne, salt and freshly ground pepper to taste, and the pimientos, if using. Stir to mix, and simmer, uncovered, for about 5 minutes, or until well blended.

Put the breadcrumbs and milk into a small saucepan and cook, stirring from time to time, for about 5 minutes. Purée in a blender or food processor. This step is not absolutely necessary but it does give a finer textured sauce. Add the breadcrumb sauce to the casserole, stirring to mix. Add the tripe. If the sauce is very thick, thin with ¼ pint or more of the reserved tripe stock. Simmer, uncovered, over very low heat, stirring from time to time, for 20 minutes to blend the flavours. Pour into a heated serving dish. Sprinkle with the grated cheese and garnish with the hardboiled egg slices. Serve with crusty bread and a green salad.

Variation: For *Guatitas con Tomatoes* (Tripe with Tomatoes), cook the tripe in the same way but omit the sweet pepper in the first sauce, and omit the breadcrumb sauce altogether. Sauté the onion and garlic, then add 6 medium tomatoes, peeled and chopped, and 2 carrots, scraped and grated. When the tomato sauce is well blended, add 6 medium potatoes, peeled and quartered, the tripe, and enough of the reserved tripe stock to cover. Simmer, covered, over low heat until the potatoes are tender. Thicken the sauce with 1 tablespoon flour mixed with a little stock to a paste, stirred into the casserole, and simmered until the sauce is lightly thickened. Omit the hard-boiled egg garnish, and sprinkle the dish with grated Parmesan cheese.

Variation: A simple dish, great as a meal in itself, *Mondongo a la Criolla* (Tripe, Creole Style) is popular throughout Latin America. This is an Argentine recipe. Soak ½ pound dried lima beans overnight, drain, and put into a saucepan with unsalted water to cover. Simmer until the beans are tender, 1 to 1½ hours. Drain and set aside. In a flameproof casserole heat ¼ pint olive oil and sauté 1 large onion, finely chopped, 1 large stalk celery, chopped, and 1 sweet red pepper, seeded and chopped, until the onion is soft. Add 2 large tomatoes, peeled and chopped, and simmer for a few minutes. Add 2 pounds honeycomb tripe cut into 1½- by ½-inch strips, 1 bay leaf, ¼ teaspoon each thyme and oregano, ¾ pint beef stock, 1 tablespoon tomato paste, and salt and pepper to taste. Simmer, covered, over low heat for 1 to 2 hours, or until the tripe is barely tender. Test often, as the cooking time for tripe varies greatly. Add ½ pound well-washed long-grain rice and simmer until the rice is tender, about 20 minutes. If necessary add a little more stock as there should be plenty of sauce. Add the beans and heat through. Serve in rimmed soup plates with plenty of freshly grated Parmesan cheese, crusty bread, and a green salad.

Two 1-pound cans of *cannellini* (white kidney beans), rinsed and drained, and 2 canned pimientos, chopped, can be used instead of lima beans and the pepper. Add just before serving and heat through.

Variation: The ground peanuts used in this Ecuadorian recipe for *Guatita* (Tripe) may seem a little startling at first. They add a delightful nutty taste, not at all overwhelming, and thicken the sauce at the same time. The annatto adds a subtle fragrant flavour while giving the dish an attractive yellow colour. A most imaginative recipe.

Cook the tripe in the same way as for *Chupe de Guatitas* (Tripe Stew, see opposite). In a frying pan heat 4 tablespoons annatto oil or lard (see page 000) and sauté 1 large onion, finely chopped, 2 cloves garlic, minced, 1 sweet green pepper, seeded and chopped, until the onion is soft. Add 1 large tomato, peeled, seeded, and chopped, season with salt, and cook until the mixture is well blended. Stir in 4 ounces ground peanuts and enough of the reserved tripe stock to thin to a medium thick sauce. Add the tripe and 1 pound potatoes, cooked and cubed, and simmer until heated through. Serve sprinkled with chopped coriander or parsley. Accompany with a green vegetable or a salad. Serves 4.

Variation: For *Caucau a la Limeña* (Tripe, Lima Style), Peruvian cooks would use hot yellow peppers, but I find fresh hot red or green peppers a perfect substitute, and where Peruvians would use 1 tablespoon of ground *palillo*, a yellow herb, I use 1½ teaspoons of turmeric, with fine results. Cook the tripe in the same way as for *Chupe de Guatitas* (Tripe Stew, see page 151). In a large, heavy frying pan that has a lid, heat ½ pint vegetable oil and add 1 or more, according to taste, fresh hot red or green peppers, seeded and pounded in a mortar or puréed in a blender, 4 medium onions, finely chopped, and 6 cloves garlic, chopped. Sauté over moderate heat until the onions are soft and beginning to brown. Add the tripe and 2 pounds potatoes, peeled and cut into ½-inch cubes. Sauté for 2 or 3 minutes, then add 1½ teaspoons ground turmeric mixed with ¼ pint tripe stock, a sprig of mint or parsley, and salt and freshly ground pepper to taste. Cover and simmer over low heat until the potatoes are almost done. Cook, uncovered, until the dish is quite dry. If necessary add a little more tripe stock during cooking, but only enough to cook the potatoes. Before serving pour a tablespoon of oil over the tripe, folding it into the mixture. Serves 4.

Lengua en Salsa Picante

TONGUE IN HOT PEPPER SAUCE   *Chile*

Fresh ox tongue is popular as a main dish in all of Latin America. This dish from Chile is not very peppery. There is just enough hot chili in the sauce to justify the name, but only enough to give a pleasant piquancy.

[Serves 6 to 8]
A fresh ox tongue, weighing about
  3 pounds
1 onion, sliced

1 sprig each parsley and coriander
1 small stalk celery
1 bay leaf
2 teaspoons salt

Wash the tongue and put into a large saucepan or flameproof casserole with all the remaining ingredients and enough cold water to cover. Bring to the boil, skim as necessary, reduce the heat, cover, and simmer until the tongue is tender, about 3 hours. Uncover and leave in the stock until it is cool enough to handle. Lift out onto a platter, remove skin and any bones or fat, and cut into ½-inch slices. Strain the stock into a jug. Rinse out and dry the casserole and return the tongue to it.

FOR THE SAUCE

2 shallots, finely chopped
¼ pint red or white wine vinegar
1 ounce butter
2 tablespoons flour
¾ pint tongue stock

1 or more fresh hot peppers,
    preferably red, seeded and finely
    chopped
2 tablespoons chopped parsley

Put the shallots into a small saucepan with the vinegar and simmer until the shallots are tender, about 3 minutes. Set aside. Heat the butter in a saucepan and add the flour. Cook, stirring constantly with a wooden spoon, for 2 minutes over low heat without letting the flour brown. Stir in the stock and simmer over low heat for 10 minutes. Stir in the vinegar and shallot mixture, the hot pepper, and parsley, and pour over the tongue. Simmer just long enough to heat the tongue through. Arrange on a platter and serve surrounded by halved cooked potatoes, or with rice served separately.

Variation: Ecuador has a similar recipe. Also called *Lengua en Salsa Picante*, the tongue is cooked in the same way but the sauce differs, and I find it makes an interesting change from the Chilean version. In 2 tablespoons vegetable oil or butter, sauté 1 medium onion, finely chopped, with 1 clove garlic, chopped, until the onion is soft. Stir in 1 tablespoon dry mustard, mixing well. Add about ½ pint stock from the cooked tongue and simmer for 5 minutes. Add 1 tablespoon capers, 2 tablespoons chopped parsley, 1 pimiento, coarsely chopped, 1 tablespoon lemon juice, and salt and pepper to taste. Pour the sauce over the sliced tongue and simmer just long enough to heat through.

Variation: The very first Mexican dish I learned to cook was *Lengua en Salsa de Tomate Verde* (Tongue in Green Tomato Sauce), using the little green husk tomatoes that have such a special, and delicious, flavour. The tongue is cooked in the same way as in the previous recipes. In a blender or food processor combine 1 medium onion, coarsely chopped, 2 cloves garlic, chopped, 8 tablespoons coriander sprigs, chopped, 1 pound canned Mexican green tomatoes, drained, and 3 or 4 canned *serrano* chilies, or 1 or 2 fresh hot green peppers, seeded and chopped, and reduce to a coarse purée. Heat 3 tablespoons lard or vegetable oil in a frying pan, pour in the purée, and cook, stirring for about 4 minutes. Add ½ pint stock from the cooked tongue, season to taste with salt, and pour over the tongue. Simmer just long enough to heat through. Serve with small new potatoes.

If fresh Mexican green tomatoes are available, peel off the brown outer husk and chop coarsely before adding to the blender or food processor.

Variation: Another favourite Mexican recipe is *Lengua en Salsa de Chile Ancho y Almendra* (Tongue in Mild Red Chili and Almond Sauce). Simply heat the tongue through in ¾ pint of the sauce (see page 301).

Variation: There is usually quite a lot of stock left over from cooking a tongue, and Latin American cooks frequently use it to make soup, saving the trimmings of the tongue for garnish. Recipes are not very formal. Vegetables such as carrots, turnips, potatoes, Swiss chard, or cabbage are cubed or chopped and may be cooked in a little butter for a few minutes before being added to the stock, or just added and simmered until tender, about 25 minutes. A little sherry is sometimes added to the finished soup, and sometimes it is sprinkled with grated cheese. Rice, vermicelli, or cornmeal is also sometimes added, in short whatever is on hand. The result is a very pleasant unpretentious soup augmented by a feeling of virtue for having avoided waste.

Patitas de Chancho a la Criolla

PIG'S FEET, CREOLE STYLE   *Peru*

Served at room temperature, this is more a salad for a luncheon main course or an hors d'oeuvre.

[Serves 4 as luncheon dish, 8 as first course]

2 pig's feet, about 2 pounds	2 cooked medium-sized potatoes,
Salt	halved and sliced
2 medium onions, very thinly sliced	6 tablespoons vegetable oil
2 medium tomatoes, peeled and	2 tablespoons white vinegar or
sliced	lemon juice, or a mixture
1 fresh hot red or green pepper,	Salt, freshly ground pepper
seeded and sliced lengthwise	Lettuce leaves for garnish

Wash the pig's feet and put them into a saucepan with salted water to cover, bring to the boil, reduce the heat, and simmer, covered, for 3 hours, or until tender. Cool in the stock, lift out, bone, and cut into 1-inch pieces, about. Discard the stock.

In a large bowl combine the pig's feet, onions, tomatoes, hot pepper strips, potatoes, oil, vinegar or lemon juice, salt and pepper to taste, and mix lightly. Allow to stand for about 15 minutes, then place in a serving dish garnished with lettuce leaves and serve at room temperature.

Patitas de Cerdo

PIG'S FEET   *Argentina*

Pig's feet, with their bland flavour and delicious gelatinous quality, are a favourite wherever pork is eaten. Latin America has some excitingly different recipes for this splendidly economical dish. I sometimes like to serve the pig's feet whole, instead of boned and cut up. I have borrowed a trick from James Beard, a dear friend always generous with help. I wrap the feet in cheesecloth and tie them with string before cooking them. It gives them a neat and tidy look, prevents broken skin, and makes for a much more attractive presentation.

[Serves 4]

8 pig's feet
2 cloves garlic

1 ripe sweet red pepper, seeded and chopped

FOR THE DRESSING

1 teaspoon Spanish (hot) paprika or
    cayenne
½ pint red wine vinegar
Salt

½ pint vegetable oil
1 ripe sweet pepper, peeled (page
    36) and seeded
Lettuce leaves

Wrap each of the pig's feet tightly in butter muslin, tie with string. Put into a large saucepan with the garlic and pepper and enough water to cover. Bring to the boil, reduce the heat, and simmer, covered, for 3 to 4 hours, or until tender. Let the pig's feet stand in the pan until cool enough to handle. Lift out and remove the muslin wrapping. Put into a shallow dish and pour on the dressing. Let stand at room temperature, turning once or twice, for at least an hour before serving.

To make the dressing mix the ground hot paprika or cayenne with the vinegar and salt to taste. Beat in the oil. Cut the pepper into strips and add. Serve the pig's feet on plates garnished with lettuce leaves, 2 per person, as a main course, or serve 1 per person as an appetizer. Accompany with crusty bread and butter.

Patitas de Cerdo con Chile Poblano

PIG'S FEET IN POBLANO PEPPER SAUCE   *Mexico*

In Mexico the dark green *chile poblano* would be used for this recipe. A sweet green pepper is a good substitute.

[Serves 4]
8 pig's feet
1 medium onion, coarsely chopped
⅛ teaspoon thyme

⅛ teaspoon oregano
1 bay leaf
1 sprig parsley or coriander

FOR THE SAUCE

1 medium onion, chopped
2 cloves garlic, chopped
6 medium tomatoes, peeled and
  chopped
4 tablespoons vegetable oil

3 sweet green peppers, peeled (page
  36), seeded, and cut into strips
Pinch of sugar
Salt, freshly ground pepper

Wrap each of the pig's feet tightly in butter muslin, tie with string. Put into a large saucepan with the onion, thyme, oregano, bay leaf, and parsley or coriander, and enough water to cover. Bring to the boil, reduce the heat, and simmer, covered, for 3 or 4 hours, or until tender. Let the pig's feet stand in the pan until cool enough to handle. Lift out and remove the muslin wrapping. Return to the saucepan.

To make the sauce put the onion, garlic, and tomatoes into a blender or food processor fitted with a steel blade and reduce to a purée. Heat the oil in a pan and add the tomato mixture and the pepper strips. Add the sugar and season to taste with salt and pepper. Simmer, uncovered, stirring from time to time, until the mixture is thick and well blended. Pour over the pig's feet and simmer until they are heated through. Serve with tortillas.

Variation: Leftover sauce from dishes like *Ternera en Pipián Verde* (Veal in Pumpkin Seed Sauce), *Pollo Verde Almendrado* (Chicken in green Almond Sauce), *Pollo en Pipián de Almendra* (Chicken Stew with Almonds), *Mole Coloradito de Oaxaca* (Chicken in Red Sauce, Oaxaca Style), or *Salsa de Chile Ancho y Almendra* (Mild Red Chili and Almond Sauce), page 300, can be used with pig's feet.

Picante de Pata Arequipeña

SPICY PIG'S FEET, AREQUIPA STYLE   *Peru*

[Serves 4]

3 pig's feet
3 sprigs fresh mint
1 or more fresh hot red or green
    peppers, seeded and ground
2 tablespoons lard or vegetable oil
2 medium onions, finely chopped

3 cloves garlic, minced
½ teaspoon oregano
2 ounces roasted peanuts, finely
    ground
Salt, freshly ground pepper
3 medium potatoes, about 1 pound,
    cooked and cut into 1-inch cubes

Wash the pig's feet and put them into a saucepan large enough to hold them comfortably, preferably in a single layer. Add the mint and enough water to cover by about 1 inch. Cover and simmer until the pig's feet are tender, about 3 hours. Let them cool in the stock, then lift out, remove the bones, and cut into 1-inch pieces. Set aside. Strain and reserve the stock.

Grind the peppers with a mortar and pestle or in a small blender jar.

Heat the lard or oil in a flameproof casserole and sauté the onions, garlic, oregano, and hot peppers until the onions are soft. Stir in the peanuts and sauté for 1 or 2 minutes longer. Season to taste with salt and pepper. Stir in 1 cup of the reserved stock and simmer for a few minutes to blend the flavours. Add the pig's feet and the potatoes and simmer just long enough to heat them through. The sauce should be thick and highly spiced but one's own taste should determine the number of hot peppers used. If the sauce is too thick, add a little more of the reserved stock. In Peru this would be served with rice. I prefer it with a green vegetable or a salad.

Coração Recheado

STUFFED OX HEART   *Brazil*

Stuffed heart has been a favourite dish of mine since childhood, so I was delighted when a Brazilian friend gave me her recipe, which is quite grand. I was also pleased to be given a Chilean version of this dish in a new guise, a simpler recipe than the Brazilian one. I like both. Calf's heart is also good. It usually weighs about 1 pound so use about one-quarter of the stuffing and reduce the cooking time to 1½ hours. It would serve 2 or 3.

[Serves 8]

1 ox heart, weighing about 4 pounds
2 ounces butter
1 medium onion, finely chopped
6 ounces corn kernels
1 ounce freshly made breadcrumbs
2 hardboiled eggs, chopped
½ sweet red pepper, peeled (see page 00), seeded and chopped
8 pimiento-stuffed olives, halved
1 small fresh hot red or green pepper, seeded and chopped
2 tablespoons chopped parsley
Salt, freshly ground pepper
½ pint dry red wine
¾ pint beef stock
1 clove garlic, chopped
2 teaspoons cornflour or arrowroot

Thoroughly wash the heart and remove the membrane inside that divides the two chambers if the butcher has not already done this. Trim away any fat. In a frying pan heat half the butter and sauté the onion until it is soft. Purée the corn in a food processor or blender and stir into the onion off the heat. Add the breadcrumbs, the eggs, sweet pepper, olives, hot pepper, parsley, and salt and pepper to taste, mixing well. Stuff the heart with the dressing. Sew it up or skewer it and lace with string. In a flameproof casserole large enough to hold the heart comfortably, heat the remaining butter and brown the heart all over. Pour in the wine and stock, add the garlic, and bring the liquid to the boil. Cover the casserole with foil, then with the lid, and cook in a preheated moderate oven (350° F., 180° C., gas 4) for about 3½ hours, or until tender. Lift the heart out onto a serving platter and remove the sewing thread or the skewers and string. Cut the heart into crosswise slices and keep warm. Reduce the cooking liquid over brisk heat to ¾ pint. Mix the cornflour or arrowroot with a little cold water, stir into the sauce, and cook, stirring, for a few minutes until the sauce is thickened. Pour a little sauce over the sliced heart and serve the rest in a sauceboat. Serve with mashed potatoes and green beans or peas.

Variation: For *Corazon Relleno* (Stuffed Heart) from Chile, prepare the heart in the same way. For the stuffing soak 4 slices firm white bread in milk, then squeeze out and mix with 1 medium onion, finely chopped, 2 tablespoons parsley, finely chopped, 4 rashers of bacon, chopped, salt and pepper to taste, and 1 egg, lightly beaten. Stuff the heart with the mixture and sew or skewer it closed. Heat 2 table-

159

spoons vegetable oil in a flameproof casserole and brown the heart all over. Add to the casserole 1 onion, coarsely chopped, 1 carrot, scraped and sliced, ½ teaspoon thyme, 1 sprig parsley, 1 bay leaf, and ¾ pint beef stock and ½ pint dry red wine. Cook as for *Coração Recheado*.

Brains

Brains are popular in Latin America, particularly French Calf's Brains in Black Butter, which sounds very splendid in Spanish as *Sesos con Salsa de Mantequilla Quemada*. But there are several interesting recipes common to a number of countries that provide us with some new ways to cook this delicacy. A preliminary soaking and peeling are always necessary, followed by a simmering in seasoned liquid, except when the brains are to be stewed as in the first of these recipes.

Sesos Guisados

STEWED BRAINS   *Colombia*

This recipe is as appetizing as it is simple.

[Serves 6]
1½ pounds brains
1 medium onion, finely chopped
1 clove garlic, chopped

3 medium tomatoes, peeled and
    chopped
½ ounce butter
Salt, freshly ground pepper

Soak the brains in several changes of water for about 2 hours. Carefully pull off the thin membrane that covers the brains. This is not difficult but requires patience. Rinse the brains in fresh cold water. Then simmer in enough water to barely cover, with the onion, garlic, tomatoes, butter, and salt and pepper to taste for 30 minutes. Lift out the brains and cut each one into 4 to 6 slices. Arrange in a warmed serving dish. Reduce the liquid in the saucepan over brisk heat until it is slightly thickened, then pour over the brains. Serve with rice or potatoes or any other starchy vegetable.

Variation: For *Sesos Rebozados* (Sautéed Brains), soak 1½ pounds brains and remove the membranes in the usual way. Then simmer, in enough water to cover, with 1 small chopped onion, 1 clove garlic, and ½ teaspoon salt for 30 minutes. Cool in the cooking liquid, lift out, and pat dry with paper towels. Cut each brain into 4 to 6 slices. Beat 2 egg whites until they stand in peaks. Fold the whites into 2 egg yolks beaten with ½ teaspoon salt. Dip the brain slices in flour, then in the beaten egg, and sauté in 2 ounces butter until golden brown on both sides. Serve with rice or potatoes and a fresh Hot Pepper Sauce (page 301), or lemon wedges.

Variation: For *Sesos en Vino* (Brains in Wine Sauce), soak and simmer 1½ pounds brains as for *Sesos Rebozados*. Cut into cubes and put into a buttered casserole. Heat 1 ounce butter and sauté 1 medium onion, finely chopped, and 1 clove chopped garlic until the onion is soft. Add to the casserole. Season to taste with salt and pepper. Fold 8 ounces diced cooked potatoes into the brains and pour ½ pint dry white wine over the mixture, adding a little more if necessary. Simmer very gently for 15 minutes to blend the flavours, sprinkle with 2 tablespoons chopped parsley, and serve surrounded by 12 triangles of white bread fried in butter.

Variation: For *Sesos con Jamón* (Brains with Ham), soak and simmer 1½ pounds brains as for *Sesos Rebozados.* Halve the brains, dip in flour seasoned with salt and pepper, and fry in butter, about 2 ounces, until golden on both sides. Sauté 6 thin slices of ham in butter and arrange on a warmed platter. Put the halved brains on top of the ham and mask with ½ pint *Môlho ao Tomate* (page 306).

Hígado en Salsa de Hongos

CALF'S LIVER IN MUSHROOM SAUCE   *Chile*

Chile's excellent wine turns an ordinary dish into a fine one in this simple recipe. Either a dry white or red wine, which I prefer, may be used.

[Serves 4]
3 ounces butter
2 tablespoons oil
1 medium onion, finely chopped
¼ teaspoon oregano

½ pound mushrooms, sliced
½ pint dry red wine
Salt, freshly ground pepper
1 pound calf's liver, cut into
  ¼-inch slices

Heat half the butter and 1 tablespoon of the oil in a frying pan and sauté the onion and oregano until the onion is soft. Add the mushrooms and cook over fairly high heat, stirring from time to time with a wooden spoon, until the mushrooms are lightly browned, about 5 minutes. Pour in the wine and cook, stirring, until the wine is reduced to half and the sauce is slightly thickened.

In another frying pan heat the remaining butter and oil and sauté the liver over moderate heat for 2 minutes. Turn the pieces and sauté for 1 minute longer. Add the liver and its juices to the pan with the mushrooms, stir to mix, and simmer for about 1 minute. Be careful not to overcook the liver—it should be pink inside. Transfer to a warmed serving dish and serve with potatoes or rice and a green vegetable.

Hígado con Vino

CALF'S LIVER IN RED WINE SAUCE   *Colombia*

The red wine marinade gives this calf's liver a special delicate flavour.

[Serves 2]
½ pound calf's liver, cut into
   ½-inch slices
Salt, freshly ground pepper

1 large clove garlic, crushed
¼ pint dry red wine
1½ ounces butter

Arrange the liver slices in a large shallow dish, season with salt and pepper and the garlic. Pour the wine over them. Leave at room temperature for 2 hours, turning the slices from time to time. When ready to cook, lift out the liver slices and pat them dry with paper towels. Reserve the marinade. In a large frying pan heat the butter and sauté the liver slices over moderate heat for about 2 minutes on the first side and 1 minute on the second side. The liver should remain pink inside. Pour the marinade into a small saucepan and reduce to half its volume. Arrange the liver on a warmed platter. Pour any liquid from the pan into the wine sauce, stir to mix, and pour over the liver.

Riñones con Vino

KIDNEYS IN WINE SAUCE   *Chile*

I love to make this simple, quick Chilean kidney dish just for myself with two lamb kidneys or one pork. It is a fine dish for a hurried supper.

[Serves 3 to 4]
1 ox kidney
Salt, freshly ground pepper
2 ounces butter
1 medium onion, finely chopped

4 tablespoons parsley, chopped
½ pint dry white wine
4 medium potatoes, freshly cooked
   and cubed

Trim off the surplus fat and cut the kidney into thin slices. Season with salt and pepper. Heat the butter and sauté the kidney slices for about 5 minutes, turning frequently. Lift out and set aside in a covered dish. In the butter remaining in the pan sauté the onion until it is soft. Add the parsley and sauté for a minute longer. Add the wine and the potatoes. Add the kidney slices and cook just long enough to heat them through without further cooking, which would toughen them. Serve immediately.

If cooking this for one and using lamb or pork kidneys, remove the thin skin and any fat from the kidneys and slice them thinly. Use one-quarter of the remaining ingredients, and cook as above.

Variation: In Argentina cooks use a similar recipe for *Riñones a la Porteña* (Kidneys, Buenos Aires Style) except that veal kidney, chopped instead of sliced, is used and is sautéed in oil instead of butter.

Variation: For the Brazilian *Rim de Vitela* (Veal Kidney) or *Rims de Carneiro* (Lamb Kidneys), the kidneys are cleaned and sliced, and sautéed in 2 tablespoons olive oil. They are then heated through in the following sauce: Sauté 1 chopped onion and ½ sweet green pepper, seeded and chopped, in 2 tablespoons olive oil until the onion is soft. Add 1 chopped tomato, 4 tablespoons chopped parsley, and salt and pepper. Simmer until well blended. Stir in 2 tablespoons dry sherry and the kidneys. Reheat the kidneys without letting the sauce boil. For those who like a fiery touch, 1 small fresh hot pepper may be added with the sweet pepper, or a dash of Tabasco with the sherry.

BARBECUES

The great cattle countries of Argentina and Brazil have marvellous outdoor feasts, elaborate and sophisticated barbecues that are superb for informal, warm weather entertaining, and easy to copy.

The *asado criollo*, the Argentine spit-roasted barbecue, originated with the gauchos—the cowboys of the *pampas*, those wide, rolling plains that stretch like a sea of grass for thousands of miles. The cowboys tended cattle, and later sheep, and when they were hungry killed an animal, spit-roasted it, and had dinner. In comparison, today's barbecue is a very grand affair. In addition to barbecued meats there are salads, sauces, bread, and wine, as well as the cowboy's favourite beverage, *mate*, the green herb tea popular in many parts of South America for its refreshing, slightly bitter taste. But the essentials are the same—meat, salt, and a fire.

The word "barbecue" comes from the Spanish *barbacoa*, derived from a Haitian word in the Taino Indian language. It meant a rude framework either for sleeping or for drying meat over a fire, and reached the United States with that meaning by 1697. By 1809 its American meaning had changed to an outdoor social entertainment at which animals were roasted whole. Because of the growing popularity of outdoor cooking, grills of various kinds can easily be bought, and it is not difficult to build a do-it-yourself grill.

To make a *parrilla* (grill) for an Argentine *asado* (roast), dig a pit about 1 foot deep and about 3 feet long by 2 feet wide. Make sure the fire bed is level and cover it with a layer of sand. Surround it with bricks at ground level or, for a more luxurious grill, extend them to waist level, and cover with an iron grate. Also needed are a long three-pronged fork, a small work table to cut up the cooked meat, canvas work gloves, an asbestos oven mitt for hot jobs, tongs for turning meats and lifting them from the grill, a bowl for the *salmuera* (brine) to baste the meats, a brush or bunch of twigs for basting, and a bottle with a sprinkler top, filled with water, to discipline unruly flames.

It takes about an hour for a fire of wood and charcoal to burn down to embers that are ready to be used, and whoever looks after the grill has to put the meats on in sequence so that they are served hot and crispy brown on the outside, red and juicy inside. It is a considerable art and one that can be mastered only by experience, common sense, and a watchful eye. Meats are not basted with a barbecue sauce. Brine is used, usually a simple solution of salt and water. When the meat is seared on one side it is basted with brine and turned, and the other side seared and basted. After that the meat is turned and basted frequently until done.

Argentine hosts are generous in their estimate of how much meat is enough. They work it out roughly as a pound a person. The *asado* always begins with grilled sausages, either a halved chorizo, or 2 or 3 slices of grilled *longaniza*, nothing else, served with a glass of dry red wine. The sausages are just to hold off starvation, not to destroy appetite, while guests wait for the meats on the grill to cook. For ten people the traditional meats for the *parrillada* (barbecue) would be 2 pounds short ribs, 2 pounds rump or chuck steak, 1½ pounds skirt steak, 1 pound blood sausage, 1 or 2 ox kidneys or a whole calf's liver, 1½ pounds sweetbreads, and 1½ pounds tripe, cut into strips about 1 inch wide. Traditionally intestines, udders, and prairie oysters are part of the roast. Intestines are grilled, then sliced. Udders are grilled, then cut into ½-inch slices. And prairie oysters are peeled, halved, grilled, and sliced.

After the sausages, the "innards" are served, and then the meats. Guests go to the grill to be served, then eat informally at simple wooden tables set with baskets of French bread and bottles or carafes of red wine. There are bowls of salad—lettuce, tomatoes, and sliced onions or spring onions in a garlic-flavoured oil and vinegar dressing, or a more robust one of potatoes, beetroot, hardboiled eggs, chopped celery, and radishes, also in a vinaigrette dressing. *Crudités* are sometimes served, raw carrot sticks, celery, and radishes. And there is always a bowl of hot pickled peppers as well as the traditional bowls of sauces—*Salsa Criolla* (Creole Sauce), a really fiery one to be taken with discretion, or sauce *Chimichurri*, an untranslatable name, hardly any milder. There is another less lethal sauce, *Salsa para Asados* (Barbecue Sauce) from nearby Uruguay, where barbecues are also popular.

The barbecue pit with a grate over it is really a sophisticated refinement. Whole animals, a lamb, kid, suckling pig, or a side of beef, can be spit-roasted in the true gaucho manner. The animals are split and impaled on iron rods that have a crosspiece to keep them flat. The rods are thrust firmly into the ground at an angle of about 20 degrees, toward a wood fire and about a foot away. They too are basted with brine and with their own fat and turned as they brown so that both sides cook evenly.

It is difficult to give more than approximate times for barbecuing as the heat of the fire and the thickness of the meats vary, as well as the degree of doneness preferred. Sausages will take about 10 minutes a side. A 2½- to 3-pound chicken, split down the back, will take about 1 hour. A medium-sized suckling pig will take 3 to 3½ hours, and baby lamb and kid about the same time. A 3-pound piece of short ribs should be cooked 10 to 15 minutes, rib side down, then turned, salted, and cooked for about 30 minutes longer. Rump or sirloin takes 20 to 30 minutes according to size. Skirt steak, over high heat, starting fat side down, takes about 7 minutes a side.

The Brazilian barbecue, *Churrasco a Gaucha* from the cattle state of Rio Grande do Sul, has its own refinements and sophisticated extras. Originally the meat was spitted on long iron skewers and stuck in the ground at an angle to the fire much as the gauchos of Argentina did. It is still done for a traditional *churrasco*, but more and more people find a barbecue pit with a grate on top more convenient. Short ribs and rump are the preferred meats. Though traditionally beef is the only meat used, many people temporarily tired of beef, like to have a *galeto*, a chicken, instead. This is split down the back and grilled whole. A whole parsley plant is used as a baster to apply the brine, seasoned sometimes with chopped onion and parsley, or crushed garlic cloves.

Slices of grilled *linguiça* (Portuguese sausage) may be served with a *Caipirinha* or a *batida* (Brazilian cocktails), page 317, as a first course. The meats are accompanied by *Farofa de Ouro* (Cassava Meal with Hardboiled Eggs) or *Farofa de Manteiga* (Cassava Meal with Butter). A nice variation is to add 4 bananas, cut into ½-inch slices and fried in an ounce of butter, to the cassava meal and mixed together. There is always a lettuce and tomato salad in an oil and vinegar dressing, and *Môlho de Tomates* (Tomato Sauce). Brazil's excellent beer is the popular drink to serve.

SAUCES FOR BARBECUES

Salsa Criolla

BARBECUE SAUCE, CREOLE SAUCE *Argentina*

[Makes about 2 pints]

1 tablespoon hot paprika or cayenne pepper
½ tablespoon dry mustard
¼ pint red wine vinegar
¼ pint olive oil
Salt, freshly ground pepper
2 sweet green peppers, seeded and finely chopped
1 medium onion, finely chopped
3 medium tomatoes, chopped

Mix the paprika or cayenne and mustard to a paste with a little of the vinegar, then stir in the rest of the vinegar. Beat in the oil. Season to taste with salt and a generous amount of freshly ground pepper. Add the remaining ingredients and stir to mix. The sauce has a lot of liquid. The solids should float in the bowl, so add a little more oil and vinegar if necessary. This is very hot.

Variation: Brazilian *Môlho ao Tomate* (Tomato Sauce). In a bowl combine 4 medium tomatoes, coarsely chopped, 2 medium onions, chopped, 2 cloves garlic, chopped, 8 tablespoons each chopped parsley and coriander, salt, pepper, ½ pint olive oil, and ¼ pint red wine vinegar. Mix lightly and serve at room temperature. Makes 1½ to 2 pints.

Chimichurri

VINEGAR SAUCE   *Argentina*

This is a popular sauce with barbecued meats or with any grilled or roasted meat or poultry.

[Makes about ½ pint]
4 tablespoons olive oil
½ pint red wine vinegar
4 tablespoons hot paprika or
   cayenne pepper

4 cloves garlic, crushed
1 teaspoon black peppercorns
1 teaspoon oregano
1 bay leaf, crumbled
½ teaspoon salt

Combine all the ingredients in a bottle, shake well to mix, and put in a cool place, or refrigerate, for 4 or 5 days for the flavour to develop. Shake a few drops on meat or poultry.

Brine

¼ pound coarse salt
¾ pint water

Mix the salt and water thoroughly and use to baste meats.

Salsa Para Asados

BARBECUE SAUCE   *Uruguay*

[Makes about 1¼ pints]
½ pint olive oil
¼ pint red wine vinegar
8 cloves garlic, chopped
2 ounces finely chopped parsley
1 teaspoon oregano

1 teaspoon thyme
2 teaspoons hot paprika or cayenne
   pepper
Salt, freshly ground pepper

Combine all the ingredients and mix thoroughly. Allow to stand for 2 or 3 hours before serving. Serve with barbecued meats. This sauce may also be used as a marinade.

POT-AU-FEUS

The pot-au-feu (literally, pot on the fire) is one of the earliest cooking methods and probably goes back to the Bronze Age. Bronze cauldrons from 3500 B.C. are not very much different from the casseroles and kettles in use today, and there is hardly a country on earth that does not have a pot-au-feu in its repertoire. In Latin America this type of stew may be called a *sancocho* (literally parboiled, a dish where foods are added to the pot after some have already been partially cooked), a *pozole* (from an Aztec word meaning beans boiled with other things), a *puchero* (a glazed earthenware pot for cooking meat and vegetables together), a *carbonada* (a meat stew from the New World), a *cocido* (a cooked meat dish), and *ajiaco* (a dish made of boiled meat and vegetables from South America). Essentially, as elsewhere, it is a whole meal cooked in a single pot on top of the stove.

In Latin America over the years versions of the pot-au-feu have served as plantation meals, useful for feeding large numbers of people. There is often an enormously long list of ingredients including the marvellous root vegetables, the yams, taros, and cassava, that flourish in this region, where many of them originated; they vary in texture and flavour and lend variety to any stew they grace. Plantains are another widely used ingredient, as are pumpkins and, of course, the greatest of all Inca achievements, the potato. Meats introduced by Spain and Portugal—beef, kid, lamb, chicken, and pork—are all used. So are beans, both the indigenous beans (*Phaseolus vulgaris*, kidney, haricot, lima, turtle, etc.) and others such as chickpeas, brought by Spain from the Middle East. In addition there are all the green vegetables, and onions, and spring onions, and garlic—a grand assemblage, needing only a degree of selection, and a knowledge of when to add them to the pot.

These dishes are still very popular in Latin America for parties and family gatherings, since it is not really possible to cook them for small numbers like two or four. They are usually presented in a grand manner with various meats on one platter, vegetables on another, the soup in a large tureen, sauces on the side, and the table set with generous-sized rimmed soup plates. With a little planning, they are easy and you don't have to spend time at the last minute in the kitchen, since the ingredients can all be prepared ahead of time, the work being mostly the peeling and cutting up of vegetables. What is essential is a large enough pot; I have often solved this problem by using two fairly big casseroles and dividing the ingredients equally between them. Since such a dish comprises the entire meal, the whole stove is available for its cooking. Permutations and combinations of ingredients have resulted in a group of wonderfully diverse dishes.

Carbonada en Zapallo

VEAL STEW IN BAKED PUMPKIN   *Argentina*

West Indian pumpkin *(calabaza)* is available in many Caribbean shops
and is ideal for this colourful and quite spectacular dish, as it is usually
possible to get just the size needed. However, any large pumpkin
can be used. The stew is served from the pumpkin itself, which plays
a dual role as both container and ingredient. It will be very soft and
mashes into the sauce, thickening it, and its flavour mingles with the
stew.

[Serves 6 to 8]

A 10- to 12-pound pumpkin
4 tablespoons vegetable oil
2 pounds veal, cut into 1-inch
   cubes
1 large onion, finely chopped
1 sweet green pepper, seeded and
   chopped
1 or 2 fresh hot peppers, seeded and
   chopped (optional)
1 large tomato, peeled and chopped
¾ pint chicken stock
½ pint dry white wine

1 pound potatoes, peeled and cut
   into 1-inch cubes
1 pound sweet potatoes, peeled and
   cut into 1-inch cubes
2 ears corn, cut into 1-inch slices
2 large pears, peeled and sliced
3 large peaches, peeled, stoned, and
   sliced
1 tablespoon chopped chives
1 tablespoon sugar
Salt, freshly ground pepper
3 ounces long-grain rice, soaked for
   1 hour and drained

Scrub the pumpkin. Cut a slice off the top to make a lid, then scrape
out the seeds and stringy fibres from the pumpkin and lid. Bake the
pumpkin on a baking sheet in a preheated moderate oven (350° F.,
180° C., gas 4) for 45 minutes.

169

Meanwhile, heat the oil in a heavy frying pan and sauté the veal pieces until they are golden all over. Lift them out into a flameproof casserole with a slotted spoon. In the fat remaining in the pan sauté the onion, pepper, and hot peppers, if using, until the onion is soft. Add the tomato and cook until the mixture is well blended, about 5 minutes. Add to the casserole with the chicken stock and wine. Bring to the boil, reduce the heat, and simmer, covered, for 40 minutes. Add the potatoes and sweet potatoes and cook 15 minutes. Add the corn and cook 5 minutes longer. Remove from the heat and add the pears, peaches, chives, and sugar. Season to taste with salt and pepper. Add the rice. Transfer the contents of the casserole to the pumpkin. Replace the lid and bake in a preheated moderate oven (350° F., 180° C., gas 4) for 30 minutes or until the rice is cooked. Transfer the pumpkin to a large serving platter and serve directly from it, taking care when scooping out the cooked pumpkin not to break the shell.

Variation: If liked, 2 quinces, peeled and sliced, may be added when the potatoes and sweet potatoes are put into the casserole.

Variation: Lean beef chuck may be used instead of veal.

Variation: Six dried apricots, soaked for 20 minutes in cold water, drained, and quartered, may be used instead of the peaches.

Carbonada Criolla

BEEF STEW, ARGENTINE STYLE   *Argentina*

This is a simpler, less spectacular version of *Carbonada en Zapallo* (Veal Stew in Baked Pumpkin). Once more it demonstrates the Argentine flair for combining meat and fruit.

[Serves 6]

4 tablespoons olive oil

2 pounds lean beef, cut into 1-inch cubes

1 large onion, finely chopped

1 clove garlic, chopped

3 medium tomatoes, peeled and chopped

½ teaspoon oregano

1 bay leaf

1 teaspoon sugar

1 tablespoon tomato paste

Salt, freshly ground pepper

½ pint beef stock

½ pint dry red wine

1 pound sweet potatoes, peeled and sliced

1 pound potatoes, peeled and sliced

1 pound pumpkin, peeled and sliced

6 small peaches, peeled

4 ears corn, each cut into 3 slices

Heat the oil in a large, heavy casserole and sauté the beef until it is lightly browned all over. Push it to the side and add the onion and garlic. Sauté the onion until it is soft. Add the tomatoes and cook for 5 minutes longer. Add the oregano, bay leaf, sugar, tomato paste, salt and pepper to taste, the stock, and the wine. Cover and simmer for 1½ hours, or until the meat is almost tender. Add the sweet potatoes and potatoes and a little more stock and wine if necessary to cover. Simmer for 10 minutes, then add the pumpkin and peaches, and simmer for a further 10 minutes. Add the corn and cook 5 minutes longer, or until all the ingredients are tender. Some cooks add 3 ounces rice or vermicelli during the last 20 minutes of cooking.

Sancocho Especial

SPECIAL BOILED DINNER   *Colombia*

The Spanish verb *sancochar* means to parboil and has come to be applied to a number of South American dishes of the pot-au-feu family in the sense of adding new ingredients to already parboiled ones in the pot. The more ingredients there are in a *sancocho*, the more of a party dish it becomes. This one is very festive. It has to be done ahead of time, as it takes about a week. Simplified by the omission of some of the vegetables and meats, it will still be very good indeed. The salt beef gives a distinctive, though not pronounced, flavour to this special *sancocho*.

[Serves 6 to 8]

1 pound beef chuck, cut into 1½-inch cubes

1 pound lean pork, cut into 1½-inch cubes

1 pound salt beef, well washed and cut into 1½-inch cubes (see below)

2 large onions, sliced

3 cloves garlic, chopped

2 large tomatoes, peeled, seeded, and chopped

1 pound yucca root (cassava), peeled and sliced

2½ pints beef stock

2½ pints chicken stock

A 3½-pound chicken, cut into serving pieces

1 pound sweet potatoes, peeled and sliced

1 pound yams, peeled and sliced

1 pound pumpkin, peeled and cubed

1 pound potatoes, peeled and sliced

2 green plantains, peeled and cut into 2-inch slices

2 ripe plantains, peeled and cut into 2-inch slices

3 ears corn, each cut into 3 slices

Salt, freshly ground pepper

3 or 4 limes, quartered

Put the beef, pork, salt beef, onions, garlic, tomatoes, yucca, and the

171

beef and chicken stock into a pot large enough to hold all the ingredients. Bring to the boil over moderate heat, skim off the froth, and reduce the heat so that the liquid barely moves. Cook, covered, for 1¼ hours. Add the chicken pieces, sweet potatoes, yams, pumpkin, potatoes, and green and ripe plantains and simmer until the chicken is tender, about 45 minutes longer. Add the corn, season to taste with salt and pepper, and cook for 5 minutes longer.

Arrange the meats on a warm platter, the vegetables on another warm platter, and pour the broth into a soup tureen. Serve in large soup plates with side dishes of quartered limes, and *Salsa do Ají* (Hot Pepper Sauce) page 299.

Salt beef, Colombia style. The salt beef, which is a special feature of this dish, is easy to do, and once done keeps indefinitely in the refrigerator. It is well worth the effort.

Cut a 3- to 4-pound piece of silverside or topside into horizontal slices about ½ inch thick, stopping short of the far side of the meat so that it opens like a book. Pour 1 pound salt over the beef, between the slices, and on the top and bottom. Place on a large platter and cover lightly with butter muslin. Leave to stand in a cool place overnight and in the morning pour off the liquid that has accumulated. There will be a lot of it the first day. Check that the meat is still heavily coated with salt, adding more if necessary. Repeat the process, leaving the beef to stand for another 24 hours and again pouring off the liquid. If necessary add more salt. Place on a piece of heavy aluminum foil, or on a platter, cover with cheese cloth, and put in the sun to dry, turning the meat over daily. It will take about a week. Shake out the excess salt, wrap the beef in foil, and store in the refrigerator. Wash well before using. I have found that Brazilian *carne sêca* (sun-dried salt beef, or jerked beef) works very well or use ordinary salt beef. If plantains are not available, use unripe (green) bananas for green plantains and barely ripe bananas for the ripe plantains. Reduce the cooking time to about 20 minutes for green bananas, 5 minutes for the barely ripe ones.

Pozole Tapatío

POZOLE, GUADALAJARA STYLE   *Mexico*

Tapatío is an affectionate term for the people of Guadalajara, the capital of Jalisco, and is also used for special dishes from the city. It comes from a colonial dance from Guadalajara, the *Jarabe Tapatío* (The Hat Dance), those who danced it being *tapatíos*. In Mexico the hominy used here would not always be bought canned but is very often prepared at home. Whole, large white corn kernels are soaked overnight, then boiled with lime. The skins are then rubbed off and the "*cabecita*," little head, at the base removed. The corn is then ready to be cooked. It is a long and time-consuming process and I have found canned whole hominy an excellent substitute. If canned hominy is not available use whole corn kernels.

[Serves 8 to 10]
6 ancho *chilies*
3 *pig's feet*
1 *head garlic, peeled*
5 *pints chicken stock*
1 *pound pork loin, cut into 1-inch cubes*

A 3½- to 4-pound chicken, cut into serving pieces
Salt
12 *ounces canned whole hominy or use whole corn kernels*

FOR THE GARNISH

1 *large onion, finely chopped*
½ *head iceberg lettuce, shredded*
1 *bunch radishes*
½ *pound Spanish fresh cheese, or Caerphilly, white Cheshire or mild Cheddar (optional)*
Oregano

Ground hot pepper, or hot pepper sauce such as Tabasco
Fresh hot tortillas, or tortillas cut into triangles and fried in hot lard or vegetable oil
3 *limes or lemons, cut into wedges*

Break off the stems and shake the seeds out of the chilies. Rinse the chilies and tear them into pieces. Put them into a bowl with ½ pint hot water and leave to soak for 1 hour, turning them from time to time. Put them into a blender or food processor and reduce to a purée. Set aside.

Put the pig's feet into a large saucepan with the garlic and chicken stock. Bring to the boil, reduce the heat, cover, and simmer for 3 hours. Add the pork loin and simmer for 1 hour, then add the chicken pieces and the puréed chilies. Add a little salt if necessary. Simmer for 40 minutes, add the hominy or corn, and cook for 5 minutes longer. By this time all the ingredients should be tender. Simmer for a little longer if necessary.

To serve put the meats and broth into a large soup tureen and set the table with large-rimmed soup plates. Put the onion, lettuce, radishes, and crumbled cheese into bowls, and the oregano and ground hot pepper or hot pepper sauce into small bowls. Serve the tortillas, in a straw basket, wrapped in a napkin. To eat, add the garnishes to each serving of meat and broth, with squeezes of lime or lemon juice.

Cozido à Brasileira

STEW, BRAZILIAN STYLE   *Brazil*

This is a dish from São Paulo that was taken by Paulistas to Minas Gerais. I have met it both in the new capital, Belo Horizonte, and the old one, Ouro Prêto. This recipe was given me by the mother of a good friend, Gilberto Rizzo, a Paulista.

[Serves 12]

2 pounds topside of beef, cut into 1-inch cubes
6 pork chops, boned
4 medium onions, grated
4 cloves garlic, crushed
4 spring onions, including the green tops
2 or 3 sprigs each parsley and fresh coriander
Beef broth
A 3-pound chicken, cut into 6 pieces
A 2-pound linguiça sausage, or use a similar sausage such as Spanish longaniza or Polish kielbasa or boiling ring
6 small whole carrots, scraped
1 small stick celery, with stalks cut into 3- to 4-inch pieces
1 small whole cabbage
6 small whole potatoes, peeled or scraped
3 small sweet potatoes, peeled and halved
1½ pounds cassava root (manioc, yucca), peeled and cut into 2-inch slices
2 pounds pumpkin, peeled and cut into 2-inch cubes
2 ears corn, each cut into 3 slices
Salt, freshly ground pepper
3 medium slightly underripe bananas, or 2 half-ripe plantains
¼ pound cassava meal (manioc, mandioca)

In a saucepan large enough to hold all the ingredients put the beef, pork chops, onions, garlic, parsley and coriander sprigs, and enough beef broth to cover. Simmer, covered, over low heat for 1 hour. At the end of that time add the chicken, sausage, and more broth as necessary to cover, and cook for 30 minutes longer. Add to the pan the carrots, celery, cabbage, potatoes, sweet potatoes, cassava root, pumpkin, corn, salt and pepper to taste, and more broth to cover.

In a separate saucepan put the bananas or plantains, cover with cold water, and simmer, covered, for 20 minutes. If using plantains, cook them for 30 minutes. When cool enough to handle, lift out and peel. Halve the bananas, or cut the plantains into thirds, and add to the ingredients in the pan just long enough to heat through. Have ready two large, deep, warmed platters. Arrange the meats on one of the platters. Place the cabbage in the centre of the second platter and cut it into wedges. Arrange the other vegetables on the platter in decorative groups.

Remove and discard the parsley and coriander sprigs from the broth. Moisten the meats and vegetables with some of the broth. Measure 1¾ pints of the broth and pour it into a saucepan. Stir in the cassava meal, then simmer, stirring constantly, over moderate heat until the cassava has thickened the liquid to a porridgelike consistency. Pour this *pirão* into a bowl and serve it as a sauce with the *cozido*.

Cocido a la Dominicana

SPANISH STEW, DOMINICAN STYLE   *Dominican Republic*

[Serves 6 to 8]

½ pound dried chickpeas, or a
   1-pound can
4 tablespoons vegetable oil
A 4-pound chicken, cut into
   serving pieces
½ pound beef, cut into 1-inch cubes
A ½ pound slice of smoked ham,
   such as prosciutto or Spanish
   Jamon Serrano, cut into 1-inch
   cubes
½ pound chorizo (hot Spanish)
   sausages, sliced, or use hot
   Italian sausages
1 medium onion, chopped

4 cloves garlic, chopped
2 pounds potatoes, peeled and sliced
1 large carrot, scraped and sliced
1 small cabbage, cut into 8 wedges
½ pound pumpkin, peeled and
   cubed
1 fresh hot red or green pepper, left
   whole with stem on
1 bay leaf
1 tablespoon white vinegar
3½ pints beef stock
Salt
6 small stoned green olives, sliced
1 tablespoon finely chopped parsley

If using dried chickpeas, soak them overnight in cold water to cover. Drain, cover with fresh water, and simmer, covered, for 1 hour. Drain, measure the liquid, and use it to replace some of the beef stock. Set aside. If using canned chickpeas, drain, rinse in cold water, and set aside.

Heat the oil and sauté the chicken pieces until golden on both sides. Transfer to a large saucepan. In the oil remaining in the pan sauté the beef cubes, ham, and sausages, and add them to the saucepan. In the remaining oil, adding a little more if necessary, though the sausages will give off quite a lot of fat, sauté the onion and garlic until the onion is soft. Add the mixture to the saucepan with the potatoes, carrot, cabbage, pumpkin, whole hot pepper, bay leaf, vinegar, the chickpeas and liquid or the canned, drained, chickpeas, the stock, and salt to taste. Cover and simmer until all the ingredients are tender, about 1 hour. The pumpkin will have disintegrated, slightly thickening the broth. Remove and discard the bay leaf and hot pepper. Transfer the stew to a warmed tureen or serving dish, add the olives, and sprinkle with the parsley.

Variation: There is an interesting variation, *Sancocho de Longaniza y Tocino* (Sausage and Bacon Stew), also from the Dominican Republic. Soak 1½ pounds bacon, in a single piece, for 15 minutes in cold water, rinse, drain, and cut into 1-inch cubes. Slice 2 pounds *longaniza* (Spanish garlic) sausages, or *linguiça* or *kielbasa* or boiling ring into 1-inch slices. Heat 4 tablespoons vegetable oil in a frying pan and sauté the bacon cubes and sausage slices until lightly browned. Transfer to a flameproof casserole. In the fat remaining in the pan sauté 1 large onion, finely chopped, 3 cloves garlic, chopped, and 1 sweet green pepper, seeded and chopped, and add to the casserole with 1 tablespoon red wine vinegar and 2 tablespoons Seville orange juice, or two-thirds orange juice and one-third lime or lemon juice. Add 5 pints beef stock, and simmer, covered, for 1½ hours, then add 1 pound cassava (yucca) root, peeled and sliced, 1 pound taro (*yautía*), peeled and sliced, 1 pound yam (*ñame*), and 1 pound West Indian pumpkin (*calabaza*), peeled and cubed. Season to taste with salt, freshly ground pepper, 1 teaspoon oregano, and hot pepper sauce (such as Tabasco) to taste. Simmer, covered, until all the ingredients are tender. In a separate saucepan, in water to cover, boil 2 green plantains in their skins for 30 minutes, cool, peel, slice, and add to the casserole just long enough to heat them through. The plantains may be omitted, if preferred, or green (underripe) bananas may be used instead, in which case boil them for 20 minutes. Put the meats and vegetables on a heated serving platter, pour the broth into a tureen, and serve in soup plates. Serves 6 to 8.

Sancocho de Gallina

CHICKEN POT-AU-FEU   *Venezuela*

Shops selling tropical foods carry an astonishing variety of root vegetables so if *apio (arracacha)* is not available, use taro (*yautía, dasheen*), or white sweet potato (*boniato*), or more than one type of yam. None of the vegetables has a dominating flavour, and all cook in about the same time so it is easy—and perfectly acceptable—to make substitutions. It is also a good way to get to know more about these delicious vegetables.

[Serves 8 to 10]

Two 3½-pound chickens, cut into
  serving pieces
5 pints chicken stock
1 leek, well washed and halved
  lengthwise
1 large onion, chopped
1 head garlic, peeled

3 white turnips, peeled and
  quartered
3 carrots, scraped and cut into 4
  slices
1 large tomato, peeled, seeded, and
  chopped
2 or 3 sprigs fresh coriander
Salt, freshly ground pepper

THE VEGETABLES

1 pound cassava root (yucca),
  peeled and cut into ½-inch slices
1 pound pumpkin, peeled and cut
  into ½-inch slices
1 pound yam, peeled and cut into
  ½-inch slices
1 pound apio (arracacha), peeled
  and cut into ½-inch slices

1 pound potatoes, peeled and cut
  into ½-inch slices
1 small cabbage, blanched and cut
  into 8 wedges
3 ears corn, each cut into 4 slices
2 green plantains (optional), or 3
  large green bananas

Put all the ingredients except those listed under vegetables into a
large saucepan. Bring to the boil, reduce the heat to a bare simmer,
and cook, covered, for 30 minutes. Add all the vegetables except the
corn and plantains, and continue cooking until the chicken and vegetables are tender, 20 to 30 minutes. Add the corn in the last 5 minutes
of cooking. In a separate saucepan boil the unpeeled green plantains
in water to cover for 30 minutes. When they are cool enough to
handle, lift out, peel, and cut into 1-inch slices. Add to the chicken
and vegetables just long enough to heat through. If using green
bananas, cook for 15 minutes, peel, slice, and add to the pot. Arrange
the chicken pieces on a large, heated serving platter and surround
with the vegetables. Strain the soup into a soup tureen. Serve in soup
plates with *Guasacaca* (Avocado Sauce) page 304, or *Salsa de Ají* (Hot
Pepper Sauce), page 299 separately.

Traditionally a large stewing hen *(gallina)* is used for this dish, but
stewing hens are no longer readily available and require long, slow
cooking. I find 3½-pound chickens very satisfactory. The dish can
also be made with 4 pounds lean beef, cut into 1-inch cubes. It is then
called *Hervido*.

Puchero Estilo Mexicano

MEXICAN POT-AU-FEU   *Mexico*

If you want to present everything in this pot-au-feu at the same time, serve the soup in bowls, the meats and vegetables on plates. The green vegetables may be varied to suit the cook. Cabbage and turnips may be added, chayotes may be used instead of courgettes.

[Serves 8 to 10]

½ *pound dried chickpeas, or a*
  1-pound can
1 *pound lean beef chuck, cut into*
  1-inch cubes
1 *pound lamb, cut into 1-inch cubes*
½ *pound raw ham, cubed*
½ *pound chorizo, sliced*
1 *large onion, chopped*
2 *cloves garlic, chopped*
⅛ *teaspoon peppercorns*
2½ *pints chicken stock*
2½ *pints beef stock*
Salt
A 3½- to 4-pound chicken, cut into
  serving pieces
4 *carrots, scraped and sliced*
4 *courgettes, sliced*
1 *pound green beans, cut into*
  ½-inch pieces

1 *pound sweet potatoes, peeled and*
  sliced
3 *ears corn, cut into 1-inch slices*
4 *tablespoons lard or vegetable oil*
1 *pound potatoes, peeled and sliced*
2 *green plantains, or 2 large green*
  (underripe) bananas, peeled and
  cut into 1-inch slices
3 *large peaches, peeled, stoned and*
  quartered
3 *large pears, peeled, cored, and*
  quartered
1 *tablespoon chopped fresh*
  coriander
Fresh hot tortillas
Guacamole (Avocado Sauce), page
  303
2 *limes or lemons, cut into wedges*
Hot pepper sauce (Tabasco or any of
  the sauces on pages 299–302)

Soak the chickpeas overnight, drain, and rinse. Put them into a large soup pot. If using canned chickpeas, drain, rinse, and set aside until later. Add to the pot the beef, lamb, ham, chorizo, onion, garlic, peppercorns, chicken and beef stock, and salt to taste, if necessary. Bring to the boil, skim any froth that comes to the surface, reduce the heat, cover, and simmer gently for 45 minutes. Add the chicken pieces and simmer for 30 minutes longer. Add the carrots, courgettes, green beans, sweet potatoes, and canned chickpeas, if using, and cook for 15 minutes longer. Add the corn and cook for 5 minutes.

Heat the lard or vegetable oil and sauté the potatoes and plantains or green bananas until tender. Lift out onto a platter and keep warm.

Take ½ pint of stock from the pot and gently poach the peaches and pears, between 10 and 15 minutes.

Check that all the ingredients are tender. Arrange the meats in the centre of a large platter and surround with the vegetables and fruits. Moisten with a little stock and keep warm. The chickpeas may be left in the soup, or put on the platter. Pour the soup into a tureen and sprinkle with the chopped coriander. Serve the soup in bowls. Serve the meats, fruits, vegetables, and the fried potatoes and plantains as a second course accompanied by hot tortillas, *Guacamole*, lime or lemon wedges, and hot pepper sauce.

Poultry

AVES

CHICKEN

There is no doubt that chicken—inexpensive and extremely versatile—is the favourite bird in the kitchens of Latin America. Most Latin American recipes are variations on a poaching theme. Chicken is gently simmered with herbs, spices, vegetables and deliciously sauced in a great variety of ways. Also, corn (maize) plays a special role in dishes like *Cuscuz de Galinha* (Garnished Steamed Chicken and Cornmeal) and *Pastel de Choclo con Relleno de Pollo* (Chicken Pie with Corn Topping)—see Substantial Dishes.

Out of a vast array of recipes I have chosen dishes that I have enjoyed, not just once, but time and again.

Pollo con Naranja

CHICKEN IN ORANGE SAUCE   *Argentina*

[Serves 4]
A 3- to 3½-pound chicken,
   quartered
Salt, freshly ground pepper
1½ ounces butter
½ pint chicken stock
½ pint orange juice
Grated rind of 1 orange
1 tablespoon flour
2 eggs
1 tablespoon double cream

Season the chicken pieces with salt and pepper. Heat the butter in a heavy casserole and sauté the chicken pieces, one or two at a time, until golden on both sides. Set aside as they are done. Pour off the fat from the casserole into a small bowl and reserve. Return the chicken pieces to the casserole, putting the legs in first with the breasts on top, as the breasts cook more quickly. Add the chicken stock, orange juice, and grated orange rind. Cover and simmer for 30 to 45 minutes, or until the chicken is done. Lift out the chicken onto a serving dish and keep warm. Mix the flour with a tablespoon of the reserved fat and stir it into the liquid in the casserole. Bring to the boil and cook, stirring, for a minute or two. Reduce the heat to low. Beat the eggs with the cream. Stir 1 cup of the thickened liquid from the casserole, 1 tablespoon at a time, into the egg mixture, then pour the mixture into the casserole and cook, stirring with a wire whisk, until the sauce is lightly thickened, a minute or two. Do not let the sauce boil, as it will curdle. Pour some of the sauce over the chicken and serve the rest in a sauceboat. Serve with rice or mashed or French fried potatoes.

Frango com Bananas

CHICKEN WITH BANANAS   *Brazil*

This chicken dish from Brazil's Mato Grosso is simmered with white wine and tomatoes, then topped with lightly fried bananas, a most attractive and unusual combination of flavours, slightly sweet, slightly sour.

[Serves 4]

A 3-pound chicken, quartered
4 tablespoons lemon juice
2 teaspoons salt
1½ ounces butter
1 medium onion, grated
2 tomatoes, peeled, seeded, and
  chopped

⅛ teaspoon sugar
½ pint dry white wine
4 tablespoons vegetable oil
6 ripe bananas, peeled and halved
  lengthwise
¼ pound grated Parmesan cheese
½ ounce butter

Season the chicken with the lemon juice and salt. Heat the butter in a flameproof casserole and stir in the onion, tomatoes, and sugar. Add the chicken pieces and any of their liquid. Simmer for 5 minutes, uncovered, turning the chicken pieces once. Add the wine, cover the casserole, and simmer until the chicken is tender, about 45 minutes.

Heat the oil in a pan and sauté the bananas until they are lightly browned on both sides. Arrange the bananas, cut side down, on top

181

of the chicken pieces and sprinkle them with the grated cheese. Dot with the butter, cut into little bits. Place the casserole in a preheated hot oven (400° F., 200° C., gas 5) and bake until the cheese is lightly browned, about 10 minutes. Serve with white rice.

Pollo en Piña

CHICKEN IN PINEAPPLE   *Guatemala*

[Serves 4 to 6]

A 3½- to 4-pound chicken, cut into serving pieces

1 ripe pineapple, weighing about 1½ pounds, peeled, cored, and coarsely chopped, or a 1-pound can unsweetened pineapple, in its own juice

2 medium onions, finely chopped

2 cloves garlic, chopped

2 whole cloves

A 1-inch piece of stick cinnamon

2 bay leaves

¼ pint olive oil

¼ pint white vinegar

¼ pint dry sherry

2 medium tomatoes, peeled and coarsely chopped

Salt, freshly ground pepper

Chicken stock, if necessary

Put the chicken pieces into a heavy casserole. If using fresh pineapple, be careful to save and use all the juice. If using canned pineapple, use the juice. Add all the rest of the ingredients, including salt and pepper to taste. If using fresh pineapple, it may be necessary to add a little chicken stock to cover the chicken pieces, as the fresh fruit will not have as much juice as the canned. Cover and simmer over low heat until the chicken is tender, about 45 minutes. If the sauce is very abundant, cook partially covered for the last 15 minutes. Serve with rice.

Ají de Gallina

CHICKEN IN PEPPER SAUCE   *Peru*

[Serves 6]

A 3½- to 4-pound chicken, quartered

1¼ pints chicken stock, about

4 tablespoons vegetable oil

2 medium onions, finely chopped

2 cloves garlic, minced

4 ounces fresh breadcrumbs

¾ pint milk

8 fresh hot red or green peppers, seeded

2 medium tomatoes, peeled and seeded

4 ounces walnuts, ground

Salt, freshly ground pepper

2 ounces grated Parmesan cheese

Put the chicken pieces into a large flameproof casserole with the stock, adding a little more if necessary to cover, and poach until the chicken is tender, about 45 minutes. Let the chicken cool in the stock. Remove the skin and bones and shred the meat into pieces about 1½ inches long and ¼ inch wide. Set the shredded chicken aside and reserve the stock.

Heat the oil and sauté the onions and garlic until the onions are golden. Soak the breadcrumbs in the milk and mash to a paste. Add the breadcrumb mixture to the casserole. In a blender or food processor reduce the peppers and tomatoes to a purée and stir into the casserole. Add the ground walnuts. Season to taste with salt and pepper, and cook, stirring, over moderate heat for about 5 minutes. Add the chicken, ½ pint of the stock, and the cheese, and cook just until heated through. The sauce should be thick. Serve the chicken and sauce on a heated platter surrounded by halved, boiled potatoes, hardboiled eggs, sliced lengthwise, and black olives.

Ajiaco de Pollo Bogotano

BOGOTÁ CHICKEN STEW   *Colombia*

[Serves 6]

2 ounces butter

A 3½-pound chicken, cut into
  serving pieces

2 large onions, finely chopped

8 medium potatoes, peeled and
  thinly sliced

3½ pints chicken stock

12 *whole, peeled* papas criollas, *if
  available (otherwise 6 new
  potatoes)*

Salt, freshly ground pepper

2 ears corn, each cut into 3 slices

3 tablespoons capers

¼ pint double cream

Heat the butter in a heavy casserole and sauté the chicken pieces with the onions until the chicken is golden on both sides. Add the thinly sliced potatoes and the stock, cover, and cook over very low heat until the chicken is about half done and the potatoes are beginning to disintegrate, about 25 minutes. Add the 6 new potatoes and continue cooking until both chicken and potatoes are tender. With a slotted spoon, remove the chicken pieces and potatoes from the casserole and keep warm. Work the stock through a sieve. It will have been thickened by the sliced potatoes. Return the stock to the casserole, season to taste with salt and pepper, add the chicken and potatoes, the corn and capers, and simmer for 5 minutes longer. Add the cream and continue cooking just long enough to heat it through. Serve in deep soup plates with *Ají de Huevo* (Avocado Sauce), page 305, on the side.

Cecilia Blanco de Mendoza's Ajiaco

CHICKEN STEW   *Colombia*

This is a very special *ajiaco* (chicken stew) with subtle seasonings that include *guascas* or *huascas*, a Colombian herb whose botanical name is *Galinsoga parviflora Lineo*. It is sold, dried and ground, in jars in Colombian markets and has a mild flavour vaguely reminiscent, to my palate, of Jerusalem artichokes, to which I am assured by a Colombian botanist, it bears no relationship whatsoever. *Guascas* will enhance any soup or stew, as the flavour is delicate and unobtrusive, but though *guascas* is an attractive extra, it is not essential to the deliciousness of this dish, which depends on a combination of flavours including spring onions and coriander.

Also in the stew are three types of potatoes: large baking potatoes, small red potatoes, and *papas criollas*. These last are delicious small Colombian potatoes that are sometimes available in Latin American markets. They have yellow flesh and stay whole through prolonged cooking. Small white new potatoes make a very good substitute, perhaps not as pretty to look at, but equal otherwise.

[Serves 6]

A 3½- to 4-pound chicken, left whole
4 whole spring onions
6 sprigs fresh coriander
1 teaspoon ground guascas
1¼ pints chicken stock or water
Salt, freshly ground pepper
4 small ears corn, cut into 1-inch slices
2 pounds large baking potatoes, peeled and cut into ¼-inch slices

2 pounds small red potatoes, peeled and cut into ¼-inch slices
1 pound papas criollas or small white new potatoes, unpeeled
¾ pint milk
1 small can Vienna sausages, sliced
4 ounces cooked baby peas
1 or 2 tablespoons capers
2 hardboiled eggs, sliced
6 tablespoons double cream

In a large pan combine the chicken, spring onions, coriander, *guascas* (if available), chicken stock or water, and salt and pepper to taste. Bring to the boil and skim off any froth that rises to the surface, reduce the heat, cover, and simmer gently until the chicken is tender, about 45 minutes. Let the chicken cool in the broth, lift it out, cut it into 6 serving pieces, and set it aside, covered. Strain the broth and add the corn to it. Bring the broth to a simmer over moderate heat and add all the potatoes. Simmer until the broth thickens. The white potatoes will disintegrate and thicken the broth, the red potatoes will retain some texture, and the *papas criollas* or new potatoes will remain whole. Add the milk and the chicken pieces and cook just long enough to heat them through. To serve, have ready six large, deep soup plates. Put a piece of chicken in each, 2 or 3 slices of Vienna sausage, 1 tablespoon peas, a few capers, a slice of egg, and the broth, making sure each gets a *papa criolla* or new potato, Pour a tablespoon of double cream over each serving. Serve with knife, fork, and soup spoon.

Pollo Borracho

DRUNKEN CHICKEN   *Argentina*

This is a typical *criollo* dish and with slight variations occurs all over Latin America.

[Serves 4]
½ ounce butter
½ pound boiled ham, cut into strips about 2 inches by ¼ inch
A 3½-pound chicken, cut into 4 serving pieces
Salt, freshly ground pepper

¼ teaspoon ground cumin
¼ teaspoon ground coriander
4 tablespoons white wine vinegar
¾ pint dry white wine
½ pint chicken stock, about
3 cloves garlic, minced
12 medium pimiento-stuffed olives
3 tablespoons capers

Melt the butter in a flameproof casserole. Make a layer of one-third of the ham. Season the chicken pieces with the salt, pepper, cumin, and coriander, and add the chicken legs to the casserole with another third of the ham on top. Arrange the chicken breasts over the ham and sprinkle with the remaining ham strips. Pour in the vinegar, wine, and enough chicken stock to cover. Add the garlic, cover, and simmer over low heat for 45 minutes, or until the chicken is tender. Rinse the olives and soak them for 15 minutes in cold water. Drain. Rinse and drain the capers. Place the chicken pieces and ham strips in a serving dish and keep warm. Measure the liquid in the casserole

185

and reduce it, over brisk heat, to ¾ pint. Moisten the chicken with a little of the liquid and serve the rest in a gravy boat. Garnish the chicken with the olives and capers.

If liked, the sauce may be lightly thickened. Mix 1 tablespoon flour with ½ ounce butter, stir into the liquid, and simmer over low heat, stirring constantly, until the sauce is thickened. Serve with plain boiled potatoes or white rice and a green vegetable or salad.

Pollo en Pepían Dulce

MAYAN CHICKEN FRICASSEE   *Guatemala*

Because Guatemala was the heart of the Mayan empire, with its capital city of Tikal, the kitchen of post-Columbian Guatemala is close to that of Yucatán in Mexico. This dish unites a medley of flavours, which the chicken absorbs during cooking. They blend harmoniously in the sauce, which is as thick as double cream and delicious with plain rice.

[Serves 6]

A 3½- to 4-pound chicken, cut into serving pieces
¾ pint chicken stock, about
1 tablespoon sesame seeds
3 ounces pepitas (Mexican pumpkin seeds)
3 sweet red peppers, seeded and coarsely chopped, or 5 canned pimientos, chopped
3 medium tomatoes, peeled and coarsely chopped

1 medium onion, chopped
2 cloves garlic, chopped
2 tablespoons lard or vegetable oil
4 tablespoons Seville orange juice, or use two-thirds orange juice and one-third lime juice
½ teaspoon ground allspice
Salt, freshly ground pepper
2 ounces seedless raisins
Butter
1 ounce chopped almonds

Put the chicken pieces into a heavy casserole, pour in the stock, adding a little more to cover, if necessary. Cover and simmer until almost tender, about 30 minutes. In a blender or food processor grind the sesame and pumpkin seeds as fine as possible and shake through a sieve. Set aside. Put the peppers, tomatoes, onion, and garlic into a blender or food processor and reduce to a coarse purée. Mix the purée with the ground sesame and pumpkin seeds. Heat the lard or vegetable oil in a pan, add the purée, and cook, over moderate heat, stirring constantly with a wooden spoon, for 5 minutes. Drain the chicken, reserve the stock, and return the chicken to the casserole. Add to the purée ½ pint of the stock, the Seville orange juice, allspice, and salt and pepper to taste. Stir to mix, and pour over the chicken. Cover and simmer gently until the chicken is tender, about 15 minutes. Add a little more stock if necessary. The sauce should be thick. Soak the raisins in cold water to cover for 15 minutes. Drain thoroughly. Heat a little butter and sauté the almonds until they are golden. Drain. Transfer the chicken and sauce to a warmed serving dish and sprinkle with the raisins and almonds. Serve with rice.

Pollo Verde Almendrado

CHICKEN IN GREEN ALMOND SAUCE   *Mexico*

I find all the Mexican green chicken dishes delicious; this one is enchanting, not only for its very subtle flavour but because the green sauce is pretty to look at.

[Serves 6]

A 3½-pound chicken, cut into serving pieces
¾ pint chicken stock
1 medium onion, chopped
1 clove garlic, chopped
2 ounces parsley sprigs, coarsely chopped
2 ounces coriander sprigs, coarsely chopped

1 heart of cos lettuce, coarsely chopped
1 or 2 fresh hot green peppers, seeded and chopped, or 2 canned jalapeño or 3 canned serrano chilies, seeded and chopped
4 ounces ground almonds
3 tablespoons vegetable oil or lard
Salt

Put the chicken pieces into a heavy casserole with the stock, bring to the boil, reduce the heat, and simmer gently, covered, for 45 minutes, or until tender. Lift the chicken out onto a platter and set aside. Pour the stock into a jug. Rinse out and dry the casserole.

In a blender or food processor combine the onion, garlic, parsley, coriander, lettuce, hot peppers, and almonds, and reduce to a coarse purée. Do not overblend as the finished sauce should have some texture, not entirely smooth. Heat the oil or lard in a large, heavy pan and pour in the purée, which will be almost pastelike because of the almonds. Cook the mixture, stirring constantly with a wooden spoon, for 3 to 4 minutes over moderate heat. Transfer it to a casserole. Stir in the stock, season to taste with salt. Add the chicken pieces, cover, and simmer just long enough to heat the chicken through.

Arroz Blanco (White Rice) is good with this. For a completely Mexican meal, serve the chicken with the rice and with tortillas, *Frijoles* (Beans), and *Guacamole* (Avocado Sauce).

187

Carapulcra

CHICKEN, PORK, AND POTATOES IN PEANUT SAUCE   *Peru*

When I decided to test *carapulcra* in New York, having enjoyed it in Peru, I was told I could regard one of its ingredients, *chuño* or *papaseca* (freeze-dried potato) as optional, to be replaced with fresh potatoes, since I couldn't buy the commercially packaged article. I decided that what the Inca women could do I could do. When the Incas, who were the first people to cultivate the potato back in 2500 B.C., faced crop storage problems, they invented freeze-drying, and there is every reason to believe that they were the first people to do so. Raw, unpeeled potatoes were put outside their houses at night in the icy cold of the Andean highlands, where they froze solid. In the morning they thawed in the sun and the water was trampled out of them by Inca women, and the process repeated until they were thoroughly dry.

The sixteenth floor of a New York high-rise is not to be compared with the Andes, whose soaring peaks topple the imagination, so I put my potatoes, 3 large Idahos, in the freezer overnight. In the morning, since I had a small terrace with a southern exposure, I put them in the sun to thaw. One cannot trample the water out of 3 potatoes—it takes a whole crop to make that possible—so I squeezed the water out of my potatoes by hand. At the end of three days they were like stone, strange skinny objects. The flesh had turned quite dark, almost black. I kept one for two years before I used it, just to see, and it was as good as ever. The others I used in this *carapulcra*. I had a lot of fun making *chuño*, but I can honestly say my Peruvian friends were right when they said it was all right to substitute fresh potatoes for it.

[Serves 6]

2 freeze-dried white potatoes, or 2 fresh potatoes

A 2½-pound chicken, cut into serving pieces

1 pound loin of pork, cut into ¾-inch cubes

¾ pint chicken stock, about

4 tablespoons lard or vegetable oil

1 large onion, finely chopped

4 cloves garlic, minced

½ teaspoon Spanish (hot) paprika or cayenne

⅛ teaspoon ground cumin

Salt, freshly ground pepper

2 ounces roasted peanuts, finely ground

6 small potatoes, freshly cooked

3 hardboiled eggs, sliced

20 medium-sized stoned black or green olives

Put the dried potatoes on to soak in warm water to cover for about 2 hours. If using the fresh potatoes instead of the dried ones, add them to the stew, peeled and diced at the same time the dried potatoes would be added. When the dried potatoes have been soaked, drain them, and chop coarsely. Set aside.

Put the chicken and pork pieces into a saucepan and add enough chicken stock to cover. Cover and simmer until tender. Drain and set the stock aside. Bone the chicken and cut the meat into cubes about the same size as the pork. Set aside with a little stock to moisten the meats.

Rinse out and dry the saucepan or use a flameproof casserole, and heat the lard or oil in it. Add the onion, garlic, hot paprika or cayenne, and cumin, and sauté until the onion is soft. Add the potato and about ½ pint of the reserved stock, cover, and simmer gently until the potato has disintegrated, thickening the mixture, about 1 hour. Season to taste with salt and pepper and stir in the ground peanuts. Cook for a minute or two, then add the chicken and pork pieces. The sauce should be thick, but add a little more stock if necessary. Simmer just long enough to heat through and blend the flavours.

Arrange the chicken and pork mixture on a heated serving platter and garnish it with the fresh, hot potatoes, the hardboiled egg slices, and olives.

Pollo en Salsa de Almendra

CHICKEN IN ALMOND SAUCE   *Mexico*

[Serves 4]
2 ounces butter
A 3- to 3½-pound chicken, cut into serving pieces
1½ pints chicken stock
1 medium onion, finely chopped
1 fresh hot red or green pepper, seeded and finely chopped, or 1 canned serrano *or* jalapeño *chili, rinsed*

4 ounces toasted almonds, finely ground
2 hardboiled eggs, chopped
2 ounces freshly made breadcrumbs
Salt, freshly ground pepper

Heat the butter and sauté the chicken pieces until lightly golden all over. Transfer the chicken to a heatproof casserole, add enough chicken stock to cover, bring to the boil, lower the heat, cover, and simmer gently until the chicken is tender, about 45 minutes. Lift out

189

the chicken pieces and keep warm. Pour the stock into a container and set it aside. Rinse out and dry the casserole.

In the fat remaining in the pan sauté the onion with the hot pepper until the onion is soft. Add the almonds, eggs, breadcrumbs, and salt and pepper to taste, and sauté for a minute or two longer. Stir in ¾ pint of the reserved chicken stock, pour the mixture into a blender or food processor, and reduce it to a purée. Do not overblend. The sauce should have some texture. Return the chicken pieces to the casserole and pour the sauce over them. Simmer just long enough to heat the chicken through. Serve with rice.

Pollo en Pipián de Almendra

CHICKEN STEW WITH ALMONDS   *Mexico*

Pipián is one of the best dishes in the Mexican kitchen and one of the hardest to define. The dictionary of the Spanish Royal Academy says it is an American stew made of meat, chicken, turkey, or other fowl with salt pork and ground almonds. Other dictionaries describe it as a kind of Indian fricassee. The *Nuevo Cocinero Méjicano*, a dictionary published in Paris in 1888, gives a more complete description. It says that *pipián* is a Mexican stew made with red or green peppers, pumpkin seeds, almonds, or oily seeds such as sesame or peanuts. The stew may be made with turkey, chicken, duck or indeed any bird, as well as with meats or fish and shellfish. There are even vegetarian versions using fruits and vegetables. It should not be salted until the moment of serving, as salt is said to make the sauce separate.

[Serves 4]

A 3-pound chicken, cut into serving pieces	6 ancho *chilies*
2 or 3 spring onions	4 ounces almonds, blanched
2 or 3 large sprigs fresh coriander	2 tablespoons lard or vegetable oil
1 carrot, scraped and halved	⅛ teaspoon ground cloves
¾ pint chicken stock, about	¼ teaspoon ground cinnamon
	¼ teaspoon oregano
	Salt

Put the chicken pieces into a large, heavy casserole with the spring onions, coriander, and carrot. Pour in the chicken stock, adding a little more if necessary to cover. Bring to the boil, reduce the heat, and simmer, covered, for 45 minutes, or until the chicken is tender. Lift the chicken pieces out of the stock. Strain and reserve the stock, discarding the solids. Rinse out the casserole and put the chicken pieces back in it. Shake the seeds out of the chilies and rinse them.

Tear them in pieces and put them to soak for 1 hour in about ¼ pint hot water, turning them from time to time. If they absorb all the water, add a little more. Reduce the chilies to a paste in a blender or food processor, using a little of the soaking water. Put them into a bowl. Toast the almonds and pulverize them in a nut grinder, blender, or food processor, shake them through a sieve, and add to the chilies, mixing thoroughly. Heat the lard or oil, add the chili and almond mixture, and sauté, stirring constantly with a wooden spoon, for 4 or 5 minutes over moderate heat. Thin with about ¾ pint of the reserved chicken stock to make a medium-thick sauce. Stir in the cloves, cinnamon, and oregano, and pour over the chicken pieces in the casserole. Cook at a bare simmer over very low heat for 15 minutes, or until the chicken is heated through and the flavours have blended. Season to taste with salt. Serve with rice, beans, tortillas, *guacamole* or other salad, and a green vegetable, if liked.

Despite the solemn warnings in ancient cookbooks and from experienced Mexican cooks, I must confess I have never found that salting the sauce earlier makes it separate, so I leave this question open.

Some cooks reserve the seeds of the *ancho* chilies, toast them, and grind them with the almonds. I have not found this a good idea. The seeds seem to coarsen the sauce and blur the delicate flavour of the almonds. Also more stock has to be added, making too much sauce.

Xinxim de Galinha

CHICKEN WITH SHRIMP AND PEANUT SAUCE   *Brazil*

This is a Bahian dish, as the use of *dendê* (palm) oil indicates. The mixture of flavours is unusual and exciting, but not difficult for the unaccustomed palate to accept.

[Serves 6]
A 3-pound chicken, cut into
  serving pieces
4 tablespoons lime or lemon juice
2 cloves garlic, crushed
Salt
2 tablespoons olive oil
1 medium onion, grated

¼ pound dried shrimp, finely
  ground
2 ounces dry roasted peanuts,
  ground
1 fresh hot red pepper, seeded and
  chopped (optional)
¼ pint chicken stock, about
4 tablespoons dendê (palm) oil

Season the chicken with the lime or lemon juice, the garlic, and salt to taste. Set aside.

191

In a heavy saucepan heat the oil and sauté the onion, dried shrimp, peanuts, and hot pepper for 5 minutes, stirring from time to time. Add the chicken pieces and their liquid, and cook for a few minutes, turning the pieces once. Add the chicken stock, cover, and simmer gently until the chicken is tender, about 30 minutes, turning once during the cooking and adding a little more stock if necessary. When the chicken is tender, taste for seasoning, pour in the *dendê* (palm) oil, and cook for a minute or two longer. The sauce should be thick and not very abundant. Serve with white rice and *Farofa de Azeite de Dendê* (Cassava Meal with Palm Oil) page 266.

Vatapá de Galinha

CHICKEN IN SHRIMP AND ALMOND SAUCE   *Brazil*

Vatapá is one of the great dishes of the Bahian kitchen of Brazil, but it does take quite a lot of work. It is an exciting dish for guests and I find their pleasure in this truly exotic food makes it well worth the effort. The coconut milk can be made ahead of time and tedious jobs like grinding the dried shrimp are made easy with the help of a food processor. I so well remember the first time I had *vatapá* in Salvador, Bahia. It was a revelation, with so many unfamiliar and delicious flavours to beguile the palate.

[Serves 6 to 8]

3 tablespoons olive oil
2 medium onions, finely chopped
4 spring onions, chopped, using white and green parts
2 large cloves garlic, chopped
4 medium tomatoes, peeled, seeded, and chopped
1 or 2 fresh hot peppers, seeded and chopped
Salt, freshly ground pepper
3 tablespoons lime or lemon juice
4 tablespoons fresh coriander, or use flat-leafed parsley

Two 2½-pound chickens, quartered
Chicken stock, if necessary
½ pound finely ground almonds
½ pound dried shrimp, finely ground
1¼ pints thin coconut milk (see page 29)
¼ pint thick coconut milk (see page 29)
1 tablespoon rice flour
4 tablespoons dendê (palm) oil

In a large frying pan heat the oil and sauté the onions, spring onions, garlic, tomatoes, and hot peppers for 5 minutes. Season the mixture to taste with salt and pepper and stir in the lime or lemon juice and the coriander. Add the quartered chickens, cover, and cook until the chickens are tender, 30 to 35 minutes. Add a little chicken stock to the pan if the mixture seems too dry. With a slotted spoon, transfer the chickens to a dish and let them cool. Skin and bone the chickens and chop the meat coarsely. Put the vegetable mixture through a sieve, pressing down hard on the vegetables to extract all the liquid. Discard the solids and reserve the liquid.

In a saucepan combine the almonds, ground shrimp, the thin coconut milk, and the reserved liquid from cooking the chicken. Bring to the boil and simmer for 15 minutes. Add the thick coconut milk and the rice flour mixed with a little water, and cook, uncovered, stirring frequently, until the mixture has the consistency of a thick béchamel. Add the chicken pieces and the *dendê* (palm) oil. Cook just long enough to heat through, about 5 minutes. Serve with *Pirão de Arroz* (Rice Flour Pudding) page 248.

Variation: To make *Vatapá de Camarão* (Prawns and Fish in a Shrimp and Almond Sauce), in place of the chicken, substitute 1 pound raw prawns, shelled and deveined, and 3 pounds fillets of any firm white fish, cut into 2-inch pieces. Add 1 tablespoon of finely chopped fresh ginger to the onion and tomato mixture, and cook the fish for 10 minutes, the prawns only until they turn pink and lose their translucent look, about 3 minutes.

Pollo Pibil

CHICKEN, YUCATÁN STYLE   *Mexico*

This is an old dish from the distant past. It would have been wrapped in banana leaves and cooked in a *pib*, an earth oven, one of the earliest methods of cooking. A modern oven does well but not as well as the *pib*. Sometimes one still gets a chance to have *pollo pibil* cooked in the traditional way and it is a grand experience.

[Serves 4]
12 *peppercorns*
½ *teaspoon oregano*
¼ *teaspoon cumin seeds*
2 *teaspoons annatto seeds*
1 *teaspoon salt*
4 *large cloves garlic*

½ *pint Seville orange juice, or use two-thirds orange juice and one-third lime juice*
A 3½- to 4-pound chicken, quartered
Banana leaves (or kitchen parchment or foil)

193

Using mortar and pestle, a blender, or a food processor, grind together the peppercorns, oregano, cumin, annatto seeds, salt, and garlic. Transfer the mixture to a large bowl and mix thoroughly with the orange juice. Add the chicken pieces, mixing well to coat them with the marinade. Cover and refrigerate for 24 hours, turning two or three times.

Wrap each piece of chicken in a square of banana leaf, kitchen parchment, or aluminum foil, about 12 inches by 12 inches, dividing the marinade equally among the pieces. Arrange the packages in a casserole, cover, and bake in a preheated moderate (325° F., 170° C., gas 3) oven for about 2 hours, or until the chicken is very tender. Serve with hot tortillas.

Pollo en Salsa de Huevos

CHICKEN IN EGG SAUCE   *Ecuador*

Ecuador was once part of the great Inca empire, which had its centre in Cuzco, Peru, and dominated the whole Andean region, stretching as far as northern Chile. Even today the dominant language of the Inca empire, Quechua, is still spoken in both countries. Coastal Ecuador was not gathered into the Inca fold, and with its vastly different climate and vegetation has a distinct regional kitchen, whose notable feature is the use of plantains, especially the *verde* (green, or unripe) plantain. The secret of the cooking lies in combining foods not usually put together, pork stuffed with shrimps, for example, or Seville orange used for the *seviches* (marinated fish). Dry mustard is used interestingly in the chicken dishes—sautéed with chopped onion first so that it adds an elusive flavour to the finished dish. Elsewhere ground walnuts make a wonderfully rich sauce for chicken, with that hint of bitterness and sweetness peculiar to walnuts. Wine, vinegar, both orange and lemon juice, eggs, red peppers, and nuts are all used one way or another with chicken, making for a very versatile yet simple cuisine, requiring no elaborate techniques.

[Serves 4 to 6]

2 ounces butter or 4 tablespoons
   vegetable oil
A 3½- to 4-pound chicken, cut into
   serving pieces
1 large onion, finely chopped

1 clove garlic, minced
1 tablespoon dry mustard
Salt, freshly ground pepper
¾ pint chicken stock
6 hardboiled eggs, finely chopped

Heat the butter in a frying pan and sauté the chicken pieces until golden on both sides. Transfer them to a casserole. In the butter remaining in the pan sauté the onion and garlic with the mustard, stirring to mix. When the onion is soft, transfer the contents of the pan to a flameproof casserole. Season with salt and pepper to taste and pour in the stock, adding a little more barely to cover the chicken, if necessary. Cover and simmer until the chicken is tender, about 45 minutes. Transfer the chicken to a warmed serving platter and keep warm. Over brisk heat reduce the sauce until it is of medium thickness. Taste the sauce for seasoning and add a little salt and pepper if necessary. Stir in the eggs and cook just long enough to heat through. Pour the sauce over the chicken and serve, or serve the sauce separately in a sauceboat. Accompany with rice or potatoes, mixed vegetable salad, or a green vegetable.

Variation: For *Pollo en Salsa de Nuez* (Chicken in Nut Sauce), omit the hardboiled eggs and add 6 ounces ground walnuts to the sauce.

Variation: For *Pollo con Aceitunas* (Chicken with Olives), use ½ pint red wine in place of ½ pint of the stock, and omit the mustard, Instead of the hardboiled eggs, add 9 ounces sliced, green, pimiento-stuffed olives to the sauce. Rinse the olives in warm water before slicing.

Variation: For *Pollo a la Criolla* (Chicken, Creole Style), omit the mustard and the hardboiled eggs, adding with the stock, ¼ pint oil, 2 tablespoons vinegar, and 1 bay leaf. Serve with fried potatoes.

Variation: For *Pollo con Pimientos* (Chicken with Sweet Red Peppers), omit the hardboiled eggs. Use ½ pint stock and ½ pint dry red wine. Increase the dry mustard to 2 tablespoons and add to the sauce one 8-ounce can of pimientos, drained and puréed in a blender. Simmer the sauce for a few minutes longer, and if necessary add enough fresh breadcrumbs to make it of medium consistency. It should not be thin.

Variation: For *Pollo al Limón* (Chicken with Lemon), omit the hardboiled eggs. Reduce the chicken stock to just over ½ pint and add ¼ pint fresh lemon juice. Traditionally the sauce is thickened by adding 2 ounces fresh breadcrumbs and stirring over moderate heat until the sauce is smooth and thick. I prefer to reduce the sauce over brisk heat, or to thicken it with 1 tablespoon flour mixed with 1 ounce of butter. The flavour is not changed, it is simply a matter of texture.

Variation: For *Pollo en Salsa de Almendras* (Chicken in Almond Sauce), omit the mustard and reduce the hardboiled eggs to 3. When the chicken is cooked, transfer it to a platter and keep it warm. Reduce the stock to just over ½ pint over brisk heat. Pulverize ¼ pound blanched almonds in a blender, add the eggs and stock, and reduce to a smooth purée. Heat the sauce, spoon a little over the chicken, and serve the rest separately. A deceptively simple dish. The eggs and almonds give the sauce a very subtle flavour.

Variation: For *Pollo en Jugo de Naranja* (Chicken in Orange Juice), omit the hardboiled eggs. Omit the mustard and use 1 tablespoon sweet paprika instead. In place of ¾ pint chicken stock, use half stock and half orange juice. Add 6 ounces coarsely chopped boiled ham to the chicken in the casserole. Before serving, reduce the sauce over brisk heat to medium thick.

Variation: For *Pollo al Jerez* (Chicken with Sherry), omit the hardboiled eggs. Reduce the amount of dry mustard to 1 teaspoon, and instead of ¾ pint chicken stock, use half stock, half sherry. Thicken the sauce with 2 ounces of breadcrumbs, or reduce it over brisk heat.

Variation: For *Pollo con Queso* (Chicken with Cheese), omit the hardboiled eggs. When adding the stock to the casserole, add 1 bay leaf and ½ teaspoon each thyme and oregano. When the chicken is done, lift it out onto an ovenproof serving dish and sprinkle it generously with grated Parmesan cheese, about 2 ounces, and dot with 1 ounce butter. Put it into a preheated moderate oven (350° F., 180° C., gas 4) until the cheese is golden brown. Strain the sauce and reduce it to half over brisk heat. Serve in a gravy boat.

In Ecuador a fresh, or bottled, hot pepper sauce would be on the table to be taken with any of these dishes according to individual taste.

Pollo con Arroz

CHICKEN WITH RICE   *Paraguay*

It would be impossible to have a book of Latin American food without including recipes for *Arroz con Pollo*, a perennial favourite, almost always translated as Chicken with Rice though literally it is Rice with Chicken. This simplest of dishes is also somewhat of a paradox. Its ingredients are not, for the most part, native to Spain, and the dish there is sometimes called *Arroz a la Valenciana* (Rice, Valencia Style). It is also often thought of as a cousin of *paella*, Spain's famous rice, chicken, and shellfish dish. The dish is quintessentially international, for the chickens originally came from India, the saffron arrived with Phoenician traders, the Arabs brought the rice from Asia, and the tomatoes and peppers are the gift of Mexico. It is tremendously popular in the Spanish-speaking Caribbean and in Mexico, as well as in South America, and differs a little from country to country not only in ingredients and technique but in the name as well. One of my favourites, in which the name is reversed to *Pollo con Arroz* (Chicken with Rice), is perhaps the simplest of all the versions I've encountered.

[Serves 4 to 6]

2 tablespoons oil, preferably olive oil

A 3- to 3½-pound chicken, cut into serving pieces

1 medium onion, finely chopped

1 sweet green or red pepper, seeded and chopped

3 tomatoes, peeled and chopped

Salt, freshly ground pepper

1¾ pints chicken stock or water

⅛ teaspoon saffron

¾ pound long-grain rice

Heat the oil in a heavy frying pan and sauté the chicken pieces until they are golden on both sides. Transfer the chicken to an earthenware or enamelled iron casserole. In the oil remaining in the pan sauté the onion and pepper until they are soft. Add to the casserole with the tomatoes, salt and pepper to taste, ¾ pint of the chicken stock or water, and the saffron, crumbled. Simmer, covered, over low heat for 30 minutes.

Lift out the chicken pieces onto a dish or plate and set aside. Pour the liquid through a sieve, reserving the solids. Measure the liquid and make the quantity up to 1¾ pints with the rest of the chicken stock. Pour it into the casserole, add the rice and the reserved solids, stir to mix, and bring to a boil over fairly brisk heat. Arrange the chicken pieces on top of the rice, cover, and cook over very low heat until the rice is tender and all the liquid absorbed, about 20 minutes. Serve directly from the casserole. If liked, artichoke hearts, about 12, may be scattered through the chicken.

Variation: Venezuela has an interesting version of this dish. It is a little more elaborate and has raisins, olives, and capers mixed with the rice. In a blender purée 4 medium tomatoes, skinned and chopped, 2 medium onions, chopped, 1 green and 1 red sweet pepper, seeded and chopped, 2 leeks, well washed and chopped, and 1 clove garlic. Season the mixture with salt and freshly ground pepper and pour it over a 3- to 3½-pound chicken, cut into serving pieces, in a flameproof casserole. Add ¼ pint dry white wine and a little chicken stock to cover, if necessary, and simmer, covered, for 30 minutes. Lift out the chicken pieces onto a plate or dish, and measure the liquid. Make up the quantity to 1¾ pints, if more liquid is needed, with chicken stock. Rinse out and dry the casserole. Heat 2 ounces butter in the casserole and stir in the rice. Stir constantly with a wooden spoon over moderate heat, taking care not to let the rice burn. Pour the chicken stock mixture over the rice. Add 3 ounces seedless raisins, 12 pimiento-stuffed green olives, halved, and 2 tablespoons capers, and stir to mix. Bring to a simmer. Arrange the chicken pieces on top of the rice, cover, and cook over low heat until the rice is tender and the liquid absorbed, about 20 minutes. Serves 4 to 6.

Variation: From Mexico I have a family recipe for *Arroz con Pollo* given me by my husband's maternal grandmother, Doña Carmen Sarabia de Tinoco. She was a fabulous cook and when she made *tamales del norte* (tamales, northern style) for a party, all the world scrambled for an invitation. I think it is a dreadful pity that grandmothers are usually so much older than their granddaughters-in-law. I could have learned so much more from a very wonderful teacher. Her recipe is interesting for having both saffron and hot peppers.

For Mexican chicken with rice, season a 3- to 3½-pound chicken, cut into serving pieces, with salt and pepper. Heat 3 tablespoons olive oil and sauté the chicken pieces until they are golden on both sides. Put the chicken pieces into an earthenware casserole heavy enough to go on direct heat, or any heavy casserole. In the oil remaining in the pan sauté 1 medium onion, finely chopped, and 2 cloves garlic, chopped, until the onion is soft. Add to the chicken. Add 4 medium tomatoes, peeled and chopped, 1 or 2 canned *jalapeño* chilies, seeded and chopped, ¼ teaspoon ground cumin, and ⅛ teaspoon saffron, crumbled. Pour in 1½ pints chicken stock or water, or enough to cover the chicken. Bring to the boil, reduce the heat to low, cover, and simmer gently for 30 minutes. Lift out and set aside the chicken pieces and measure the stock. Make up the quantity to 1¾ pints. In the oil remaining in the pan sauté ¾ pound rice until the rice grains are well coated. Do not let the rice brown. Add the rice to the casserole, pour in the stock, and stir to mix. Bring to the boil, add the chicken pieces, reduce the heat, cover, and cook over very low heat until the rice is tender and all the liquid absorbed. Garnish with 2 pimientos, cut into strips. Serve directly from the casserole.

Two ounces of dry sherry may, with advantage, be poured over the chicken and rice at the end of the cooking and the dish cooked for a minute or two longer. The *jalapeño* chilies may be left out, if preferred. Serves 4 to 6.

Pollo Ticuleño

CHICKEN, TICUL STYLE   *Mexico*

This is a Mayan dish from Yucatán. The delicate chicken breast makes a fine contrast to the robust flavour of black beans and tortilla, all enhanced by the tomato sauce. Put the beans on to cook about 3 hours ahead of time, so they will be ready when needed. The dish really needs no accompaniment other than the garnishes and, for lovers of the *picante*, *Ixni-Pec*, the hot pepper sauce from Yucatán (page 301).

[Serves 4]

FOR THE TOMATO SAUCE

3 medium tomatoes   *Salt, freshly ground pepper*
1 small onion

FOR THE CHICKEN

¼ pound butter   4 tortillas, fried crisp in vegetable
2 whole chicken breasts, boned   oil
   and halved   6 ounces black beans cooked as for
Flour   Panuchos (see page 65)
1 egg, lightly beaten   4 tablespoons freshly grated
8 ounces dry breadcrumbs, about   Parmesan cheese, about

FOR THE GARNISH

1 onion prepared as for Panuchos   8 to 12 radish flowers
   (see page 65), but thinly sliced   1 or 2 medium tomatoes, sliced
   instead of chopped   (optional)
6 ounces cooked green peas
2 ripe plantains, halved crosswise,
   then lengthwise, and fried until
   golden brown in vegetable oil

To make the tomato sauce, peel and chop 3 medium tomatoes and add to a blender or food processor with 1 small onion, chopped. Reduce to a purée. Pour the mixture into a small saucepan and simmer, uncovered, over very low heat for 15 minutes, or until thick and well blended. Season with salt and freshly ground pepper to taste.

   Chop the butter coarsely and put it into a small, heavy saucepan. Melt the butter over very low heat. Skim off the foam that rises to

199

the top and carefully pour the butter into a heavy frying pan, discarding the milky sediment. Roll the chicken breasts in flour, dip in the egg, then in breadcrumbs. Heat the clarified butter and sauté the breasts for about 4 minutes on each side, taking care not to overcook them. Spread the tortillas with the beans, place the chicken breasts on top of the tortillas, pour a little tomato sauce over them, and sprinkle with the grated cheese. Place 1 tortilla on each of four warmed serving plates and garnish with the onion, peas, plantains, radishes, and, if liked, sliced tomatoes.

Pollo Escabechado

PICKLED CHICKEN   *Chile*

In this recipe the chicken literally stews in the oil, which is poured or spooned off the sauce at the end of the cooking time. It makes for a very delicate, moist, and tender bird. Though the name of the dish translates as pickled chicken, the small amount of vinegar used leaves just a pleasant echo on the palate. Since the chicken is served cold, it is done ahead of time, which makes it perfect for a family meal in summer. It is an attractive dish in its pale, translucent jelly, lovely for a cold buffet accompanied by salads such as *Ensalada de Aguacate* (Avocado Salad), *Ensalada de Habas* (Fresh Broad Bean Salad), or *Ensalada de Verduras* (Vegetable Salad).

[Serves 6 to 8]
A 4-pound roasting chicken, cut
  into serving pieces
½ pint vegetable oil
¼ pint white wine vinegar

1 teaspoon salt
6 peppercorns
1 bay leaf
2 medium onions, thinly sliced
2 carrots, scraped and thinly sliced

Place all the ingredients in a heavy casserole, cover, and cook over very low heat until the chicken is tender, about 1½ hours. Allow to cool. Place the chicken pieces on a serving platter with the vegetables arranged around them. Remove and discard the peppercorns and bay leaf. Pour the liquid in the casserole into a bowl, then spoon off all the oil (it is easier to do it this way). Save the oil, incidentally, for sautéing other meats and poultry. Pour the stock over the chicken pieces and refrigerate. The liquid will set into an aspic. If a firmer jelly is preferred, add to the stock ½ tablespoon unflavoured gelatine softened in water and stir to dissolve, over low heat, before pouring it over the chicken. In very hot weather I find this is sometimes necessary. If any oil escapes being spooned off, it will separate out when the jelly sets. Just tip the dish and pour it off, or remove it with a piece of blotting paper or paper towel.

To serve, decorate a platter with lettuce leaves, sliced tomatoes, cooked green peas and beans, and sliced pimiento or other suitable vegetables such as artichoke hearts.

Variation: *Pollo a la Paisana* (Country Chicken), also from Chile, can, I suppose, be considered a variation of *Pollo Escabechado* (Pickled Chicken) though it is served hot not cold and is a much simpler dish. It is in fact simplicity itself and is most useful when one is both busy and hungry for delectable food. The chicken emerges from the pot wonderfully moist and tender and with a subtle flavour that the cook can vary by the use of different vinegars. Tarragon vinegar and Japanese rice vinegar both spring to mind and I have used them with great success, though I doubt whether Japanese rice vinegar is a commonplace item in Chile. I claim cook's privileges for this departure from strict tradition.

For *Pollo a la Paisana* (Country Chicken), cut a 3½- to 4-pound chicken into serving pieces and put it into a heavy earthenware or enamelled cast iron casserole with 4 spring onions, cut into 1-inch pieces and using both white and green parts, 4 cloves garlic, left whole, salt and freshly ground black pepper to taste, 1 or 2 sprigs parsley, 6 tablespoons olive oil, and 2 tablespoons vinegar. Cover and cook over very low heat until the chicken is tender, 45 minutes to 1 hour. Serve with either matchstick potatoes or French fries and a lettuce or watercress salad or a green vegetable. Serves 4 to 6.

TURKEY

Pavo Relleno

STUFFED TURKEY   *Mexico*

Until recently when industrialization brought gas and electric stoves into the kitchens of Mexico to replace the charcoal stoves of the past, there was very little oven cooking done, except for the baking of breads and cakes. This roast turkey with its hearty meat stuffing is an exception. I was a little taken aback the first time I encountered

201

it; it seemed such a double richness, meat and bird. But I very soon adopted it with enthusiasm, for it is delicious. In Mexico the bird would be served with a garnish of chopped lettuce, sliced tomatoes, and avocado, in oil and vinegar dressing, and olives and radish roses, but I prefer these garnishes served separately as a salad.

[Serves 6 to 8]

½ *recipe* Picadillo *(Seasoned Chopped Beef), page 139*
A 6- to 8-pound turkey, ready to cook

Butter
½ *pint dry white wine*
3 *tablespoons flour*
Salt, freshly ground pepper

Make the *Picadillo* stuffing and allow it to cool. Fill the cavities of the bird with the stuffing and close them with skewers. Truss the bird and place it breast side up on a rack in a roasting pan. Have ready a double thickness of butter muslin large enough to cover the bird. Soak it in melted butter and drape it over the bird. Roast in a pre-heated moderately slow oven (325° F., 170° C., gas 3) for 2 to 2½ hours, or until the bird is done, basting through the cheesecloth several times with pan drippings or melted butter. While the bird is roasting, make a stock by covering the neck, giblets, and liver with water and ½ pint white wine and simmer 45 minutes to 1 hour. Remove butter muslin 30 minutes before the bird is done so that it will brown, basting twice during this period. Lift the bird onto a platter and remove the trussing strings and skewers. Let it rest 15 minutes before carving. Skim all but 3 tablespoons of fat from the roasting pan and stir in the flour, blending thoroughly over moderate heat. Stir in ½ pint of the stock and blend well, adding a little more if the gravy is too thick. Season to taste with salt and pepper and serve separately in a sauceboat.

Variation: For another popular stuffing, substitute 2 pounds minced pork for the beef. Omit the oregano and thyme and add ⅛ teaspoon of cloves and half that amount of ground cinnamon. Ground cumin (⅛ teaspoon) may be added to either stuffing. This spice is very popular in Mexican cooking and I find it makes a pleasant change.

Pavita Rellena a la Criolla

HEN TURKEY WITH CREOLE STUFFING   *Argentina*

Quinces, when they are available, may be used instead of peaches in this delicious turkey stuffing.

[Serves 10 to 12]
8 slices firm white bread
Milk
1 ounce butter
1 medium onion, finely chopped
2 pounds sausage meat
1 bay leaf, crumbled
1 teaspoon oregano
1 tablespoon parsley, finely chopped
2 hardboiled eggs, finely chopped

3 tablespoons stoned green olives,
  chopped
1 pound stoned, peeled, and
  chopped peaches
Salt, freshly ground pepper
3 eggs, lightly beaten
A 10- to 12-pound turkey,
  preferably a hen turkey
Olive oil
Butter for basting

Soak the bread in milk, squeeze out, and fluff. In a saucepan heat the butter and sauté the onion until it is golden. Add the sausage meat and cook until it has lost all its colour, mashing with a fork to break it up. Remove the saucepan from the heat. Add the bread, herbs, hardboiled eggs, olives, and peaches. Season to taste with salt and a generous amount of pepper. Stir in the lightly beaten eggs. Stuff the bird with the mixture and truss it in the usual way. Rub the bird all over with olive oil and bake in a preheated moderate oven (325° F., 170° C., gas 3) for 3 to 3½ hours, or until it is done. Baste every 30 minutes with ¼ pound melted butter and when this is used up, the drippings in the pan. If necessary, use a little more butter. If any dressing is left over, bake it separately in a foil-covered container. If liked, make a gravy by simmering the giblets and neck in water to make 1¼ pints of stock, stir 4 tablespoons flour into 4 tablespoons fat from the roasting pan, add the stock, and cook, stirring, until the gravy is thickened.

Pavo Guisado
TURKEY STEW, DOMINICAN STYLE   *Dominican Republic*

Perhaps because it remained out of the mainstream, the cooking of the Dominican Republic has preserved some of the best dishes of the Spanish colonial period.

[Serves 8 to 10]
An 8- to 8½-pound turkey, cut
  into serving pieces
4 cloves garlic, crushed
Salt, freshly ground pepper
2 tablespoons red wine vinegar
¼ pint vegetable oil
½ pint tomato purée

1 sweet green pepper, seeded and
  chopped
24 small stoned green olives
4 tablespoons capers
3 pounds potatoes, peeled and sliced
1 pound fresh peas, shelled, or a
  10-ounce package frozen peas,
  thawed

Season the turkey pieces with the garlic, salt and pepper to taste, and the vinegar. Leave for 1 hour at room temperature. Heat the oil in a heavy casserole or Dutch oven large enough to hold the turkey pieces comfortably. Pat the turkey dry with paper towels, and reserve any marinade that remains. Sauté the turkey pieces, two or three at a time, until lightly browned on both sides. Arrange the turkey in the casserole and add the marinade. Add the tomato purée, the pepper, and enough water to cover. Cover and simmer over moderate heat for 1 hour. Add the olives, capers, and potatoes, and cook for 20 minutes longer. Add the peas, and cook for about 10 minutes longer, or until both the turkey and vegetables are tender. If using frozen peas, add only for the last 5 minutes of cooking. To serve arrange the turkey pieces on a warmed serving platter and surround with the potatoes. If the liquid is very abundant, reduce it over brisk heat and pour over the turkey.

MOLE DISHES

TURKEY OR CHICKEN

Mole Poblano de Guajolote

TURKEY IN CHILI AND CHOCOLATE SAUCE   *Mexico*

This is Mexico's most famous dish and though it is native to the state of Puebla, it is served all over the republic on truly festive occasions. It can be absolutely sensational for a party when served with tortillas, Mexican rice and beans, and *Guacamole* (Avocado Sauce). I always put a small bowl of canned *serrano* or *jalapeño* chilies on the table for the bold souls who claim no dish is hot enough for them. Actually *Mole Poblano* is not hot though I have come across versions of it where a *chipotle* chili or two had been added, introducing both heat and this chili's very exotic flavour. For a more everyday dish, chicken or pork may be used instead of turkey.

There is a charming but apocryphal legend, that a group of nuns at the convent of Santa Rosa in Puebla invented the dish in early colonial times to honour a visiting viceroy and archbishop. But, in fact, it had long been a royal dish of the Aztec court; since it contained chocolate, it was forbidden to women, and among men it was reserved for royalty, the military nobility, and the higher ranks of the priesthood. It is on record that the Spanish conquistador Hernán Cortés was served a version of the dish at the court of Aztec Emperor Moctezuma. All the same I do think we owe the sisters a debt. They recorded the recipe, which might otherwise have been lost, and they substituted familiar ingredients for some of the more exotic herbs and spices used in the emperor's day. I'd be prepared to swear that in the past allspice (a native spice) was used instead of cloves and cinnamon brought by Spain from the East, but since the flavour is much the same, why fuss?

Since *mole*, which comes from the Nahuatl word *molli*, means a sauce made from any of the chilies, hot, pungent, or sweet, there are more *moles* in Mexico than one can count. Out of the innumerable array, I have had to content myself with just this one. However it can be made with chicken instead of turkey, either halving the amount of sauce for one chicken or using two 3- to 3½-pound chickens, cut into serving pieces. It is also delicious made with pork: use 3 pounds lean, boneless pork cut into 2-inch pieces and simmer gently in water barely to cover for 1 hour. Add the pork to the sauce and simmer, covered, until the pork is tender, about 30 minutes. Left-over *mole* makes splendid filling for tacos.

[Serves 10]

An 8-pound turkey, cut into serving pieces	*2 cloves garlic, chopped*
	Salt
1 medium onion, chopped	*3 ounces lard*

FOR THE SAUCE

6 ancho *chilies*	*3 ounces raisins*
6 mulato *chilies*	*4 tablespoons sesame seeds*
4 pasilla *chilies*	*½ teaspoon ground coriander seed*
2 medium onions, chopped	*½ teaspoon ground anise*
3 cloves garlic, chopped	*2 whole cloves*
3 medium tomatoes, peeled, seeded, and chopped	*A ½-inch piece of stick cinnamon*
2 tortillas, or 2 slices toast, cut up	*¼ pound lard*
4 ounces blanched almonds	*1½ ounces plain chocolate*
2 ounces peanuts	*Salt, freshly ground pepper*
	1 tablespoon sugar (optional)

Put the turkey pieces into a large heavy saucepan with the onion, garlic, and water to cover. Season with salt, bring to the boil, lower the heat, and simmer, covered, for 1 hour, or until the turkey is barely tender. Drain off and reserve the turkey stock. Lift out the turkey pieces and pat them dry with paper towels. Heat the lard in a large pan and sauté the turkey pieces until they are lightly browned on both sides. Set them aside.

205

To make the sauce, remove the stems and seeds from the *ancho*, *mulato*, and *pasilla* chilies. Tear them into pieces, put them in a bowl, and pour hot water over them barely to cover, about ¾ pint. Let them stand for 30 minutes, turning the pieces from time to time. In a blender or food processor combine the chilies and the water in which they have soaked with the onions, garlic, tomatoes, and tortillas or toast, and blend the mixture until it forms a paste. Do this in two lots if necessary. Transfer the paste to a bowl. Rinse out and dry the container of the blender or food processor and add the almonds, peanuts, raisins, 2 tablespoons of the sesame seeds, the coriander seed, the anise, the cloves, and the cinnamon stick, broken up, and blend the mixture well. Mix thoroughly with the chili paste. Measure the lard left in the pan from sautéing the turkey and add enough to bring the quantity up to 2 ounces. Add the chili paste and sauté over moderate heat, stirring, for 5 minutes. Transfer the mixture to the saucepan in which the turkey was cooked. Stir in ¾ pint of the reserved turkey stock and the chocolate, cut into pieces. Season to taste with salt and pepper. Cook the mixture over low heat, stirring until the chocolate is melted and adding more turkey stock if necessary to make the sauce the consistency of double cream. Stir in the sugar, if liked. Add the turkey and simmer it, covered, for 30 minutes. Arrange the turkey and sauce in a serving dish. In a small pan toast the remaining sesame seeds and sprinkle them over the turkey. Serve with tortillas, *Arroz Blanco*, *Frijoles*, and *Guacamole*.

For an authentic Mexican fiesta meal, start with *Seviche de Sierra* (Mackerel Marinated in Lime Juice) and finish with *Cocada* (Coconut Custard).

DUCK

Arroz con Pato

DUCK WITH RICE   *Peru*

It is not surprising that this is Peru's favourite duck dish. The coriander and cumin unite in a most subtle way with the dark beer in which the rice is cooked, and the rich flavour of the duck permeates the whole.

[Serves 6]

A 4½- to 5-pound duck, cut into 6 serving pieces
Vegetable oil
1 large onion, finely chopped
3 fresh hot red or green peppers, seeded, coarsely chopped, and puréed in a blender or food processor

6 large cloves garlic, crushed
2 tablespoons fresh coriander, chopped
1 teaspoon ground cumin
Salt, freshly ground pepper
1¾ pints chicken stock
¾ pound long-grain rice
¾ pint dark beer
¼ pound cooked green peas

GARNISH

Sliced tomatoes and fresh hot peppers, seeded and cut into flower shapes

Prick the skin of the duck all over with the tines of a fork. Film the bottom of a heavy pan with a small amount of oil and sauté the pieces of duck—about 10 to 15 minutes—until they are lightly browned all over in their own fat, which will run out during the cooking. Transfer them to a heavy casserole. Pour off all but 3 tablespoons of fat from the pan, and in the remaining fat sauté the onion, peppers, and garlic until the onion is golden. Add the vegetables to the casserole with the coriander, cumin, salt and pepper to taste, and the chicken stock, which should just cover the duck. Add a little more if necessary. Cover and simmer over low heat until the duck is almost done, about 45 minutes. Drain off the stock and measure it. Add the rice to the casserole with ¾ pint of the stock and the dark beer. Cover, bring to the boil, reduce the heat to low, and cook until the rice is tender and quite dry. Fold in the peas. Serve hot on a large platter garnished with tomato slices and fresh hot peppers.

Pato al Vino

DUCK IN WINE   *Colombia*

Spices from the New and Old Worlds—allspice, cinnamon, and cloves—combine to give this duck a full, rich flavour. It may be cooked on top of the stove, but I find it much more satisfactory to use the oven as do many modern Latin Americans.

[Serves 4]

A 4½- to 5-pound duck	4 allspice berries
Salt, freshly ground pepper	1 whole fresh hot red or green
1 ounce butter	pepper
2 large onions, finely chopped	½ pint dry red wine
1 bay leaf	½ pint duck stock, made by
2 whole cloves	simmering giblets, neck, and
A 1-inch piece of stick cinnamon	liver for 1 hour

Pull the loose fat from inside the duck and prick the bird all over with a fork to help release the excess fat. Season inside and out with salt and pepper. Heat the butter in a heavy casserole and sauté the duck until it is golden brown all over. Lift out and set aside. Spoon off all but 4 tablespoons fat from the casserole. Add the onions and sauté until soft. Return the duck to the casserole. Tie the bay leaf, cloves, cinnamon, allspice berries, and hot pepper in square of butter muslin and add to the casserole with the red wine and duck stock. Season to taste with more salt and pepper if necessary and bring to the boil on top of the stove. Cover with aluminum foil, then with the casserole lid, and cook in a preheated moderate oven (350° F., 180° C., gas 4) for 1½ hours, or until the duck is tender. Lift out onto a serving platter and keep warm. Remove and discard the cheesecloth bag. Spoon excess fat from the sauce, and if it is very abundant, reduce it over brisk heat for a few minutes. Spoon a little sauce over the duck and serve the rest separately. Serve with *Arroz con Coco y Pasas* (Rice with Coconut and Raisins), page 245, and a green salad.

Variation: *Pato Borracho* (Drunken Duckling) is a popular duck dish all over Latin America. Cook as for *Pato al Vino* but use white wine instead of red. Omit the cloves, cinnamon, allspice, and hot pepper, and use instead a bouquet garni of parsley and thyme tied in a butter muslin square with the bay leaf. Add 3 cloves of chopped garlic to the onions, and when they are soft, add 4 tomatoes, peeled, seeded, and chopped.

Variation: *Pato com Ameixas* (Duckling with Prunes), from Brazil, is a full-flavoured, robust dish. Cook as for *Pato al Vino* but omit the cloves, cinnamon, allspice, and hot pepper. When sautéing the onions, add 2 cloves garlic, chopped. When the onions are soft, add 3 large tomatoes, peeled, seeded, and chopped, and ½ teaspoon thyme. Instead of ½ pint red wine, add ¾ pint dry white wine and the 10 ounces of duck stock, and ½ pint stoned prunes, quartered. Just before serving stir in 4 tablespoons dry Madeira.

Pato en Jugo de Naranja

DUCK IN ORANGE JUICE   *Mexico*

This is a very old colonial dish that has remained popular, with slight variations, throughout Latin America, though it seems to have originated in Mexico. I have chosen a modern version where the duck is braised in the oven, instead of on top of the stove.

[Serves 4]

1 duck weighing about 4 pounds	¼ teaspoon thyme
1 ounce butter	¼ teaspoon marjoram
1 medium onion, finely chopped	1 bay leaf
2 cloves garlic, chopped	1½ ounces raisins
3 medium tomatoes, peeled, seeded, and chopped	1 tablespoon white wine vinegar
	½ pint orange juice
	1 ounce toasted, slivered almonds

Pull out the loose fat from inside the duck and prick the bird all over with a fork to help release the excess fat. Heat the butter in a large frying pan and brown the duck lightly all over. Transfer it to a flame-proof casserole large enough to hold it comfortably. Spoon off all but 2 tablespoons of fat from the pan and sauté the onion and garlic until the onion is soft. Add to the casserole with all the remaining ingredients except the almonds. Add the duck giblets to enrich the sauce. Bring the liquid in the casserole to the boil on top of the stove. Cover the casserole with foil, then with the lid, and cook in a preheated moderate oven (325° F., 170° C., gas 3) for 1½ hours, or until the duck is tender. Lift the bird out and carve it. Put it onto a serving platter and keep warm. Spoon off the fat from the sauce, take out and discard the giblets and bay leaf. If the sauce is very abundant, reduce it over brisk heat for a few minutes. Spoon a little of the sauce over the duck and sprinkle with the almonds. Pour the rest of the sauce into a sauceboat and serve separately with rice and green peas or green beans.

PIGEON

Latin America has a marvellous way with pigeons, which everyone loves. They range from the beautifully simple Mexican favourite *Pi-*

chones al Vino (Pigeons with Wine) to the exotic *Pichones con Salsa de Camarones* (Pigeons in Shrimp Sauce) of Peru. They make an ideal dinner party dish, with each guest served a plumply elegant bird. You may also substitute fresh poussins.

Pichones con Salsa de Camarones

PIGEONS IN SHRIMP SAUCE   *Peru*

The shrimp sauce turns this into an excitingly different dish, the apparently contradictory flavours deliciously complementing each other.

[Serves 6]
4 tablespoons clarified butter (page 312)
6 pigeons, each weighing about 8 ounces
1 medium onion, finely chopped
1 clove garlic, chopped
2 tablespoons flour
½ pint dry white wine

¾ pint chicken stock
Pinch of nutmeg
Salt, freshly ground pepper
½ pound raw shrimp, peeled and coarsely chopped
2 eggs, lightly beaten
2 tablespoons finely chopped fresh coriander

Heat the butter in a frying pan and sauté the pigeons until they are golden on both sides. Transfer to a heavy casserole. In the butter remaining in the pan sauté the onion and garlic until the onion is soft. Add the flour and cook, stirring, for a minute or two. Add the wine, stir, add the stock and the nutmeg, and simmer, stirring, until the mixture is smooth. Season to taste with salt and pepper and pour over the birds. Cover the casserole with foil, then with the lid, and simmer over moderate heat until the birds are tender, about 1½ hours. Lift out the birds and arrange on a serving dish. Keep warm. Add the shrimp to the liquid in the casserole and cook for about 2 minutes. Then stir in the eggs and the coriander and cook, stirring, over low heat until the sauce is lightly thickened. Do not let the sauce boil once the eggs are added, or it will curdle. Spoon a little of the sauce over the birds and serve the rest separately in a sauceboat. Serve with white rice or boiled potatoes and a green vegetable or a salad.

Pichones al Vino

PIGEONS WITH WINE   *Mexico*

Dry sherry is sometimes used in this recipe and though it is pleasant

I prefer the equally traditional dry red wine. Baked *boniato* (white sweet potato) is a splendid accompaniment.

[Serves 4]

4 pigeons, each weighing about 8 ounces

2 cloves garlic, chopped

16 spring onions, trimmed and cut into 1¼-inch pieces, using both green and white parts

4 medium-sized carrots, scraped and thinly sliced

½ teaspoon thyme

½ teaspoon marjoram

⅛ teaspoon freshly ground black pepper

⅛ teaspoon ground allspice

1 whole clove

Salt

1 small fresh hot pepper, seeded and chopped

4 tablespoons olive oil

2 tablespoons red wine vinegar

½ pint dry red wine or dry sherry

¼ pint chicken stock

Arrange the birds in a flameproof casserole just large enough to hold them comfortably. Add all the ingredients except the chicken stock and mix well. Marinate in the refrigerator overnight, turning once or twice. When ready to cook, add the stock, using a little more if necessary barely to cover. Bring to a simmer on top of the stove, then cook, covered, in a preheated moderate oven (350° F., 180° C., gas 4) until tender, about 1½ hours. Arrange the birds on a warmed serving dish, spoon a little of the sauce over them. Serve the rest of the sauce separately.

Pichones Saltados

PIGEON STEW   *Peru*

This is a deceptively simple dish, very easy to cook yet with a fine, rich flavour.

[Serves 4]

4 pigeons, each weighing about 8 ounces

Salt, freshly ground pepper

¼ pint olive oil

1 large onion, finely chopped

1 fresh hot red or green pepper, seeded and chopped

2 tablespoons flour

2 teaspoons sweet paprika

½ pint dry white wine

½ pint chicken stock

Season the birds inside and out with salt and pepper. Heat the oil in a flameproof casserole and sauté the birds over moderate heat until they are golden brown all over, about 15 minutes. Lift out and set

211

aside. Add the onion and the hot pepper to the oil remaining in the casserole and sauté until the onion is soft. Stir in the flour and the paprika and cook, stirring, for a minute longer. Add the wine, stir to mix, then stir in the stock. Return the birds to the sauce, cover the casserole with a piece of foil, then with the lid, and simmer over low heat until the birds are tender, about 1½ hours. Lift them out onto a serving dish. Taste the sauce and add more salt and pepper if necessary. Pour a little sauce over the birds and serve the rest in a sauceboat. Serve with rice, mashed potatoes, or a purée of any starchy root vegetable such as sweet potato or yams, or with a purée of pumpkin, and a green vegetable.

Pichones en Jugo de Naranja

PIGEONS IN ORANGE JUICE   *Colombia*

Orange juice and white wine combine to make a delicate sauce for the richness of the pigeons, a balancing of flavours that is typical of Colombian cooking.

[Serves 6]
2 ounces butter
6 pigeons, each weighing about 8
  ounces
1 medium onion, finely chopped

½ pint dry white wine
½ pint orange juice
Salt, freshly ground pepper
Pinch of cinnamon
2 teaspoons cornflour

Heat the butter in a pan and sauté the birds until golden brown all over. Transfer them to a heavy casserole. In the butter remaining in the pan sauté the onion until it is soft. Pour in the wine and the orange juice, bring to the boil, and stir, scraping up all the brown bits. Season to taste with salt and pepper and add the cinnamon. Pour the mixture over the pigeons, cover, and simmer over low heat until they are tender, about 1½ hours. Transfer the birds to a serving dish and keep warm. Mix the cornflour with a little cold water and stir into the casserole. Simmer, stirring, until the sauce is lightly thickened. If the sauce seems very abundant, reduce briskly over fairly high heat for a few minutes before adding the cornflour. Serve with any root vegetable or rice and a green vegetable.

Substantial Dishes

PLATILLOS FUERTES

There are a number of hearty dishes in the Latin American cuisine that combine fish, meat, or poultry with beans, rice, corn, potatoes, or other root vegetables. These once served as a course in a meal as soup or appetizers do now. To our modern appetites they are main dishes, so I have put them into a category of their own. I have included the festive dish *Feijoada Completa* (Black Beans with Mixed Meats) here because beans are such an important part of it. This is not a very sharply defined category but I think it is a useful one.

Feijoada Completa

BLACK BEANS WITH MIXED MEATS *Brazil*

This exuberant mixture of black beans, meats, vegetables, and garnishes is Brazil's national dish. It was created in Rio de Janeiro but has now spread all over the country. It is magnificent for parties and well worth the work involved. And it is versatile as one can eliminate or substitute many of the meats if some are not available. Polish or Spanish sausage (*kielbasa*, boiling ring, or *longaniza*) can substitute for *linguiça*, fresh pork hocks can be used instead of pig's feet, ears, and tail. Any fresh hot peppers can be used in the hot pepper sauce. To serve the *Feijoada*, the meats are sliced and arranged on one or more platters, the beans, which should be quite soupy with an almost saucelike consistency, are served in a tureen or large serving bowl with a soup ladle or generously sized serving spoon, and accompanied by *Arroz Brazileiro* (Brazilian Rice), *Couve a Mineira* (Kale, Minas Gerais Style), *Farofa de Manteiga* (Cassava Meal with Butter) or *Farofa de Ouro* (Cassava Meal with Hardboiled Eggs), as well as 6 peeled and sliced oranges arranged in a serving dish, *Mólho de Pimenta e Limão* (Hot Pepper and Lime Sauce) and *Salada de Palmito* (Hearts of Palm Salad).

The table looks very splendid with this array of food. Guests put a serving of everything onto a single plate, then sprinkle *farofa* over the lot. *Cachaça*, Brazilian rum, is traditionally served with *Feijoada* but to the uninitiated this can be traumatic. Ideally either *batidas* or *Caipirinhas*, two *cachaça* drinks made with lime or lemon juice, are served before the meal, and chilled beer with it.

Brazilian friends say *Feijoada* should be eaten for Saturday lunch so that one may sleep it off. I've done that but I find I prefer *Feijoada* for dinner, or for a festive Sunday luncheon party. It is a truly international dish since the beans and hot peppers come originally from Mexico, the cassava (manioc) meal from pre-Portuguese Brazil, the meats and sausages from Europe by way of Portugal, and the cooking genius that put it all together from Africa.

An admirable dessert to accompany this feast is *Quindins de Yáyá* (Coconut Cupcake Dessert), which is deliciously rich and sweet.

[Serves 10 to 12]

4 pig's ears
1 pig's tail
Salt
3 pig's feet, split
A 1-pound piece carne sêca (sun-dried salted beef), see page 27
A 3-pound smoked ox tongue
A ½-pound piece of lean bacon
1¾-2 pounds black beans
A 1-pound piece of lean beef chuck or bottom round

1 pound linguiça sausage (see page 37)
1 pound fresh pork sausages
1 ounce lard or 2 tablespoons vegetable oil
2 onions, finely chopped
2 cloves garlic, minced
2 tomatoes, peeled, seeded, and chopped
1 fresh hot pepper, seeded and minced, or ⅛ teaspoon Tabasco (optional)
Salt, freshly ground pepper

Two days ahead of time put the pig's ears and tail into a mixing bowl and sprinkle thoroughly with salt. Cover and refrigerate for 2 days. Lift out of the bowl, discard the liquid, and rinse the meats thoroughly in cold water. Put into a large saucepan with water to cover, bring to the boil, lower the heat, and simmer for 10 minutes. Drain. Set aside until ready to cook.

The night before put the pig's feet on to cook in cold water to cover and simmer, covered, for 1½ hours. Cool and refrigerate in a covered container in the cooking liquid until ready to use.

Also on the night before cut the salted beef in half lengthwise. Put it with the tongue, and the bacon to soak overnight in cold water to cover. Start soaking early in the evening and change the water 2 or 3 times if possible. Thoroughly wash and pick over the beans and put them to soak in cold water to cover.

When ready to cook, allowing 4 hours for the actual cooking time, put the beans and their soaking liquid into a casserole large enough to hold all the ingredients. Drain and add the pig's feet. Reserve the jellied liquid from the pig's feet for some other time to make stock. Add enough cold water to cover by 2 inches. Bring to the boil, then simmer over low heat, covered, for 1½ hours.

While the beans are cooking, put the tongue, salted beef, and bacon into a large saucepan with fresh cold water to cover, bring to the boil over moderate heat, then simmer, covered, over low heat for 1 hour. When the beans have cooked for 1½ hours, add the bacon and beef to the bean pot but continue to simmer the tongue separately. At the same time add the fresh beef, pig's ears and tail to the beans. Add hot water as necessary to cover and simmer, covered, for 2 hours longer. By this time the tongue will be tender. Remove from the heat and allow to cool. As soon as it is cool enough to handle, peel it and remove any gristle and bones. Add the tongue to the beans with hot water if necessary to keep the beans covered. Stir the pot with a wooden spoon from time to time to prevent the beans from sticking.

Fill the pot in which the tongue was cooked with fresh water, bring to the boil, and add the *linguiça* and the fresh pork sausages. Bring back to the boil and simmer for 1 minute. Drain and add the sausages to the beans, which by now will have been cooking for 3½ hours.*

Heat the lard or oil and sauté the onions and garlic until the onions are soft. Add the tomatoes and the hot pepper or Tabasco, if liked, and simmer until the mixture is well blended. Season to taste with salt and pepper. Remove 1 cup of the cooked beans and add, mashing them into the sauce. Stir the mixture back into the beans and simmer for 15 minutes longer, or until the beans have been cooking for 4

*The *Feijoada* can be cooked ahead to this point and kept overnight in a cool place, or refrigerated, until half an hour before it is to be served. Bring it to room temperature before adding the onion, tomato, and mashed bean mixture.

215

hours. The beans should be very soft, almost falling apart. Lift out the meats and continue to simmer the beans, uncovered, over low heat. Remove any bones from the meats. Slice the pig's ears and tail into 4 or 5 pieces. Slice all the meats and arrange on a platter with the tongue in the centre, its traditional position. Use two platters if necessary. Moisten the meats with a little bean liquid and keep warm. Pour the beans into a tureen or large serving bowl.

Tutú a Mineira

BLACK BEANS, MINAS GERAIS STYLE   *Brazil*

This is a sort of junior *Feijoada,* much simpler than that grand feast but nonetheless a hearty dish. It is really a dish of mashed beans and cassava (manioc) meal generously garnished with meat and eggs. It is a very old dish going back to the days of slavery and was a great favourite with small children. Somehow the infants, lisping the word purée, converted the sound into *tutú* and that is what it has been called ever since.

[Serves 6]
1 *recipe* Feijão Preto *(Black Beans), page 239*
4 *large eggs*
A *¾-pound* linguiça, *or similar sausage such as* longaniza *or*

kielbasa *or boiling ring*
½ *ounce lard*
8 *slices bacon, chopped*
2 *medium onions, finely sliced*
1½ *ounces cassava (manioc) meal*

Have ready the black beans, freshly cooked. Put the eggs into a large saucepan and boil them for 8 minutes. Shell under cold running water. Halve the eggs and set them aside. Put the sausage in a saucepan with cold water to cover and simmer for 30 minutes. Drain and cut into ½-inch slices. Heat the lard and sauté the sausage slices and bacon until the bacon is crisp. Transfer the sausage and bacon to a dish lined with paper towels and keep warm. In the fat remaining in the pan sauté the onions and keep them warm.

Put the beans into a large saucepan and mash over low heat. Stir in the cassava meal and cook, stirring, until the mixture has the consistency of rather heavy mashed potatoes, adding a little more cassava meal if necessary. Transfer the mashed beans to a deep, hot serving dish and pat them down lightly to an even layer. Pour the onion and bacon fat mixture over the beans. Arrange the sausage and bacon at opposite ends of the dish and put the hardboiled eggs in a row down the middle. Serve with *Couve a Mineira* (Kale, Minas Gerais Style), page 256, and, if liked, a hot pepper sauce.

Variation: Some cooks serve the *Tutú* with eggs fried in butter instead of hardboiled eggs. Roast pork, cut into small slices, may be substituted for the chopped bacon or the *Tutú* may be served with *Roupa Velha* (Old Clothes) page 135, a traditional Brazilian shredded beef dish.

Ocopa Arequipeña

POTATOES WITH CHEESE, WALNUT, AND
HOT PEPPER SAUCE   *Peru*

Having "invented" the potato, the Incas developed splendid recipes using this most versatile of all root vegetables. I am sure dishes like the *ocopas* and the *causas* are pre-Columbian, slightly changed, I think for the better, by food introduced by the Conquest—walnuts, for example. In colonial times (and still today for a really traditional Peruvian meal), these were considered dishes to have before the main course. As far as I am concerned, they make a complete meal with the addition of a light dessert. They are very useful when one wants a vegetarian meal or something a little different made with fish or prawns. In Peru *mirasol* pepper would be used. Hot dried red peppers are an excellent substitute.

[Serves 6]

6 hot red dried peppers, about 1½ to 2 inches long
¼ pint peanut oil
1 medium onion, thickly sliced
2 cloves garlic, finely chopped
¼ pound walnuts, ground
¼ pound Spanish fresh cheese or Caerphilly or white Cheshire, crumbled

½ pint milk
1 teaspoon salt, or to taste
Lettuce leaves
6 warm, freshly cooked medium potatoes, peeled and halved lengthwise
6 hardboiled eggs, halved lengthwise
12 black olives
Strips of pimiento for garnish

Shake the seeds out of the peppers and put them to soak in 4 tablespoons hot water for 30 minutes. Drain and set aside. Heat the oil in a small frying pan and sauté the onion and garlic over very low heat until the onion is golden. Put the oil, onion, garlic, hot peppers, walnuts, and fresh cheese in a blender or food processor. Add the milk and salt and blend to a smooth sauce, about the consistency of

217

a heavy mayonnaise. Add milk and oil in equal quantities to thin the sauce if necessary.

Arrange a bed of lettuce leaves on a large, warmed platter. Arrange the potatoes, cut side down, on top of the lettuce. Mask the potatoes with the sauce, then garnish the dish with the eggs, cut side up, the black olives, and the strips of pimiento.

Variation: For *Ocopa de Camarones* (Shrimp and Potatoes with Cheese, Walnut, and Hot Pepper Sauce), reduce the walnuts to 2 ounces and add to the blender or food processor ½ pound cooked, chopped shrimp or prawns. In addition garnish the platter with ¼ pound cooked, peeled prawns, preferably medium-sized.

Papas a la Huancaina

POTATOES WITH CHEESE AND HOT PEPPER SAUCE   *Peru*

This is from Huancayo, in the Peruvian highlands at 11,000 feet. It is a typical highlands dish, very Indian, especially in the use of the local herb *palillo*, which colours food a bright yellow. Turmeric, used sparingly, is an admirable substitute.

[Serves 8 as a first course, 4 as a light luncheon dish]

4 tablespoons lemon juice
⅛ teaspoon cayenne pepper
Salt, freshly ground pepper
1 medium onion, thinly sliced
8 medium potatoes
¾ pound coarsely chopped Spanish fresh cheese or mild Cheddar or white Cheshire
1 or more fresh hot yellow peppers, seeded and chopped, or use red or

green peppers
1 teaspoon palillo, or ½ teaspoon turmeric
½ pint double cream
¼ pint olive oil
Lettuce leaves
4 hardboiled eggs, halved
2 or 3 ears of corn, cooked and cut into 8 slices
8 black olives

In a bowl combine the lemon juice, cayenne pepper, and salt and pepper to taste. Add the onion, separated into rings, and set it aside to pickle at room temperature.

Boil the potatoes in their skins until tender. Drain, peel, and keep warm. In a blender or food processor combine the cheese, hot peppers, *palillo* or turmeric, and the cream. Blend until smooth. Heat the oil in a frying pan, pour in the cheese mixture, reduce the heat to low, and cook, stirring constantly with a wooden spoon, until the sauce is smooth and creamy.

Garnish a platter with the lettuce leaves. Arrange the potatoes on the platter and pour the sauce over them. Arrange the eggs, corn slices, and olives around and in between the potatoes. Drain the onion rings and arrange them over the potatoes.

Causa a la Chiclayana

POTATOES WITH FISH AND VEGETABLES   *Peru*

This is a very decorative dish and looks lovely on a buffet with lettuce leaves framing the serving platter and the mound of mashed potatoes garnished with strips of red pepper, onion rings, wedges of cheese, and black olives, in the centre surrounded by the fried fish, sliced green bananas, corn, and slices of tropical root vegetables. The potatoes are transformed into something quite exciting with the vinaigrette dressing. It makes a hearty and satisfying one-dish meal.

[Serves 6]

4 tablespoons finely chopped onion
¼ pint lemon juice
⅛ teaspoon cayenne pepper
Salt, freshly ground pepper
3 pounds boiling potatoes, peeled and halved
¾ pint olive oil
1 pound sweet potatoes, peeled and cut into 6 slices
1 pound cassava (yucca) root, peeled and cut into 6 slices
3 green plantains or green bananas
2 ears corn
Flour
2 pounds striped bass fillets, cut
into 2-inch pieces, or any firm white fish
3 fresh hot red peppers, about 4 inches long, or use hot green peppers
3 medium onions, cut into ⅛-inch slices
¼ pint white vinegar
Lettuce leaves
½ pound Spanish fresh cheese (queso blanco or queso fresco) or white Cheshire, cut into 6 wedges
Lettuce leaves
Black olives

In a small bowl combine the finely chopped onion, lemon juice, cayenne pepper, and salt and pepper to taste. Set aside. Cook the potatoes in salted water until they are tender, but not mushy. Drain well and mash. Add ½ pint of the olive oil to the onion and lemon juice. Pour this dressing over the potatoes, mixing thoroughly. Make a mound of the potatoes in the centre of a large round platter and keep warm, not hot.

Boil the sweet potatoes and cassava in salted water for 20 minutes, or until they are tender. Drain and keep warm. It does not matter if

219

the cassava slices have broken up. In a separate saucepan boil the plantains, unpeeled but cut in half if necessary to fit the pan, until tender, about 30 minutes. Green bananas will take less time, about 15 minutes. Peel and cut into 12 slices. Keep warm with the sweet potatoes and cassava. Drop the corn into a large saucepan of boiling salted water and boil for 5 minutes. Cut each ear into 3 slices and put with the other vegetables.

Season the flour with salt and pepper. Dredge the fish pieces in the seasoned flour, shaking to remove the excess. Heat 4 tablespoons of the olive oil and fry the pieces of fish until they are golden brown on both sides, about 3 or 4 minutes. Drain on paper towels and keep warm.

Cut the peppers into ⅛-inch strips and put, with the sliced onions, into a saucepan of boiling water. Blanch for a few minutes then drain well. Add the remaining olive oil, the vinegar, and salt and pepper to taste. Bring to the boil over low heat and cook, covered, for 2 or 3 minutes.

To serve, garnish the platter round the edge with lettuce leaves. Arrange the fish fillets, corn, sweet potato, cassava, and plantains or bananas on the lettuce leaves. Pour the onion and pepper mixture over the potatoes and garnish the mound with the wedges of cheese and black olives..

Variation: For *Causa a la Limeña* (Potatoes with Prawns and Vegetables), add a seeded and finely chopped fresh hot red or green pepper to the chopped onion pickle. Omit the plantains and fish. Instead drop 6 large prawns (or more if using smaller prawns) into boiling salted water and cook until just tender, 3 to 5 minutes. Hardboil 3 eggs and cut them in halves lengthwise. To serve arrange lettuce leaves round the edge of the mound of potatoes and arrange the cassava and sweet potato slices on the lettuce leaves. Make a circle on the edge of the mound of potatoes with the corn, then another circle on the potatoes with the cheese and prawns alternately, and finally place the eggs and the black olives on top of the potatoes. Serves 6.

Ocopa de Pichones

POTATOES AND EGGS IN PIGEON AND WALNUT SAUCE   *Peru*

This is a most exotic and delectable dish, ideal for a summer lunch or dinner when hot food is unappetizing and the palate longs for something light yet substantial. The flavour of the pigeon is subtly enhanced by the walnuts, cheese, and oil-stewed onion, to make a most sumptuous sauce for the potato and hardboiled egg. Start with a corn or sweet red pepper soup and follow the *Ocopa* with *Mazamorra Morada* (Peruvian Fruit Compote), page 285, for dessert. A dry white wine or a rosé makes extremely pleasant drinking.

[Serves 6]

4 pigeons, each weighing about 8 ounces
Salt, freshly ground pepper
6 medium onions
4 medium tomatoes
1 large hot dried red pepper, or 2 small

4 tablespoons olive oil
4 ounces walnuts
8 ounces fresh cheese, or Spanish queso fresco or queso blanco
Milk
6 eggs
6 medium potatoes

FOR THE GARNISH

Lettuce leaves
Black and green olives

4 fresh hot red peppers (optional)

Split the pigeons in half and season on both sides with salt and pepper. Thinly slice 4 of the onions and put them in the bottom of a heavy casserole. Arrange the pigeons on top of the onions. Peel the tomatoes and cut them into thin slices, about ⅛ inch. Make a layer of the tomatoes over the pigeons. Cover the casserole with foil and then with the casserole lid. Cook over very low heat, using an asbestos mat if necessary to keep the contents from burning. Cook until the pigeons are tender, about 3 hours, shaking the casserole from time to time. Let the pigeons cool thoroughly in the casserole. Lift the birds out and bone them. Chop the meat coarsely and set aside. Reserve the pan juices. Rinse out and dry the casserole. Shake the seeds out of the hot dried pepper and put it to soak in warm water.

Cut the remaining 2 onions into thick slices, about ¾ inch. Heat the oil in the casserole and add the onion slices. Cook over low heat, turning once, until they are golden brown on both sides. Allow to cool slightly, then put into a blender or food processor fitted with a steel blade, with the oil, the pigeon meat, and the pan juices. Drain the pepper, chop, and add. Add the walnuts and cheese and reduce to a purée, adding milk as necessary to make the sauce the consistency of a thick mayonnaise. Purée in batches if necessary.

Hardboil the eggs, shell them, and halve them lengthwise. Boil the potatoes and drain them. Arrange the eggs, yolk side up, and the potatoes while still warm on a large warmed serving platter. Pour the sauce over them. Decorate the edge of the platter with lettuce leaves and arrange the olives on top of the potatoes and eggs. Slice the peppers from the tip to the stem and into 4 or 5 sections, which will then curl back, forming flowers. Place them round the edge of the dish. This is optional but I like to do it, as there is always someone who really enjoys nibbling on hot peppers.

If serving this as an appetizer, halve the potatoes lengthwise and serve half a potato and half a hardboiled egg per person. Serves 12.

Cuscuz de Galinha

GARNISHED STEAMED CHICKEN AND CORNMEAL   *Brazil*

This *Cuscuz* from São Paulo is made of cornmeal. The original *couscous*—the national dish of the Maghreb, the North African countries of Morocco, Tunisia, and Algeria—is made of wheat. There are other differences, which help to illustrate the Brazilian cook's ability to absorb foreign influences and to transform what is borrowed. This is a delicious dish, easy to make and wonderfully festive looking.

[Serves 6 to 8]

A 3½-pound chicken, cut into serving pieces
2 tablespoons lemon juice
2 ounces butter
4 spring onions, chopped, using white and green parts
2 medium tomatoes, peeled, seeded, and chopped
Salt, freshly ground pepper

½ pint dry white wine
¼ pint chicken stock
1 tablespoon olive oil
½ pound chorizo or other spiced smoked pork sausage, cut into ¼-inch slices
8 tablespoons chopped parsley
1 or 2 fresh hot red peppers, seeded and chopped

Put the chicken pieces in a bowl with the lemon juice. Mix well and let stand 15 minutes. Lift out the chicken pieces, pat dry, and reserve the liquid. Heat the butter in a flameproof casserole and sauté the chicken pieces lightly. Add the spring onions and tomatoes and season to taste with salt and pepper. Pour in the wine and chicken stock. Bring to a simmer, cover, and cook over low heat until the chicken pieces are tender. Let them stand, off the heat, until they are cool enough to handle. Lift them out of the stock, skin and bone them, and shred the meat into pieces about 1 inch by ¼ inch. Strain the stock and discard the solids. Make up to ½ pint with chicken stock if necessary. Return the chicken to the stock.

Heat the olive oil in a frying pan and sauté the sausage until browned on both sides. Drain on paper towels and add to the chicken with the parsley and hot peppers. Set aside.

FOR THE CORNMEAL MIXTURE

1 pound white, or if not available, yellow cornmeal
½ pound butter
2 medium tomatoes, thinly sliced
A 10-ounce can hearts of palm, drained and thinly sliced

3 hardboiled eggs, sliced
12 stoned black olives, halved
6 ounces cooked fresh green peas or cooked frozen peas
2 oranges, preferably Seville oranges, peeled and thinly sliced

Toast the cornmeal in a heavy frying pan over moderate heat, stirring constantly with a wooden spoon, until it is golden, about 5 minutes. Sprinkle ½ pint boiling water over the cornmeal and stir to mix. Cook, stirring, for 2 minutes. Melt the butter in a small saucepan and pour it over the cornmeal, mixing well. Stir the cornmeal, little by little, into the chicken, sausage, and stock mixture, combining it gently but thoroughly. Test the mixture to see if it holds its shape when pressed into a ball. If it is too crumbly, add a little warmed chicken stock and mix, testing again to see that the mixture keeps its shape.

If using a *cuscuzeiro (couscoussière)* butter the upper part. Otherwise, butter the inside of a fine-holed colander. Place a tomato slice in the centre of the colander or *couscoussière*. Divide the remaining tomato, the hearts of palm, eggs, and olives into 3 equal parts. Divide the peas into 2 parts. Arrange one-third of the tomatoes, palm hearts, eggs, and olives in a decorative pattern around the bottom and sides of the colander. They will stay in place because of the butter. Put one-third of the cornmeal mixture into the colander and pat it down lightly. Sprinkle with half of the peas and another third of the garnish. Cover with another third of the cornmeal. Add the remaining peas and the remaining garnish and top with the remaining cornmeal. Cover with a cloth napkin, then cover the colander tightly with foil, tucking the foil firmly under the rim. Pour boiling water into a deep pot large enough to hold the colander comfortably (or into the bottom half of the *couscoussière*), taking care that the water is not deep enough to reach the bottom of the colander. Cover and steam over low heat for 1 hour, adding a little boiling water during the cooking period if necessary. Turn off the heat and let the colander stand for a few minutes. Remove the napkin and unmould the *Cuscuz* onto a serving dish. It will look like a steamed pudding decorated with the tomato, hearts of palm, and so on. Garnish the dish with the sliced oranges.

Pastel de Choclo con Relleno de Pollo

CHICKEN PIE WITH CORN TOPPING   *Bolivia*

This is simply delicious, with a combination of flavours that is new to our palates though none of the ingredients is hard to find. As it can be prepared ahead of time, it makes an ideal party dish.

[Serves 6]

A 3½-pound chicken, cut into serving pieces
¾ pint chicken stock, about
4 tablespoons seedless raisins
3 tablespoons olive or vegetable oil
2 medium onions, finely chopped

3 medium tomatoes, peeled and chopped
Salt
1 or 2 pinches ground cinnamon
2 hardboiled eggs, coarsely chopped
12 small pimiento-stuffed olives, rinsed and halved

FOR THE TOPPING

¼ pound butter or lard, or a mixture of both
1½ pounds corn kernels

1 tablespoon sugar, or less to taste
2 teaspoons salt, or to taste
4 eggs
Sweet paprika

Put the chicken pieces into a large saucepan, pour in the stock, adding a little more if necessary to barely cover. Bring to the boil, cover, and simmer over low heat until the chicken is tender, about 45 minutes. Let it cool in the stock. When it is cool enough to handle, lift it out of the stock, remove the skin and bones, and cut the meat into 1-inch pieces. Set aside. Reserve the stock for another use. Put the raisins to soak in cold water to cover for 10 minutes. Heat the oil and sauté the onions until they are soft. Add the tomatoes and cook for about 5 minutes longer, or until the mixture is well blended. Season with salt, drain, and add the raisins, cinnamon, chopped eggs, olives, and chicken. Set aside.

To make the topping, melt the butter or lard in a small saucepan. Put the corn kernels in a blender or food processor and reduce to a purée. Pour into a saucepan and stir in the melted butter or lard. Stir in the sugar and salt. Cook over very low heat, beating the eggs in one by one. Cook, stirring with a wooden spoon, until the mixture has thickened. Allow to cool slightly.

Butter a 3 pint soufflé dish and spoon in about one-third of the corn mixture, patting it up to cover the sides of the dish. Carefully spoon in the chicken mixture, then cover with the rest of the corn.

Sprinkle with sweet paprika. Bake in a preheated moderate (350° F, 180° C., gas 4) oven for 1 hour, or until the topping is set and lightly browned. Serve hot.

The pie may be prepared ahead and refrigerated until ready to bake, in which case let it come to room temperature before baking.

Pudín de Choclo

CORN SOUFFLÉ   *Ecuador*

This is less like a French soufflé than like an American corn pudding. It is a rich-tasting dish, but not heavy, nice for a light meal, or as the first course of a grand one.

[Serves 6]

6 ounces kernels of young corn, or frozen corn, thawed
½-pound mild Cheddar, or white Cheshire, cubed
2 ounces butter, cut into small pieces
Salt, white pepper
5 eggs, well beaten
Butter

Combine the corn, cheese, and butter in a blender or food processor. Season to taste with salt and pepper and pour in the eggs. Blend on high speed until the mixture is smooth. Pour into a buttered 2½ pint soufflé dish and set the dish in a pan of hot water in a preheated moderate (350° F., 180° C., gas 4) oven. Bake for 1 hour, or until a knife inserted in the soufflé comes out clean.

Chouriço, Brócolos, y Creme de Milho

SAUSAGE AND BROCCOLI WITH PURÉED CORN   *Brazil*

This dish from the state of Minas Gerais is a fine one-dish family meal. The corn purée makes a lovely sauce for the broccoli.

[Serves 4]

1½-pounds broccoli
2½ ounces butter
Salt, freshly ground pepper
Oil
¾ pound chorizo or other spiced smoked pork sausage
1½ pounds raw corn kernels

Rinse the broccoli in cold water and cut off and discard the tough stems. Chop the broccoli. In a saucepan heat 2 ounces butter, add the broccoli, stir, and cook for 2 minutes. Add 1 tablespoon water, cover, and cook until the vegetable is tender, about 8 minutes. Season with salt and pepper. Put in a serving dish and keep warm.

225

Film the bottom of a pan with oil and sauté the chorizos until browned all over, about 5 minutes. They will cook in their own fat. Drain on paper towels and slice, or halve crosswise. Arrange the sausage around the broccoli and keep warm.

Purée the corn in a blender or food processor. In a saucepan melt the remaining butter, add the corn, and cook stirring constantly with a wooden spoon for about 5 minutes over low heat. Season with salt and pepper. Pour the corn purée over the broccoli.

Mucbi-Pollo

CHICKEN AND PORK TAMAL PIE   *Mexico*

This is a very old, traditional Mayan dish from Yucatán, a sort of corn pie wrapped in banana or plantain leaves and baked in a *pib* or earth oven, though nowadays it is usually cooked in an ordinary gas or electric oven. As banana or plantain leaves are fairly difficult to come by, kitchen parchment or aluminum foil may be used as substitutes. If the herb *epazote* is not available, its absence from the dish is no great matter since it is the annatto that gives the *tamal* pie its characteristic flavour and appearance. Traditionally a whole chicken, cut into serving pieces, is used but there seems to be no logical reason why the chicken should not be boned for ease in assembling and serving the dish. I have had it both ways and there is no difference in flavour, which is what matters.

[Serves 4 to 6]

FOR THE FILLING

1 large onion, chopped
3 medium tomatoes, peeled and
   chopped
2 cloves garlic, chopped
½ teaspoon oregano
¼ teaspoon cumin

2 tablespoons ground annatto
Salt
A 2½-pound chicken, quartered
1 pound lean pork, cut into 1-inch
   cubes
½ pint chicken stock, about
4 ounces masa harina

Put the onion, tomatoes, garlic, oregano, cumin, annatto, and salt to taste in a blender or food processor and reduce them to a purée. Put the chicken and pork into a saucepan or casserole and pour the purée over them. Add enough chicken stock to cover, about ½ pint. Cover and simmer until the chicken is tender, about 45 minutes. Lift out the chicken pieces and set aside. Continue to cook the pork until it is tender, about 30 minutes longer. Bone the chicken and cut it into large pieces. Set it aside with the pork. Strain the stock. Put the *masa harina* in a small saucepan and add enough of the stock to make a very thick sauce, stirring over low heat for a minute or two. Pour the sauce over the chicken and pork.

FOR THE DOUGH

1 *pound* masa harina	1½ *tablespoons annatto seeds*
½ *pint annatto oil or lard, page* 310	*Chicken stock*
	Salt

Put the *masa harina* in a bowl, stir in the annatto oil or lard and the seeds, and when thoroughly mixed add just enough hot chicken stock and a pinch of salt to make a thick, smooth dough. Cut a 12- by 24-inch strip of kitchen parchment or aluminum foil, or use a banana leaf, if available. Spread half of the *masa harina* dough on the parchment or foil, leaving room at the sides. Arrange the chicken, pork, and sauce on top of the dough. Cover with the rest of the dough. Fold up the parchment into a parcel and put it into a greased baking pan, fold side down. Bake in a preheated hot oven (400° F., 200° C., gas 6) for 30 minutes. Unwrap to serve. The outside will be crisp, the inside, with the chicken and pork filling, moist. Serve with *Ixni-Pec* (Hot Pepper Sauce), page 301.

Chilaquiles de Estudiante

STUDENT'S TORTILLA CASSEROLE   *Mexico*

My husband says this dish reminds him of his days at the university in Mexico, when he was perpetually hungry but often lacked the time to get home for the main meal at midday and found no one very interested in feeding him at night, when only *merienda*, a light supper, was served. *Chilaquiles* is essentially a leftover dish using anything the kitchen has to offer, usually leftover chicken, or turkey *mole*, or any pork. This one is very special indeed, quite approaching elegance. I suspect that only a very warm-hearted family cook, who understood that acquiring knowledge provokes appetite, would have gone to the trouble of preparing it for the evening meal of a hungry student and three of his friends, equally hungry, since it serves 4. I also suspect the cook must have overbought the pork for the midday meal to have had a pound left over. Made on purpose with no students around, it makes a fine lunch or supper dish.

[Serves 4]

FOR THE TORTILLAS

1 recipe tortillas (page 63)   *4 tablespoons vegetable oil or lard*

Make the tortillas the previous day, if possible, as they should have time to dry out a little. Simply wrap them in a cloth and leave them in the kitchen. If they are freshly made, dry them in the oven with the pilot light on for an hour or two. When ready to use, cut the tortillas with kitchen shears into strips about ½ inch wide. Heat the oil or lard and fry the tortilla strips in batches, but do not let them brown. Drain on paper towels and set aside. Reserve the oil.

FOR THE FILLING

*1 pound of cooked pork, cut into
 1-inch pieces*
*2 medium tomatoes, peeled and
 chopped*
1 medium onion, chopped
2 cloves garlic, chopped

3 tablespoons seedless raisins
*16 small pimiento-stuffed olives,
 halved*
1 tablespoon red wine vinegar
½ teaspoon sugar
Salt and pepper to taste

Shred the meat. Put the tomatoes, onion, and garlic in a blender or food processor and reduce to a purée. Measure the oil remaining in the pan and if necessary make up the quantity to 2 tablespoons. Add the tomato mixture and cook, stirring, for 2 or 3 minutes. Add the pork, raisins, olives, vinegar, sugar, and salt and pepper to taste, and simmer over low heat until the mixture is quite thick, about 5 minutes. Make a layer of half the tortilla strips in a greased ovenproof casserole, preferably earthenware, and spread the pork mixture on top. Cover with the remaining tortilla strips. Set aside.

FOR THE SAUCE

4 ancho *chilies*
1 medium onion
1 clove garlic
⅛ teaspoon cinnamon
Pinch of ground cloves

1 teaspoon sugar
Salt, freshly ground pepper
3 tablespoons vegetable oil or lard
*2 medium tomatoes, peeled and
 chopped*

Pull the stems from the chilies, shake out the seeds, rinse in cold water, and tear into pieces. Put into a bowl with ¼ pint warm water and soak, turning from time to time, for about 1 hour. Put the chilies and any soaking water into a blender or food processor with the onion and garlic and reduce to a purée. It should be quite thick and heavy. Do not over-blend, as it should have some texture. Add the cinnamon, cloves, sugar, salt, and pepper. Heat the oil or lard and add the *ancho* mixture. Cook, stirring, for about 5 minutes. Purée the tomatoes in the blender and add to the pan and simmer for 2 or 3 minutes longer. Add ¾ pint of chicken stock or water. Stir to mix, heat through, and pour over the contents of the casserole. Bake the casserole in a preheated moderate oven (350° F., 180° C., gas 4) until heated through, about 30 minutes. Serve directly from the casserole. Accompany with a green salad.

Arroz com Porco

RICE WITH PORK *Brazil*

This dish is typical of São Paulo and the regions the Paulistas developed.

[Serves 6]

FOR THE MARINADE

¼ pint dry white wine
¼ pint white vinegar
1 large clove garlic, crushed
1 medium onion, grated
Salt, freshly ground pepper
1 tablespoon chopped fresh
　coriander

1 fresh hot red pepper, chopped, or
　½ teaspoon hot pepper sauce
　(such as Tabasco or Môlho de
　Pimenta e Limão, *page 302*)
2 pounds pork, loin or shoulder,
　cut into 1-inch cubes

FOR THE STEW

2 tablespoons vegetable oil
1 medium onion, chopped
1 sweet green pepper, seeded and
　chopped
1 clove garlic, chopped
1 tablespoon chopped fresh
　coriander

¾ pound long-grain rice
Salt, freshly ground pepper
¼ pound boiled ham, diced
¼ pound freshly grated Parmesan
　cheese plus 2 tablespoons
½ ounce butter

In a large bowl combine the wine, vinegar, garlic, grated onion, salt

229

and pepper to taste, coriander, and hot pepper or hot pepper sauce. Add the pork and mix lightly. Cover the bowl and refrigerate for about 8 hours, stirring once or twice. Lift out the pork pieces and pat them dry with paper towels. Strain and reserve the marinade. Discard the solids.

Heat the oil in a casserole and sauté the pork pieces until they are lightly browned. Add the onion, green pepper, garlic, and fresh coriander, and sauté for 3 or 4 minutes longer. Add the strained marinade, cover, and simmer until the pork is tender, about 1 hour.

About 20 minutes before the pork is done, wash the rice, drain, and put it into a heavy saucepan with 1½ pints cold water. Bring to the boil over high heat, stir in ½ teaspoon salt, cover, and cook over low heat until the rice is tender and all the liquid absorbed, about 20 minutes.

Taste the pork for seasoning, adding a little more salt and pepper if needed. Add the ham and stir in the ¼ pound cheese.

Arrange half the rice on an ovenproof serving platter. Spread the pork mixture over the rice, which should be quite dry. Arrange the rest of the rice over the pork. Sprinkle the rice with the 2 tablespoons of Parmesan cheese and the butter, cut into small bits. Put the platter into a preheated moderately hot (375° F., 190° C., gas 5) oven until the top is lightly browned, about 10 minutes. Serve with a freshly made tomato sauce (*Môlho ao Tomate,* see page 306).

Flan de Legumbres

VEGETABLE SOUFFLÉ   *Ecuador*

Vegetables are handled imaginatively by Ecuadorian cooks. This mixture of eggs and vegetables makes a satisfying meal when served with soup and dessert.

[Serves 4 to 6]

6 rashers bacon, cut into julienne
3 ounces fresh breadcrumbs
¼ pint milk
3 tablespoons tomato sauce
¼ pint chicken stock
2 tablespoons melted butter
1 tablespoon chopped parsley

Salt, freshly ground pepper
¾ pound cooked mixed vegetables
    such as corn, peas, carrots,
    cauliflower, green beans, and
    green pepper, all chopped
3 eggs, well beaten
a knob of butter

Cook the bacon over moderate heat until crisp, and drain on paper towels. Combine the bacon with the breadcrumbs, milk, tomato sauce, chicken stock, melted butter, parsley, and salt and pepper to taste. Fold in the mixed vegetables. Fold in the eggs and pour the mixture into a buttered 2½ pint soufflé dish. Stand the dish in a baking tin, half-filled with hot water, in a preheated moderate oven (350° F., 180° C., gas 4) and cook for 1 hour, or until a knife inserted into the soufflé comes out clean.

Repollo Relleno

STUFFED WHOLE CABBAGE   *Bolivia*

A whole stuffed cabbage with a highly seasoned meat stuffing makes a most delectable luncheon or family supper dish. I've come across it with variations in the filling in the Andean countries of Bolivia, Peru, Venezuela, and Colombia. Its obvious ancestor is *sou-fassum*, the stuffed cabbage of Provence. When I cook it, I borrow a trick from Richard Olney, who wraps his *sou-fassum* in butter muslin, making it a lot easier to handle than when it is merely tied round with a piece of string. I save the leftover stock for making soup.

[Serves 6 to 8]
1 large Savoy cabbage, weighing
   about 3 pounds
1 recipe Picadillo (Seasoned
   Chopped Beef), page 139, using

*pork instead of beef and omitting
the apples and almonds
Beef or chicken stock*
1 recipe Salsa de Jitomate
   (Tomato Sauce), page 306

Trim the cabbage, removing any wilted outer leaves. Drop it into a large saucepan full of briskly boiling water and let it simmer for 10 minutes. Lift out the cabbage into a colander and let it drain thoroughly. When it is cool enough to handle, place on a large square of double butter muslin and carefully open the outer leaves, spreading as flat as possible without breaking them off. Cut out the heart of the cabbage, discard the core, chop fine, and add it to the seasoned chopped pork, mixing thoroughly. Cut away as much of the core as possible while leaving the cabbage intact. Form the meat into a ball and pack it into the centre of the cabbage. Press the outer leaves back into shape, re-forming the cabbage. Gather up butter muslin and tie it up with string. Put the cabbage into a large saucepan into which it fits comfortably and pour in enough stock to cover. Bring to the boil, reduce the heat, and simmer the cabbage for 3 to 3½ hours. Lift out into a round serving dish or soup tureen, untie, and slide out butter muslin, lifting the cabbage with a spatula to do so. Spoon a little tomato sauce over the cabbage and serve the rest in a sauceboat. To serve cut the cabbage into wedges. Accompany with rice.

Variation: Reduce the amount of pork to 1 pound and add 1 pound potatoes, peeled and cut into ¼-inch cubes. Serve with crusty bread instead of rice.

Variation: In Venezuela, cooks add 1 teaspoon *Aliño Criollo* (Creole Style Seasoning Powder), page 310, to the meat mixture.

Variation: In Brazil, where stuffed cabbage is also popular, a mixture of pork and beef, seasoned with ½ teaspoon nutmeg, is used. Two slices of chopped bacon may be added as well as 4 tablespoons well-washed raw rice.

Carne Rellena

STUFFED STEAK   *Venezuela*

This is an unusual dish and looks quite spectacular, as the egg and vegetables show attractively in each slice. The flavour matches the looks. The stuffed omelet makes a rich accompaniment to the tender, juicy steak.

[Serves 6]

A 3-pound skirt steak, or two 1½-pound steaks
4 large cloves garlic, crushed
Salt
4 tablespoons olive oil
4 eggs

Vegetable oil
A 10-ounce tin green asparagus tips
2 whole pimientos, cut into strips
1 ounce butter
½ pint dry red wine

Trim the steak of any fat and place in a baking dish or any shallow dish large enough to hold it comfortably. Mix the garlic with 2 teaspoons salt and the olive oil and rub the mixture into both sides of the steak. Let it stand at room temperature for about 2 hours.

Break the eggs into a bowl and beat them lightly with 1 teaspoon salt and 2 tablespoons water. Heat a 7-inch omelet pan and pour in just enough vegetable oil to film the surface. The pan should be about the same width as the steak. A rectangular Japanese omelet pan is ideal for this; if using a round pan, trim the omelet later to fit the steak. Pour the eggs into the pan and make an omelet in the usual way, stirring vigorously with the flat of a fork over moderate heat until the eggs begin to set, then cook until the eggs have set. Slide the omelet out of the pan and place it on top of the steak. If using

2 smaller steaks, make 2 omelets. Trim the omelet to fit. On top of the omelet lay alternate horizontal rows of asparagus tips and pimiento strips, starting and ending about ½ inch from the edge. Roll up the steak and tie it securely with string. Put the steak into a baking tin and dot it with the butter. Bake in a preheated moderate oven (350° F., 180° C., gas 4) for 45 minutes for rare steak, basting it several times with the wine. Cook for 15 minutes longer if a well-done steak is preferred.

Lift the steak out onto a warmed serving platter and remove the string. Reduce the wine and pan juices quickly over brisk heat and pour into a sauceboat. Cut the steak into 1-inch slices, and serve with plain white rice, *Caraotas Negras* (Black Beans), and fried plantains or bananas.

Molondrones con Camarones

OKRA WITH PRAWNS   *Dominican Republic*

This is a lovely dish from the Dominican Republic with okra, bananas, prawns, and coriander making an unusual combination of flavours.

[Serves 3 to 4]

¼ pint vegetable oil
1 medium onion, finely chopped
1 pound small, fresh okra pods, cut into ¼-inch slices
3 underripe bananas, peeled and cut into ½-inch slices
2 medium tomatoes, peeled and chopped

4 tablespoons lemon juice
1 small fresh hot red or green pepper, seeded and chopped
1 tablespoon fresh green coriander, chopped
Salt, freshly ground pepper
1 pound medium-sized prawns, shelled and deveined

Heat the oil and sauté the onion until it is soft. Add the okra and sauté for 2 to 3 minutes longer. Add the bananas, tomatoes, lemon juice, hot pepper, coriander, and salt and pepper to taste. Simmer the mixture for about 5 minutes, or until the okra is tender. Add the prawns and cook for about 3 minutes longer, or until the prawns turn pink. Serve with rice.

Queso Relleno

STUFFED CHEESE   *Mexico*

This dish, though popular for a long time in its birthplace, the Caribbean island of Curaçao (where it is called *Keshy Yena* in the patois of the island), was introduced to Yucatán by Dutch and German coffee men sometime in the last century. Its foreign origins are obvious in that a Dutch Edam cheese is the main ingredient, hollowed out and stuffed with a rich pork mixture. For some reason Yucatecans almost invariably use saffron rather than annatto, which is more characteristic of their kitchen, and they usually steam rather than bake the cheese; the sauce, too, is a further Mayan enhancement. The dish looks quite spectacular when brought to the table as the cheese expands during the cooking and, when cut into wedges and served, the soft cheese shell combines deliciously with the pork filling. All that is needed as an accompaniment is a salad.

[Serves 6 to 8]
A 4-pound Edam cheese
6 eggs
2 pounds lean pork, minced
Salt
2 ounces lard or 4 tablespoons
   vegetable oil
1 medium onion, finely chopped
1 red pepper, seeded and chopped,
   or use 2 canned pimientos

2 cloves garlic, chopped
2 tomatoes, peeled, seeded, and
   chopped
½ teaspoon oregano
¼ teaspoon ground cloves
Freshly ground pepper
2 ounces small, stoned green olives
2 ounces seedless raisins
2 tablespoons capers
2 ounces dry sherry

FOR THE SAUCE

1½ ounces butter
3 tablespoons flour
The reserved pork stock
⅛ teaspoon powdered saffron, or
   thread saffron ground in a
   mortar with a pestle

1 sweet red pepper, seeded, and
   chopped, or use 2 canned
   pimientos, chopped
Salt, freshly ground pepper
2 ounces small, stoned green olives,
   halved

Peel the red wax covering off the cheese. Cut an inch-thick slice from the top and hollow it out slightly. Scoop out the cheese, leaving a shell ½ to ¾ inch thick. Reserve the scooped-out cheese for another use. Put the shell and lid in a large bowl of cold water to cover, and soak for 1 hour. Hardboil the eggs and drop them into cold water. When they are cool enough to handle, shell them. Carefully remove the whites, leaving the yolks whole. The best way to do this is with the fingers. Finely chop the whites and set both whites and yolks aside.

Put the pork into a saucepan with enough water to cover and salt to taste. Cover and simmer until the meat is tender, about 30 minutes.

Heat the lard or vegetable oil and sauté the onion, pepper, and garlic until the onion is soft. If using the pimientos, add with the tomatoes. Add the tomatoes and cook until the mixture is quite thick, about 5 minutes. Drain the pork and reserve the stock. Add the onion and tomato mixture to the pork with the oregano, cloves, salt and pepper to taste, the chopped egg whites, olives, raisins, capers, and sherry, mixing well. Remove the cheese shell and lid from the water, drain, and pat dry. Divide the meat mixture into three parts. Put one-third of it into the cheese, patting it down firmly. Halve the egg yolks. Make a layer of 6 halved yolks on top of the meat. Spoon in another third of the meat mixture and pat down lightly. Make a layer of the remaining 6 halved egg yolks, and top with the rest of the meat mixture. Place the lid on the cheese and rub the cheese all over with lard or oil. Wrap it in a double layer of muslin, then place on a rack in a steamer, and steam over boiling water for 40 minutes.

Meanwhile prepare the sauce: Heat the butter in a saucepan. Add the flour and cook, stirring constantly with a wooden spoon, for a minute. Do not let the flour brown. Add the reserved pork stock, making up the quantity with water to ¾ pint, if necessary. Add the saffron, the pepper or pimientos, salt and pepper to taste, and the olives. Cook, stirring frequently, for 15 minutes. Pour over the cheese just before serving.

Lift the cheese out of the steamer and remove the muslin. Place the cheese on a warmed serving platter and pour the sauce over it. To serve, cut the cheese in wedges.

Torta de Plátano

SAVOURY GREEN BANANA CAKE   *Mexico*

There is a hint of sweetness in this very original old colonial dish from Oaxaca in Mexico: the bananas go well with the robust flavour of the beans, a combination that is both unusual and good with meat and poultry when served instead of rice or potatoes.

[Serves 6 to 8]
1 pound cooked kidney or black beans
1 medium onion, finely chopped
1 bay leaf
2 ounces lard or 4 tablespoons vegetable oil

Salt, freshly ground pepper
6 green (unripe) bananas, or 4 green plantains
2 ounces grated Parmesan cheese
2 ounces butter
2 eggs, lightly beaten

235

If dried beans are used, simmer 6 ounces well-washed and picked-over kidney beans in water to cover with ½ medium onion, chopped, and a bay leaf, until the beans are tender, about 2 hours. If the beans dry out during the cooking, add a little hot water. Drain, reserve ¼ pint of the cooking liquid, remove and discard the bay leaf. Purée the cooked beans with about ¼ pint of the cooking liquid in a blender or food processor and reduce them to a purée. Heat the lard or oil in a heavy frying pan and sauté the onion until it is very soft. Add the beans and cook, stirring with a wooden spoon, until they form a soft paste. They should not be dry. Season to taste with salt and pepper. Set aside.

Cut through the skins of the bananas lengthwise and peel them. Put them into a saucepan with salted water to cover, bring to the boil over moderate heat, reduce the heat, and simmer, uncovered, until they are tender, 10 to 15 minutes. Plantains will take about 30 minutes. Drain and mash with a fork while they are still warm. Mash in the grated cheese and 1½ ounces butter. Stir in the eggs, mixing well. Butter a soufflé dish and make a layer of half the banana mixture, cover with the bean mixture, and top with the remaining banana mixture. Dot with the remaining tablespoon of butter, and bake in a preheated moderate oven (375° F., 190° C., gas 5) for 30 minutes. Serve directly from the dish.

Variation: Some cooks add 4 tablespoons of flour to the banana mixture with the cheese but I find this makes the topping very dense and heavy. However, for another Mexican version of the dish, *Frijoles con Plátanos* (Beans with Bananas), which is made with ripe bananas, flour is necessary (1 tablespoon flour for each banana), as the ripe fruit has more sugar and less starch. For this the banana mixture is fried in oil, 1 tablespoon at a time as a fritter, until browned on both sides, about 5 minutes. To serve put 1 teaspoon hot mashed black beans in the centre and fold the fritter over. These can be eaten with cream cheese as a dessert but are delicious with plainly cooked meats or poultry as a side dish.

Variation: In Oaxaca the *torta* is sometimes made into *Empanadas* (Turnovers). Pat the cooked green banana mixture plus 4 tablespoons flour into flat cakes 2 to 3 inches in diameter, stuff with a little of the bean mixture, fold over, pressing the edges together to seal in the filling, and fry in lard or vegetable oil until golden on both sides.

Variation: I came across a similar dish in Guatemala, *Empanadas de Plátano* (Banana Turnovers), also called, more picturesquely, *Niños*

Envueltos (Babies in a Blanket). Green plantains were preferred to green bananas though both were used, and flour was added, but the beans used were black beans, never any other kind. Sometimes the turnovers were stuffed with fresh cream cheese instead of, or as well as, the mashed beans, and the turnovers were deep fried. I once had them sprinkled with sugar and served with cream as a dessert. They were remarkably pleasant.

BEANS

Beans are important in Latin America not only because so many of the world's varieties of this useful vegetable originated there but because they supplied valuable protein in a region where there were none of the sources of high protein that Europe had, such as cattle, sheep, goats, pigs, and so on. Fortunately beans were not pushed out of the kitchen by the Conquest. They are just as popular today as they ever were. They are an essential part of Mexico's main meal, served after the main course and before dessert, in small bowls. They are quite soupy and are eaten with a spoon, accompanied by tortillas, which can also be used to scoop up the beans. I like to serve them, as do many modern Mexicans, with the meal. So essential are beans to the Latin American kitchen that there is a saying when unexpected guests arrive: *"Pónle más agua a los frijoles,"* meaning "Add more water to the beans." They are immensely popular as *frijoles refritos*, refried beans. It took me some time to understand why they are called "refried" when clearly they are fried only once. It is partly a matter of euphony since *frijoles fritos* sounds awful whereas *frijoles refritos* makes a pretty sound. It is also a nice economy of language as the beans are first boiled then fried, with the "re" standing for twice and pointing out the double cooking.

Venezuelans make a charming joke about their black beans, *Caraotas Negras*. They call them *"caviar criollo,"* creole caviar, and serve them mashed, usually with *Arepas* (Corn Bread) as an hors d'oeuvre. They are also an essential part of the national dish, *Pabellón Caraqueño*. They are the heart of Brazil's national dish, *Feijoada Completa* (Black Beans with Mixed Meats).

Because they were so important, cooks evolved their own special ways of seasoning the slowly simmered beans. I cook my beans according to the rules laid down by my husband's grandmother. I think of her recipe as Seven Precious Beans because seven ingredients are added to the beans, which she, along with lots of other cooks in Mexico, insist must never be presoaked. There are exceptions, notably black beans for *Feijoada*. Soaking instructions are given for the exceptions in the recipes in which they occur. Added are onion, garlic, hot pepper, oil or lard, salt, *epazote* or bay leaf, and tomato. Beans themselves have a good, full flavour and when well seasoned and slowly cooked over the most gentle heat are quite irresistible.

Lentils, which like beans are members of the legume family and also a very ancient food, are very popular all over Latin America though not to the point of rivalling beans.

Frijoles

BEANS   *Mexico*

[Serves 6 to 8]

1 pound red kidney, black, pinto, or pink beans

2 medium onions, finely chopped

2 cloves garlic, chopped

2 canned serrano chilies, or 1 jalapeño chili, chopped, or 1 teaspoon dried hot red peppers, crumbled

1 sprig epazote, or 1 bay leaf

2 tablespoons lard or vegetable oil

Salt

1 medium tomato, peeled and chopped

Wash and pick over the beans but do not soak. Put the beans into a large saucepan with cold water to cover by about 1 inch. Add half the chopped onions and garlic, the chilies, and the *epazote* or bay leaf. Cover, bring to the boil, and simmer gently, adding hot water as needed. When the beans begin to wrinkle, after about 15 to 20 minutes of cooking, add 1 tablespoon of the lard or vegetable oil. When the beans are tender (cooking may take 1½ to 3 hours), add salt to taste and continue to simmer for 30 minutes longer but without adding any more water. There should not be a great deal of liquid when the beans are done.

In a frying pan heat the remaining lard and sauté the remaining onions and garlic until soft. Add the tomato and sauté for 2 or 3 minutes longer. Take about ½ cup of beans and liquid from the saucepan and add them, by the tablespoon, to the pan, mashing the beans into the tomato mixture over moderate heat to form a fairly heavy paste. Stir this back into the beans in the saucepan, and simmer over low heat for a few minutes to thicken the remaining liquid.

Variation: For *Frijoles Refritos* (Refried Beans), cook the beans as above but use a large frying pan to sauté the onions, garlic, and tomato. Over moderate heat, gradually mash in all the beans, tablespoon by tablespoon, together with any liquid. Add a tablespoon of lard from time to time until the beans form a heavy, creamy paste. The amount of lard or vegetable oil used is a matter of taste.

For *antojitos* the beans are used as a spread. If the beans are served as a side dish, they are formed into a roll, sprinkled with grated cheese, and stuck with *tostaditas*, triangles of crisply fried tortilla.

Caraotas Negras

BLACK BEANS   *Venezuela*

[Serves 6]
1 pound black (turtle) beans
3 tablespoons olive oil
1 medium onion, finely chopped
1 sweet red pepper, seeded and
   chopped, or 2 pimientos, chopped

4 cloves garlic
1 teaspoon ground cumin
1 tablespoon sugar
Salt

Wash and pick over the beans. Put the beans to soak for 2 to 4 hours in a saucepan in enough cold water to cover by 2 inches. Add enough water to cover the beans by 1 inch as they will have absorbed much of the soaking water, bring to the boil, cover, and cook until the beans are tender, about 2 hours. In a frying pan heat the oil and sauté the onion and pepper until both are soft. Add the garlic, cumin, sugar, and the pimientos, if using instead of red pepper. Sauté for a minute or two, then stir into the beans. Season with salt to taste, and cook, partially covered, over low heat for ½ hour longer. The beans will be quite dry. Serve as a side dish or with *Pabellón Caraqueño* (Steak with Rice, Black Beans, and Plantains) page 134.

Feijão Preto

BLACK BEANS   *Brazil*

[Serves 6 to 8]
1 pound black (turtle) beans
2 tablespoons bacon fat

1 medium onion, grated
1 clove garlic, crushed
Salt, freshly ground pepper

Thoroughly wash the beans and put them into a heavy saucepan. Cover with cold water and soak them for about 4 hours. Add enough water to cover the beans by about 1 inch, bring to the boil, lower the heat, and simmer the beans, covered, until they are tender, about 2 hours. Heat the bacon fat in a frying pan and add the onion and garlic. Sauté until the onion is soft, then scoop out a cupful of the beans with their cooking liquid and add to the frying pan. Continue cooking, at the same time mashing the beans over low heat until the mixture is smooth and thick. Stir the mixture into the pot with the beans, season to taste with salt and pepper, and cook, uncovered, over very low heat for 30 minutes longer.

Porotos Granados

CRANBERRY BEANS WITH CORN AND PUMPKIN *Chile*

This very popular Chilean dish is also very Indian since its main ingredients are all indigenous foods—beans, tomatoes, corn, and pumpkin. In Chile fresh *porotos* (cranberry beans, sometimes called shell beans) are available almost all year round. If they are not available, dried cranberry or haricot beans can be used. *Calabaza*, the West Indian pumpkin, is best to use if available.

[Serves 4 to 6]

1 pound fresh cranberry beans, or ½ pound dried cranberry or haricot beans
3 tablespoons olive oil
2 tablespoons sweet paprika
1 large onion, finely chopped
4 medium tomatoes, peeled and chopped
½ teaspoon oregano
Salt, freshly ground pepper
1 pound pumpkin, peeled and cut into 1-inch cubes
4 ounces corn kernels

Wash the fresh beans and put them into a saucepan with cold water to cover, bring to the boil, lower the heat, and simmer, covered, until the beans are tender, about 45 minutes. If using dried beans, rinse them and put them to soak in cold water for 3 or 4 hours. Simmer the beans in unsalted water to cover until they are barely tender, 1½ to 2 hours. Drain the fresh or dried beans and set aside. Reserve the cooking liquid.

Meanwhile heat the oil in a frying pan and stir in the paprika over moderate heat with a wooden spoon, taking care not to let it burn. As soon as the paprika and oil are thoroughly mixed, stir in the onion and sauté until the onion is tender. Add the tomatoes, oregano, salt, and freshly ground pepper, and simmer the mixture, stirring from time to time, until it is thick and well blended. Add this mixture and the pumpkin to the saucepan with the beans, stir to mix, and add enough of the reserved cooking liquid barely to cover. Cover and simmer gently for 15 minutes. The pumpkin will disintegrate and thicken the sauce. Stir in the corn and simmer for 5 minutes longer. Serve in soup plates with a little *Pebre* (Chilean Hot Pepper Sauce), page 298, if liked.

Frijoles con Puerco Estilo Yucateco

BEANS WITH PORK, YUCATÁN STYLE   *Mexico*

[Serves 6]

1 pound black beans
2 pounds lean pork, cut into
   1½-inch cubes
2 large onions, finely chopped

1 whole fresh hot pepper, or 1
   canned hot pepper
½ teaspoon chopped epazote, if
   available
2 or 3 sprigs fresh coriander
Salt, freshly ground pepper

FOR THE GARNISH

1 large onion, finely chopped
8 tablespoons fresh coriander,
   chopped

12 small radishes, chopped
6 lemon wedges

FOR THE TOMATO SAUCE

4 medium tomatoes
2 fresh or canned hot green peppers

Salt

Thoroughly wash and pick over the beans. Put the beans into a large saucepan or flameproof casserole with water to cover by about 2 inches. Bring the beans to the boil, cover, reduce the heat, and simmer for 1 hour. Strain the beans, measure the liquid, and make it up to 3 pints. Return the beans and liquid to the saucepan. Add the pork, onions, hot pepper, *epazote*, if available, coriander sprigs, and salt and pepper to taste. Simmer, covered, until the meat and beans are both tender, about 1½ hours. Discard the hot pepper and coriander sprigs. Lift out the pork pieces with a slotted spoon and place them in the centre of a warmed platter. Strain the beans and arrange them round the pork. Pour the bean liquid into a soup tureen. Serve the soup in bowls and the beans and pork on plates at the same time. Serve the garnishes in bowls at the table to be eaten with both the soup and the beans.

To make the tomato sauce: Peel and chop 4 medium tomatoes and simmer them for 15 minutes with 2 fresh or canned hot green peppers and salt to taste. Pour the mixture into a blender or food processor and reduce to a purée. Pour back into the saucepan and heat through. Pour into a bowl and serve over the meat.

Frijoles Estilo Mexicano

BEANS, MEXICAN STYLE *Mexico*

This does not mean beans as cooked all over the republic of Mexico. It means as cooked in the state of Mexico and the federal district, where the capital, Mexico City, is located.

[Serves 8]
1 pound pinto, pink, or red kidney beans
1 onion, chopped

1 sprig epazote *or 1 bay leaf*
3 tablespoons lard or vegetable oil
Salt

Wash and pick over the beans and put them into a heavy saucepan with the onion and *epazote,* if available, or the bay leaf. Add enough water to cover the beans by 1 inch. Simmer the beans, covered, until they begin to wrinkle, after about 15 to 20 minutes of cooking. Add 1 tablespoon of the lard or oil and continue to cook the beans, covered, adding hot water as necessary until they are tender (1½ to 3 hours). Add salt to taste. Discard the *epazote* or bay leaf. Remove the beans with a slotted spoon to a bowl. Measure 4 tablespoons beans and mash them until smooth. Stir the mashed beans into the liquid in the saucepan. In a frying pan heat the remaining lard or oil and sauté the remaining beans until they are dry, about 5 minutes. Add them to the liquid in the saucepan and simmer the mixture, stirring frequently, until the liquid is thickened.

Lentejas

LENTILS *Colombia*

[Serves 6]
½ pound lentils
2 tablespoons olive oil
2 medium onions, finely chopped
2 cloves garlic, chopped

2 large tomatoes, peeled, seeded, and chopped
Salt, freshly ground pepper
Pinch of sugar
1 teaspoon chopped fresh coriander

Put the lentils in a large saucepan with water to cover by about 1 inch and cook until they are almost tender, about 1 hour. The quick-cooking variety (noted on package) will be done in about 25 minutes. Drain and set aside.

Heat the oil and sauté the onions and garlic until the onions are softened. Add the tomatoes, salt, pepper, sugar, and coriander, and simmer gently until the mixture is thick, about 10 minutes. Stir the sauce into the lentils and cook over very low heat for 10 minutes longer to blend the flavours. Serve instead of potatoes or rice.

Angú de Farinha de Milho

MOULDED CORNMEAL   *Brazil*

Brazilians are fond of this simple corn pudding. Traditionally it is served with *Picadinho de Porco* (Pork Hash), and *Couve à Mineira* (Kale, Minas Gerias Style), accompanied by *linguiça* sausages. It may also accompany any meat or poultry dish, or fish and shellfish.

[Serves 6]   *¼ pound cornmeal*
1¼ pints water   *1½ ounces butter plus butter for*
1 teaspoon salt   *   the mould*

In a heavy saucepan bring the water and salt to the boil and pour in the cornmeal in a thin, steady stream, stirring constantly with a wooden spoon. Cook over moderate heat until the mixture is smooth and thick. Stir in the butter. Butter a 3-pint mould and turn the cornmeal mixture into it. Pat it down, then unmould onto a serving dish.

Bacon fat may be used instead of butter.

RICE

Rice is enormously popular in Latin America and cooks pride themselves on their ability to cook rice to perfection, as this is often considered the measure of their skill in the kitchen. There are many ways to cook plain white rice and all of them produce rice that emerges tender, and with every grain separate. In Peru, Colombia, and Ecuador, cooked rice is drier than ours and is called *Arroz Graneado*.

Graneado has a dual meaning in Peruvian Spanish—choice or select, and grainy. It is an attractive texture. There are also more elaborate rice dishes like *Arroz a la Mexicana* (Rice, Mexican Style), which is served as a separate course, *sopa seca*, or dry soup, at *comida*, the big midday meal. It comes after soup and before the main course. I serve it with the main course as our meals are not as elaborate as they are traditionally in Mexico. In coastal Colombia rice is cooked in coconut milk and garnished with raisins, giving it a tantalizing hint of sweetness. In addition to plain white rice and more elaborate rice dishes, Brazil makes rice into moulded puddings that are served with the traditional dishes of Bahia. It is important always to use a heavy saucepan with a tightly fitting lid. If the rice is not to be used immediately, cover the saucepan with a folded tea towel, then the lid to prevent condensed moisture from making the rice mushy. The rice will stay hot for about 15 minutes.

Arroz Blanco

WHITE RICE   *Mexico*

[Serves 6]   *2 cloves garlic, finely chopped*
9 ounces long-grain rice   *1¼ pints cold water*
4 tablespoons vegetable oil   *Salt*
1 small onion, finely chopped   *1 fresh hot green pepper (optional)*

Wash the rice thoroughly in several changes of water, drain, and put into a saucepan with hot water to cover. Let stand 15 minutes. Drain in a sieve, letting it stand for about 10 minutes. Heat the oil in a saucepan, add the rice, onion, and garlic, and sauté over low heat, stirring constantly with a wooden spoon, until the rice begins to take on a pale gold colour and the oil is absorbed, 3 or 4 minutes. Add the water and salt to taste. Bring to the boil over high heat, reduce the heat to as low as possible, and cook, covered, until the rice is tender and all the liquid absorbed, about 20 minutes. I sometimes like to add a whole fresh hot green pepper when adding the water. It is discarded when the rice is cooked. This gives just a hint of peppery flavour.

Variation: For *Arroz Graneado* (Peruvian Style Rice), pour 2 tablespoons vegetable oil into a saucepan and add 1 clove crushed garlic. Sauté over low heat for 1 or 2 minutes, being careful not to let the garlic burn. Add 1¾ pints water, 1 teaspoon lemon juice, and salt to taste, and bring to the boil. Stir in 12 ounces long-grain rice, washed and drained, bring back to the boil, cover, and cook on the lowest possible heat until the rice is tender and all the liquid absorbed, about 25 minutes. Serves 4 to 6.

Variation: *Arroz Blanco* (White Rice) from Venezuela is traditionally served with *Pabellón Caraqueño* (Steak with Rice, Black Beans, and Plantains) but may accompany any fish, meat, or poultry dish. Thoroughly wash and drain 9 ounces long-grain rice. Heat 1½ ounces butter in a saucepan and stir in the rice, 1 medium onion, finely chopped, ½ red or green sweet pepper, seeded and chopped, and 1 clove garlic, chopped. Sauté, stirring, over low heat for 3 or 4 minutes, or until the butter is absorbed. Do not let the rice brown. Add 1¼ pints water and salt to taste, bring to the boil, and cook, covered, over very low heat for about 20 minutes, or until all the liquid is absorbed and the rice tender. Serves 6.

Variation: *Arroz de Amendoim* (Peanut-Coloured Rice) is not only the colour of roasted peanuts, but has a fine, nutty flavour. Thoroughly wash the rice and let it drain in a sieve for 30 minutes. Pour 2 tablespoons peanut oil into a saucepan, add the rice, and sauté, stirring constantly with a wooden spoon, over low heat until the rice is a light brown about 10 minutes. Be careful not to let the rice get too dark in colour as it will have a bitter taste. Add 2 tablespoons lemon juice, 1 teaspoon salt, and 1¼ pints water. Bring to the boil over high heat, then simmer, covered, over very low heat, 15 to 20 minutes, or until the rice is tender and all the liquid absorbed. Serves 6.

Variation: For *Arroz Brasileiro* (Brazilian Style Rice), thoroughly wash and drain ¾ pound long-grain rice. Heat 3 tablespoons vegetable oil or lard in a saucepan and sauté 1 onion, finely chopped, and 1 clove garlic, chopped, until the onion is soft. Add the rice and cook, stirring, until the fat has been absorbed. Add 1½ pints water and salt to taste, bring to the boil, cover, and simmer over very low heat until the rice is tender and all the liquid absorbed, about 20 minutes. An attractive variation is to add 1 peeled, seeded, and chopped tomato to the rice just before adding the water, or add 6 tablespoons tomato purée. Serves 6, but should be enough for 8 to 10 when served with a *Feijoada Completa* (Black Beans with Mixed Meats) page 213.

Arroz con Coco y Pasas

RICE WITH COCONUT AND RAISINS   *Colombia*

There are two versions of this dish, *Arroz con Coco y Pasas* (Rice with Coconut and Raisins) and *Arroz con Coco Frito y Pasas* (Rice with Fried

Coconut and Raisins). Either makes an excellent and unusual accompaniment to meat dishes. They are typical of the cooking of coastal Colombia, where coconut is very much used.

[Serves 6]
½ pound raisins
2 pints coconut milk (see page 29)
¾ pound long-grain rice
2 teaspoons sugar
½ ounce butter
Salt

Put the raisins into a heavy saucepan with a tightly fitting lid, pour in the coconut milk, and let the raisins soak for 30 minutes. Add the rice, sugar, butter, and salt to taste. Cover, bring to the boil, stir once, reduce the heat to very low, and cook the rice, covered, until it is tender and dry (20 to 25 minutes).

Variation: For *Arroz con Coco Frito y Pasas* (Rice with Fried Coconut and Raisins), heat the thick milk made from 1 coconut, about ½ pint or less, in a saucepan over moderate heat, stirring from time to time until the oil separates from the grainy golden residue. In Colombia this is called *titoté*. Add 1 tablespoon brown sugar and cook, stirring, for a few minutes longer. Add 1¾ pints thin coconut milk and ½ pound raisins and simmer over low heat for 10 minutes. Add ¾ pound long-grain rice and salt to taste and cook, stirring frequently, for 10 minutes longer. Stir in 2 ounces butter, or omit this step if preferred. Cover the rice and cook over very low heat until all the liquid is absorbed and the rice is dry and grainy, 20 to 25 minutes.

Arroz a la Mexicana

RICE, MEXICAN STYLE   *Mexico*

[Serves 6 to 8]
¾ pound long-grain rice
2 tomatoes, peeled, seeded, and
    chopped
1 medium onion, chopped
1 clove garlic, chopped
1½ ounces lard or 3 tablespoons
    vegetable oil
1½ pints chicken stock
2 carrots, scraped and thinly sliced
6 ounces fresh raw peas or frozen
    peas, thawed
1 hot green pepper, seeded and
    chopped, or 2 serrano (hot,
    green) chilies, seeded and
    chopped
1 tablespoon chopped fresh
    coriander or flat parsley

Thoroughly wash the rice in several changes of water and let it soak for 15 minutes. Drain thoroughly in a sieve. Put the tomatoes, onion, and garlic in a blender or food processor and reduce to a purée. Heat the lard or vegetable oil in a flameproof casserole and sauté the rice, stirring constantly, until it is golden. Be careful not to let it brown. Add the tomato mixture and cook it, stirring occasionally, until all the moisture has evaporated. Stir in the chicken stock, carrots, peas, and green pepper. Bring the mixture to the boil, cover it, and simmer over very low heat until the rice is tender and all the liquid absorbed, about 20 minutes. Serve the rice garnished with the chopped coriander or parsley.

Variation: Slice 2 chorizo sausages, fry in a little oil, drain, and garnish the rice with the sausages, 1 large avocado, sliced, and 2 hardboiled eggs, sliced.

Variation: *Arroz Guatemalteco* (Rice, Guatemalan Style) is traditionally served with *Carne en Jocón* (Beef in Tomato and Pepper Sauce), but it may also be served with any dish that would be accompanied by plain rice, such as a meat or poultry stew. Heat 2 tablespoons peanut oil or butter in a heavy saucepan, add ¾ pound mixed vegetables (carrots, celery, sweet red peppers, chopped finely, and green peas), salt and pepper, and 1¾ pints chicken or beef stock. Bring to a boil, cover, and reduce the heat to low. Cook until the rice is tender and all the liquid absorbed, about 20 minutes. Serves 6 to 8.

Angú de Arroz

MOULDED RICE   *Brazil*

Brazilians like to make moulded puddings of rice or rice flour, which are served at room temperature as an accompaniment to dishes like *Vatapá* or with Bahian fish, shellfish, or meat dishes. They make a pleasant change from plain white rice and look very attractive when unmoulded.

[Serves 6 to 8]   *A scant ½ pint thin coconut milk*
¾ *pound short-grain rice*   *(see page 29)*
1 *teaspoon salt*   *Butter*

Thoroughly rinse the rice until the water runs clear. Put the rice into a saucepan with 1¾ pints water and leave it to soak overnight. Stir in the salt, cover, bring to the boil, and cook over low heat for 20 minutes, or until the liquid has been absorbed and the rice is mushy. Stir in the coconut milk and cook, mashing the rice with a wooden spoon, for 2 minutes. Turn the rice into a buttered mould and allow to cool. Unmould the rice by covering with a platter and turning over quickly. If it doesn't turn out readily, hit the bottom of the mould with the flat of your hand. Serve at room temperature.

Variation: For *Pirão de Arroz* (Rice Flour Pudding), which goes with the same dishes as does *Angú de Arroz*, combine ¼ pound rice flour, 1 teaspoon salt, and 1 pint coconut milk made by combining both thick and thin coconut milk (see page 29) in a saucepan. Cook over low heat, stirring constantly with a wooden spoon, until the mixture is smooth and thick, about 5 minutes. Pour the mixture into a buttered bowl and let it stand for a few minutes. Turn out onto a serving dish and serve at room temperature. Serves 6 to 8.

Arroz de Haussá

HAUSSÁ RICE   *Brazil*

This is an Afro-Brazilian speciality named for the Haussa tribe of Nigeria, who are great rice eaters. The beef used is Brazilian sun-dried salt beef, *carne sêca*. It makes a fine main course for rice lovers.

[Serves 4]
1 pound carne sêca *see page 27*
2 ounces butter
2 medium onions, thinly sliced

1 recipe Arroz Brasileiro
    (Brazilian Style Rice), page 245
1 recipe Môlho de Acarajé *(Black-
    Eyed Pea Fritter Sauce), page 43*

Soak the beef overnight in cold water to cover. Drain, put into a saucepan with fresh cold water to cover, bring to the boil over moderate heat, and drain. When the beef is cool enough to handle, chop it coarsely, or shred it with the fingers. Heat the butter and sauté the onions until they are lightly browned. Add the beef and cook, stirring, until it is lightly browned and heated through. Arrange the rice in the centre of a serving dish and surround it with the beef and onion mixture. Serve with *Môlho de Acarajé* (Black-Eyed Pea Fritter Sauce), a hot sauce.

Vegetables and Salads

VERDURAS Y ENSALADAS

One of the great excitements of Latin American markets is the vegetable stalls with great heaps of orange carrots, little green courgettes, bright red tomatoes, bursting with ripeness, green beans, corn, young onions looking like giant spring onions, great, green pumpkins cut to show the vivid yellow flesh inside, bright green okra pods, new potatoes so clean and unblemished they look as though they had sprung from some celestial soil, avocados, black- and green-skinned, green globes of cabbage, peas ready shelled for the buyer, deep red beetroot, peppers—vivid green, red, yellow, and orange, in more shapes and sizes than seems possible—spinach, Swiss chard, and a bewildering array of root vegetables—the sweet potatoes, the yams, the taros and malangas, dark brown and light brown, enormous or tiny, smooth-skinned and tough-skinned, knobbly or nicely symmetrical in shape—and the dried beans, black, red, creamy yellow, pink, and speckled, in lavish heaps.

It is no wonder that vegetables play such an important role in the Latin American kitchen—so much so that they are often served as a separate course. What I have learned from South America has changed my own cooking habits considerably. Now I love to serve whole platters of cooked vegetables, lightly dressed with oil and vinegar, at room temperature, either as an accompaniment or as a first course, and I have picked up so many new uses for our more unfamiliar produce that vegetables are never uninspired.

Aguacates Rellenos

STUFFED AVOCADOS   *Ecuador*

Avocados are much more widely used in soups and sauces than here but they're most popular as a first course, stuffed. For a grand occasion, especially a meal in the Latin American tradition, this is fine. I also find that, accompanied by a glass or two of dry white wine and a dessert of cheese, stuffed avocados make a delicious lunch or light supper.

[Serves 6]
3 large avocados
½ pound cooked ham
3 hardboiled eggs, chopped

Salt, freshly ground pepper
Mayonnaise
Cos or iceberg lettuce, shredded

Carefully peel the avocados, cut into halves lengthwise, and remove and discard the pits. In a bowl combine the ham and hardboiled eggs, season to taste with salt and pepper, and fold in enough mayonnaise to bind the mixture. Fill the hollows of the avocados with the mixture. Make a bed of lettuce on six salad plates and put half an avocado on each. Serve as a first course or light luncheon dish. A vinaigrette sauce may be used instead of mayonnaise.

Avocados discolour quickly, so if it is necessary to prepare this ahead of time, dip the avocados in lemon juice, or leave them unpeeled, though they will look less elegant. Chopped cold roast pork or chicken may be used instead of the ham mixed with 6 ounces cooked mixed vegetables instead of the hardboiled eggs. This is a dish that welcomes the improviser. Ecuadorian cooks sometimes substitute tomato sauce or béchamel for mayonnaise, though I find this less attractive.

Variation: For *Paltas Rellenas con Mariscos* (Avocados Stuffed with Prawns or Shrimp) from Chile, peel and halve 3 avocados and arrange them on a bed of lettuce on six salad plates. Make 1 recipe *Salsa Golf* (Tomato- and Cognac-Flavoured Mayonnaise), page 311, and mix half of it with 1 pound cooked prawns, quartered if large, or use shrimp.

Pile the shellfish mixture into the avocados and serve the rest of the mayonnaise in a sauceboat.

Variation: Venezuela varies the Chilean shrimp-stuffed avocado slightly and calls it *Aguacates Rellenos con Camarones*. The avocados are not peeled, just halved, with the pits removed. The flesh is mashed lightly with a fork and a little vinaigrette dressing is mixed in. They are then stuffed with shrimp in vinaigrette. If small avocados are used, this does make a very nice first course.

Variation: For *Paltas Rellenas* (Stuffed Avocados) from Peru, halve and remove the pits from 3 avocados. Mash a fourth avocado with 1 fresh hot pepper, seeded and chopped, and about ¼ pint vinaigrette dressing made with mustard. Toss the dressing with 3 ounces each cooked diced green beans and carrots, 3 ounces cooked green peas, 3 ounces finely chopped celery, 6 small pimiento-stuffed olives, chopped, and 2 hardboiled eggs, finely chopped. Fill the avocados with the mixture and mask them with mayonnaise. Garnish with slices of hardboiled egg and a little finely chopped parsley. If liked, garnish also with a fresh hot red pepper, cut into a flower shape by slicing it into thin strips almost its full length, stopping short of the stem end. Put the peppers into ice water for several hours, or until the cut ends curl back.

Variation: A simpler version of the Peruvian dish, which is very rich, comes from Cuba. For *Aguacates Rellenos* (Stuffed Avocados), peel the avocados and dip them in lemon juice to prevent discolouring. Cut them in half lengthwise and discard the pits. Arrange each half on a bed of lettuce and fill with a mixture of diced cooked vegetables, using any of the following: potatoes, carrots, beetroot, peas, green beans, asparagus tips, finely chopped green or red sweet peppers, or chopped cucumbers. Toss the vegetables in a vinaigrette dressing before putting into the avocados, and mask with mayonnaise.

Variation: For *Paltas Rellenas con Salsa Cruda* (Avocados with Uncooked Tomato Sauce) from Bolivia, peel and halve the avocados lengthwise, or simply halve them and remove and discard the pits. Fill them with a sauce made by combining 2 medium tomatoes, peeled and chopped, 1 medium onion, finely chopped, ½ sweet green pepper, seeded and chopped, salt and freshly ground pepper to taste, 1 teaspoon vinegar, and 1 tablespoon vegetable oil. This should be made at the last minute if possible, as the sauce loses its fresh flavour if it stands for long.

251

Variation: For *Paltas Rellenas con Pollo* (Avocados Stuffed with Chicken) from Chile, peel 3 large avocados, dip them in lemon juice, halve them lengthwise, and remove and discard the pits, or simply halve them without peeling. Peel and mash a fourth large avocado and mix it with 1 whole cooked chicken breast, finely chopped. Season to taste with salt, pepper, and lemon juice and fill the avocados with the mixture.

Variation: In Chile leftover cooked rice is also used as a filling. The avocados are prepared as above. Season the mashed avocado with salt, pepper, and ¼ pint vinaigrette dressing made with lemon juice. Mix with the rice, about 3 ounces, and 12 pimiento-stuffed green olives, sliced. Fill the avocados with the mixture.

Calabacitas Picadas

CHOPPED COURGETTES   *Mexico*

Courgettes are surely Mexico's favourite green vegetable, perhaps because they have so long a history in the country, going back to 7000 B.C. They are available all year round and are picked when they are only 3 to 4 inches long. Though vegetables in Mexico are traditionally served as a separate course before the main dish, I find they go admirably with meat, poultry, or fish, and in today's Mexico more and more people are serving them in this way.

[Serves 4 to 6]

3 tablespoons vegetable oil
1 medium onion, finely chopped
1 clove garlic, chopped
3 medium tomatoes, peeled, seeded, and chopped
1 sprig coriander or epazote

2 small fresh hot green peppers, seeded and chopped, or canned serrano or jalapeño chilies
Salt, freshly ground pepper
1 pound small, young courgettes, cut into ½-inch cubes
6 ounces corn kernels (optional)

Heat the oil in a saucepan and sauté the onion and garlic until the onion is soft. Add the tomatoes, coriander or *epazote*, the hot peppers, salt and pepper to taste, the courgettes, and the corn, if using. Cover and simmer over very low heat until the courgettes are tender, 30 to 40 minutes, which may seem excessively long. It is because the acid in the tomatoes slows up the cooking of the courgettes.

The corn makes the dish more robust. I add it when the main dish is a light one and leave it out when I want a more purely green vegetable dish to go with a hearty meat.

Calabacitas Poblanas

COURGETTES, PUEBLA STYLE   *Mexico*

The state of Puebla in Mexico, home of the country's most famous dish, the *mole poblano*, is noted for its cooking and for the wonderfully rich flavour of the *poblano* chili, a large, deep green pepper that can be mild or quite hot. Since I cannot get *poblanos*, I use sweet green peppers, with very good results, for this unusual vegetable dish.

[Serves 4 to 6]

3 sweet green peppers, toasted,
   peeled (see page 36), and seeded
1 medium onion, chopped
1 clove garlic, chopped

3 tablespoons vegetable oil
1 pound small, young courgettes,
   cut into ½-inch cubes
Salt, freshly ground pepper
5 tablespoons double cream

Chop the peppers coarsely and purée them in a blender or food processor with the onion and garlic. Heat the oil in a saucepan and sauté the purée, stirring constantly with a wooden spoon, for 3 or 4 minutes. Add the courgettes, and season to taste with salt and pepper. Add a little water, about ¼ pint is all that should be needed, cover, and simmer until the courgettes are tender, about 30 minutes. Check to see if more water is needed—there should be only just enough liquid to cook the courgettes. Stir in the double cream and simmer, uncovered, just long enough to heat it through. Serve as a green vegetable with any plainly cooked meat, poultry, or fish.

Variation: Topped with slices of cheese (Spanish *queso blanco*, mild Cheddar or similar cheese), about 2 ounces per person, this makes an attractive vegetarian luncheon dish. Serves 2 as a main course.

Guiso de Repollo

CABBAGE IN SAUCE   *Bolivia*

Cabbage, that universal vegetable, is found all over Latin America often cooked in borrowed ways. Green, white, and red varieties are all available. Cole slaw turns up everywhere, usually as *ensalada de repollo crudo* (raw cabbage salad) and I have found *choucroute* (sauerkraut), another popular borrowed dish, as *chuckrut*. But there are also attractive and original recipes for cabbage that are worth our borrowing. The Bolivian *Guiso de Repollo* (Cabbage in Sauce) is a hearty dish that needs only a grilled lamb chop, a small steak, or a piece of fried

253

chicken to make a complete main course since it combines cabbage with potatoes in a pleasantly spicy tomato sauce.

[Serves 4]

1 small white or green cabbage, weighing about 1 pound

Salt

3 tablespoons vegetable oil

1 medium onion, finely chopped

3 medium tomatoes, peeled and chopped

1 fresh hot red or green pepper, seeded and chopped

Salt, freshly ground pepper

1 tablespoon tomato purée

2 tablespoons fresh coriander or parsley, chopped

4 medium potatoes, freshly cooked and halved

Wash the cabbage and shred it finely. Drop it into a large saucepan of boiling salted water, bring back to the boil, and simmer for 5 minutes. Drain thoroughly and set aside. Heat the oil and sauté the onion until it is soft. Add the tomatoes and hot pepper and cook until the mixture is well blended, about 5 minutes. Season with salt and pepper. Stir in the tomato purée and the coriander or parsley. Fold in the cabbage, add the potatoes, and cook until the mixture is heated through.

Variation: For the Brazilian version of the dish, *Repôlho com Vinho* (Cabbage with Wine), omit the potatoes. Sauté 1 sweet green pepper, seeded and chopped, with the onion in olive oil. When adding the tomato purée, stir in 3 tablespoons chopped parsley, and when adding the cabbage, stir in ¼ pint dry white wine.

Espinacas con Anchoas

SPINACH WITH ANCHOVIES   *Venezuela*

Here anchovies add a salty accent to the blandness of the spinach. I borrow a Japanese trick of squeezing the excess moisture out of the spinach by rolling the drained spinach in a *sudare* (a matchstick bamboo mat like a place mat), and squeezing gently. Swiss chard can be used in any of the spinach recipes.

[Serves 6]

2 pounds spinach or Swiss chard

3 tablespoons olive or vegetable oil

Freshly ground pepper

A small can anchovy fillets, drained and mashed

Wash and drain the spinach or Swiss chard and trim any coarse stems. Drop the spinach into a large saucepan of briskly boiling water.

Bring back to the boil over high heat and boil for 5 minutes. Drain the spinach, rinse quickly under cold water, and drain again. Squeeze out the excess moisture. Chop the spinach coarsely. Heat the oil in a large frying pan, add the spinach, and sauté, stirring frequently, for about 3 minutes. Season generously with freshly ground pepper. Add the mashed anchovies, tossing to mix well. Serve as a vegetable with any plainly cooked meat or poultry, or topped with fried or poached eggs as a dish by itself.

Espinacas Saltadas

SPINACH WITH TOMATOES   *Peru*

[Serves 6]
2 pounds spinach or Swiss chard
3 tablespoons vegetable oil
1 medium onion, finely chopped
2 cloves garlic, chopped
4 medium tomatoes, peeled and
  chopped

1 fresh hot red or green pepper,
  seeded and chopped
Salt, freshly ground pepper
Grated rind of ½ lemon

Cook the spinach or Swiss chard as for *Espinacas con Anchoas* (Spinach with Anchovies) and set aside. Heat the oil and sauté the onion and garlic until the onion is soft. Add the tomatoes and hot pepper, season with salt and pepper, and cook until the mixture is well blended, about 5 minutes. Add the grated lemon rind. Stir the spinach into the tomato mixture and cook just long enough to heat through. Serve as a vegetable with any plainly cooked meat, poultry, or fish. For a more robust dish add 6 medium potatoes, boiled and tossed in butter.

Variation: For this version from the Dominican Republic, cook the spinach as above and set aside. Heat 1 ounce butter and sauté 1 medium onion, finely chopped, until it is soft. Add 1¼ pounds tomatoes, peeled and chopped, salt, pepper, a pinch of sugar, a pinch of ground cloves, and a bay leaf, and simmer until the mixture is thick and well blended. Add the spinach and cook until heated through.

Variation: For *Espinacas con Crema* (Spinach with Cream) from Mexico, cook the spinach as above and set aside. Peel, seed, and chop 2 sweet green peppers (page 36) and purée in a blender or food processor with 1 medium onion, chopped. Heat 3 tablespoons oil in a frying pan, add the purée, and sauté for 3 or 4 minutes, stirring with a wooden spoon. Add the spinach and season with salt and pepper.

Stir in ¼ pint double cream and simmer just long enough to heat through. Serve as a vegetable dish or as a dish by itself garnished with 6 halved hardboiled eggs.

Acelgas en Crema

SWISS CHARD IN CREAM SAUCE   *Argentina*

Both the white and green parts of the chard are used here. When only the green part is called for, I use the white part the next day, cut into 1-inch pieces, boiled in salted water until tender (about 10 minutes), and served either with a plain béchamel sauce or with a cup of grated cheddar stirred into the sauce. Not Latin American, but it avoids wasting this attractive vegetable.

[Serves 6]
1½ ounces butter
1 medium onion, finely chopped
1 medium carrot, cut into julienne
   strips
1 medium-sized potato, cut into
   ½-inch cubes
1½ pounds Swiss chard
Salt, freshly ground pepper
3 tablespoons double cream

Heat the butter in a saucepan and sauté the onion, carrot, and potato until the vegetables are tender. Wash and drain the Swiss chard and cut both white and green parts into thin strips crosswise. Add to the saucepan, stir to mix, and season to taste with salt and pepper. Cover and simmer over very low heat until the chard is tender, about 10 minutes. Stir in the heavy cream and simmer, uncovered, for a few minutes longer.

Couve a Mineira

KALE, MINAS GERAIS STYLE   *Brazil*

[Serves 6]
2 pounds kale
Salt
2 ounces bacon fat
1 clove garlic (optional)

Wash the kale under cold running water. Trim the leaves from the stems and shred them finely. Put the leaves in a large bowl and pour boiling salted water over them. Allow to stand for 5 minutes, then drain thoroughly. Heat the bacon fat with the clove of garlic, if liked. Add the kale and sauté for a minute or two. Season to taste with salt, cover the pan, and cook until the kale is tender, about 15 minutes. Discard the garlic and serve.

Variation: For a slightly different, but equally traditional, dish cut 4 ounces salt pork into ¼-inch cubes and sauté until they have given up all their fat and are crispy and brown. Lift them out and reserve. Cook the kale as above in the fat and just before serving fold in the pork.

Coliflor en Salsa de Almendra

CAULIFLOWER IN ALMOND SAUCE   *Chile*

[Serves 6]
1 medium-sized cauliflower, about
   8 inches across
Salt

1 recipe béchamel (White Sauce),
   page 313
2 ounces finely ground almonds

Trim the cauliflower and cut a cross in the bottom of the stem end. This speeds up the cooking of the stalk so that it is tender at the same time as the flowerets. Drop, stem end down, into a large saucepan of boiling salted water, cover, and simmer for 15 to 20 minutes, or until just tender. Lift out and place in a serving dish, preferably round, to show off the cauliflower.

Meantime make the béchamel. Stir in the ground almonds, and cook, stirring, over low heat for about 2 minutes to blend the flavours. Mask the cauliflower with the sauce and serve as an accompaniment to any plainly cooked meat, poultry, fish, or shellfish.

Variation: Use ground walnuts instead of the almonds—less delicate but very rich tasting.

Variation: Mask the cauliflower with 1 recipe *Salsa de Choclos* (Sweetcorn Sauce), page 308, for a marvellous combination of flavours.

Variation: Heat 4 tablespoons olive or vegetable oil and add 2 large cloves garlic, crushed in a garlic press, and 2 tablespoons finely chopped parsley. Sauté for a minute or two, then stir in 1 tablespoon red wine vinegar, salt, and freshly ground pepper, and pour, hot, over the cooked cauliflower. This pleasant, simple dish is from Bolivia.

Variation: Put the freshly cooked cauliflower into a flameproof serving dish and mask with 1 recipe *Môlho ao Tomate* (Tomato Sauce), page 306. Sprinkle with 1 ounce freshly grated Parmesan cheese and run under a grill just long enough to brown the cheese. I have found it makes a pleasant change to leave out the cheese and instead sprinkle the cauliflower with 2 tablespoons finely chopped fresh coriander or parsley.

Variation: This dish from the Dominican Republic is robust enough to serve 4 as a main course at lunch. Heat 2 ounces butter and sauté 1 finely chopped onion until it is soft. Stir in 1 clove garlic, crushed in a garlic press. Add 4 medium tomatoes, peeled and chopped, 1 tablespoon tomato purée, 1 tablespoon lemon juice, a pinch of sugar, salt and pepper to taste, and 1 bay leaf. Simmer for about 10 minutes, remove and discard the bay leaf and fold in 1 large freshly cooked potato, cubed, 1 medium-sized cauliflower, cooked and separated into flowerets, and 6 ounces cooked cut green beans. Cook the mixture just long enough to heat through. Serve with freshly grated Parmesan cheese separately.

Chayotes Rellenos

STUFFED CHAYOTES   *Costa Rica*

Chayotes are a favourite vegetable from the Caribbean to Brazil. Often they are just peeled, sliced, and simmered until tender in salted water, drained, and served with butter and perhaps a few grinds of black pepper. This is a more elaborate recipe and is served as a separate course before the main dish. It makes a good lunch or light supper dish if the servings are doubled. In Brazil almost identical ingredients are made into a pudding, *Pudim de Chuchu*.

[Serves 3 to 6]

3 chayotes, peeled and halved
Salt
7 ounces freshly made breadcrumbs
8 ounces grated mild Cheddar
  cheese

Freshly ground pepper
2 eggs, lightly beaten
3 tablespoons grated Parmesan
  cheese
Butter

Parboil the chayotes in salted water for 10 minutes. Drain thoroughly, then scoop out the flesh, leaving a ½-inch shell and taking care not to break the vegetables. Chop the flesh coarsely and mix with 6 ounces of the breadcrumbs, the Cheddar cheese, salt and pepper, and the eggs. Pile the mixture back into the shells. Mix the remaining breadcrumbs with the Parmesan cheese and sprinkle over the chayotes. Dot with butter and bake in a preheated hot oven (450° F., 230° C., gas

8) for 15 to 20 minutes, or until the dish is heated through and the top nicely browned.

Variation: *Pudim de Chuchu* is an interesting example of how very similar ingredients can result in a very different dish. This is closer to a soufflé than anything else. Peel and halve 2 large chayotes, each weighing about ¾ pound. Simmer in salted water to cover until tender, about 15 minutes. Drain and allow to cool. Remove the edible seed. Chop the vegetable coarsely and set aside. In a bowl mix together 2 ounces freshly made breadcrumbs, 4 ounces grated cheese such as Gruyère, or Cheddar, salt and freshly ground pepper, 2 tablespoons melted and cooled butter, and 3 lightly beaten egg yolks. Beat 3 egg whites until they stand in stiff peaks. Fold into the chayote mixture. Pour into a buttered mould and bake in a preheated moderate oven (375° F., 190° C., gas 5) for about 30 minutes, or until a knife inserted in the pudding comes out clean. Serve with *Mōlho ao Tomate* (Tomato Sauce), page 306, as a light lunch or supper dish, or as a separate course, or to accompany any plainly cooked meat, poultry, or fish. Serves 3 to 4.

Tayotes Revueltos con Huevos

CHAYOTES SCRAMBLED WITH EGGS   *Dominican Republic*

Chayotes are called tayotes in the Dominican Republic, where the cuisine is remarkably rich and varied. This dish is most versatile since it could serve for a late breakfast, light lunch, or supper, or accompany plainly cooked meat, poultry, or fish. The cooked seed of the chayote is delicious. I always claim it as cook's perks.

[Serves 2]

1 large chayote, weighing about ¾ pound
Salt
3 tablespoons vegetable oil
1 medium onion, finely chopped
1 clove garlic, finely chopped

2 medium tomatoes, peeled and chopped
1 small fresh hot red or green pepper, seeded and chopped
Freshly ground pepper
1 tablespoon tomato purée
4 eggs, lightly beaten

Peel and halve the chayote and cook in salted water to cover until tender, about 15 minutes. Remove the seed and eat it. Drain thoroughly and cut into ½-inch cubes. Set aside. Heat the oil in an 8-inch frying pan and sauté the onion over medium heat until it is soft. Add the garlic, tomatoes, and the hot pepper and simmer until the mixture is well blended and most of the liquid evaporated. Season with salt and pepper and stir in the tomato purée. Add the chayote and cook until heated through. Add the eggs and cook, stirring with the flat of a fork to reach all the surfaces of the pan until the eggs are set. Serve immediately.

Variation: For a more robust dish, add 4 ounces chopped ham with the cubed chayotes.

Aubergine

The type of aubergine found in Latin America is the beautiful shiny deep purple kind, and it is a much-loved vegetable throughout Latin America. It may be simply sliced and fried in oil, or dipped in beaten egg and breadcrumbs, or in batter, before frying. It is served stuffed with a cheese and ham mixture, or with a *picadillo* (hash) made of pork or beef, or cooked with shrimp. Recipes do not differ a great deal from country to country. Stuffed aubergine may be served as a separate course or as a main dish for lunch or supper. A perennial favourite is *Caviar de Berengena* (Aubergine Caviar), sometimes called *berengena Rusa* (Russian aubergine), served as a cold hors d'oeuvre or salad. It is amusing to note that this dish is known in both the Caucasus and the Middle East as poor man's caviar.

Berenjena Rellena con Picadillo

AUBERGINE STUFFED WITH HASH   *Chile*

[Serves 2]

1 medium aubergine, weighing
    about 1 pound
Salt
4 tablespoons vegetable oil
½ pound chopped pork or beef
1 medium onion, finely chopped
1 clove garlic, chopped

3 medium tomatoes, peeled, seeded,
    and chopped
1 tablespoon tomato purée
1 tablespoon red wine vinegar
2 tablespoons parsley or fresh
    coriander, chopped
Salt, freshly ground pepper
2 tablespoons grated Parmesan

Cut the aubergine in half lengthwise and score with a small sharp knife in both directions at ½-inch intervals. Sprinkle with salt and leave for 30 minutes. Squeeze the aubergine gently to remove the bitter juice, rinse quickly in cold water, squeeze again, and pat dry. With a grapefruit knife cut round the aubergine, leaving a ½-inch shell. Pull out the flesh and cut away any bits left in the shells. Chop the aubergine coarsely and set aside. Heat the oil in a frying pan and sauté the pork or beef with the onion and garlic until the onion is soft and the meat lightly browned. Add the aubergine and sauté, stirring, for 2 or 3 minutes longer. Add the tomatoes, the tomato purée, vinegar, parsley or coriander, and salt and pepper. Stir to mix and simmer for 5 minutes longer. Spoon the mixture into the aubergine shells, sprinkle with the cheese, and arrange on a baking sheet or in a baking pan. Bake in a preheated moderate oven (350° F., 180° C., gas 4) for 30 minutes.

Variation: For *Berenjena Rellena con Queso* (Aubergine Stuffed with Cheese), sauté 1 medium onion, finely chopped, in 1½ ounces butter. Add the chopped aubergine and sauté for a few minutes longer. Stir in 2 ounces freshly made breadcrumbs, 4 ounces grated Cheddar cheese, 2 ounces ham, coarsely chopped, salt, pepper, ⅛ teaspoon cayenne, and 1 egg, lightly beaten. Pile the mixture into the aubergine shells, sprinkle with 2 tablespoons Parmesan cheese, dot with butter, and bake in a preheated moderate oven (375° F., 190° C., gas 5) for 30 minutes. Serve with *Môlho ao Tomate* (Tomato Sauce), page 306.

Variation: For *Berinjela com Camarão* (Aubergine with Shrimp) from Brazil, sauté 1 medium onion, finely chopped, 1 clove garlic, chopped, 1 small fresh red or green pepper, seeded and finely chopped, and the aubergine in 3 tablespoons olive or vegetable oil until the onion is soft. Stir in ½ pound raw, coarsely chopped shrimp and sauté for 1 minute longer. Add 2 ounces freshly made breadcrumbs, 8 tablespoons chopped parsley or fresh coriander, 10 ounces tomatoes, peeled, seeded, and chopped, 1 tablespoon tomato purée, and salt and pepper. Mix thoroughly, then pile into the aubergine shells. Sprinkle with 2 tablespoons grated Parmesan cheese, dot with butter, and bake in a preheated moderate oven (350° F., 180° C., gas 4) for 30 minutes.

Caviar de Berenjena
AUBERGINE CAVIAR   *Dominican Republic*

Serves 4

1 large aubergine, weighing about 2 pounds
1 medium onion, finely chopped
1 sweet red pepper, peeled (page 36), seeded, and chopped
2 medium tomatoes, chopped

2 tablespoons fresh coriander, chopped
Salt, freshly ground pepper
4 tablespoons olive oil
1 tablespoon red wine vinegar or lime or lemon juice
Lettuce leaves and black olives

Bake the aubergine on the middle rack of a preheated moderate oven (375° F., 190° C., gas 5) for about 45 minutes, or until tender. Cool, peel, and chop coarsely. Add the onion, sweet pepper, tomatoes, coriander, salt and pepper, and mix well. Beat the oil and vinegar together and stir into the aubergine mixture. Serve garnished with lettuce leaves and black olives as an hors d'oeuvre with crackers, or as a salad.

Berenjenas con Vainitas

AUBERGINE WITH GREEN BEANS   *Venezuela*

A very pretty dish, it is also the sort of combination of vegetables that is popular in Latin America. Excellent with grilled meat, poultry, or fish, it also makes a fine salad, tossed with vinaigrette instead of butter, and served slightly chilled or at room temperature.

[Serves 6]

2 pounds aubergines
Salt
6 tablespoons vegetable oil
1 medium onion, finely chopped
4 medium tomatoes, peeled and
    chopped
Pinch of sugar
Freshly ground pepper
20 small pimiento-stuffed olives
1 pound green beans, cut into
    1-inch pieces
1 ounce butter, or 4 tablespoons
    vinaigrette (page 313)
2 tablespoons finely chopped parsley

Cut the aubergines into ½-inch slices, then cut each slice into fingers crosswise. Put into a colander, sprinkle with salt, and leave for about ½ hour to drain the bitter juice. Rinse in cold water, squeeze lightly, and pat dry with paper towels. Heat the oil, add the onion and aubergine. Sauté, turning the aubergine pieces once or twice, until the onion and aubergine are both soft. Add the tomatoes, salt to taste, sugar, and pepper. Stir in the olives and cook for about 5 minutes longer, or until the mixture is fairly dry. Cook the beans in boiling salted water until they are tender, 10 to 15 minutes. Drain thoroughly, return to the saucepan with the butter, and toss over moderate heat until the butter is melted. Arrange the aubergine mixture in the centre of a serving dish, surround it with the beans, and sprinkle with the parsley.

Stuffed Peppers

CHILES RELLENOS

Stuffed peppers are eaten all over Latin America but it is in Mexico, where they use the lovely dark green *poblano* pepper, that they are most famous (I substitute sweet green peppers instead with fine results). The best known of all the stuffed peppers is *Chiles en Nogada* (Peppers in Walnut Sauce) from Puebla. They are traditionally served on St. Augustine's Day, August 28, and also on September 15, Mexican Independence Day, the colours of the dish—red, white, and green—being the colours of the Mexican flag. Fresh walnuts, which are in season in late August and early September, are used in the sauce, but packaged walnuts will do.

Chiles en Nogada

PEPPERS IN WALNUT SAUCE   *Mexico*

[Serves 6]
6 poblano *or large sweet green*
  peppers, peeled (page 36)
1 *recipe* Picadillo *(Seasoned*
  Chopped Beef), made with pork
  and 1 of the apples replaced by a
  peach (page 139)

2 eggs, separated
½ teaspoon salt
Flour
Vegetable oil for frying

FOR THE SAUCE

4 ounces walnuts, finely ground
8 ounces cream cheese
½ pint single cream
1 tablespoon sugar (optional)

Pinch of ground cinnamon
  (optional)
Salt

FOR THE GARNISH

Seeds from 1 pomegranate

Slit the peppers down one side and remove the seeds, taking care not to break the peppers. Stuff with the *Picadillo*. Beat the egg whites until they stand in firm peaks. Beat the egg yolks lightly with the salt and fold into the whites. Pat the peppers dry with paper towels and dip them in the flour, then in the egg. Heat enough oil in a heavy pan to come to a depth of at least ½ inch. Fry the peppers, in more than one batch so as not to crowd the pan, until they are lightly golden all over. The egg will seal in the filling. Drain on paper towels. Arrange them on a shallow platter.

In a blender or food processor fitted with a steel blade, combine the walnuts, cream cheese, cut into bits, and half the cream. Traditionally sugar and cinnamon are added but this is not to everyone's taste so it may be left out. (I personally prefer the sauce without.) Add a little salt and blend the mixture until it is smooth with the consistency of heavy mayonnaise, adding as much of the cream as necessary. Mask the peppers with the sauce, and garnish with the pomegranate seeds.

Variation: Of all the stuffed peppers, the one simply known as *Chiles Rellenos* (Stuffed Peppers) is most often served. Taste and texture combine to make this a splendid dish. Prepare the peppers and stuff them with *Picadillo* (Seasoned Chopped Beef), page 139, or *Picadillo de la Costa* (Seasoned Meat, Coastal Style), page 140. Coat with the egg mixture and fry in oil until golden brown. Drain on paper towels. Make 1 recipe *Salsa de Jitomate* (Tomato Sauce), page 305, and thin it to the consistency of a heavy broth with chicken stock, about ½ pint, and pour it into a large saucepan. Add the stuffed peppers. The broth will come about halfway up them. Simmer just long enough to heat through and serve with the broth. The peppers can be prepared ahead of time and added to the tomato broth to heat through just before serving.

Variation: For *Chiles Rellenos con Frijoles* (Peppers Stuffed with Beans), prepare the peppers and stuff them with about 1 pound of *Frijoles Refritos* (Refried Beans), page 239. Coat in the egg mixture in the usual way and fry in oil. Drain on paper towels. Arrange in an ovenproof dish, pour ¼ pint double cream over them, and sprinkle with 4 ounces shredded Cheddar cheese. Heat the dish in a preheated moderate oven (350° F., 180° C., gas 4) for 30 minutes, or until it is heated through and the top lightly browned.

Variation: Make the peppers in the usual way but stuff with slices of mild Cheddar cheese, and serve with *Salsa de Jitomate* (Tomato Sauce), page 305.

Variation: The Chileans have a good way of using up leftover cooked beef or pork. Prepare the peppers for stuffing in the usual way. To make the filling sauté 1 finely chopped medium onion in 1 ounce butter, add 1 pound cooked meat, chopped or shredded, ¾ pound cooked corn kernels, 2 ounces freshly made breadcrumbs, 8 tablespoons chopped parsley, 1 fresh hot red or green pepper, seeded and finely chopped, ½ teaspoon oregano, and salt and pepper to taste. Stir to mix and sauté for a minute or two. Stuff the peppers and fry in the egg batter in the usual way. Serve with *Pebre* (Chilean Hot Pepper Sauce) page 298, or with *Salsa Chilena* (Chilean Sauce), page 309, or with *Salsa de Jitomate* (Tomato Sauce) page 305.

Papas Chorreadas

POTATOES WITH CHEESE, TOMATO, AND
ONION SAUCE   *Colombia*

This is a rich, beautifully flavoured potato dish.

[Serves 6]
6 *large potatoes, scrubbed*
½ *ounce lard and* ½ *ounce butter,*
  or 1 ounce butter
1 *medium onion, finely chopped*

2 *large tomatoes, peeled and*
  chopped
Salt, freshly ground pepper
¼ *pint double cream*
¼ *pound grated Cheddar cheese*

Boil the potatoes until they are tender. Drain the potatoes, peel, and
keep them warm. Heat the lard and butter and sauté the onion until
it is softened. Add the tomatoes and salt and pepper to taste, and
cook, stirring, for about 5 minutes. Stir in the cream and cheese and
cook, stirring, until the cheese is partially melted. Pour the sauce over
the potatoes.

Llapingachos

POTATO CAKES   *Ecuador*

This is a typical *sierra* (mountain) dish with a number of variations.
It may be served as a first course, 2 cakes to a serving, accompanied
by lettuce, avocado slices, and tomato. The potato cakes may be
topped with fried eggs, and on the coast it is usual to add slices of
fried, ripe plantains and *Salsa de Maní* (Peanut Sauce). Often served
with slices of fried bass as a main course, the *Llapingachos* are then
accompanied by hot white rice and tomato, lettuce, avocado, cauliflower, green beans, and green peas, all at room temperature, as a
salad.

[Serves 6]
2 *pounds potatoes, peeled and sliced*
Salt
2 *ounces butter*
2 *medium onions, finely chopped*

½ *pound Cheddar or similar*
  cheese, shredded
Lard, butter, or oil, or annatto lard
  or oil (page 310) for frying

Boil the potatoes in salted water until soft. Drain and mash. Heat the
butter and sauté the onions until they are very soft. Add the onions
to the mashed potatoes, mixing well. Shape the potatoes into 12 balls.
Divide the cheese into 12 parts and stuff each of the potato balls with

the cheese, flattening them as you do so into cakes or patties about 1 inch thick. Chill in the refrigerator for about 15 minutes. In enough lard, butter, or oil (with or without annatto as you please) to cover the bottom of a frying pan, sauté the potato cakes until they are golden brown on both sides. The onions may be omitted, or the potato may be mixed with the cheese instead of the cheese being used as a stuffing.

Tropical Root Vegetables

Tropical root vegetables like the taros, malangas, cassava (yucca), yams, sweet potatoes (including the white sweet potato better known as *boniato*), *arracacha, apio,* and Jerusalem artichokes add a new dimension to any meal whether it is a Latin American one or not. Generally speaking they can be cooked as potatoes are, peeled and boiled, then dressed with butter, salt, and freshly ground pepper, or mashed to a purée with butter and a little milk or cream, or baked in the oven, unpeeled like potatoes in their jackets. It is not possible to give exact cooking times for all the root vegetables as they vary so much in size, shape, and texture. However, as a guide, a *boniato* weighing 1 pound takes about 1½ hours in a preheated moderate oven (350° F., 180° C., gas 4). There is one yam called a *mapuey* that has a dry texture and positively thirsts for butter. I like to bake or boil it and serve the butter with a lavish hand. Other root vegetables have a moist texture and are nice just with sauce or gravy from the main course. Pumpkins though they're not root vegetables, are also marvellous baked or boiled and mashed with butter, or with sauce or gravy. Many of the tropical root vegetables discolour quickly when exposed to the air, so it is wise to peel them under running water and drop them into cold water as soon as they are peeled.

The best way to get to know these enchanting vegetables is to buy and cook them. Markets specializing in tropical foods carry them and the men and women in the markets are usually a mine of information. The various types are discussed in the ingredients section.

Farofa de Azeite de Dendê

CASSAVA MEAL WITH PALM OIL   *Brazil*

Cassava root, whether eaten as a root vegetable or made into cassava meal is much appreciated throughout Latin America. A Brazilian meal would not be complete without some form of *farinha de mandioca* (cassava, or manioc, meal). It may be toasted in a pan on top of the stove or in the oven until it is a very light brown. It is then put into a *farinheira*, a sort of shaker, and sprinkled on meat, poultry, and vegetables at the table. As I don't have the traditional shaker, I serve it from a small bowl, and spoon it over foods. It has a light, nutty flavour, quite subtle. The *farofas* are more elaborate and are served with any main course.

[Serves 6 to 8]

½ *pound cassava (manioc) meal*   4 *tablespoons* dendê *(palm) oil*

In a frying pan, over low heat, toast the cassava meal until it begins to turn a very pale brown. Stir frequently so that it does not burn. Stir in the *dendê* (palm) oil and cook until it is well blended and the mixture is bright yellow. Transfer to a serving bowl. Serve with *Xinxim de Galinha* (Chicken with Shrimp and Peanut Sauce) page 191, or with any meat or poultry.

Variation: For *Farofa de Manteiga* (Cassava Meal with Butter), use butter instead of *dendê* (palm) oil. If liked 1 small onion, finely chopped, may be sautéed in the butter, then scrambled with 1 egg, lightly beaten. The cassava meal is then added, seasoned with salt, and garnished, when ready to serve, with a little finely chopped parsley.

Farofa de Ouro

CASSAVA MEAL WITH HARDBOILED EGGS   *Brazil*

½ *pound cassava (manioc) meal*   3 *hardboiled eggs, peeled and*
¼ *pound butter*   *chopped*
Salt

In a heavy frying pan, preferably iron, toast the cassava meal until it turns a pale beige, stirring constantly with a wooden spoon so that it colours evenly. Put the butter into a small saucepan and melt it over low heat. Pour the butter over the cassava meal, stirring to mix evenly. Season to taste with salt and stir in the eggs. Serve in a bowl as an accompaniment to meats or poultry, or with *Feijoada Completa* (Black Beans with Mixed Meats) page 213.

Variation: Garnish the *Farofa* with 6 ounces small stoned black or green olives. If liked, chop 6 rashers bacon and fry until crisp. Drain and discard the fat. Fold the bacon bits into the cassava meal after the butter has been added.

Picante de Yuca

CASSAVA ROOT WITH CHEESE SAUCE   *Peru*

One of the most original cassava dishes is this Peruvian one where the vegetable is masked by a lively cheese sauce made hot with fresh peppers. The peppers used should be quite large ones, 3 or 4 inches in length, not the tiny very hot ones, as they lend flavour as well as heat. The number of peppers can, of course, be reduced according to individual taste but Peruvians like their food hot and this is how they would have it. They would also use an herb called *huacatay*, of the marigold family, in the sauce, but it is not available here and there is no substitute. The flavour is unusual, a little rank, and it is certainly an acquired taste. I find the sauce good without it. The dish makes an attractive accompaniment to plainly cooked meats or poultry and is also good by itself. The recipe makes about 1½ pints of sauce, which is lovely with corn on the cob or over green vegetables such as green beans or cauliflower to make a vegetarian luncheon dish.

[Serves 6]

½ pound Spanish fresh cheese crumbled, or use grated Cheddar cheese

10 fresh hot red or green peppers, seeded and chopped

½ pint olive or vegetable oil

Salt, freshly ground pepper

2 pounds cassava (yucca) root, peeled and sliced

2 hardboiled eggs, sliced

Black olives

Lettuce leaves

Put the cheese into a blender or food processor with the peppers and the oil and reduce it to a heavy cream. Season to taste with salt and pepper and set aside. Boil the cassava (yucca) root in salted water until it is tender, about 30 minutes. Drain and arrange the slices on a serving platter and pour the sauce over them while they are still hot. Garnish the platter with the eggs, olives, and lettuce leaves.

Budín de Yuca

CASSAVA ROOT SOUFFLÉ   *Guatemala*

Guatemala has an interesting way of making cassava root into a soufflé, which can be served instead of rice or other starchy vegetables with meat and poultry dishes, or with *Môlho ao Tomate* (Tomato Sauce), page 306, or *Salsa de Jitomate* (Tomato Sauce), page 305, and grated Parmesan cheese as a first course or light luncheon dish.

[Serves 4]
1 pound cassava (yucca) root
Salt, freshly ground pepper
3 ounces butter

½ pint milk, about
4 egg yolks
5 egg whites

Peel the cassava (yucca) root under cold running water, as it discolours quickly. Slice it and drop it into a saucepan of salted water. Bring to the boil, lower the heat, cover, and simmer until tender, about 30 minutes. Drain the cassava, mash, season to taste with salt and pepper, and beat in the butter. Heat the milk and stir it gradually into the mashed vegetable until it has the consistency of mashed potatoes. Use a little more hot milk if necessary. Beat in the egg yolks one by one. Beat the egg whites with a pinch of salt until they stand in firm peaks. Fold them into the vegetable mixture lightly but thoroughly and pour into a 3 pint soufflé dish. Bake in a preheated moderate oven (350° F., 180° C., gas 4) for 35 minutes or until well puffed and lightly browned.

SALADS

Ensalada Mixta

MIXED SALAD   *Ecuador*

Of all the countries in Latin America, Ecuador has the most imaginative and original approach to vegetables. Cooks there never cease to astonish me with the variety of their salads, many of which I find pleasant for a simple lunch if served in double portions. Because it is only 15 miles from the equator, Quito, Ecuador's capital, has equal day and night so that all year round 12 hours of sunshine encourage fruits and vegetables to grow. This part of the country also has a fantastically deep subsoil and good rainfall so that the raw materials for making salads are of superb quality. At 9,500 feet above sea level, water boils at a lower temperature and vegetables do not get overcooked, and since at this altitude it is always cool in the shade, salads are served at room temperature rather than chilled. I find this enhances flavour, though at sea level in hot summer an unchilled salad will be a wilted and drooping one.

[Serves 4]
4 ounces chopped lettuce
2 hardboiled eggs, chopped
½ pound cooked, cubed potatoes

¾ pound cooked green beans, cut into ½-inch pieces
¼ pint vinaigrette dressing (page 313)

Combine all the ingredients in a salad bowl and toss lightly to mix.

Variation: For *Ensalada de Hongos* (Mushroom Salad), combine equal amounts of cooked corn kernels, cooked chopped carrots, cooked green beans, cut into ½-inch pieces, cooked green peas, and sliced mushrooms, and toss in vinaigrette dressing.

Variation: For *Ensalada de Garbanzos* (Chickpea Salad), combine cooked chickpeas with half the amount of cooked, coarsely chopped Brussels sprouts and toss in vinaigrette dressing made with mustard (page 313). Chopped lettuce and cubed boiled potatoes may be added and the Brussels sprouts omitted.

Variation: For *Ensalada de Alcachofas* (Artichoke Heart Salad), mix together equal amounts of cooked, sliced artichoke hearts and sliced apples with Mayonnaise (page 311) to taste.

Variation: For *Ensalada de Papas* (Potato Salad), omit the lettuce, add ½ pound chopped celery and 1 medium tomato, peeled and chopped.

Variation: For *Ensalada de Tomate* (Tomato Salad), combine 4 medium tomatoes, peeled and chopped, with 4 hardboiled eggs, chopped, and 2 ounces chopped lettuce. Toss with vinaigrette dressing made with lemon juice.

Variation: For *Ensalada de Pepinos* (Cucumber Salad), peel 2 cucumbers if they are waxed, if not leave them unpeeled and slice very thinly. Put them in a bowl with 1 teaspoon salt, mixing well, and let stand for 30 minutes. Rinse and drain thoroughly. Peel and chop 2 medium tomatoes and combine with the cucumbers. Toss with a vinaigrette dressing.

Variation: For *Ensalada de Papas y Pimientos* (Potato and Sweet Red Pepper Salad), combine ½ pound cooked sliced potatoes, 2 sweet red peppers, peeled and sliced, 2 medium-sized mild onions, sliced, or 1 large, halved and sliced, and 1 cucumber peeled, seeded, and sliced with ¼ pint Vinaigrette dressing (page 313), made with lemon juice and seasoned with 2 pinches nutmeg. Let the salad stand for 1 hour before serving. Mix lightly just before serving.

Ensalada de Habas

FRESH BROAD BEAN SALAD   *Ecuador*

Fresh young broad beans are often hard to get. If the beans are older, shell them, drop them into boiling water, let them stand a few minutes, then peel off the tough outer skin. I find English canned broad beans or Italian canned broad beans labelled fava beans a good substitute. These need no cooking and should just be rinsed and drained. I sometimes use baby lima beans. The 12-ounce package of frozen baby limas serves 4.

[Serves 4]
1 pound young broad beans, shelled
1 ounce butter

Salt, freshly ground pepper
1 tablespoon white vinegar or
*   lemon juice*

Cook the beans in water to cover until they are tender, about 15 minutes. Drain and cool. Melt the butter in a saucepan, add the beans, season to taste with salt and pepper, and cook for about 1 minute, turning the beans with a rubber spatula so that all are coated with the butter. Remove from the heat and pour the vinegar or lemon juice over them, stirring to mix. Serve at room temperature as an accompaniment to meats or poultry.

Salada de Palmito

HEARTS OF PALM SALAD   *Brazil*

[Serves 6 to 8]
Two 1-pound cans hearts of palm

FOR THE MÔLHO PARA PALMITO (Hearts of Palm Dressing)

1 tablespoon lime or lemon juice
1 tablespoon Dijon mustard
Salt, freshly ground pepper
4 tablespoons vegetable oil

Thoroughly drain the hearts of palm and cut them into ½-inch slices. Set aside.

In a bowl beat together the lime or lemon juice with the mustard and salt and pepper to taste. Gradually beat in the oil. Pour the dressing over the palm heart slices and toss lightly.

Ensalada de Aguacate

AVOCADO SALAD   *Colombia*

This salad is simplicity itself as well as being surprisingly good.

[Serves 6 to 8]
6 tablespoons olive oil
2 tablespoons white wine vinegar
Salt, freshly ground pepper
2 large, ripe avocados

In a salad bowl beat together the oil and vinegar. Season to taste with salt and pepper. Peel the avocados and remove the pits. Cut the flesh into cubes and toss lightly with the dressing. If liked, serve in a bowl lined with lettuce leaves.

Chojín

RADISH AND FRIED PORK RIND SALAD   *Guatemala*

[Serves 6 to 8]
24 small red radishes, ½ pound
  about, finely chopped
12 fresh mint leaves, finely chopped
¾ pound chicharrones (fried pork
  rinds), finely chopped
Salt to taste
4 tablespoons Seville orange juice,
  or use two-thirds orange juice to
  one-third lemon juice

Combine all the ingredients in a bowl and serve as a salad first course. If possible, use a Latin American type of *chicharrón*, as it has more flavour.

Variation: For *Picado de Rábano* (Radish Salad), omit the *chicharrones* (fried pork rinds) and serve as a salad.

Ensalada de Coliflor

CAULIFLOWER SALAD   *Mexico*

This cauliflower salad looks quite grand on a buffet, the white of the vegetable just visible beneath the pale green of the masking avocado sauce, very summery and pretty especially when garnished with radish roses.

[Serves 4 to 6]
1 medium-sized cauliflower, cooked
  and placed in a serving dish
  (page 257)
½ recipe for Guacamole
  (Avocado Sauce), *page 303*, or
  Guacamole del Norte *(Avocado
  Sauce, Northern Style), page 304*

Allow the cooked cauliflower to cool, then mask it with the avocado sauce. Serve immediately as avocado tends to darken. Garnish with radish roses.

Variation: Dominican Republic cooks have their own way of doing this. Mash 1 large avocado with salt, pepper, 1 tablespoon white wine vinegar, 3 tablespoons vegetable oil, and 1 ounce finely ground almonds. Mask the cauliflower with the mixture. The oil and vinegar used in this recipe help to keep the avocado sauce from darkening. Garnish with radish roses.

Ensalada de Nopalitos

CACTUS SALAD   *Mexico*

This is Mexico's most traditional salad. It is lovely for summer as the juicy yet crisp young cactus pieces are very refreshing.

[Serves 6]
Two 10-ounce cans nopalitos
3 medium tomatoes, peeled, seeded,
  and chopped
½ medium white onion, finely
  chopped

2 tablespoons fresh coriander,
  chopped
¼ pint vinaigrette dressing (page
  313)

273

Rinse the cactus pieces gently in cold water and drain them thoroughly. Combine all the ingredients in a salad bowl and mix lightly. Chill before serving.

Variation: For a more elaborate salad, line the bowl with lettuce leaves, add the salad, and garnish it with canned *jalapeño* chili rinsed, patted dry, and cut into strips, about ¼ pound crumbled fresh cheese (*queso fresco* or *queso blanco* or cottage cheese), or 3 tablespoons grated Parmesan cheese, with ¼ teaspoon oregano sprinkled on top of the salad.

Ensalada de Topinambur

JERUSALEM ARTICHOKE SALAD   *Mexico*

A good change from potato salad. Choose the largest artichokes available to give the finished salad a more attractive look, and be careful not to overcook them as they should be crisp not mushy.

[Serves 6]
2 pounds Jerusalem artichokes
Salt
1 recipe vinaigrette (Oil and
  Vinegar Dressing), page 313

Wash and scrape the artichokes and cook in salted water until tender, about 10 to 15 minutes. Drain and slice. Allow to cool, then toss with the vinaigrette.

For a richer salad, mix the artichokes with Mayonnaise (page 311), or *Salsa Golf* (Tomato- and Cognac-Flavoured Mayonnaise), page 311.

Ensalada de Verduras

VEGETABLE SALAD   *Ecuador*

This is a favourite way of serving vegetables in Ecuador and is often presented as a separate course, before the main course. The vegetables are arranged in rows on a large platter and are served freshly cooked at room temperature. I have had them without any dressing, simply seasoned with salt during the cooking, with a dressing only of oil, salt, and pepper, and with a vinaigrette made with 3 parts oil to 1 part vinegar or lemon juice, and seasoned with salt and pepper. The platter may be decorated with shredded lettuce or garnished with slices of hardboiled egg, or with olives, green or black. The vegetables should be cooked and tossed with the dressing separately. The dressing should not be abundant. The vegetables may be arranged as the cook sees fit: in rows, in heaps, or in circles. The vegetables listed below are the ones most frequently used. I like to serve the platter of mixed vegetables to accompany a main course, especially an Ecuadorian one.

Green peas
Diced beetroot
Cauliflower, separated in florets
Green beans, cut into ½-inch slices
Corn kernels
Diced carrots
Diced potatoes
Diced celery

Asparagus, cut into 1-inch pieces
Artichoke hearts, halved or
  quartered
Tiny sliced raw courgettes or larger
  courgettes, cooked and diced
Sliced raw tomatoes
Sliced avocados

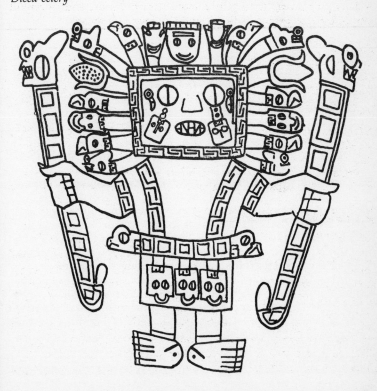

Breads and Desserts

PANES Y POSTRES

The people of pre-Columbian America had no breads as we know them but they had their own special flat breads made from corn, *Arepas* and *Tortillas* (already discussed as appetizers). In the colonial period other breads like *Sopa Paraguaya* were invented. Modern Latin American bakeries produce commercial breads like our own as well as *pan dulce*, the sweet breakfast breads of Spain. They are truly international. I have chosen breads that are either indigenous or colonial, like a delicious banana bread from Guatemala, *Pan de Banano;* Mexico's bread rolls, *Bolillos;* Venezuela's corn pancakes, *Cachapas de Jojoto;* and Paraguay's rich and splendid corn bread, *Sopa Paraguaya.* They are not hard to make and add an authentic and different touch to a Latin American meal.

There were few indigenous desserts; people mostly finished a meal with fresh fruits. Some, like pineapple, papaya, the *zapotes* and *anonas,* and *tuna* (fruit of the *nopal* cactus), were unknown to Europe at the time. The Aztecs stuffed tamales with strawberries, that universal fruit; honey was used as a sweetening by both Mayas and Aztecs; and the Incas made desserts from pumpkin and sweet potatoes, but they lacked wheat flour, butter, cream, and sugar to make the pies, puddings, and rich desserts of Europe. It was not until the colonial period and the introduction of sugar cane that desserts began to flourish. Spanish nuns in Peru and Mexico, especially in Puebla, made colonial desserts famous. In Brazil, primarily in Bahia, cooks in the great houses of the sugar plantations created a whole new world of cakes and sweet things for desserts. They drew on the Portuguese tradition of using lots of egg yolks and sugar. Out of this huge array I have chosen a small selection of favourites which I think are suited to the modern palate.

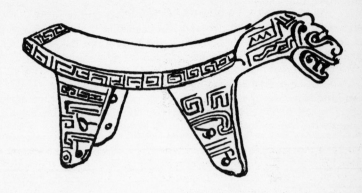

BREADS

Sopa Paraguaya

PARAGUAYAN CORN BREAD *Paraguay*

This is a wonderfully hearty corn bread with two kinds of cheese to enrich it and onions sautéed in butter to add to the flavour. It is traditionally served with *So'O-Yosopy* (Beef Soup) and with grilled steaks, but is fine with any meat or poultry dish, or by itself.

¼ pound butter
2 medium onions, finely chopped
½ pound cottage cheese
½ pound Cheddar cheese, grated
½ pound cornmeal
12 ounces grated corn kernels, or a

1-pound can cream-style sweet corn
1 teaspoon salt, preferably coarse
½ pint milk
6 eggs, separated

Grease a baking tin, about 10 by 13 inches, and sprinkle with 1 tablespoon flour. Shake to remove the excess.

Heat 2 ounces of the butter and sauté the onions until they are softened. Set aside. Cream the remaining butter and add to the cot-

277

tage cheese, blending thoroughly. Add the Cheddar cheese and the onions. In another bowl combine the cornmeal, corn, salt, and milk, and mix thoroughly. Combine the corn mixture with the cheese mixture, blending thoroughly.

Beat the egg whites until they form soft peaks and beat the yolks separately. Combine the two and stir them into the cornmeal and cheese mixture. Pour the batter into the baking tin. Bake in a preheated hot (400° F., 200° C., gas 6) oven for 45 minutes, or until a cake tester comes out clean.

A pinch of ground aniseed may be added to the mixture, if liked. Another pleasant variation is to cut 2 ounces Cheddar into tiny cubes and stir this into the batter at the last moment, if liked. This gives a slightly different texture to the finished bread.

Pan de Banano

BANANA BREAD *Guatemala*

This easy-to-make banana bread is lovely for a snack. Spread with honey or topped with fresh fruit, it can be dressed up with cream or ice cream to make an attractive dessert.

[Makes one 9-inch loaf]	1 teaspoon ground cinnamon
¼ pound butter	1 tablespoon lemon juice
¼ pound sugar	1 egg, well beaten
1 pound ripe bananas (2 or 3 large)	6 ounces plain flour
½ teaspoon salt	2 teaspoons baking powder

Soften the butter at room temperature and cream it with the sugar in a mixing bowl until light and fluffy. Mash the bananas and add to the butter and sugar mixture. Add the salt, cinnamon, lemon juice, and egg. Sift the flour with the baking powder and fold it into the liquid mixture. Pour the batter into a greased (9- by 5-inch) loaf pan. Bake in a preheated moderate oven (350° F., 180° C., gas 4) for 1 hour, or until a cake tester comes out clean. Serve with honey as a cake bread, or as a pudding with cream or ice cream.

Tortillas *Mexico*

[Makes about eighteen 4-inch tortillas]

To make tortillas, see page 63.

Tortillas that are served instead of bread with Mexican meals may be made slightly larger, 5 or 6 inches across, though the 4-inch ones are perfectly acceptable. When they are eaten in this way, or made into soft tacos (stuffed, rolled tortillas), they should be brought to the table wrapped in a napkin, then placed in a small woven reed or straw basket. The napkin is always folded back over the tortillas when one is taken so as to keep them warm and soft. In Mexico no one ever takes the top tortilla of the stack, always the second or third to be sure of getting a good hot one. Leftover tortillas are never wasted, as they are the prime ingredient of *chilaquiles,* fried strips of day-old tortilla baked in a chili sauce. They are also used as a garnish in certain soups.

Arepas

CORN BREAD   *Venezuela and Colombia*

The *Arepas* of Venezuela and Colombia are made from corn processed into flour in the same way as the flour for Mexican corn tortillas, but the *arepa* is not a flexible pancake like the tortilla. It looks rather like a pure white round bread roll. The outside is crisp, the inside doughy. In Caracas I have had *Arepas* served with cream cheese as an unusual first course. The doughy inside is pulled out of the *arepa* and it is then filled with the delicious local runny cream cheese. French *crème fraîche* is a good substitute, as it is very like the Caracas cream cheese. I've found that cream cheese softened at room temperature and mashed with a little double cream also serves nicely as a substitute for the Venezuelan original. Easy to make and taking little time, *Arepas* make a pleasant change from everyday bread and are especially good with Venezuelan dishes. When eaten as bread, the doughy inside is split open, pulled out with the fingers, and the remaining shell is buttered, or the *Arepas* are simply split and buttered. I often top the butter with a little cream cheese as I find the combination irresistible.

[Makes 8 to 10]
10 ounces corn flour for Arepas   1 teaspoon salt
  (see page 38)   ¾ pint water, about

In a bowl mix the *arepa* flour with the salt. Stir in the water to make a stiffish dough. Add a little more if necessary. Let the dough stand for 5 minutes, then form into balls flattened slightly to 3 inches across and about ½ inch thick. Cook on a heavy, lightly greased griddle over moderate heat for 5 minutes a side, then bake in a preheated moderate oven (350° F., 180° C., gas 4) for 20 to 30 minutes, turning them two or three times during cooking. They are done when they sound hollow when tapped. Serve hot. Traditionally they are wrapped in a napkin and served in a straw basket.

Variation: For *Arepas de Queso* (Corn Bread with Cheese), add 4 ounces finely chopped or crumbled *queso fresco* or *queso blanco* (Spanish fresh cheese), or grated Cheddar cheese.

Variation: For *Arepas de Chicharrones* (Corn Bread with Pork Rinds), add 4 ounces *chicharrones* (fried pork rinds), crumbled.

Variation: For *Arepas Santanderinas* (Corn Bread, Santander Style), mix 2 tablespoons lard into the flour before adding the water, working it in thoroughly with your fingers, then make as usual.

Variation: For *Arepas Fritas* (Fried Corn Bread), mix 4 ounces grated cheese with the flour. Beat an egg yolk with the water and salt, and mix it with the flour and cheese, kneading the dough thoroughly (about 5 minutes). Roll out into thin circles about 4 inches in diameter and fry in lard or oil until lightly browned on both sides. These may be made smaller, about 1½ inches in diameter, and served as an accompaniment to drinks.

Variation: For *Arepas Fritas Infladas* (Puffed Fried Corn Bread), add to the dough 4 ounces grated cheese, 2 ounces plain flour, ¼ teaspoon ground anise, and 1 tablespoon sugar, preferably brown. Knead the dough until it is very smooth, about 5 minutes. Form it into small balls and roll them out on a lightly floured board to make thin 3-inch pancakes. Deep fry in hot oil. They should puff up. Serve immediately. I find it easier to lift them with a slotted spoon as they are very soft.

Cachapas de Jojoto

CORN PANCAKES   *Venezuela*

These are pleasant eaten instead of bread with a meal. Miniaturized (about 1½ inches across) and wrapped round a piece of Spanish fresh cheese, (*queso fresco* or *queso blanco*), or Cheddar, they make an attractive cocktail nibble.

[Makes about 12]
9 ounces corn kernels, if frozen
    thoroughly defrosted
¼ pint double cream
1 egg

3 tablespoons plain flour
¼ teaspoon sugar
½ teaspoon salt
1 ounce butter, melted
Butter for frying

Put all the ingredients into a blender or food processor and mix until smooth. Grease an omelet pan by rubbing a piece of crumbled wax paper over the butter, then rubbing the pan with the paper. Repeat this process for each pancake. Drop the mixture, 2 tablespoons at a time, into the pan and fry until lightly browned on both sides, turning once. Serve hot.

Variation: For *Cachapas de Hojas* (Corn Mixture Steamed in Leaves), put 2 tablespoons of the corn mixture into the centre of a dry corn husk and fold it up into a package. Arrange the corn husks in a steamer, and steam, covered, over boiling water until firm, about 30 minutes. *Cachapas de Budare* (Corn Mixture in Banana Leaves) are made by stuffing a piece of banana leaf with the corn mixture, folding the leaf into a package, and cooking it over moderate heat on a griddle, turning it twice, then standing it at the side of the griddle to finish cooking. Ideally the *Cachapas* should be baked on a *budare*, a special Venezuelan griddle, and finished at the back of a wood-burning stove. It is possible to improvise using aluminum foil and a heavy griddle, setting both over very low heat on top of two asbestos mats. Faced with the difficulty of getting fresh banana leaves, I have contented myself with *Cachapas de Jojoto*, which are extremely good and present no difficulties at all.

Bolillos

MEXICAN BREAD ROLLS *Mexico*

These are the marvellous *petits pains* of Mexico, acquired during the short, unhappy reign of Maximilian and Carlota, wished on the Mexicans by Napoleon III and vigorously resisted by the infant republic. Mexico preferred to remain independent but was in no way reluctant to accept the world's best bread—French bread. To this day I find that *Bolillos*, the spindle-shaped rolls that are sold fresh twice a day in the bakeries of Mexico, are equalled only by bread in France. I find I can make a good approximation of them with little trouble if I get a good, hard wheat flour.

[Makes 18]
¼ ounce active dry yeast, or ½ ounce fresh yeast

1½ teaspoons salt
1¼ pounds sifted bread flour*
Butter for the bowl

*Bread flour is one with a higher mixture of hard wheat. Plain flour may be substituted.

Put the yeast into a large bowl and soften it in ¼ pint lukewarm water. When it has liquefied completely, stir in ½ pint lukewarm water and the salt, and stir to mix. Gradually mix in the flour to make a dough that comes away from the sides of the bowl with a little stickiness. Knead the dough on a lightly floured board for 10 minutes, or until it is smooth and elastic and has lost all its stickiness. Put the dough in a buttered bowl, cover it with a clean cloth, and leave it to rise in a warm place until it has doubled in bulk, about 2 hours.

The oven with just the pilot light lit is a good place to put the dough to rise in cold weather. This is a slow-rising dough and it is important to allow it enough time.

At the end of this time punch the dough down, cover it, and let it rise a second time until again doubled in bulk, about 1 hour. Turn it out onto a lightly floured board and knead it for about 5 minutes. Divide the dough in half. Roll each piece out into an oblong, about 18 inches by 6 inches. Roll each piece up like a jelly roll. Cut each roll into 9 slices, making 18 in all. Pinch the ends of each slice to form a spindle shape and arrange on a buttered baking sheet. Cover and let the rolls rise until they have doubled in bulk, about 1 hour. Brush them lightly with water and bake in a preheated hot oven (400° F., 200° C., gas 6) for about 30 minutes, or until they are golden brown.

DESSERTS

Flan de Piña

PINEAPPLE CUSTARD   *Colombia*

This is a very old family recipe given to me by my friend Cecilia Blanco de Mendoza, an authority on traditional Colombian cooking.

[Serves 6]   ½ *pound sugar*
2 *ounces sugar*   4 *eggs*
½ *pint unsweetened pineapple juice*

In the top of a double boiler over boiling water melt 2 ounces sugar over moderate heat, stirring constantly, until it has melted and is a rich caramel colour. Dip the bottom of the container into cold water for a second or two, then turn it so that the caramel coats sides as well as bottom. Set aside.

In a saucepan combine the pineapple juice and ½ pound sugar and cook, stirring, until the liquid is reduced to half and is quite thick. Cool the syrup. Beat the eggs until they are thick and lemon-coloured. Pour the syrup into the eggs in a thin, slow stream, beating all the time. Pour the mixture into the prepared caramelized container. On the top of the stove cook the custard, covered, over barely simmering water for about 2 hours, or until it is set. Cool and refrigerate until ready to serve. Before serving unmould by running a knife between the custard and the container, then place a serving dish over the mould and invert quickly.

Mousse de Castanhas de Caju e Chocolate

CASHEW NUT AND CHOCOLATE MOUSSE   *Brazil*

[Serves 6 to 8]
2 ounces plain chocolate
¼ pound sugar
5 egg yolks

¼ pound roasted cashew nuts,
  finely ground
½ pint double cream
5 egg whites

Break the chocolate into small pieces and put with 2 to 3 tablespoons of water into the top of a double boiler over boiling water. Add the sugar and stir until the chocolate is melted and the sugar dissolved. Remove the pan from the heat and beat in the egg yolks, one at a time, beating well after each addition. Stir in the ground cashew nuts. Beat the cream until it stands in firm peaks and fold it into the chocolate mixture. Beat the egg whites until they stand in firm peaks and fold into the chocolate mixture, lightly but thoroughly. Pour into a 2 pint soufflé dish and refrigerate overnight or for several hours. Serve, if liked, with sweetened whipped cream.

Capirotada

BREAD PUDDING   *Mexico*

This is a very special bread pudding, a great favourite in Mexico during Lent and a marvellous dessert at any time, especially for a holiday buffet. I make my *Capirotada* from a recipe given me by my husband's grandmother, and I use brown sugar flavoured with cinnamon and cloves for the syrup in which it is drenched before baking. A good friend, the writer Elizabeth Borton de Treviño, sent me a grandly extravagant recipe for the syrup, which she was given by a friend, Señora Estela Santos Coy de Cobo, who had it from her grand-mother. It is a blend of disparate flavours—orange rind, tomato, onion, cloves, green or red pepper—which one would never expect to work, yet work it does, lusciously.

[Serves 6 to 8]

FOR THE SYRUP

1 pound piloncillo *or brown sugar*
A 2-inch piece of stick cinnamon
1 small onion, stuck with 3 cloves
1 medium red or green sweet pepper, seeded and halved

Peel from 1 medium orange, shredded
8 tablespoons fresh coriander, chopped
1 small tomato, peeled, seeded, and chopped
1¾ pints water

Combine all the ingredients in a saucepan, bring to the boil, reduce the heat, and simmer, partially covered, for 30 minutes. Allow to cool a little. Strain, discard the solids, and set the syrup aside.

FOR THE PUDDING

Butter
¾ pound of ½-inch cubes toasted French or firm white bread
3 apples, peeled, cored, and thinly sliced

6 ounces raisins
¼ pound chopped blanched almonds
½ pound Cheddar, or similar cheese, coarsely chopped

Butter a 3-pint ovenproof casserole or soufflé dish and make a layer of cubes of toast. Add a layer of apple slices, raisins, almonds, and cheese. Repeat until all the ingredients are used up. Pour the syrup over the dish. Bake in a preheated moderate oven (350° F., 180° C., gas 4) for 45 minutes, or until heated through. Serve hot.

Variation: For a slightly richer dish sauté the bread cubes in ¼ pint vegetable oil or 4 ounces butter.

Variation: For a simpler syrup simmer 1 pound brown sugar with a 2-inch piece of stick cinnamon, 2 cloves, and 1¾ pints water to make a light syrup. Remove the cinnamon and cloves before using.

Creme de Abacate

AVOCADO CREAM   *Brazil*

Apart from avocado ice cream, which I confess I do not care for, this is the only dessert using avocados that I have come across. It was part of our kitchen repertoire during the years we lived in Jamaica, and later on I was puzzled by this as it was so clearly not a Jamaican dish. The mystery was solved by my mother, who told me it had been given her by the Brazilian lady who was the previous tenant of the house we rented—a sort of parting gift.

[Serves 6]
3 large, ripe avocados, chilled

4 tablespoons fresh lime juice
6 tablespoons castor sugar

Halve the avocados, remove the stones, and mash them in their shells with a fork. Turn them out into a bowl and mash until smooth with the lime juice and sugar. Pile the mixture into glass serving dishes and garnish, if liked, with a little grated lime peel or a slice of lime.

Mazamorra Morada

PERUVIAN FRUIT COMPOTE   *Peru*

Mazamorra is a dish made with cornflour and sugar or honey. This *Mazamorra* is made with *maíz morado*, the purple corn of Peru that gives off a most beautiful deep purple colour when it is simmered in water. It has a delicate, flowery, lemony taste. Purple corn is not readily available outside Peru but I have found I can get the same lovely colour by using blackberries. This is a luscious and refreshing dessert, lovely for a summer buffet.

[Serves 8 to 10]
½ pound purple corn kernels
2½ pints water
1 pound sugar
6 cloves
A 3-inch piece of stick cinnamon
½ small pineapple, peeled, cored, and cubed
2 quinces, peeled and sliced
2 pears, peeled and sliced

2 peaches, stoned, peeled, and sliced
1 pound cherries, stoned
½ pound dried apricots, halved
½ pound dried peaches, quartered
4 tablespoons cornflour
Juice of 2 lemons, about 6 tablespoons
Ground cinnamon (optional)

Put the purple corn kernels into a saucepan with the water, bring to the boil, and simmer until the corn is cooked, about 30 minutes, and the water is a deep purple. Strain and discard the corn. Measure the liquid and add more water to make 2½ pints, if necessary. Return the purple water to the saucepan and add the sugar, cloves, cinnamon stick, pineapple, quinces, pears, peaches, cherries, dried apricots, and dried peaches. Bring the liquid to a simmer, cover the saucepan, and cook gently over low heat until the fruit is tender, about 15 minutes. Remove and discard the cloves and cinnamon. Dissolve the cornflour in 4 tablespoons water and stir it into the fruit mixture. Cook until the liquid is thickened, then stir in the lemon juice. Chill the compote and serve it sprinkled with a little cinnamon, if liked.

Variation: Cook the fruit in plain water. Add 2 apples, peeled and sliced, and ½ pound blackberries to the other fruit, otherwise make the dish in the same way.

Dulce de Queso

CHEESE SWEET   *Colombia*

[Serves 4 to 6]
1 pound mozzarella cheese
1 pound dark brown sugar

½ pint water
A 2-inch piece of stick cinnamon

Let the cheese come to room temperature. Using a very sharp knife, cut the cheese horizontally into ¼-inch slices and arrange them in a shallow Pyrex dish. In a small saucepan combine the sugar, water, and cinnamon, and bring to the boil, stirring to dissolve the sugar. Boil for 5 minutes without stirring. Pour the syrup over the cheese and serve immediately. For a softer cheese, put the prepared dish in a preheated oven (350° F., 180° C., gas 4) for 5 minutes.

Cocada

COCONUT CUSTARD   *Mexico*

[Serves 6]
¾ pound sugar
A 2-inch piece of stick cinnamon
Liquid from a medium-sized
    coconut, ¼ pint, about

½ pound grated coconut (page 28)
1¼ pints milk
4 whole eggs, lightly beaten
1 ounce butter, or 2 ounces toasted
    slivered almonds

In a saucepan combine the sugar, cinnamon stick, and coconut water. Stir the mixture over low heat until the sugar is dissolved. Add the coconut and continue to cook the mixture, stirring, until the coconut is transparent, about 5 minutes. Remove and discard the cinnamon stick. Stir in the milk, mixing thoroughly. Simmer, over moderate heat, stirring from time to time, until the mixture has thickened and a spoon drawn across the bottom leaves a clean path. Pour ¼ pint of the mixture into the eggs, beating constantly with a whisk. Pour the egg mixture back into the saucepan and cook, stirring constantly, over low heat until it has thickened. Do not let it boil. Remove from the heat and pour into a flameproof serving dish (a 2-pint soufflé dish is fine), cool, then refrigerate for several hours. Just before serving, dot the pudding with the butter, and put it under the grill until the top is lightly browned, or garnish with the slivered almonds.

Variation: For *Dulce de Coco* (Coconut Sweet) from Colombia, soak ¼ pound raisins in hot water for 15 minutes, drain, and put into a heavy saucepan with 1 pound grated coconut, the coconut water made up to ½ pint with water, 4 tablespoons lemon juice, ¾ pound sugar, and a 3-inch piece of stick cinnamon. Bring to the boil, reduce the heat, and simmer until the syrup forms a thread when tested in cold water. Remove and discard the cinnamon stick. Beat 3 egg yolks in a bowl until they are thick and lemon-coloured. Beat in 3 tablespoons of the coconut syrup, a tablespoon at a time. Gradually pour the yolk mixture into the coconut mixture and cook over low heat, stirring constantly, for 5 minutes without letting it boil. Cool and refrigerate several hours before serving. Serves 6.

Variation: *Doce de Leite Baiana* (Bahian Style Coconut and Milk Pudding) is a simpler, but still delicious, version of coconut custard. Combine 1 pound finely grated fresh coconut with 1¾ pint milk and 1 pound light brown sugar in a heavy saucepan and cook over moderate heat until the mixture is thick and has the consistency of custard. Stir the mixture from time to time with a wooden spoon until it begins to thicken, then stir constantly. Transfer the pudding to a serving dish and serve at room temperature. Serves 6 to 8.

Variation: Elizabeth Borton de Treviño gave me this recipe, given her by the Acapulco cook of the Limantour family at their *quinta* Los Bichitos. It needs less watching than top-of-the-stove versions and has a rather denser texture. For this *Cocada*, simmer 1¼ pints milk with ¾ pound sugar in an uncovered saucepan for 20 minutes, or until the mixture is slightly thickened. Let it cool. Lightly beat 6 eggs, then beat them into the milk mixture. Stir in ½ teaspoon almond extract and ¾ pound freshly grated coconut. Pour into a buttered Pyrex dish. Set in a pan of water so that the water comes 2 inches up the side and bake in a preheated moderate oven (350° F., 180° C., gas 4) for 1½ hours, or until a cake tester comes out clean. Cool and chill before serving. Serves 6 to 8.

Variation: *Pudim de Côco* (Coconut Pudding) from Brazil is a rather richer version of coconut custard. Combine ½ pound sugar with 5 tablespoons water in a small saucepan and simmer until it spins a thread. Remove from the heat and stir in 2 ounces butter. Cool. Stir in ½ pound grated coconut. Thoroughly beat 5 egg yolks until they are very light, and fold into the coconut mixture. Pour into a buttered 1½ pint baking dish or soufflé dish, set in a pan of water so that the water extends 2 inches up the side, and bake in a preheated moderate oven (350° F., 180° C., gas 4) for 1 to 1½ hours, or until a cake tester comes out clean. Serve at room temperature. Traditionally the pudding is served with cheese. Use Spanish fresh cheese (*queso fresco* or *queso blanco*), Cheddar, or similar cheese. Serves 6.

Manjar de Coco com Môlho de Ameixas

COCONUT BLANCMANGE WITH PRUNE SAUCE   *Brazil*

[Serves 6]

FOR THE BLANCMANGE

1 pound finely grated fresh coconut   *Sugar to taste*
1¾ pints milk   *4 tablespoons cornflour*

In a saucepan combine the coconut and milk and bring to a simmer. Remove from the heat and steep for 30 minutes. Strain the liquid through butter muslin-lined sieve into a bowl, squeezing the cloth to extract all the liquid. There should be 1¾ pints. If necessary add a little milk to make up the quantity. Season with sugar to taste. Rinse out and dry the saucepan. Mix a little of the coconut milk with the cornflour and stir it into the rest of the milk. Pour the mixture into the saucepan and cook, stirring constantly with a wooden spoon, over moderate heat until it is smooth and thick, about 5 minutes. Pour it into a 2 pint mould rinsed out with cold water and refrigerate until set. Unmould onto a serving plate and surround with the prune sauce.

FOR THE SAUCE

½ pound stoned prunes   *¾ pound sugar*
¼ pint tawny port   *¼ pint water*

Put the prunes into a bowl with the port and let them macerate for 30 minutes. In a medium saucepan combine the sugar and water. Simmer for 5 minutes to make a fairly heavy syrup. Add the prunes and port and simmer for 5 minutes longer. Cool, chill, and use to garnish the *Manjar de Coco.*

Quindins de Yáyá

COCONUT CUPCAKE DESSERT   *Brazil*

[Makes 24]
½ *pound freshly grated coconut*   1 *egg white, well beaten*
1 *ounce softened butter*   *Butter*
¾ *pound light brown sugar*   4 *ounces sifted plain flour*
8 *large egg yolks*   *(optional)*

In a large bowl mix together the coconut, butter, and sugar, beating to mix thoroughly. One by one beat in the egg yolks, beating thoroughly after each addition. Fold in the egg white beaten until stiff peaks form. Some cooks add a little flour, in which case beat in the flour after all the other ingredients have been combined. The addition of flour gives a lighter, more cakelike texture. Butter your patty pans. Pour in the mixture and stand them in a baking pan with hot water to reach about halfway up the sides of the tins. Bake in a preheated moderate oven (350° F., 180° C., gas 4) for about 45 minutes, or until a toothpick inserted into the cakes comes out clean.

Torta de Zapallo

PUMPKIN CAKE   *Ecuador*

Calabaza (West Indian pumpkin), which is used so much all over Latin America as a vegetable and in soups and stews, is also used in some delectable puddings, cakes, and fritters.

[Serves 8]   1 *ounce butter*
1½ *pounds peeled and cubed*   2 *ounces dark rum*
   pumpkin   6 *ounces seedless raisins*
½ *teaspoon cinnamon*   ¼ *pound grated Münster or mild*
½ *pound sugar*   *Cheddar cheese*
¼ *pint double cream*   3 *large eggs, well beaten*

Cook the pumpkin in water to cover until tender, about 15 minutes. Drain thoroughly. Put the pumpkin in a saucepan and stir in the cinnamon, sugar, cream, and ½ ounce of the butter. Mash the pumpkin and cook it over low heat until the sugar has dissolved and the mixture is fairly firm, not watery. Remove from the heat and allow to cool. Add all the remaining ingredients, except the reserved butter. Using the butter, grease a 3 pint soufflé dish and pour in the mixture. Bake in a preheated moderate oven (350° F., 180° C., gas 4) until the cake is firm to the touch, about 1 hour. An ounce of rum may be poured over the cake while it is still hot, if liked. Serve as a pudding from the soufflé dish plain, or with whipped or sour cream.

Pudim de Abóbora

PUMPKIN PUDDING *Brazil*

[Serves 6]
4 *large eggs*
½ *teaspoon salt*
¼ *pound light brown sugar*
½ *teaspoon ground ginger*
¼ *teaspoon ground cinnamon*

¼ *teaspoon ground cloves*
¼ *teaspoon ground nutmeg*
1½ *pounds cooked mashed pumpkin*
½ *pint evaporated milk or single cream*
Butter for the mould

Break the eggs into a large bowl and beat them lightly. Beat in the salt, brown sugar, ginger, cinnamon, cloves, nutmeg, pumpkin, and evaporated milk or cream. Butter a 2-pint mould or pudding basin and pour in the custard. Set it in a pan of hot water so that the water extends 2 inches up the side and bake in a preheated moderate oven (350° F., 180° C., gas 4) until a toothpick inserted into the custard comes out clean, about 1½ hours.

Picarones

SWEET FRITTERS *Peru*

[Serves 8 to 12]
½ *pound pumpkin, peeled and sliced*
½ *pound sweet potato, preferably white sweet potato (boniato), peeled and sliced*

1 *teaspoon salt*
¼ *teaspoon ground aniseed*
1 *pound plain flour, sifted*
¼ *ounce dried yeast*
Vegetable oil for deep frying

Cook the pumpkin and sweet potato in water to cover until they are tender. Drain the vegetables, mash them, and force them through a sieve. Mix in the salt, aniseed, and flour. Soften the yeast in 4 tablespoons of lukewarm water and mix it into the flour to make a fairly firm dough, adding a little more water if necessary, though the pumpkin and sweet potato will probably supply enough moisture. Knead the dough until it is smooth and satiny, about 5 minutes. Place it in a bowl, cover with a cloth, and allow to stand in a warm, draught-free place for 2 to 3 hours, or until it has doubled in bulk. Pull off pieces of dough by tablespoons and shape them into rings. Deep fry them in hot oil until they are browned on both sides. Drain on paper towels and serve with *Miel de Chancaca* (Sugar Syrup).

MIEL DE CHANCACA (Sugar Syrup)

1 pound dark brown sugar
½ pound sugar
¾ pint water

1 piece lemon peel
1 piece orange peel

Combine all the ingredients in a saucepan and simmer until the syrup is quite thick. Remove and discard the orange and lemon peel. Serve as a dipping sauce with the *Picarones*.

Pristiños

PUMPKIN FRITTERS

Ecuador

[Serves 6]
½ pound plain flour
1 teaspoon baking powder
1 teaspoon salt
2 tablespoons grated Parmesan
 cheese

¼ pound butter, softened at room
 temperature
½ pound cooked, mashed pumpkin
Oil or lard for deep frying

Sift the flour, baking powder, and salt into a bowl. Add the cheese. Work the butter into the mixture with your fingers, then the pumpkin with a fork. The pumpkin should supply enough moisture to make a soft but not sticky dough. Turn the dough onto a floured board and roll out to a ½-inch thickness. Cut it into strips 1 inch wide and 6 inches long. Form each strip into a ring, pinching the ends lightly together. Deep fry in hot oil or lard until golden brown on all sides. Drain on paper towels and serve with cinnamon syrup.

CINNAMON SYRUP

1 pound dark brown sugar
A 1-inch piece of stick cinnamon

In a saucepan combine the sugar with ½ pint water and the cinnamon stick. Stir the mixture to dissolve the sugar and simmer over moderate heat for 5 minutes. Discard the cinnamon stick.

Milk Pudding

There is a dessert made from milk simmered with sugar until it is thick that is popular throughout Latin America. It has a variety of names—*Manjar Blanco, Natillas Piuranas, Arequipe, Dulce de Leche, Cajeta de Celaya*—and the cooking technique varies slightly from country to country. I think milk pudding is about the most practical translation. Making this can be time-consuming, about 1½ hours, if one stands at the stove and conscientiously stirs the mixture with a wooden spoon, but I have found that if the heat is kept low one can make the pudding, stirring from time to time, while doing other things in the kitchen. Once the mixture begins to thicken, however, it does need constant stirring or the texture suffers and is grainy instead of smooth. But this is only in the last 5 minutes or so. Everyone in Latin America knows the *truco*, or trick, of boiling an unopened can of sweetened condensed milk until it caramelizes, but most cooks prefer the results of the longer method. However, there is a very quick Colombian version using sweetened condensed milk and evaporated milk that is delicious, and a nice compromise. It is amazing how great a difference in taste and texture is produced by small differences in proportions and cooking methods for this most delicate of desserts.

Natillas Piuranas

BROWN SUGAR PUDDING   *Peru*

Ideally this should be made with goat's milk but I have found that using a mixture of milk and cream or evaporated milk gives a very good result.

[Serves 4 to 6]
1 pound dark brown sugar
4 tablespoons water
1¼ pints milk

½ pint single cream or evaporated milk
½ teaspoon baking soda
2 ounces finely ground walnuts

In a large, heavy saucepan combine the brown sugar and the water and cook over low heat, stirring constantly with a wooden spoon, until the sugar is dissolved. In another saucepan combine the milk, cream or evaporated milk, and the baking soda. Stir to mix and bring almost to the boil over fairly high heat. Pour into the dissolved sugar, stirring to mix thoroughly, and cook, stirring frequently, until the mixture is thick and caramel-coloured and the bottom of the pan can be seen when the spoon is drawn across it. Stir in the walnuts, mixing well. It will take about 1 hour. Serve either chilled or at room temperature.

Manjar Blanco

MILK PUDDING *Chile*

[Serves 6] 1¼ *pounds sugar*
3½ *pints milk* *A 2-inch piece of vanilla bean*

In a heavy saucepan combine all the ingredients and bring to a simmer. Cook, stirring from time to time, over low heat until the mixture begins to thicken. Remove the piece of vanilla bean. Simmer, stirring constantly with a wooden spoon, until the mixture is thick enough so the bottom of the pan can be seen when the spoon is drawn.across it. It will take about an hour. Do not overcook or the pudding will turn into candy. Turn into a serving bowl and serve either slightly chilled or at room temperature.

Variation: For *Dulce de Leche* (Milk Sweet or Dessert) from Paraguay, combine 4 pints milk, 1 teaspoon vanilla essence, ½ teaspoon baking soda, and 1 pound sugar in a saucepan and stir from time to time, off the heat, until the sugar is dissolved. Bring to a simmer and cook over very low heat, to prevent the milk from boiling over, stirring occasionally with a wooden spoon until the mixture is thick and caramel-coloured. When the mixture begins to thicken, stir constantly. The pudding is ready when the bottom of the saucepan can be seen when the spoon is drawn across it, or when a spoonful on a plate no longer runs but retains its shape. The pudding may be varied by increasing the amount of sugar by ½ pound or by increasing the amount of milk by ¾ pint. Serves 6 to 8.

Variation: For *Arequipe* (Milk Pudding) from Colombia, there is a recipe almost identical to the one above from Paraguay but using 5 pints milk to 2 pounds sugar.

Variation: There is another *Arequipe* that is very successful and a splendid shortcut. Put ¾ pint evaporated milk and ¾ pint sweetened condensed milk into a heavy saucepan, stir to mix thoroughly, bring to a simmer, and cook, stirring constantly, until the mixture is thick and golden and the bottom of the pan can be seen when the spoon is drawn across it. Serve with wedges of cheese, preferably Spanish fresh cheese, Cheddar, Edam, or Gouda.

Variation: For *Dulce de Leche Con Huevos* (Milk Sweet with Eggs), simmer 3½ pints of milk with 1 pound sugar, a vanilla bean, and a 2-inch piece of stick cinnamon until the mixture begins to thicken. Remove the vanilla bean and cinnamon stick. When the pudding is thick, remove from the heat and stir in 4 well-beaten egg yolks. Return the pudding to the heat and cook, stirring, for 2 minutes. Remove from the heat. Beat 4 egg whites until they stand in peaks and add to the pudding, off the heat. Return the pudding to the heat and cook, stirring constantly, until it is again thick. Off the heat beat the pudding until it is cool. Turn into a dessert dish and chill until ready to serve. Serves 6 to 8.

Variation: The best milk puddings of Mexico come from the rich mining and farming state of Guanajuato. The most famous of them is *Cajeta de Celaya,* which means literally box from the town of Celaya and refers to the small wooden boxes in which the sweet is packaged. Put 1¼ pints each cow's and goat's milk, mixed with ½ teaspoon baking soda and 2 teaspoons cornflour, in a heavy saucepan with 1 pound sugar and a fig leaf, if available, and simmer the mixture in the usual way until thick. Discard the fig leaf and pour the pudding into a serving bowl. Serve chilled or at room temperature. Goat's milk is sometimes available in health shops.

For *Cajeta Envinada* (Milk Pudding with Wine), stir ¼ pint sherry, muscatel, or Madeira into the finished sweet. For *Cajeta de Leche Quemada* (Pudding of Burned Milk), the sugar is carmelized before the milk is added. To do this the sugar is put into a heavy saucepan over low heat and stirred constantly with a wooden spoon until it melts and turns coffee colour. The milk should be added little by little, off the heat, and stirred well to mix. The pudding is then cooked in the usual way. It is a deep, rich amber colour. There is a little *truco* here that some cooks use—they substitute light brown sugar for white sugar. For *Cajeta de Almendra Envinada* (Milk Pudding with Almonds and Wine), add 1 ounce ground almonds and ¼ pint sherry, muscatel, or Madeira. Serve the pudding by itself, or with ice cream or slices of pound cake or sweet biscuits. Serves 6.

Torta del Cielo

HEAVENLY CAKE   *Mexico*

This cake is served on all kinds of special occasions in Yucatán: engagement parties, weddings, baptisms, first communions, birthdays, and so on. There are many versions, some using no flour at all, just ground almonds. This is the version I prefer and I find it aptly named.

[Serves 12]
8 ounces blanched almonds
2 ounces fine flour
1 teaspoon baking powder

10 eggs, separated
10 ounces sugar
1 teaspoon vanilla extract
Pinch of salt

Cut a piece of wax paper to fit a 10-inch springform pan and oil it lightly. Fit it into the bottom of the pan. Do not oil the sides.

Grind the nuts and shake them through a sieve. Sift the flour with the baking powder into a bowl and mix thoroughly with the nuts. In another bowl beat the egg yolks, adding the sugar gradually until they are light, thick, and lemon-coloured and form a ribbon when lifted from the bowl. Stir in the vanilla. Beat the egg whites with the pinch of salt until they stand in firm peaks. Sprinkle the flour and nut mixture onto the egg yolks, add the whites, and, using a rubber spatula, lightly fold them all together. Do not overmix, fold only until the last patches of white disappear. Pour the mixture into the prepared pan and bake in a preheated moderate oven (375° F., 190° C., gas 5) for 50 minutes, or until a cake tester comes out clean. Invert on a wire rack and allow to cool thoroughly for 1 to 2 hours. Remove from the pan and peel off the wax paper. Turn right side up and dust with icing sugar. The cake may be served with whipped cream, ice cream, fruit salad, or by itself. It may be frosted with a butter cream frosting, if liked.

Variation: Use 1 pound ground almonds and omit the flour and baking powder. Beat the egg whites until they stand in firm peaks, then beat in the yolks, two at a time, adding 2 extra yolks. Then beat in the almonds, 1 ounce at a time, and 1 pound icing sugar, 4 ounces at a time. Stir in the vanilla.

Quimbolitos

STEAMED PUDDINGS *Ecuador*

[Serves 6]
2 ounces butter
6 tablespoons sugar
2 eggs, well beaten
4 tablespoons milk
2 ounces plain flour

2 ounces cornflour
2 teaspoons baking powder
2 ounces grated Parmesan cheese
2 ounces seedless raisins
2 tablespoons cognac or light rum

Soften the butter at room temperature. In a bowl cream together the butter and sugar until the mixture is light and fluffy. Add the eggs mixed with the milk. Sift together the flour, cornflour, and baking powder, and stir into the batter mixture. Stir in the cheese, raisins, and cognac or rum.

Cut aluminum foil into six 8- by 12-inch rectangles. Drop a scant 3 tablespoons of the mixture into the centre of each, and fold up into an envelope. Arrange in a steamer and cook over boiling water for 45 minutes. Serve hot, with or without cream. In Ecuador the *Quimbolitos* are cooked in *achira* leaves, the leaf of the taro plant, perhaps better known as *dasheen* or *yautía*. Nothing seems to be lost by cooking them in foil, however.

Torta de Castanhas-Do-Pará

BRAZIL NUT CAKE   *Brazil*

This rich yet light cake from Brazil makes a splendid dessert. I like it as a change from *Quindins de Yáyá* (Coconut Cupcake Dessert) to follow *Feijoada Completa* (Black Beans with Mixed Meats). Brazil nuts take the place of flour in the cake itself, an airy thing of egg whites. The egg yolks make a luscious filling, while the chocolate frosting adds the final luxurious touch.

[Serves 12 to 14]

FOR THE CAKE

12 egg whites	*8 ounces Brazil nuts, finely ground*
½ pound sugar	*Butter*

Beat the egg whites until they stand in firm, unwavering peaks. Gradually beat in the sugar. Fold in the nuts, gently but thoroughly. Have ready two 8-inch cake tins lined with buttered paper. Pour in the cake batter and bake in a preheated moderate (350° F., 180° C., gas 4) oven for 40 minutes. The cakes will puff up but will fall as they cool. When they are cool, spread generously with the filling and sandwich the cakes together. Cover with chocolate frosting.

FOR THE FILLING

½ pound sugar	*6 egg yolks*
¼ pint water	

Combine the sugar and water in a small saucepan and cook over moderate heat until the syrup reaches the soft ball stage, when a little of the syrup dropped on a saucer holds its shape but flattens out.

Beat the egg yolks until they are thick and lemon-coloured, then beat in the cooled syrup. Pour into the top of a double boiler and cook, stirring constantly with a wooden spoon, over low heat until the mixture is thick. Cool before using to fill the cake.

FOR THE FROSTING

2 ounces plain chocolate, broken
   into bits
4 ounces sugar

4 tablespoons coffee or water
½ egg white, beaten until stiff

In the top of a double boiler over moderate heat, combine the chocolate, sugar, and coffee or water, and cook, stirring, until the sugar is dissolved and the mixture smooth. Cool. Beat in the egg white. Spread over the cake. Refrigerate the cake until the frosting is firm.

   For a simpler frosting melt 2 ounces plain chocolate in 2 tablespoons coffee or water in the top of a double boiler over moderate heat. Off the heat, beat 2 ounces unsalted butter, cut into bits, into the chocolate mixture. Continue to beat the mixture until it is cool. Spread over the cake.

Sauces

Because the sauce is incorporated into so many Latin American dishes, there is not a large body of separate sauces. At the same time it could be said with justification that Mexican cuisine is one of sauces with infinite variations played on a theme. The same is true of Peruvian cooking. No one has ever codified these sauces and it might, if it could be done, complicate rather than simplify matters. Every country has some form of hot pepper sauce, always present on family tables, so that the amount of fire in one's food is discretionary, though Peruvian dishes tend to be pretty hot in their own right. French sauces, sometimes with names that startle a little, have migrated to Latin America, and so has the technique of the *sofrito*, that useful mixture of sautéed onion and garlic, which began in Spain and Portugal and was expanded during the colonial period from its simple original form to include peppers and tomatoes, gifts of the New World. The avocado-based sauces are well represented, as are sauces with tomato.

Pebre

CHILEAN HOT PEPPER SAUCE   *Chile*

The number of hot peppers used in this sauce is discretionary. Some people like it very hot, and it is then just called *Salsa Picante* (Hot Sauce). As many as 8 hot peppers might be used. Others prefer it mild. Hot red peppers may be used instead of green.

1 medium onion, finely chopped
1 clove garlic, minced
2 tablespoons finely chopped fresh
  coriander
1 tablespoon finely chopped parsley
1 or more fresh hot green peppers,
  seeded and finely chopped

3 tablespoons olive oil
1 tablespoon lemon juice
Salt to taste

Combine all the ingredients in a bowl and let stand for about 1 hour before serving for the flavour to develop. Serve with any meat and with *Porotos Granados* (Cranberry Beans with Corn and Pumpkin).

Salsa de Ají Colorado

RED PEPPER SAUCE   *Chile*

24 fresh hot red peppers, seeded
  and cut into strips
½ pint wine vinegar
1 clove garlic, chopped

1 teaspoon salt
¼ pint vegetable oil

Put the pepper strips into a bowl and add the vinegar. Leave overnight, stirring with a wooden spoon once or twice. Drain, reserving the vinegar. Put the peppers into a blender or food processor with the garlic, the salt, and enough of the vinegar to reduce them to a purée. Beat in the oil, adding about 4 tablespoons of the vinegar to give the sauce the consistency of mayonnaise. For a milder sauce discard the vinegar in which the peppers were soaked and use fresh vinegar. A lot of the heat of the peppers will have soaked out into the vinegar.

Serve with *Chancho a la Chilena* (Pork Loin, Chilean Style) or with any plainly cooked meat, poultry, or fish, or with cold meats.

Salsa de Ají

HOT PEPPER SAUCE   *Colombia*

½ pound fresh hot red or green
  peppers
1 teaspoon salt, or to taste

1 medium onion, finely chopped

Remove the seeds from the peppers and chop them coarsely. In a blender or food processor grind them to a pulp with the salt. Add the chopped onion and mix well.

Salsa de Ají Picante

HOT PEPPER SAUCE   *Ecuador*

There are many versions of hot pepper sauce. This one is from the coast.

Fresh hot red or green peppers	*Lemon juice*
Red onion	*Salt*

Seed the peppers and cut them into small strips. Combine the peppers with an equal amount of finely chopped red onion in a wide-mouthed glass jar. Cover the vegetables with lemon juice, add salt to taste, and let the sauce stand for 3 or 4 hours before using. The lemon juice may be diluted by adding a little hot water.

Salsa de Chile Ancho y Almendra

MILD RED CHILI AND ALMOND SAUCE   *Mexico*

The Mexican kitchen is extraordinarily rich in sauces, *mollis* in Nahuatl, the language of the Aztec empire, modified to *moles* in Spanish. This mild and gentle sauce was probably made originally with peanuts, which were indigenous, having found their way north from Brazil, instead of almonds. Certainly almonds make a subtler sauce than do peanuts, though both are good.

The sauce is used with salt cod, another import, in *Bacalao en Salsa de Chile Ancho y Almendra* (Salt Cod in Mild Red Chili and Almond Sauce) page 111. It is excellent with poultry, pork, or veal (chicken stock is fine for all three). The meat is poached in stock or water until it is almost tender. The sauce is then thinned with a little of the stock and the meat is simmered in the sauce until it is tender and the flavours are blended, about 5 minutes.

6 ancho chilies	*¼ teaspoon oregano*
1 medium onion, chopped	*¼ teaspoon sugar*
¼ pound toasted almonds, ground	*Salt*
⅛ teaspoon ground cinnamon	*4 tablespoons vegetable oil*
⅛ teaspoon ground cloves	*1 pint chicken, beef, or fish stock*

Pull the stems off the chilies, shake out and discard the seeds, rinse in cold water, tear into pieces, and put into a bowl with 1 cup hot water. Let soak for about 1 hour, longer if the chilies are very dry, turning them from time to time. Put the chilies, any soaking water, and the onion into a blender or food processor and reduce to a purée. Add the almonds to the chili mixture with the cinnamon, cloves, oregano, sugar, and salt to taste. The mixture will be quite heavy, almost a paste. Heat the oil in a heavy pan and sauté the chili mixture, stirring constantly with a wooden spoon, for 5 minutes over moderate heat. Add the appropriate stock, stir to mix, and simmer for a few minutes longer.

The sauce, which should be of medium consistency, is now ready to use with salt cod, poultry, pork, or veal. It may also be used with fresh fish, preferably fillets, in which case the uncooked fish may be simmered in the sauce until done, or put into a greased, shallow flameproof casserole with the sauce poured over it and baked in a preheated moderate oven (350° F., 180° C., gas 4) until tender, about 20 minutes.

Ixni-Pec

HOT PEPPER SAUCE   *Mexico*

Pronounced roughly schnee-peck, this is the fresh, hot pepper sauce that always appears on Yucatecan dining tables in a small bowl or sauceboat. It should be taken with discretion for, though it has a lovely flavour, it is very hot. The pepper used is the yellow *habanero*. I have found that pickled hot peppers from the Caribbean, usually from Trinidad or Jamaica, have an almost identical flavour and make a splendid substitute.

4 tablespoons each finely chopped onion, tomato, and hot chili pepper, rinsed if pickled
Seville orange juice, or use two-

thirds orange juice to one-third lime juice
Salt

In a bowl combine the onion, tomato, and hot pepper and add enough orange juice to make it soupy, about 4 tablespoons. Season to taste with salt. Serve with Yucatecan dishes or whenever a hot pepper sauce is called for. The sauce should be eaten the same day or the next.

Variation: Though *Ixni-Pec* is very hot indeed, I have encountered an even hotter sauce called simply *Salsa Picante* (Hot Sauce). It consisted of green *habaneros* peeled by toasting over a flame, seeded and chopped and diluted with a little Seville orange juice.

Môlho de Pimenta e Limão

HOT PEPPER AND LIME SAUCE   *Brazil*

The peppers used in Brazil are the small, very, very hot *malagueta* peppers not usually available here. Any very hot pepper can be substituted but I have found pickled Caribbean peppers, usually from Jamaica or Trinidad, a good substitute.

3 or 4 hot red or green peppers,   *1 clove garlic, chopped*
  seeded   *Salt*
1 onion, chopped   *¼ pint lime or lemon juice*

Crush the peppers, onion, and garlic with salt to taste in a mortar with a pestle, adding the lime or lemon juice little by little, or purée in a blender or food processor. Serve in a bowl to accompany meat, poultry, or fish dishes and with *Feijoada Completa* (Black Beans with Mixed Meats) page 213.

Môlho de Pimenta e Azeite de Dendê

HOT PEPPERS IN DENDÊ (PALM) OIL   *Brazil*

This is a common sauce on Bahian tables. The pepper used is the tiny, ferociously hot *malagueta* pepper.

6 or more small fresh hot red or   Dendê *(palm) oil, to cover*
  green peppers

Put the peppers in a small bowl and pour in enough oil to cover them. Let them stand for several hours before using. The oil will be quite hot and flavoured by the peppers, while the heat of the peppers themselves will be slightly reduced.

Variation: For *Môlho de Pimenta e Azeite de Oliva* (Hot Peppers in Olive Oil), use olive oil instead of palm oil. This is a more usual hot sauce in other parts of Brazil, where palm oil is not used.

Ajíes en Leche

HOT PEPPERS IN MILK   *Venezuela*

The hot peppers used in Venezuela are medium-sized round or lantern-shaped ones, extremely hot and very well flavoured. Any hot peppers may, of course, be used.

½ pint milk
½ teaspoon salt
6 fresh hot red or green peppers,
   stemmed and halved lengthwise

1 slice onion
1 clove garlic
3 or 4 fresh mint leaves (optional)

Pour the milk into a saucepan, add the salt, bring to the boil and immediately remove from the heat. Allow to cool. Put the hot peppers, onion, garlic, and mint leaves in a glass jar and pour the milk over them. Let stand overnight. To serve, pour into a bowl and eat the peppers as a sauce with any meat, poultry, or fish dish.

Guacamole

AVOCADO SAUCE   *Mexico*

In Mexico *Guacamole* is eaten with everything—meat, poultry, fish, shellfish, beans, cheese, and by itself with *tostaditas,* triangles of fried tortilla. *Antojitos* are unthinkable without it. Very old recipes give *Guacamole* simply as avocado with chili and I have had it simply mashed with a little salt. However, recipes from the seventeenth century on give it as a mixture of tomatoes, fresh green coriander, onion, and chopped *serrano* chilies, the small hot green mountain peppers very much used in the Mexican kitchen. I find the canned *serranos* are a better choice than fresh hot peppers of another variety, since it is their flavour as well as their heat that is needed. Fresh *serranos* are sometimes available in West Indian shops.

There is a lot of superstition about preventing *Guacamole* from darkening when exposed to air. One is that putting the avocado pit in the centre of the finished sauce will do this. Long and careful research has convinced me of the falseness of this claim but I must confess I like the look of the brown pit sitting in the bowl of creamy green sauce. Next to making the sauce at the last minute the best solution is to cover the bowl tightly with plastic wrap and refrigerate it.

There are two basic versions of *Guacamole*, one with tomatoes, the other *Guacamole del Norte* (Avocado Sauce, Northern Style) made with Mexican green husk tomatoes, which does not discolour quite so quickly, perhaps because the green tomato is more acid than ordinary tomatoes. Certainly sprinkling lime or lemon juice on a cut avocado does help prevent darkening. Also a very ripe avocado will darken more quickly than one that is just at its moment of ripe perfection but not a minute over it.

I find that the best way to mash an avocado is to cut it in half, unpeeled, remove the pit, and holding the pear in the left hand mash the flesh with a fork, scoop it out with a spoon and mash any solid bits that have escaped. This gives the finished purée a good texture.

2 *large ripe avocados, stoned and*
  mashed
2 *medium tomatoes, peeled, seeded,*
  and chopped
1 *tablespoon onion, finely chopped*
3 *canned* serrano *chilies, or 1*

teaspoon seeded and finely
chopped fresh green pepper
1 *tablespoon fresh green coriander,*
  chopped
Salt to taste

Mix all the ingredients thoroughly and place in a serving dish with the pit of one of the avocados in the centre, if liked. Serve as a dip with triangles of fried tortilla, or as a sauce.

Variation: For *Guacamole del Norte* (Avocado Sauce, Northern Style), substitute half of a 10-ounce can of Mexican green tomatoes (about 6), drained and mashed, for the tomatoes. If fresh green husk tomatoes are available, peel off the papery husk and drop them into boiling water. Cook for 2 minutes, drain, and allow to cool. Chop finely. Then proceed as for *Guacamole*.

Guasacaca

AVOCADO SAUCE   *Venezuela*

There was a great deal of trade between Mexico and South America in pre-Conquest times and it is entirely possible that this is a migrant version of an original *guacamole* somewhat modified in later colonial days.

4 *tablespoons olive oil*
1 *tablespoon red wine vinegar*
Salt to taste
½ *teaspoon finely chopped, seeded,*
  fresh hot red pepper, or ½
  teaspoon ground hot red pepper
1 *large avocado, peeled and diced*

1 *medium tomato, peeled and*
  chopped
1 *medium ripe red sweet pepper, or*
  use a green pepper, finely
  chopped
1 *small onion, finely chopped*

In a bowl combine the oil, vinegar, salt, and hot pepper, and beat with a fork to mix thoroughly. Add the rest of the ingredients, tossing to mix. Serve with grilled meat.

Variation: Add 1 tablespoon of finely chopped fresh green coriander or parsley.

Variation: Add 1 hardboiled egg, finely chopped.

Ají de Huevo

AVOCADO SAUCE   *Colombia*

This is another migrant recipe that evolved when the Chibcha of Colombia used to export their exquisite gold work to Mexico. I suspect the reverse trade included more than recipes. It is interesting to see how this one differs from the original Mexican recipe and from the next-door Venezuelan one. The name of the sauce really defies translation. *Ají* is the South American word for hot pepper. *Huevo* is egg. Literally one gets "hot pepper of egg." Avocado sauce is a better way of describing it.

1 large avocado, stoned and mashed
1 hardboiled egg yolk, mashed
1 tablespoon finely chopped fresh
    green coriander
1 fresh hot green pepper, seeded
    and chopped

1 finely chopped spring onion,
    using white and green parts
1 hardboiled egg white, finely
    chopped
1 tablespoon white wine vinegar
Salt, freshly ground pepper

Mix the avocado and egg yolk thoroughly. Add all the rest of the ingredients and mix well. Serve as a sauce with *Sobrebarriga Bogotana* (Skirt Steak, Bogotá Style) page 133 or *Ajiaco de Pollo Bogotano* (Bogotá Chicken Stew).

Salsa de Jitomate

TOMATO SAUCE   *Mexico*

1 medium onion, chopped
1 clove garlic, chopped
3 large tomatoes, peeled and
    chopped
2 canned serrano chilies, chopped
    or 2 fresh green chilies

⅛ teaspoon sugar
Salt to taste
2 tablespoons vegetable oil
1 tablespoon chopped fresh green
    coriander

Combine the onion, garlic, tomatoes, and chilies in a blender or food processor and purée briefly. The purée should retain some texture and not be too smooth. Season with the sugar and salt. Heat the oil, pour in the tomato mixture, and cook, stirring, over moderate heat until it is thick and well blended, about 5 minutes. Stir in the coriander.

Môlho ao Tomate

TOMATO SAUCE   *Brazil*

3 tablespoons olive oil
6 large, ripe tomatoes, coarsely
   chopped
1 clove garlic, minced

3 or 4 fresh basil leaves, chopped,
   or 1 teaspoon dried basil
Salt, freshly ground pepper

Heat the oil in a saucepan and add the tomatoes, garlic, and basil.
Simmer over low heat for 3 or 4 minutes, stirring occasionally. Season
to taste with salt and pepper and stir in 4 tablespoons warm water.
Simmer over low heat, stirring from time to time, until the mixture
is quite thick. Work the mixture through a sieve.

Salsa Cruda

UNCOOKED TOMATO SAUCE   *Mexico*

This sauce appears on Mexican tables as often as salt and pepper. It
is served with cooked meats, poultry, fish, eggs, and beans and is
added to tacos (stuffed tortillas) and other *antojitos* (appetizers). The
beautifully ripe, red tomatoes of Mexico have very thin skins and
though these can simply be peeled off by hand, they are usually left
on for *Salsa Cruda*. I peel the tomatoes for this sauce only if they have
thick skins.

2 large ripe tomatoes, finely
   chopped
1 small onion, finely chopped
2 or more fresh hot green peppers,
   seeded and chopped, or use
   canned serrano chilies, seeded
   and chopped

1 tablespoon chopped fresh green
   coriander
Pinch of sugar
Salt to taste

Mix all the ingredients together. Serve in a bowl or gravy boat. It is
best made at the last minute and served at room temperature.

Salsa de Tomatillo

MEXICAN GREEN TOMATO SAUCE   *Mexico*

This is, I think, the most distinctive of all the Mexican sauces and the
most delicious. It is made with the green husk tomato available

canned from stores specializing in Mexican foods. Green husk tomatoes must not be confused with green (unripe) ordinary tomatoes. They are in the same family but a different species altogether (see page 37).

A 10-ounce can Mexican green tomatoes, drained
1 tablespoon finely chopped white onion
½ clove garlic, chopped

2 or more canned serrano chilies, chopped or fresh green chilies
1 tablespoon fresh green coriander, chopped
Salt to taste

Thoroughly mix all the ingredients, mashing the green tomatoes, or whirl very briefly in a blender or food processor. Serve in a bowl or gravy boat.

Variation: Some cooks omit the onion and garlic and increase the amount of coriander to taste. Whirl very briefly in a blender or food processor.

Salsa de Perejil

PARSLEY SAUCE   *Chile*

½ pint olive or vegetable oil
4 tablespoons red or white wine vinegar or lemon juice

1 teaspoon prepared mustard
½ cup finely chopped parsley
Salt, freshly ground pepper

Mix all the ingredients together. Serve with fish or shellfish or as a dressing with tomatoes.

For *erizos* (sea urchins), make the dressing with lemon juice, omit the mustard, and add one small finely chopped onion.

Ají de Queso

CHEESE SAUCE   *Ecuador*

1 large tomato, peeled, seeded, and coarsely chopped
1 fresh hot red or green pepper
½ pound Spanish fresh cheese (or cottage cheese)

Salt, freshly ground pepper
1 medium onion, finely chopped
1 hardboiled egg, chopped

In a blender or food processor combine the tomato, pepper, and cheese and reduce to a purée. Be careful not to overblend. Season to taste with salt and pepper and put into a bowl. Sprinkle with the onion and egg. Serve as a sauce with potatoes and cooked green vegetables.

Salsa de Maní

PEANUT SAUCE   *Ecuador*

Serve this with *Llapingachos* (Potato Cakes) page 205.

2 tablespoons annatto oil or lard
  (see page 310)
1 onion, finely chopped
1 clove garlic, chopped
1 medium tomato, peeled, seeded,
  and chopped

2 ounces finely ground peanuts, or
  2 tablespoons peanut butter
Salt, freshly ground pepper

Heat the annatto oil or lard and stir in the onion, garlic, and tomato. Cook over moderate heat until the onion is tender and the mixture well blended. Stir in the peanuts, season to taste with salt and pepper, and cook for a few minutes longer. The sauce should be thin enough to pour. If necessary, add a little tomato juice or water and cook just long enough to blend.

Salsa de Choclos

SWEETCORN SAUCE   *Chile*

This is a colonial sauce developed at a time when corn was a make-do vegetable, not yet esteemed in its own right, as it was later on. The sauce is light and delicious, the flavour of the fresh sweetcorn coming through beautifully. It can be used as a sauce with meats or poultry, but I prefer it over green vegetables and especially with cauliflower.

¾ pound sweetcorn kernels; if
  using frozen corn, thaw
  thoroughly
½ pint milk

1 teaspoon sweet paprika
Salt, freshly ground white pepper
1 or 2 eggs, lightly beaten
  (optional)

In a blender or food processor combine the corn, milk, sweet paprika, salt, and pepper and reduce to a smooth purée. Pour into a saucepan and cook, stirring constantly, over low heat for 5 minutes, or until the mixture is well blended. If necessary, thicken the sauce by stirring in 1 or 2 eggs, lightly beaten, and cooking over low heat, stirring, until the sauce is thickened. I find corn varies considerably, so I use my judgment about thickening the sauce, using no eggs, or 1 or 2 as required.

Salsa Chilena

CHILEAN SAUCE   *Chile*

Serve this with plainly cooked meat or any cold dish.

¾ pint beef stock
1 medium onion, finely chopped
2 medium tomatoes, peeled and
  chopped

2 tablespoons lemon juice
Salt, freshly ground pepper
4 tablespoons olive or vegetable oil

Put the stock and onion into a saucepan and simmer, uncovered, over moderate heat until the onion is tender. Pour into a blender or food processor and reduce to a purée. Set aside.

Put the tomatoes into the blender or food processor and reduce them to a purée. Pour the purée into a small saucepan and cook, stirring, until it is thick. Stir the tomato into the stock and onion mixture. Add the lemon juice and salt and pepper to taste. Allow to cool, then gradually beat in the oil. The sauce should be thick. If necessary, beat in more oil.

Salsa Criolla

CREOLE SAUCE   *Argentina*

Serve this with roasted or grilled meats.

2 medium onions, finely chopped
3 medium tomatoes, finely chopped
1 fresh hot green pepper, seeded
  and finely chopped
1 clove garlic, chopped

2 tablespoons finely chopped parsley
Salt, freshly ground pepper
¼ pint olive oil
3 tablespoons red wine vinegar

In a bowl combine the onions, tomatoes, pepper, garlic, and parsley, mixing lightly. Season with salt and pepper. In a small bowl beat together the oil and vinegar with a fork, then pour the mixture over the vegetables. Stir to mix.

Color Chilena

PAPRIKA OIL   *Chile*

This oil is used a great deal in Chilean cooking, and since it keeps indefinitely can be made in quantity. However, if you want to make less, paprika can simply be added to oil in the ratio of 1 teaspoon paprika to every 2 tablespoons oil, with garlic used proportionately.

¾ pint vegetable oil or 1 pound lard	*3 cloves garlic*
	5 tablespoons sweet paprika

Heat the oil or lard in a saucepan and add the garlic cloves. Sauté the garlic until it is brown, then lift out and discard. Off the heat, stir in the paprika until it is well mixed with the oil. Cool and pour into a covered container.

Aceite o Manteca de Achiote

ANNATTO OIL OR LARD *Colombia*

This is used a good deal as both a colouring and a flavouring in the Caribbean, Colombia, Ecuador, and Venezuela (see page 25).

4 tablespoons annatto seeds	*4 tablespoons vegetable oil or lard*

Combine the annatto seeds and oil in a small, heavy saucepan and place over moderate heat until the seeds begin to give up their colour, a deep orangey-red. If the seeds are fresh, the colour will be abundant and deep and will be given off very quickly, within about 1 minute. Watch for the moment when the colour starts to change to golden and remove immediately from the heat. Strain and pour into a covered container. The oil or lard will keep indefinitely.

Aliño Criollo

SEASONING POWDER, CREOLE STYLE *Venezuela*

This mixture of ground herbs and spices, which varies slightly from cook to cook, is used as a seasoning in many Venezuelan dishes, and I have found it a pleasant addition to stews and casseroles even outside the Venezuelan or Latin American kitchen. It can be bought ready-made from spice shelves in Venezuelan supermarkets as *Aliño Preparado* (Prepared Seasoning). I make it without garlic so that it keeps, but I add a large clove of crushed garlic to 2 tablespoons of the powder when I use it in cooking.

1 tablespoon garlic salt	*¼ teaspoon ground black pepper*
1½ teaspoons ground cumin	*1 tablespoon oregano*
1 tablespoon ground annatto seeds	*3 tablespoons sweet paprika*

Thoroughly mix all the ingredients and put into a small glass jar. Store in a cool, dark place. Keeps indefinitely.

Mayonnaise

This is my preferred recipe for mayonnaise. Any standard recipe may be used, and blender mayonnaise is perfectly acceptable. However, I find this is richer with a better texture, and since it takes only minutes to make I will give it in detail.

2 large egg yolks
½ teaspoon Dijon mustard
Salt, freshly ground pepper
½ pint corn, peanut, or olive oil, about

4 teaspoons vinegar or lemon juice, or 2 teaspoons each vinegar and lemon juice

Put the egg yolks into a rimmed soup plate. I find this makes beating easier than using a bowl, though a bowl, of course, will do. Beat the egg yolks lightly with a fork, and beat in the mustard, and salt and pepper to taste. Drop by drop beat in the oil until the yolks thicken. When about half the oil is beaten in and the mixture is very thick, beat in the vinegar or lemon juice, or a mixture of the two. Beat in the remaining oil, pouring it in a thin, steady stream. Taste the mayonnaise and add more vinegar or lemon, or salt and pepper, if liked. If the mayonnaise is too thick for personal taste, thin with a teaspoon or so of hot water.

If the mayonnaise fails to thicken, or separates, place an egg yolk in a bowl and beat in the failed mayonnaise, tablespoon by tablespoon, to restore the sauce.

The type of vinegar used is a matter of choice, but it should never be a coarse vinegar. Wine vinegar is the most commonly used, but I do find that a Japanese rice vinegar gives a delicious result, as of course do the herb-flavoured tarragon or basil vinegars.

Salsa Golf

TOMATO- AND COGNAC-FLAVOURED MAYONNAISE   *Chile*

This is a delicious mayonnaise. I have come across it served in Colombia as a dressing for avocado and described as an international recipe; it may also be used with any cold fish or shellfish. It is generally credited to Chile, where perversely it is sometimes called *Salsa Americana*. I can find no explanation whatever for its being called *Salsa Golf*

2 egg yolks
1 teaspoon Dijon mustard
Pinch of cayenne pepper, or dash of
    Tabasco
Salt to taste
2 teaspoons lemon juice

1 tablespoon white wine vinegar
½ pint vegetable oil
4 tablespoons olive oil
2 tablespoons tomato ketchup or
    thick tomato purée
1 tablespoon cognac

Put the egg yolks, mustard, cayenne or Tabasco, salt, lemon juice, and vinegar in a bowl, and beat until thick and well blended. Beat in the vegetable and olive oil, drop by drop, until the mayonnaise begins to thicken, then beat in the remaining oil in a thin, steady stream. Add the tomato ketchup or purée and the cognac. The finished mayonnaise will be a delicate pink.

For *Palta Rellena* (Stuffed Avocado), peel and halve an avocado and remove the pit. Fill the centre of each half with *Salsa Golf*. Serves 2 as an appetizer, 1 as a luncheon.

BASIC PROCEDURES

BEURRE MANIÉ TO THICKEN A SAUCE

Thoroughly mix ½ ounce butter, softened at room temperature, with 1 tablespoon flour. The most convenient way to do this is to put the flour and butter in a cup and mix with a fork. Stir bit by bit into the liquid to be thickened, over moderate heat. This is enough to lightly thicken the average stew. Quantities can be adjusted as required.

TO CLARIFY BUTTER

Cut the butter into chunks and put into a heavy saucepan over moderate heat. Skim the foam off the surface as it rises. When the butter has melted and looks quite clear let it stand for a few minutes for all the solids to sink to the bottom. Strain the butter through a sieve lined with damp muslin. The residue need not be thrown away but can be poured over green vegetables or stirred into a stew.

TO PEEL AND SEED TOMATOES

Ripe tomatoes picked off the vine in one's own garden can often be peeled simply by pulling off the skin with the fingers. I've often peeled market-bought tomatoes in Latin America this way and hot-house tomatoes are sometimes peelable in this manner. Otherwise, choose ripe, red tomatoes and drop them into boiling water, one at a time, for 10 seconds. Lift out, rinse quickly under cold water, and peel with a paring knife from the stem end. To remove the seeds, cut the tomato in half crosswise and squeeze out the seeds gently.

Béchamel

WHITE SAUCE

1 ounce butter   *Salt, white pepper*
2 tablespoons flour   *Pinch of nutmeg*
¾ pint milk

In a small, heavy saucepan melt the butter. Stir in the flour with a wooden spoon and cook, stirring, over low heat for 2 minutes. Gradually pour in the milk, stirring constantly to mix, and bring to the boil. Simmer, stirring frequently, for 5 minutes. Season to taste with salt, white pepper, and nutmeg.

For a thick béchamel, use just under ½ pint of milk. For a medium sauce, use ⅝ pint, and for the more usual, creamy sauce, use ¾ pint.

If the sauce should be lumpy, which is unlikely if it is properly made, simply whirl it in a blender or food processor.

Vinaigrette

OIL AND VINEGAR, OR FRENCH DRESSING

2 tablespoons wine vinegar or other   1 teaspoon Dijon mustard
  mild vinegar   *8 tablespoons peanut, corn, or olive*
Salt, freshly ground pepper   *oil*

Put the vinegar in a bowl with the salt and pepper to taste and the mustard and beat with a fork to mix well. Then beat in the oil, little by little, until the sauce is well blended. Taste for seasoning, adding more vinegar, or salt and pepper.

Lemon juice may be used instead of vinegar. For a mustard-flavoured vinaigrette, increase the amount of Dijon mustard to 2 tablespoons.

313

Drinks

BEBIDAS

Latin America does very well with drinks from tea, coffee, wine, and beer, which were introduced there, to native chocolate, *mate*, tequila, *pisco*, rum, and the beerlike drinks, *pulque*, *chicha*, and *tepache*. There is lots of Scotch whisky, gin, and vodka as well as the soft drinks of both the antique and colonial past, and modern soft drinks.

Thanks to Germans, who missed the beer of their homeland, all of Latin America has very good beer indeed. And thanks to French, Spanish, Portuguese, Italians, Germans, and Swiss, who missed their native wines, Chile and Argentina, and to a lesser extent Brazil, Uruguay, Paraguay, and Mexico, have either good or acceptable wines.

Brazil's coffee is notable and one drinks it as *cafezinho*, very strong demitasse with a lot of sugar, often as not with *bôlos* (cakes), while in Colombia, whose coffee is also notable, what one takes in a demitasse is called a *tinto*. Other fine coffees are produced in smaller quantities in Guatemala, El Salvador, Costa Rica, and Mexico. For breakfast Brazil takes its coffee as *café com leite*, the same strong coffee of the demitasse diluted with hot milk, the *café con leche* of the rest of the continent. Mexico adds brown sugar, cinnamon stick, and cloves to make its *Café de Olla* (Pot Coffee).

Tea is not as popular as coffee, though it is esteemed for afternoon tea. Also popular are the herbal teas, the *tisanas* like mint and chamomile, and, of course, *mate*. Chocolate is a popular drink especially in Mexico, where it is packaged already sweetened, flavoured with cinnamon and cloves, and mixed with ground almonds.

314

Many of the local soft drinks or beerlike drinks are either not available here, or are impractical to make at home, but I have sometimes come across a concentrated bottled form of *guaraná* in shops selling Brazilian foods. This is made from a Brazilian shrub and is delicious as a soft drink as well as being a good mix for gin, vodka, or rum.

Many of the mixed drinks of Latin America are as international as Scotch and soda, or gin and tonic. I have chosen local drinks I have enjoyed in their home countries and which I have been able to make here.

Pisco Sour

PERUVIAN BRANDY SOUR   *Peru*

Pisco, Peruvian brandy, is used in this sour, which is also popular in Chile, where they use the very similar Chilean *pisco*. *Pisco* is also popular in Bolivia. The small tropical lemon-limes used in the drink have a very subtle flavour. Our limes and lemons are rather more strongly flavoured, and a little more sugar may be needed.

[Serves 1]

1 teaspoon egg white	2 ounces pisco (Peruvian brandy)
1 teaspoon castor sugar	2 or 3 ice cubes
2 teaspoons lime or lemon juice	Angostura bitters

Combine all the ingredients except the Angostura bitters in a cocktail shaker and shake vigorously. Strain into a glass and shake a few drops of Angostura bitters on top.

Biblia con Pisco

PERUVIAN BRANDY EGGNOG   *Bolivia*

[Serves 1]

1 whole egg	⅛ teaspoon ground cinnamon or
1 tablespoon castor sugar	nutmeg
1½ ounces pisco (Peruvian brandy)	

Beat the egg with the sugar, either by hand or with an electric beater, until the sugar is dissolved. Beat in the *pisco*. Pour into a goblet, chill thoroughly, sprinkle with cinnamon or nutmeg, and serve. If preferred, 1 or 2 ice cubes may be added instead of chilling the drink.

Yungueño

PERUVIAN BRANDY WITH ORANGE JUICE   *Bolivia*

[Serves 1]

1½ ounces pisco (Peruvian brandy)   ¼ teaspoon castor sugar
1½ ounces orange juice   5 ounces cracked ice

Combine all the ingredients in a cocktail shaker and shake vigorously. Pour, unstrained, into a wine glass or a tumbler.

Gin Fizz   *Uruguay*

It was said to me once that the greatest glory of Uruguay was the gin fizz (pronounced jeen feez) made in the capital city of Montevideo. This may well be true, and I think the secret lies in the delicate flavour of the tropical lemon-limes of the region. I find using a little more sugar with our lemons balances the flavour and gives almost the same result.

[Serves 1]

2 teaspoons castor sugar   2 ounces gin
2 tablespoons lemon juice   5 ounces crushed ice

Combine the sugar and lemon juice in a cocktail shaker and stir until the sugar is dissolved. Add the gin and crushed ice and shake very thoroughly. Strain into a narrow straight-sided glass, or into a small tumbler.

Coco Fizz   *Mexico*

[Serves 4]

¾ pint coconut water   10 ounces crushed ice
3 tablespoons castor sugar   5 tablespoons lime juice
½ pint gin   soda water

In a cocktail shaker combine the coconut water and the sugar and stir until the sugar is dissolved. Add all the remaining ingredients, except the soda water, and shake vigorously. Pour into four glasses and add a splash of soda to each.

Coconut water is the liquid in the green coconut; there is some coconut water in mature coconuts, about ½ pint usually, enough for 2 drinks.

Cola de Lagarto

LIZARD'S TAIL   *Mexico*

[Serves 1]
¼ *pint dry white wine*   *1 teaspoon castor sugar*
5 tablespoons vodka or gin   *1 teaspoon crème de menthe*
1 tablespoon lime juice   *3 or 4 ice cubes*

Combine all the ingredients in a cocktail shaker and shake vigorously.
Strain into a chilled tumbler.

Caipirinha

RUM SOUR   *Brazil*

The name of this drink means literally "country bumpkin," perhaps
because the lime is coarsely chopped and the drink served unstrained,
unlike the *Batida de Limão* (Lime Batida), where only juice is used and
the drink is strained, refined. Or perhaps because it is a splendid
drink for that country feast, *Churrasco à Gaucha*, the Brazilian barbecue.

[Serves 1]   *2 ounces* Cachaça *(Brazilian rum)*
½ *lime*   *or white rum*
1 teaspoon castor sugar   *5 ounces crushed ice*

Coarsely chop the lime and transfer it to the mixing glass of a cocktail
shaker with the sugar, adding more if liked. Press thoroughly to
extract all the juice and oil from the lime peel. Add the rum and ice.
Shake vigorously and pour, unstrained, into a cocktail glass.

Batida de Limão

LIME BATIDA   *Brazil*

[Serves 1]   *2 ounces* Cachaça *(Brazilian rum)*
2 tablespoons lime or lemon juice   *or white rum*
1 teaspoon sugar   *5 ounces crushed ice*

Combine all the ingredients in a cocktail shaker and shake vigorously.
Strain into a cocktail glass.

Variation: For *Batida de Coco* (Coconut Milk Batida), substitute 2 tablespoons thick coconut milk (see page 29) for the lime juice.

Variation: For *Batida de Maracujá* (*Granadilla* or Passion Fruit Batida), substitute 2 tablespoons of *granadilla* or passion fruit juice for the lime juice and increase the sugar to 1½ teaspoons.

Variation: For *Batida de Abacaxi* (Pineapple Batida), substitute 2 ounces pineapple juice for the lime juice.

Vampiros

TEQUILA BLOODY MARYS   *Mexico*

[Serves 4]
½ pint tomato juice
¼ pint orange juice
2 tablespoons lime juice

2 tablespoons chopped onion
½ teaspoon Worcestershire sauce
Salt, cayenne pepper to taste
6 ounces white tequila

Combine all the ingredients, except the tequila, in a blender and blend until smooth. Pour into a jug and chill for at least 4 hours. To serve pour 1½ ounces white tequila into each of four glasses and pour in ¼ pint of the tomato mixture. Stir to mix. If liked, the drink may be served over ice cubes.

Margarita   *Mexico*

[Serves 1]
½ shell of lime or lemon
Salt
1½ ounces white tequila
½ ounce Triple Sec or Curaçao

1 ounce lime or lemon juice
2 or 3 ice cubes

Rub the rim of a cocktail glass with the rind of the lime or lemon. Pour salt into a saucer and spin the rim of the glass in it. Combine the remaining ingredients in a bar glass and stir until thoroughly chilled. Strain into the prepared cocktail glass.

Tequila Sunrise   *Mexico*

This and its variation, Tequila Cocktail, are very popular tequila drinks.

[Serves 1]
½ lime
2 ounces white tequila
½ teaspoon crème de cassis

1 teaspoon grenadine syrup
soda water
Ice cubes

Squeeze the lime, pour the juice into an 8-ounce glass together with the shell of the lime. Add the tequila, *crème de cassis*, and grenadine syrup. Add enough soda to fill the glass three-quarters full, stir to mix, then drop in 2 or 3 ice cubes.

Variation: For Tequila Cocktail, combine 1½ ounces tequila with the juice of 1 lime, and ½ ounce grenadine syrup or to taste. Stir to mix and pour over crushed ice in a cocktail glass. Serve with two short straws. Serves 1.

Aperitivo Chapala   *Mexico*

There is a lot of controversy over this drink, a chaser for tequila, created by the widow Sanchez at her restaurant at Lake Chapala. Her original was made without tomato juice and had Seville orange juice and grenadine syrup. I find ordinary orange juice just as good. The hot pepper gives it a nice lift. I was served it as *Aperitivo Chapala* when I stayed at the lake so I have kept that name here.

[Makes about 6 servings]
½ pint orange juice
3 tablespoons grenadine syrup

½ teaspoon salt
½ teaspoon cayenne pepper or any ground hot red pepper

Mix all the ingredients thoroughly and chill. Serve in small, straight-sided tequila glasses with another glass of tequila served separately. Drink alternately sip by sip. Traditionally the drink is accompanied by small, dried, fried fish.

Sangrita   *Mexico*

Sangrita made with tomato juice is also a splendid accompaniment to tequila. I like the modern way of serving it, combining the Sangrita and the tequila over ice cubes.

[Makes 18 to 24 servings]
1½ pints tomato juice
½ pint orange juice
¼ pint lime juice
½ small white onion, chopped
1 teaspoon sugar
1 teaspoon salt, or to taste

2 teaspoons seeded and chopped fresh hot green or red pepper, or 1 teaspoon cayenne pepper
White tequila
Halved limes
Salt

Combine the tomato juice, orange juice, lime juice, onion, sugar, salt and hot pepper or cayenne in a blender or food processor and blend until smooth. Strain into a jug and chill thoroughly. Serve in small, straight-sided tequila glasses with another glass of tequila served separately. Squeeze a little lime juice into either the Sangrita or the tequila and drink sip by sip, or put a little salt on the lime and take a little suck of it as liked.

Sangría
Mexico

This is the Spanish wine drink that Mexico has both adopted and adapted to its own use. It is light and pleasant, especially in hot weather.

[Makes about 10 servings]
½ pint orange juice
¼ pint lime or lemon juice
2 ounces castor sugar, or to taste

1 bottle dry red wine, preferably
   Spanish
Ice cubes

In a jug combine the orange juice, lime or lemon juice, and the sugar and stir until the sugar is dissolved. Taste and add a little more sugar if liked. Pour in the wine, stir to mix, and chill thoroughly in the refrigerator. To serve, put 2 or 3 ice cubes in a goblet or tumbler and fill with Sangría.

Agua de Jamaica
SORREL OR ROSELLA DRINK
Mexico

This is a popular soft drink and is made from the sepals of a tropical flower known in Mexico as *flor de Jamaica* and in Jamaica as sorrel, elsewhere as rosella. It can be bought dried in West Indian shops usually as rosella or sorrel. It is also sold as hibiscus tea in health food shops.

[Makes about 10 servings]
2 ounces rosella sepals
3¼ pints water
Sugar to taste

Rinse the rosella sepals and put them into a large saucepan with the water. Bring to a boil over moderate heat, remove from the heat, and allow to cool. Strain into a jug. Sweeten to taste and chill thoroughly. Serve in tumblers with ice cubes.

Mate   *Paraguay*

Mate, from the Quechua word, is a mildly stimulating, nonalcoholic drink made from the powdered dried leaves of the South American evergreen *Ilex paraguayensis*. It can be bought in many health food shops and made according to package directions. It is not necessary to have the special silver-trimmed gourd and the *bombilla*, a special silver straw, to sip it through. A teapot and a cup do just as well, and it may be drunk either hot or cold. The *mate*, the name for the gourd in which the tea is made, is called a *chimarrao* in southern Brazil, where the drink is as popular as it is in Paraguay, Uruguay, and Argentina. In South America, especially in Argentina, the rules for making *mate* can be quite complicated, and many lovers of the tea insist that the water must be just under the boil.

To make the tea, heat a teapot by rinsing it out in boiling water, add 1 tablespoon *mate* per cup, pour in boiling water, let the tea steep for 5 minutes, strain, and serve either plain, or with sugar and/or milk, if liked. To drink cold, make the *mate* double strength and pour it over ice cubes. Serve plain or with sugar and lemon.

Café de Olla

POT COFFEE   *Mexico*

In Mexico, which is coffee country, this is served in small pottery mugs each holding ¼ pint as an after-dinner coffee. In Mexico *piloncillo*, the local brown sugar, would be used. Our dark brown sugar is about the same. Coffee for breakfast, *Café con Leche* (Coffee with Milk), is very strong, served in large cups, and diluted half and half with hot milk.

[Serves 6]
1¼ pints water
3 ounces dark brown sugar
2-inch piece of stick cinnamon
3 whole cloves
3 tablespoons finely ground coffee

Combine the water, sugar, cinnamon, and cloves in an earthenware or any heatproof coffee pot and bring the water to the boil over moderate heat. Add the coffee, bring again to the boil, simmer for 1 minute, stir, cover, and leave in a warm place for a few minutes for the grounds to settle. Pour through a strainer into earthenware mugs, or use any demitasse cups.

Shopping Guide

The Guide to Good Food Shops, edited by Susan Campbell and published by Macmillan, can be very useful in tracking down unusual ingredients.

Hobbs and Co.
29 South Audley Street
London W1

Mail order for Mexican chili peppers, annatto, etc.

Lourdes Nichols
Chimalistac
Upper Hollis
Great Missenden
Buckinghamshire
Tel. Great Missenden 4348

Tortilla presses, masa harina, Mexican black beans and other Mexican foods. Mail order.

John Haral Ltd.
12 Inverness Street
London NW1
Tel. 01-485 6544

Brazilian black beans

J.A. Mako Horticultural
Enterprises
P.O. Box 34082
Dallas, Texas 75234
USA

Authentic Mexican chili pepper seeds, epazote seeds and green

tomato seeds for those who want to grow their own. Mail order.

Casa Moneo
210 West 14th Street
New York, NY 10011
USA

Mail order for all ingredients

Lisboa Deli
54 Goldbourne Road
London W11

Brazilian and Portuguese foods

Cornucopia
64 St Mary's Road
London W5

Shepherds Bush market
London W14

Stalls and shops selling a wide range of tropical fruits, vegetables and dry goods.

Charlies
Esmond Road
London NW6

Tropical fruits, vegetables and dry goods.

Index

abalone filling for little pies, 52
allspice (or pimiento), 25
almond sauce: cauliflower in, 257
  chicken in, 189, 190, 195
almonds, chicken stew with, 190
almond and shrimp sauce, chicken
    in, 192
  prawns and fish in, 192
ancho chili sauce, 143
anchovies, spinach with, 254
annatto, 25
annatto oil or lard, 25, 310
Argentinian food, 21
Argentinian recipes
  barbecue sauce, Creole style, 166
  beef stew, Argentine style, 170
  chicken, drunken, 185
  chicken in orange sauce, 180
  Creole sauce, 309
  hake in vinaigrette sauce, 96
  hen turkey with Creole stuffing,
    202
  kidneys, Buenos Aires style, 163
  meat soup, 82
  pig's feet, 156
  pork loin baked in milk, 138
  pumpkin soup, 77–8
  skirt steak, stuffed, rolled, 131–2
  striped bass, Buenos Aires style,
    101
  striped bass, stuffed, 99
  Swiss chard in cream sauce, 256
  tripe, Creole style, 152
  turnovers, 57
  veal stew in baked pumpkin, 169
  vinegar sauce, 167
arrowroot, 25

artichoke heart salad, 270
aubergine: cavier, 261
  with green beans, 262
  with shrimp, 261
  stuffed with cheese, 261
  stuffed with hash, 260
avocado(s): about, 26
  cream, 284
  leaves of, toasted, 26
  salad, 272
  sauces, 303
  soup, 69
  stuffed, 250, 312
  stuffed with chicken, 251
  stuffed with marinated prawns, 47
  stuffed with rice, 252
  stuffed with shrimp or prawns,
    250
  with uncooked tomato sauce, 251

banana(s), 26
  beans with, 236
  bread, 278
  chicken with, 181
  how to fry, 134
  savoury green banana cake, 235
  turnovers, 236
  See also plantain(s)
banana leaves, 26
  corn mixture in, 281
barbecue(s), 23, 163
  sauces for, 166
  spit-roasted whole animals, 165
barbecue sauce, 166
  Creole style, 166
bass marinated in lime juice, 48, 49
beans, 14, 27, 237–43

beans (*continued*)
  with bananas, 236
  cooking rules for, 27
  cranberry beans, 240–1
  Mexican style, 242
  peppers stuffed with, 264
  with pork, Yucatán style, 245
  refried, 239
béchamel, 312
beef: barbecued, 164
  chopped, seasoned, 139
  and dried fruit stew, 126
  in fruit sauce, 127
  salted, Colombia style, 172
  soup, 81
  stew, 115, 170
  in tomato and pepper sauce, 116
  and tomato stew, 117
beurre manié, 312
biblia con pisco, 315
black beans, 237
  about, 17, 27
  cooked, 238
  in fried stuffed tortillas, 66
  Minas Gerais style, 216
  with mixed meats, 213
  soup with prawns, 89
black-eyed pea fritters, 42
boiled dinner, special, 171
bolillos, 281
Bolivian food, 20
Bolivian recipes
  avocados with uncooked tomato
    sauce, 251
  aubergine with shrimp, 261
  cabbage, stuffed, 231
  cabbage in sauce, 253
  Peruvian brandy eggnog, 315
  Peruvian brandy with orange
    juice, 316
boniato, 37, 266
brains: with ham, 161
  sautéed, 160
  stewed, 160
  in wine sauce, 161
Brazilian food, 21

Brazilian recipes
  avocado cream, 284
  black beans, cooked, 239
  black beans, Minas Gerais style,
    216
  black beans with mixed meats
    (*feijoada*), 213
  black-eyed pea fritters, 42
  black-eyed pea fritter sauce, 43
  Brazil nut cake, 296
  cabbage, stuffed, 232
  cabbage with wine, 257
  cashew nut and chocolate mousse,
    283
  cassava meal with butter, 267
  cassava meal with hardboiled
    eggs, 267
  cassava meal with palm oil, 266
  chicken with bananas, 101
  chicken in shrimp and almond
    sauce, 192
  chicken with shrimp and peanut
    sauce, 191
  coconut blancmange with prune
    sauce, 288
  coconut cupcake dessert, 289
  coconut milk batida, 317
  coconut and milk pudding, Bahia
    style, 287
  coconut pudding, 287
  crabs, stuffed, 50
  duck with prunes, 208
  fish stew, 94
  fish in tangerine sauce, 94
  garnished steamed chicken and
    cornmeal, 222
  hearts of palm salad, 271
  hearts of palm soup, creamed, 70
  hot pepper and lime sauce, 302
  hot peppers and dendê oil, 302
  kale, Minas Gerais style, 256
  lamb kidneys in wine sauce, 163
  lime batida, 317
  old clotl.es, 135
  ox heart, stuffed, 158
  passion fruit batida, 318

pastry for fried turnovers, 56
pastry for little pies, 53
pineapple batida, 318
pork hash, 144
prawns in coconut milk, 107
prawns and fish in coconut, nut
    and shrimp sauce, 105
prawns and fish in a shrimp and
    almond sauce, 193
prawn stew, 105
prawn stew, Bahian, 104
pumpkin pudding, 290
pumpkin soup, 77
rice, Brazilian style, 245
rice, Haussá, 248
rice, moulded, 247
rice with pork, 229
rum sour, 317
salt cod, Bahia style, 110
salt cod and cabbage, Minas Gerais
    style, 111
salt cod with eggs, 112
sausage and broccoli with puréed
    corn, 225
softshell crabs in coconut milk, 93
stew, Brazilian style, 174
sweet potato soup, 81
tomato sauce, 306
tripe with vegetables, Brazilian
    style, 149
veal kidneys in wine sauce, 163
breadfruit chips, 46
bread pudding, 283
broad bean(s), 27
salad, fresh, 271
broccoli and sausage with puréed
    corn, 225
brown sugar pudding, 292
burned milk, pudding of, 294
butter, clarified, 313

cabbage: salt cod and, Minas Gerais
    style, 111
  in sauce, 253
  stuffed whole, 231
  with wine, 257

cake(s): Brazil nut, 296
  heavenly, 294
  pumpkin, 289
Caribbean Islands, food of, 15
cashew nut and chocolate mousse,
    283
cassava, 27, 266
cassava meal, 28
  with butter, 267
  with hardboiled eggs, 267
  with palm oil, 266
cassava root, 27
  cassava chips, 46
  with cheese sauce, 268
  soufflé, 268
cauliflower: in almond sauce, 257
  in corn sauce, 257
  salad, 273
chard, Swiss, in cream sauce, 256
chayote(s): about, 28
  pudding, 259
  scrambled with eggs, 259
  soup, 71
  stuffed, 258
cheese recipes: aubergine stuffed
      with cheese, 261
  cheese sauce, 307
  cheese sweet, 286
  chicken with cheese, 196
  corn bread with cheese, 280
  courgettes with cheese, 253
  filling for little pies, 56
  peppers stuffed with cheese, 264
  potato cakes, 265
  potatoes with cheese, tomato, and
      onion sauce, 265
  potatoes with cheese and hot
      pepper sauce, 218
  stuffed chayotes, 258
  stuffed cheese, 233
chicken, 180–201
  in almond sauce, 189, 190, 195
  avocados stuffed with, 251
  with bananas, 81
  barbecued, 166
  chayote soup with, 72

chicken (*continued*)
  with cheese, 196
  country chicken, 201
  Creole style, 195
  drunken, 185
  in egg sauce, 194
  filling for little pies, 55
  garnished steamed chicken and
    cornmeal, 222
  in green almond sauce, 187
  with lemon, 195
  Mayan chicken fricassee, 186
  in nut sauce, 195
  with olives, 195
  in orange juice, 196
  in orange sauce, 180
  in pepper sauce, 182
  pickled, 200
  pie with corn topping, 224
  in pineapple, 182
  and pork and potatoes in peanut
    sauce, 188
  and pork tamal pie, 226
  pot-au-feu, 176
  with rice, 196
  with sherry, 196
  in shrimp and almond sauce, 192
  with shrimp and peanut sauce, 191
  stew, 184
  stew with almonds, 190
  stew, Bagotá style, 183–4
  with sweet red peppers, 195
  Ticul style, 199
  Yucatán style, 193
chickpeas, 27
  salad, 270
  soup, 83
  toasted, 44
Chilean food, 20
Chilean recipes
  aubergine stuffed with cheese, 261
  aubergine stuffed with hash, 260
  avocados stuffed with chicken, 251
  avocados stuffed with rice, 252
  avocados stuffed with shrimp, 250
  beef and tomato stew, 117

calf's liver in mushroom sauce, 161
cauliflower in almond sauce, 257
chicken, country, 201
chicken, pickled, 200
cranberry beans with corn and
    pumpkin, 240
fish soup, 87
fish stew, 89
Jerusalem artichoke soup, 80
kidneys in wine sauce, 162
lamb casserole, 122
lamb stew with green peas, 123
meatballs, 142
milk pudding, 293
paprika oil, 309
pork loin, Chilean style, 138
pumpkin, 240
pumpkin soup, 77
rabbit in orange sauce, 148
rabbit in peanut sauce, 147
sauce, Chilean, 309
sauce, hot pepper, 298
sauce, parsley, 307
sauce, red pepper, 299
sauce, sweetcorn, 308
skirt steak, rolled, 137
tomato- and cognac-flavoured
    mayonnaise, 311
tongue in hot pepper sauce, 153
tripe stew, 151
turnovers, little, 53
chili sauces: ancho, 143
  chipotle, 144
  morita, 144
chipotle chili sauce, 144
chocolate: and cashew nut mousse,
    283
  and chili sauce, turkey in, 204
clam soup, 84
coco fizz, 316
coconut(s): about, 28
  blancmange with prune sauce, 288
  coconut sweet, 287
  cupcake dessert, 289
  custard, 286
  and milk pudding, Bahian style, 287

pudding, 287
coconut milk, 17
  batida, 317
  cream of coconut soup, 75
  how to make, 29
  okra soup with, 85
  prawns in, 107
  rabbit stew with, 146
  rice with coconut and raisins, 245
  shad fillets in, 102
Colombian food, 17
Colombian recipes
  annatto oil or lard, 25, 310
  avocado salad, 272
  avocado sauce, 305
  bean fritters, 44
  beef, salted, 172
  beef and dried fruit stew, 126
  brains, stewed, 160
  calf's liver in red wine sauce, 162
  cassava chips, 46
  cheese sweet, 286
  chicken stew, 184
  chicken stew, Bogotá, 183
  clam soup, 84
  coconut soup, cream of, 75
  coconut sweet, 287
  corn bread, 279
  Creole potatoes, fried, 46
  duckling in wine, 207
  fried fish with red wine sauce, 95
  hot pepper sauce, 299
  lentils, cooked, 242
  milk pudding, 293
  okra and pompano soup, 85
  pigeon in orange juice, 212
  pineapple custard, 282
  plantain chips, 44
  pork-filled turnovers, 60
  potatoes with cheese, tomato, and
    onion sauce, 265
  pumpkin soup, 77
  rabbit stew with coconut milk, 146
  rice with coconut and raisins, 245
  rice with fried coconut and raisins,
    246

shad fillets in coconut milk, 102
  shrimp and potato omelette, 109
  skirt steak, 133
  skirt steak, Bogotá style, 133
  special boiled dinner, 171
coriander, 29
corn: cranberry beans with pumpkin
    and, 240
  pancakes, 280
  puréed, sausage and broccoli with,
    225
  sauce, 308
  sauce, cauliflower in, 257
  soufflé, 225
  soup, 79
  toasted, 44
corn bread: with cheese, 280
corn bread, Paraguayan, 277
cornmeal, garnished steamed
    chicken and, 222
  moulded, 243
corn mixture: in banana leaves, 281
  steamed in leaves, 281
corn topping, chicken pie with, 224
Costa Rican recipe
  chayotes, stuffed, 258
crabs, stuffed, 50
cranberry beans with corn and
    pumpkin, 240
Creole sauce, 166, 309
Cuban recipes
  avocados, stuffed, 251
  corn soup, 79
  fish in oil and vinegar sauce, 95
  turnovers, 58
cucumber salad, 270
custard(s): coconut, 286
  pineapple, 282

dendê (palm) oil, 31
Dominican Republic, food of, 16
Dominican Republic, recipes of
  aubergine caviar, 261
  cauliflower salad, 273
  chayotes scrambled with eggs, 259
  okra with prawns, 233

Dominican Republic (*continued*)
  pork chops with dried fruit, 129
  sausage and bacon stew, 167
  Spanish stew, Dominican style,
    175
  turkey stew, Dominican style, 203
drunken chicken, 185
drunken duck, 208
duck, 206
  drunken, 208
  in orange juice, 209
  with prunes, 208
  with rice, 206
  in wine, 207

Ecuadorian food, 18
Ecuadorian recipes
  artichoke heart salad, 270
  avocados, stuffed, 250
  bass marinated in lime juice, 48
  beef in fruit juice, 127
  broad bean salad, fresh, 271
  cheese sauce, 307
  chicken, Creole style, 195
  chicken in almond sauce, 195
  chicken with cheese, 196
  chicken in egg sauce, 194
  chicken with lemon, 195
  chicken in nut sauce, 195
  chicken with olives, 195
  chicken in orange juice, 196
  chicken with sherry, 196
  chicken with sweet red peppers,195
  chickpea salad, 270
  chickpeas, toasted, 44
  corn, toasted, 44
  corn soufflé, 225
  cucumber salad, 270
  hot pepper sauce, 300
  mixed salad, 269
  mushroom salad, 270
  ox tongue, 154
  peanut sauce, 308
  peanut soup, 79–80
  pork loin in orange juice, 137
  pork loin with shrimp, 136

  pork stew, 119
  potato cakes, 265
  potato salad, 270
  potato soup, 78
  potato soup with prawn fritters, 78
  potato and sweet red pepper
    salad, 270
  pudding, steamed, 295
  prawns, marinated, 48
  pumpkin cake, 289
  pumpkin fritters, 291
  pumpkin soup, 77
  spring soup, 90
  striped bass and shrimp stew, 86
  striped bass stew, 87
  tripe with peanut sauce, 152
  vegetable salad, 274
  vegetable soufflé, 230
egg(s): chayotes scrambled with, 259
  hardboiled, cassava meal and, 267
  milk sweet with, 294
  salt cod with, 112

fish and shellfish, 20
  fish with coriander, 94
  fish in oil and vinegar sauce, 95
  fish with potatoes and vegetables,
    219
  fish and prawns in coconut, nut,
    and shrimp sauce, 106
  fish with red wine sauce, fried, 95
  fish stew, 89, 93, 98, 104
  fish in tangerine sauce, 94
  fish with tomatoes and onions, 97
  fish, Veracruz style, 100
French dressing, 312
fritters: black-eyed pea, 42
  prawn, 78
  pumpkin, 291
  sweet, 290
fruits: meat stews with, 126
  Peruvian fruit compote, 285

gin fizz, 316
green beans, aubergine with, 262
Guatemalan recipes

banana bread, 278
banana turnovers, 236
beef in tomato and pepper sauce, 116
cassava root soufflé, 268
chicken fricassee, Mayan, 186
chicken in pineapple, 182
oysters marinated in lime juice, 50
radish and fried pork rind salad, 272
radish salad, 272
rice, Guatemalan style, 247

hake in vinaigrette sauce, 96
hash: aubergine stuffed with, 260
    pork, 144
Haussá rice, 248
heart: skewered, 41
    stuffed, 158
hearts of palm: about, 31
    salad, 271
    soup, creamed, 70

Jerusalem artichoke(s): about, 32
    salad, 274
    soup, 80

kale, Minas Gerais style, 256
kid: roast, 122
    stew, 115
kidneys: Buenos Aires style, 163
    in wine sauce, 162

lamb: casserole, 122
    in chili and vinegar sauce, 124
    Creole style, 121
    kidneys, 163
    in mild red chili sauce, 125
    roast, 122
    stew, 125
    stew with green peas, 123
lentils, cooked, 242
lime: batida, 317
    and hot pepper sauce, 302
    juice, fish and shellfish marinated in, 48

soup, 76
liver, calf's, 161
    in mushroom sauce, 161
    in red wine sauce, 162
lizard's tail, 317
    en jugo de Naranja, 137-8

mackerel marinated in lime juice, 49
malangas, 37, 266
Margarita, 318
Mayan chicken fricassee, 186
mayonnaise, 311
    tomato- and cognac-flavoured, 311
meat(s), 113-79
    about, 113
    fillings for turnovers, 54-61
    mixed meats, black beans with, 213
    spit-roasted whole animals, 165
    See also barbecue(s); beef; brains;
        kid; kidneys; lamb; liver, calf's;
        meat stews; minced meat dishes;
        ox; pig's feet; pork; rabbit; skirt
        steak; tongue; tripe; veal
meatballs, 140
    broth for, 141
    chili sauces for, 143
    peppery, 142
meat stews, 115-30
    beef and dried fruit stew, 126
    beef in fruit sauce, 127
    beef stew, 115
    beef and tomato, 117
    beef in tomato and pepper sauce, 116
    with fruits, 126-30
    kid stew, 115
    lamb, Creole style, 121
    lamb casserole, 122
    lamb in chili and vinegar sauce, 124
    lamb with green peas, 123
    lamb in mild red chili sauce, 125
    lamb stew, 115, 125
    Peruvian fresh ham, 120
    pork, 115, 119

meat stews (*continued*)
  pork, spicy, 119
  pork chops with dried fruit, 129
  pork with peppers and greengage
    plums, 130
  rabbit, 146
  veal with olives, 128
  veal in prune sauce, 128
  veal in pumpkin seed sauce, 118
  with vegetables, 115–26
Mexican food, 11
Mexican recipes
  avocado sauce, 303
  avocado sauce, northern style, 304
  avocado soup, 69
  avocado stuffed with marinated
    prawns, 47
  beans, cooked, 238
  beans, Mexican style, 242
  beans, refried, 239
  beans with bananas, 236
  beans with pork, Yucatán style,
    241
  black bean soup with prawns, 89
  bread pudding, 283
  bread rolls, 281
  cactus salad, 273
  cake, heavenly, 294
  cauliflower salad, 273
  chayote soup, 71
  cheese, stuffed, 233
  chicken, Ticul style, 199
  chicken, Yucatán style, 193
  chicken in almond sauce, 190
  chicken in green almond sauce,
    187
  chicken and pork tamal pie, 226–7
  chicken with rice, 198
  chicken stew with almonds, 190
  chickpeas, toasted, 44
  chickpea soup, 83
  chopped beef, seasoned, 139
  coco fizz, 316
  coconut custard, 286
  coffee pot, 321
  courgettes, chopped, 252

  courgettes, Pueblo style, 253
  courgettes, with cheese, 253
  courgette soup, 74
  duck in orange juice, 209
  fish, Veracruz style, 100
  fish with coriander, 94
  fish in oil and vinegar sauce, 95
  green banana cake, savoury, 235
  hot pepper sauce, 301
  lamb in chili and vinegar sauce,
    124
  lamb in mild red chili sauce, 125
  lime soup, 76
  lizard's tail (drink), 317
  mackerel marinated in lime juice,
    49–50
  Margarita, 318
  meatballs, 143
  mild red chili and almond sauce,
    300
  milk pudding, 294
  milk pudding with wine, 294
  minced pork and veal with fruits,
    140
  peppers, stuffed, 262
  peppers in walnut sauce, 263
  pigeon with wine, 210
  pig's feet in poblano pepper sauce,
    157
  pork stew with peppers and
    greengage plums, 130
  pot-au-feu, 178
  pozole, Guadalajara style, 172
  pumpkin blossom soup, 73
  pumpkin blossom soup, cream of,
    74
  pumpkin blossom and tomato
    soup, 74
  rice, Mexican, 246
  rice, white, 244
  salt cod in mild red chili and
    almond sauce, 111
  sangría, 320
  sangrita, 319
  shrimp or prawns, Acapulco style,
    106

sorrel or rosella drink, 320
striped bass in sauce, 99
student's tortilla casserole, 227
sweet red pepper soup, 72
tequila Bloody Mary, 318
tequila sunrise, 318
tomato sauce, 305
tomato sauce, green, 305
tomato sauce, uncooked, 306
tomato soup, 72
tongue in green tomato sauce, 154
tongue in mild red chili and
    almond sauce, 155
tortillas, 63–5, 278
tortillas, fried stuffed, 65
tortillas, stuffed miniature, 66
tripe, mountain style, 150
turkey in chili and chocolate sauce,
    204
veal with olives, 128
veal in prune sauce, 128
veal in pumpkin seed sauce, 118
milk: hot peppers in, 302
    puddings, 292–4
minced meat dishes, 139–45
    meatballs, 140–4
    pork hash, 144
    seasoned chopped beef, 139
morita chili sauce, 144
mushroom salad, 270

Nicaraguan recipe
    chayote soup with chicken, 72
nopal (prickly pear cactus), 32

oils: annatto, 25, 310
    dendê (palm), 31
    paprika, 309–10
okra: and pompano soup, 85
    with prawns, 233
olives: cassava meal with, 267
    chicken with, 195
    veal with, 128
omelette, shrimp and potato, 109
orange(s), 32
    juice, chicken in, 196

juice, duck in, 209
juice, Peruvian brandy with, 316
juice pigeon in, 212
juice, pork loin in, 137
juice, prawns and shellfish
    marinated in, 48, 49
sauce, chicken in, 180
sauce, rabbit in, 148
ox heart: skewered, 41
    stuffed, 158
ox tongue: in green tomato sauce,
    154
    in hot pepper sauce, 153
    in mild red chili and almond sauce,
    155
    stock, use of, 155
oysters marinated in lime juice, 50

paprika oil, 309
Paraguayan food, 21
Paraguayan recipes
    beef soup, 81
    chicken with rice, 196
    corn bread, 277
    courgette soup, 74
    fish stew, 98
    meatballs, peppery, 142
    meatballs in stock, 142
    milk sweet or dessert, 293
    pumpkin soup, 77
parsley sauce, 307
passion fruit batida, 318
peanut-coloured rice, 245
peanut sauce, 308
    chicken, pork, and potatoes in, 188
    rabbit in, 147
    tripe in, 152
peanut and shrimp sauce, chicken
    with, 191
peanut soup, 79
pepitas (pumpkin seeds), 33
peppers, 12, 33–6, 41
peppers, dried, 33
    how to use, 34, 41
peppers, fresh, 34
    hot, 34

peppers (*continued*)
  sweet, 35
peppers, stuffed, 262
  with beans, 264
  with cheese, 264
  in walnut sauce, 263
peppers, sweet bell: about, 35
  how to peel, 36
  and potato salad, 270
  striped bass in sweet pepper
    sauce, 101
  stuffed, 262
  sweet red pepper soup, 72
Peruvian food, 19
Peruvian recipes
  avocados, stuffed, 251
  bass marinated in lime juice, 29
  beef stew, 115
  brown sugar pudding, 292
  cassava root with cheese sauce,
    268
  chicken in pepper sauce, 182
  chicken, pork, and potatoes in
    peanut sauce, 188
  duck with rice, 206
  fish in oil and vinegar sauce, 95
  fritters, sweet, 290
  fruit compote, Peruvian, 285
  ham, fresh, 120
  ham sandwiches, Peruvian, 121
  kid stew, 115, 116
  lamb, Creole style, 121
  lamb or kid, roast, 122
  lamb stew, 125
  ox heart, skewered, 41
  Peruvian brandy eggnog, 315
  Peruvian brandy with orange
    juice, 316
  Peruvian brandy sour, 315
  pigeon in shrimp sauce, 210
  pigeon stew, 210
  pig's feet, Creole style, 155
  pig's feet, spicy, Arequipa style,
    158
  pork, spicy, 119
  prawn stew, 88

rabbit in peanut sauce, 147
rabbit stew, 146
rice, Peruvian style, 244
rice with shellfish, 108
spinach with tomatoes, 254
striped bass with vegetables, 93
tripe, Lima style, 153
pies: chicken, with corn topping, 224
  chicken and pork tamal, 226
pigeon, 209–12
  in orange juice, 212
  in shrimp sauce, 210
  stew, 211
  and walnut sauce, potatoes and
    eggs in, 220
  with wine, 210
pig's feet, 155
  cheesecloth wrapping for, 156
  Creole style, 155
  in poblano pepper sauce, 157
  spicy, Arequipa style, 158
pineapple: batida, 318
  chicken in, 182
  custard, 282–3
pisco sour, 315
plantain(s): about, 36
  babies in a blanket, 236
  chips, 45
  green plantain soup, 80
  how to fry, 134
  See also banana(s)
pompano and okra soup, 85
pork: beans with, Yucatán style, 241
  cheese stuffed with, 233
  and chicken tamal pie, 226
  chops with dried fruit, 129
  hash, 144
  loin, 136
  loin, Chilean style, 138
  loin baked in milk, 138
  loin and chicken and potatoes in
    peanut sauce, 188
  loin in orange juice, 137
  loin with shrimp, 136
  Peruvian fresh ham, 120
  with rice, 229

spicy, 119
stew, 115, 119
stew with peppers and greengage
    plums, 130
turnover fillings, 59, 60
whole cabbage stuffed with, 231
pork rind, fried, 28
and radish salad, 272
potato(es), 18, 36
cakes, 265
with cheese and hot pepper sauce,
    218
with cheese, tomato, and onion
    sauce, 265
with cheese, walnut, and hot
    pepper sauce, 217
with chicken and pork in peanut
    sauce, 188
and eggs in pigeon and walnut
    sauce, 220
with fish and vegetables, 219
fried Creole potatoes, 46
salad, 270
shrimp and, with cheese, walnut,
    and hot pepper sauce, 218
with prawns and vegetables, 220
and shrimp omelette, 109
soup, 78
and sweet red pepper salad, 270
pot coffee, 321
pozole, Guadalajara style, 172
prawns: Acapulco style, 106
avocados stuffed with, 250
black bean soup with, 89
in coconut milk, 107
fish and, in coconut, nut and
    shrimp sauce, 105
and fish in a shrimp and almond
    sauce, 193
fritters, 78
marinated, 48
marinated, avocado stuffed with,
    47
okra with, 233
with potatoes and vegetables, 220
stew, 88, 104, 105

Puerto Rican recipes
breadfruit chips, 46
plantain chips, 45
pumpkin,
baked, veal stew in, 169
cake, 289
cranberry beans with corn and, 240
fritters, 291
pudding, 290
soup, 77
pumpkin blossom(s), 31
soup, 73
soup, cream of, 74
soup with tomatoes, 74
pumpkin seed sauce, veal in, 118

rabbit, 145
how to cut up, 145
in orange sauce, 148
in peanut sauce, 147
stew, 146
stew with coconut milk, 146
radish: and fried pork rind salad, 272
salad, 272
red snapper, baked, 102
refried beans, 239
rice, 243
about, 243
avocados stuffed with, 252
Brazilian style, 245
chicken with, 198
with coconut and raisins, 245
duck with, 206
with fried coconut and raisins, 246
Guatemalan style, 247
Haussá rice, 248
Mexican style, 246
moulded, 247
peanut-coloured, 245
Peruvian style, 244
with pork, 229
rice flour pudding, 248
with shellfish, 108
white, 244
root vegetables, tropical, 266
    See also cassava; Jerusalem

root vegetables (*continued*)
artichoke(s); malangas; sweet
potato(es); taros; yams
rum sour, 317
salt cod: about, 26, 110
Bahia style, 110
and cabbage, Minas Gerais style,
111
Creole style, 111
with eggs, 112
in mild red chili and almond sauce,
111
sandwiches, Peruvian ham, 121
sangría, 320
sangrita, 319
sauce(s), 298–313
ancho chile, 143
avocado, 303
for barbecues, 166
for black-eyed pea fritters, 43
cheese, 307
Chilean, 309
Chilean hot pepper, 298
chili and chocolate, 205
chipotle chili, 144
Creole, 166, 309
French dressing, 312
green tomato, 306
hot pepper, 299, 300, 301
hot pepper and lime, 302
hot peppers in dendê oil, 302
hot peppers in milk, 302
hot peppers in olive oil, 302
how to thicken, 313
mayonnaise, 311
mild red chili and almond, 300
morita chili sauce, 144
parsley, 307
peanut, 308
pigeon and walnut, 220
red pepper, 299
sweetcorn, 308
tomato, 305
tomato, uncooked, 306
white, 312
sausage: and bacon stew, 176

and broccoli with puréed corn, 225
seasoning powder, Creole style, 25,
310
shad fillets in coconut milk, 102
shrimp: Acapulco style, 106
aubergine with, 261
avocados stuffed with, 250
in black-eyed pea fritters and
sauce, 42
dried, 37
pork loin with, 136
and potatoes, with cheese, walnut,
and hot pepper sauce, 218
and potato omelette, 109
and striped bass stew, 86
stuffing, Bahian style, 55
shrimp and almond sauce: chicken
in, 192
prawns and fish in, 192
shrimp and peanut sauce, chicken
with, 191
shrimp sauce, pigeon in, 210
skirt steak, 131–6
baked, 132
barbecued, 164
Bogotá style, 133
casseroled, 132
old clothes, 135
with rice, black beans and
plantains, 134
rolled, 132
stuffed, 232
stuffed, rolled, 131
sorrel or rosella drink, 320
soufflé(s): cassava root, 268
corn, 225
vegetable, 230
spinach with anchovies, 255
with cream, 255
with tomatoes, 254
spring soup, 90
steamed pudding, 295
stew(s): about, 115
chicken, 180–96
fish, 89, 98, 104
meat, 115–30

pot-au-feus, 168–79
pigeon, 211
prawn, 88, 104, 105
striped bass and shrimp, 86
tripe, 151
turkey, Dominican style, 203
stock, 69
prawn, 108
tongue, use of, 155
striped bass: Buenos Aires style, 101
in sauce, 99
and shrimp stew, 84
stuffed, 99
in sweet pepper sauce, 101
with vegetables, 93
stuffings for turkey, 202
sugar syrup, 291
sweet potato(es), 266
about, 37
soup, 81
white (*boniato*), 37, 266

tacos, 64
taros, 37, 266
tequila: Bloody Mary, 318
sunrise, 318
tomato(es), 14
beef and, stew, 117
and cognac-flavoured
mayonnaise, 311
green, 14, 37
peeling and seeding, 313
pumpkin blossom soup with, 74
salad, 270
sauce, 305
soup, 72
spinach with, 254
tripe with, 152
uncooked sauce, 306
tongue: in green tomato sauce, 154
in hot pepper sauce, 153
in mild red chili and almond sauce,
155
stock, use of, 155
tortillas, 38, 61–7, 278
about, 13–14

chalupas, 64
dough for, 63, 67
fillings for, 65, 66, 67
fried stuffed, 65
how to cook, 63
sopes, 64
student's tortilla casserole, 227
stuffed miniature, 66
tacos, 64
tostadas, 65
totopos, 64
tripe, 148–53
about, 148
Creole style, 152
Lima style, 153
mountain style, 150
in peanut sauce, 152
stew, 151
with tomatoes, 152
with vegetables, Brazilian style,
149
turkey, 201–6
in chili and chocolate sauce, 204
hen, with Creole stuffing, 202
stew, Dominican style, 203
stuffed, 201
turnover(s), 51–61, 236
about, 51
banana, 236
pastry for, 53
pastry for fried turnovers, 56, 58, 59
pastry for little pies, 53
turnover fillings, 52–61
abalone, 52
beef, 54, 59
beef with pears and peaches, 58
beef with potatoes and onions, 57
cheese, 56
chicken, 55
meat, 54
pork, 59, 60
sardine, 54
shrimp, Bahian style, 55

Uruguayan recipes
barbecue sauce, 167

Uruguayan recipes (*continued*)
    gin fizz, 316
    meatballs, 140
    stuffed rolled skirt steak, 131

veal: kidney, 163
    with olives, 128
    in prune sauce, 128–9
    in pumpkin seed sauce, 118
    stew in baked pumpkins, 169
vegetable(s), 249–69
    meat stews with, 115–26
    potatoes with fish and, 219
    in pot-au-feus, 168
    salad, 274
    soufflé, 230
    See also aubergine; avocado(s);
      cabbage; cauliflower; chard,
      Swiss, in cream sauce;
      chayote(s); courgettes;
      Jerusalem artichoke(s); kale,
      Minas Gerais style; peppers,
      stuffed; potato(es); root
      vegetables, tropical; spinach
Venezuelan foods, 16
Venezuelan recipes
    aubergine with green beans, 262
    avocado sauce, 304
    avocado soup, 70

avocados stuffed with shrimp, 251
black beans, cooked, 239
cabbage, stuffed, 232
chicken pot-au-feu, 176
chicken with rice, 197
corn bread, 279
corn pancakes, 280
hot peppers in milk, 302
meatballs, 144
plantain chips, 45
red snapper, baked, 102
rice, white, 244
salt cod, Creole style, 111
seasoning powder, Creole style,
    25, 310
spinach with anchovies, 254
steak, stuffed, 232
steak with rice, black beans, and
    plantains, 134
striped bass in sweet pepper
    sauce, 101
turnovers, little, 58
vinaigrette, 313
vinegar sauce, 167

walnuts, 194
walnut sauce, peppers in, 263

yams, 38, 266